Maria Call
Sound Healing,
Living A Duet For
Mankind

Helena Hawley

www.capallbann.co.uk

Maria Callas and I, Sound Healing, Living A Duet For Mankind

Cover design by Paul Mason
Cover Painting by Helena Hawley

Published by:

Capall Bann Publishing
Auton Farm
Milverton
Somerset
TA4 1NE

Contents

Acknowledgements

Of all the many people who have helped me, I feel I owe the most thanks to Marguerite Vidal. She helped guide me in the work we did together with Maria, assisted me with the French language when I was in France with her, not to mention proof reading this English edition of it, as well as giving her time freely in many other little ways.

I will not forget the wonderful support Maria and I have had from Joan Ocean on various occasions, and how she unwittingly provided the perfect setting for Maria to come through me for the first time in her home.

Then there was Samarpan, whose recognition of both of us, and whose healing words and wisdom contributed so much to our progress together.

Amongst the others who made this book what it is are those who allowed me to use their real names in the stories in which they were involved. In no particular order, they include Richard Lutz, husband of Marguerite Vidal, Michael and Gila Galitzine, Monique Schmidt, Dany Serrat, Geneviève Granger, Jean-Luc, Douglas Webster, Jack Davis, Chris James, Simone Bak, Katerina Elander Vickers, Wendy Broad, Julia Day, Sonia in the Azores, Licinia M. da Rosa, Noëlle, Margot Maddison, Ujjavel, Gabrielle, Georgia, Celeste Eaton, Sandi Duffy and Felicity Jones.

I acknowledge most gratefully the support of my loyal publishers who have agreed to publish this, thus making it available for all those interested in reading it.

My greatest thanks of all, without a doubt, are for the soul who was formerly known as "Maria Callas", for she has enriched my life beyond belief.

Helena Hawley

Introduction

Even in my wildest dreams, or most imaginative moments, I could never have made all this lot up! I remind myself of that sometimes, not to convince myself it really happened, but because I find it so amazing! This was not the direction I was expecting my life to go in! It is better than that. I often wonder how it was that I wandered into this amazing adventure. It is, of course, my mind that asks me these questions. Therefore I know that if my intellect cannot fully comprehend how or why all this happened to me, it does not matter. There is much that our brains cannot take in or comprehend in life, and I do not intend that to prevent me accepting and enjoying the divine gifts that enter my life.

I offer "our" story, Maria's and mine, to the world, or those in it who care to read this book. The veil between dimensions grows thinner now. I find it helpful to be aware of these things in my search for the truth.

I have written this story just as it took place, expressing my feelings, doubts, elations and struggles to accept it at times. It has challenged me to reach out further than I thought I could go. It is my wish that this book inspire others walking their spiritual pathways in the service of the Light.

So many times I tried to do some work on another book, "Book Four" as I called it, but it never worked! Something in my life would always happen to take me away from it, even though my computer was full of wonderful material for it about animals and so on.

Whereas when I started to put this book together, I not only found the time, but I have felt totally supported by the Universe and all that is in its production. This book is meant to be!

This is what Marguerite Vidal, who has probably had more involvement in the drama than anyone else, had to say about it.

"Helena, the story you will tell in your book is not only your story and Maria's story; it's the story of mankind. Each one will be able to understand something about his own life when reading your words or what Maria said. There are so many things to discover and to be aware of! I see in this book, which you are finishing, the opportunity for each reader to lift the veil of the outward aspect of his life and look at what is behind it... or inside. I thank Maria for giving us this present... for offering us her life and feelings as a living woman first and now as a living spirit who can share her new point of view, her understandings. Yes, that's true, we walk hand in hand with those in the spirit world. Thank you, Helena.

LOVE,
 Marguerite"

Chapter 1

The Beginning

I had no idea whatsoever of the adventure that was in store for me. It came as a complete surprise.

It was July 2001. I had just travelled from the island of Bimini in the Bahamas to Hawaii to join Joan Ocean's "Into the Future" seminar, which was to include meditaions and swimming with dolphins as well. While travelling, it had become increasingly obvious to me that I was developing the symptoms of a nasty cold. At first it was all in my head and nose, and then it migrated to my throat, where it resided as a horrible noisy cough, the last thing I wanted to take with me to a seminar with countless silent meditations. I feared that the noise would be a constant irritation and disturbance to the rest of Joan's group.

It was the second day. We were not only meditating, but Joan wanted us to tone as well. I lay down for this, and immediately saw a lion coming close to me. This animal symbolised courage, and protection. Having lain down beside me, he stayed there to look after my physical self during the out-of-body experiences that followed.

The toning was about to begin. A red arrow appeared, sent by beings of Light, and it landed in the centre of my throat chakra. I remembered how Patrick Kempe had told me that arrows were sometimes used to bring messages, so I looked to see what message this one was bringing me. Hanging from its shaft was a notice. There was my message written in clear black writing on white paper. There were only three words, namely, "OPEN IT UP!" written in capitals. I interpreted this to mean that when we toned, I was supposed to join in, in spite of the cold-smitten state of my throat. I did try cautiously and as quietly as possible, to sing some suitable low notes, which I hoped no one would hear other than me. They sounded pretty awful! The arrow's message was a clue concerning what would follow shortly, but at the time I merely supposed that my chakra needed opening up for better bodily and spiritual health, or communication skills.

Twenty-four hours later

This was one of the biggest surprises of my life. Now I was about to find out what "OPEN IT UP!" was really about.

Following a lovely dolphin swim, I sat with the rest of Joan's group to listen to the brief Joan gave us concerning the imminent meditation. I was trying to sit there quietly and un-noticed, when one of my coughing fits started. It went on and on and on. Had I been alone, it would not have bothered me much, but sitting there trying to stifle the cough and listen quietly without disturbing everyone else, thus making it hard for people to hear what on earth Joan was trying to say, made it a stressful situation for me. I felt really distressed about this. The group, on the other hand, were extremely tolerant and loving towards me. They knew I was trying to stifle the sound, but wanted me to feel free to cough out loud, and not worry about the noise. The amount of love being directed towards me from all of them, as we made our way to the meditation room, was enormous.

We were to tone and meditate lying down, but Joan offered me a special chair, as we felt that lying down would make my cough even worse. I gratefully accepted both the chair and the offer to put it near the door, so that if I felt I absolutely had to leave the room, I could do so easily. All this love and consideration made me feel much happier and more relaxed about it all.

The music started on Joan's tape, and I clairvoyantly saw myself surrounded by the group, who were sending me love and healing. The effect was to raise my spiritual body upwards, so that I felt they were helping me to learn to fly in the Light.

Joan started her introduction, guiding us in our visualisation, but my guides had other plans. They took me aside to a place a little way up to the left of where I perceived the group to be. At first, I lay in a hammock being comforted. Next I was led to a healing table surrounded by clouds

6

of pale blue and strong white light, descending on me from above. I gladly accepted the invitation to lie on this table, where I experienced the wonderful feeling of a new (to me) high vibrational energy entering and enveloping my physical body. This was complete in time for me to be present with the group for the toning.

I had serious doubts that I could manage it after my coughing fit, and started softly and warily with a suitably deep note. The sound I was making was not at all clear, but in spite of this, I kept feeling something urging me to sing higher notes. It was at this point that the miracle happened. It seemed that the very special energy field that the spirit healers had created for me, as I had lain on their healing table, made me a suitable vehicle for someone to sing through. With my body and auric field still tingling pleasantly from it, I felt full of Light. I was soon aware of "outside help" with my singing, and reacted by asking that this entity, who clearly knew how to sing, to produce the notes that would be the best possible help for those in the group to move into the optimum state for the meditation.

Never in my life had I experienced my vocal chords opening up so much. Clairvoyantly, I saw a narrow slit in my throat expand until the space created was almost circular. I needed to use so much air for this to happen, that at the end of it, I found myself quite out of breath. The entity that did the singing had also organised my breathing. "She", as she turned out to be, chose the notes that I sang, to the extent that I did not know until I heard them what notes they would be. I was present in my body, but not actually doing it. I just sat there quietly listening. Step by step, she sang higher and higher notes, perhaps not so very high, but far beyond anything that I thought I could manage. When the time came to stop, she withdrew, and using my own voice, I sang my way down an arpeggio to a comfortable pitch for me, at which point I ceased singing. I sat there almost in shock, but of the pleasant kind, for I had difficulty acknowledging that something so wonderful could happen to me.

On the Boat

The following day we went out on the boat to look for dolphins. While I was standing on it gazing at the blue water, for it was a lovely day, I became aware of a discarnate presence talking to me. She was the one who had sung through me the previous morning. She told me that her name was Maria. She showed me how she had looked as a slightly portly middle-aged lady with her still dark hair tied back, dressed in black, and totally engrossed in her music. She knew everything about how to use the vocal chords correctly, had sung opera, and also taught music. It was her entire life. The limelight may have been a consequence of her beautiful voice and abilities when she sang opera in her younger years, but it was never achieving that which had motivated her. She sang for the love of music itself. (This last bit of information turned out to be a mixture of correct facts concerning Maria herself, and information about someone currently living on Earth that she was trying to give me. I have written what I mistakenly believed to be correct at the time. Furthermore, it was a level of the truth I was capable of believing. I was nowhere near ready to accept who she really was or had been in her past life.)

After her transition into the spirit world, she became interested in the music of the spheres, and how to use sound in the service of the Light. Her object when working with me was to put together her singing techniques learnt during her earthly lifetime with her knowledge of the workings of heavenly music, and bring it all to Earth. For this, she needed to use my body, and had found in me a willing subject. As she had evolved considerably since her incarnation here, it had helped that my vibrational rate had been raised to make us more compatible prior to her coming the first time.

Later I realized that the love had assisted me to open up enough to receive her, and to trust, for I felt safe. All the same, I thought I was a very odd choice for her. I had been truly astounded to discover that it was actually possible for my vocal chords to be opened up enough for her to produce such a powerful sound. I thought that in a body of fifty-five years, though only just fifty-five, previously unused vocal chords would have atrophied by now, and that unlike those of a younger body, they would lack the elasticity necessary. On the rare occasions when I had tried to sing to myself, using my limited range of notes, I had often thought that my only hope of singing freely, instead of with a broken or constantly cracking voice, and a tight throat, would be if I could channel someone else, but never in my wildest dreams had I ever thought that this would actually happen on the scale I had just experienced.

Maria told me how she knew about my childhood dream to sing. I had wanted to be a singer, a soloist, and believed that I could never live happily without music. At a low level, I had studied piano and violin, and would not have minded becoming a concert soloist with one of those, preferably the violin, had I had the ability. I had no time or interest in light popular music, and adored anything classical that I felt I resonated with.

Up until the age of about twelve, I was often one of the chosen ones to sing solos in school concerts, because it did not unnerve me to sing alone and be heard. On account of this, I had received some basic tuition about not breathing in the middle of a phrase, singing in tune, and annunciating the words clearly, but this included nothing concerning correct voice production, or what ever it is that opera singers have to study. I was "choir leader", because with my fairly strong voice it was easy for the others to follow me.

Aged thirteen, I left that school, and moved on to a school for older girls. That is where it all started to go wrong. The acoustics in the school chapel were entirely different from those I was accustomed to, and in my struggle to get the usual sound, I strained the middle notes of my limited range. I lost confidence, and very soon, could not sing alone any more. The notes cracked, or my vocal chords seized up into a painful silence due to self-consciousness, something I had known little about in early childhood. I had an almost total lack of belief in my ability.

The singing teacher advised me that if I were to spend the next two years just singing very softly, then maybe my voice would return. Reluctantly I tried this, but to no avail, and gave up all hope of ever singing properly again. Since then, I had never sought singing tuition on the grounds that I was not worth anyone's time, because my voice was no good. I lacked the ability, so the whole thing was doomed to failure anyhow. It would never be possible for me with my poor voice to sing well. Also, how could I justify it? What would it be, some kind of self-indulgent money wasting ego trip? I needed to spend time and money in a more useful fashion than that, I had told myself many times. These latter thoughts about it came to me after I had grown up.

Maria told me that she knew about all of this, and I felt so deeply touched by her love, that tears came to my eyes. She loved the little girl in me. The one who felt unloved, and full of childhood dreams. It was this almost motherly acceptance of who and what I was, which moved my heart the most.

Back at the Ranch

At the next group sharing, I told the group about Maria, so that they would know as much about what was going on as possible. After the first time, I did not know if she would ever sing through me again. Nothing had been said by Maria about the future.

Meanwhile, I was getting some positive feedback from various members of the group. One of them told me that there had been a childhood issue, which she had felt she ought to deal with in the meditation, but she could not face it yet. Then after Maria came through and sang, it left her in exactly the right space to look at it, for which she thanked Maria. I was amazed, and began to see this as a way of helping humanity. To be able to do that would be a greater gift than being a professional opera singer for me. Of course, I acknowledge the wonderful service that opera singers give to people in the entertainment world, but to allow Maria to sing through me, bringing her heavenly music and deep knowledge of how to use sound to help those aspiring to spirituality, would be an enormous joy.

For the toning in the following meditation, Maria came again. I had started rather tentatively on a fairly low note, and noticed how the sound coming out was freer than usual for me. This gave me more confidence in my voice than I was accustomed to, even though it was just I singing. The song Joan had played to us before we started had words in it about going higher, so I intuitively surmised, that if Maria came, she would want to sing high notes. I tried an ascending arpeggio to raise the pitch an octave, and found that fairly easy. I was still on quite a low note. I let the pitch waver about a bit, remembering to use more air than I usually do, and then the sound changed. Maria had arrived. She was gently taking over with my full consent and encouragement.

Sometimes I doubted her presence a little, but then I noticed that I was not controlling the direction of the pitch, only allowing it. Once, she did an upward slide, which was so completely even, that it compared with sliding my finger up a violin string. That was more than enough evidence for me that I was not doing it. She took me higher and higher. As we went up, the nature of the sound changed, but nothing was forced, so I felt no strain in my throat afterwards. The high notes sounded very clear, as I gained confidence in Maria's ability to sing them. I realized, that she was not just doing it, but teaching me, which is why she had let me start on my own to see if I would remember anything from the previous day's lesson.

After the meditation following the toning, someone told me that Maria had taken her straight into the space necessary for her meditation, which had made it very easy for her to be there.

The next day, Maria came again. She seemed to wait until I had worked my way up to the bottom of what may have been her natural range in her previous life, and then joined in with me. She soared up to the heights again, and her music was very free. I never knew which way it was going next.

Suddenly I became aware that everyone else had finished singing, so "we" cut the sound immediately in mid-flow. This toning was to have been preparation for a serious meditation, but everyone having heard what had happened, was in fits of laughter. Surprised, I watched them rolling around on the floor, some trying to stop hopeless giggles unsuccessfully, and other just letting their laughter flow. "Laughter is a great healer", I thought to myself, but I felt a real concern that as it was going on for so long, as it was seriously holding up the start of Joan's led meditation. I did not see how she could possibly take any of us anywhere with so much noise in the room. They looked very happy, but this was Joan's workshop, not mine, and I did not wish to disrupt it. To my great relief, eventually the group became quiet enough for Joan to carry on.

Afterwards the feedback from the group about Maria was about how much joy she brought, and how much they appreciated her coming. Joan was happy, and I need not have worried that "we" were causing any trouble.

On the Boat again

The next day, we had our second trip out on the boat. We were not having much success to start with in our search for dolphins, so Joan decided to have a group toning session. Sometimes that does not make any difference, and other times it helps to create harmony in the group and raise the vibrations with sound, which helps to attract dolphins. It may depend on how the dolphins feel that particular day, where they are at the time, and what else they have on their agenda.

As Maria had been through several times by now, people were starting to look forward to her voice, and I was feeling that this was a lot to live up to, especially as I had no means of ensuring that she would want to be there and help. I need not have worried, for she came through powerfully, her voice soaring all over the place. Much to my amusement, I learnt afterwards, that Joan had warned the captain that we had an opera singer on board, and therefore there was no need to be frightened by the noise! She also drew my attention to the fact that others had benefited, as with a background of plenty of sound from Maria, they had become bolder, and were enjoying their own singing more.

Following that, we found dolphins. It is my opinion that Maria had helped bring about this encounter, but one must not lose sight of the fact that the love from the group, any telepathic communication that I did not know about, and the desires of the dolphins themselves must also be taken into account.

Later on in the morning, I had my first brief swim with pilot whales. They tend to be trailed by oceanic white-tip sharks, who can be quite aggressive towards humans if one is unlucky, so only three of us were allowed to join Joan in the water at the same time. We stayed near the boat, to which we all returned safely, having seen not only the pilot whales, but also two sharks swimming along in deep water well below us. Everyone, including the whales and the sharks, remained calm, and I never felt we were ever in any danger.

The captain had been nervous about it, as he was new to the job, so no doubt he did not start breathing again until we were all safely back on the boat. I would trust Joan who is a very responsible person, albeit an adventurer, to follow her inner guidance in making the right decisions for us anywhere. The energies in the water with the pilot whales were quite different from those I have felt with the dolphins or the humpback whales. It may well have been a combination of theirs and ours I was feeling, but I cannot describe it in words properly. A first time is always special, and I doubt I will forget watching the three pilot whales gliding smoothly along, about a metre below the surface not far ahead of us, before they disappeared out of sight.

Back in the Group Room

That afternoon, we were toning again. Maria's voice was powerful, but a little bit quieter than the morning I thought. She told me that my vocal chords needed to be trained gently, not too much at once. This time, she seemed to be leading the whole group. She opened it by singing the first note, and even indicated when we should stop by a suitable drop in the pitch, as I felt her withdraw. The harmony that Maria and the group created together sounded beautiful. I had listened to it full of joy, and its beauty combined with Maria's love made me feel tearful again. I was moved by it all.

The Future with Maria?

I did not know if Maria was planning a future with me or not, but one thing was clear to me. I was very interested. It was possible that in the autumn, or at some time, I would go to Europe to do a book promotion tour. When speaking of this in the group sharing, I put out my idea that whereas some speakers talk, and then show slides to their public, I could talk, and then "make a noise", as I put it, when thinking of Maria's beautiful music. Knowing that I was a part of this sound as well, I did not like to call it singing. I was too modest. Later, it occurred to me that it could even be used to introduce short meditations. One person confided in me, that in her opinion, she felt sure that a professional teacher would love to work with my voice. This was very helpful, because if the sound coming out of me sounded good even to others to justify training it, then maybe it would be worthwhile getting singing lessons when I was at home. I could not be sure, and decided just to remain open about this possibility. Maria seemed to be teaching me, and giving me some of my lost confidence back, but maybe a little earthly help as well could be useful.

13

After the Seminar

On 20th July, Joan's seminar came to a close. The following day I moved down to Dolphin house near the beach.

On various occasions I meditated, and toned alone at the beginning, usually trying to choose my moment, so that it would not disturb other people. When I was overheard, I received very positive feedback about it.

On Tuesday night, there was to be a meditation up at Sky Ranch. Joan would not be leading this one, but I felt moved to attend it. Perhaps because I had already meditated alone that day, I found that this was to be a "resting" meditation, where the biggest benefit to me was that I had to stop doing everything else, and just be quiet and still for half an hour. So it was after a good rest, the lady leading us announced that we were to tone a little. My cold was almost gone, and chanting was becoming easier for me each day.

Maria came through with a lovely sweet sound, which could easily be heard above everybody else. She knew exactly when to stop, and as a group we were creating beautiful harmonies. Again, I had the feeling she was leading it to some extent. Now I knew why I was there. It was for the toning. Afterwards, someone told me that he had opened his eyes in the middle of it, because he wanted to know where the sound was coming from. I had made it clear to all afterwards that it was not me, but someone who liked to sing through me, and how this was all very new for me, and she advised that whenever I could, it would be beneficial to chant with another person, because with two of us, it would create a resonance.

I would have to wait and see where this new interest would take me after I had returned home. It was something both special and joyful.

Chapter 2

Singing

After my return from Hawaii, I made inquiries about a singing teacher to Jackie, one of my neighbours who sang in a local choir. She discovered it was harder than she thought to find out about one from her friends. Eventually she came round to the door with some details on it that someone had given her, hoping the person might be suitable.

The first thing I did was to lose the piece of paper, but recovered it just after finishing some tasks that were urgent, leaving me freer to organise something new for myself without too much stress. I left a message on the lady's answering machine. I waited, but there was no reply from her, so I tried again.

This time I had a real person on the end of the line, and asked, "Is that Felicity Jones?" "Yes," said the voice. She explained that she was busy for the next few days, but would get back to me around the middle of the following week. She tried to telephone me one morning, but I thought it was a fax coming through, so we failed to connect. Later on in the day, when I came back into the house again, I decided to see who had called. I checked the number, and saw that it had been Felicity trying to get in touch again. I made another attempt. Success! A singing lesson was arranged for the following morning.

The Lesson

So it came to pass on 19th October 2001, that at nine thirty prompt, Felicity Jones walked through my front door to give me my first lesson. She looked quizzically at me, and said something like, "Strange! I thought I was going to find that you were someone I had already met, or seen around somewhere." I looked at her, and confirmed that we had not met before, and after a short discussion, the lesson commenced.

About half way through, I recognised her face and hair. When Maria had shown me a picture of someone who had taught music, whom I naturally thought (having had no idea how she had actually looked) must be Maria herself, it was not. Instead she had been showing me my future singing teacher. Felicity was a good match for the picture I had been shown. She was a lady on her spiritual pathway, and her hairstyle, hair colour, skin colour, and age were all just as I had seen them that day when standing on the boat in the waters surrounding Hawaii. Music was her life! I had never even considered finding a singing teacher at that point, so no wonder I assumed that all the information Maria was giving me was about herself, not someone else as well.

This discovery that she was recommended by Maria as the right one to give me some guidance, gave me an absolute knowing that she was indeed someone to whom I was being guided. Therefore I did not hesitate to arrange more lessons with her. Felicity had never sung opera to my knowledge, and although she emphasised that she had not been trained herself, it was evident that she had studied the subject enough to know a lot more about it than I did. She not only gave private lessons, but was also training a choir. She was a very encouraging teacher, which helped my confidence, and she had endless patience with me.

When Felicity had spoken to me on the telephone before she met me, to my surprise, she remarked that my speaking voice was very resonant, as though I ought to be singing opera, whereas she taught "tercet" music. I had never heard of this before. I thought she was right concerning what I would like to do, but I had to begin somewhere. The name tercet refers to music written for three voices, usually in parts, which may or not be accompanied.

Near the beginning of this lesson, she told me that the reason she did not need a piano, something which had surprised me, was because she preferred to teach "a cappella" music, which means sung unaccompanied. In nature, the songs Felicity taught me to sing were spiritual, and often in Latin. They had "parts", were sometimes sung like canons, and were very beautiful for their simplicity, harmonies and words.

I began to see how the musical tuition I had received as a child at a convent school had prepared me for this, although without the prompting from Maria, I would never have looked for a teacher, or had enough belief in my own potential to have the nerve to ask for help.

My biggest problem during these lessons, or practices on my own, was the unreliability of my voice. One minute I would be singing away happily, and the next my voice would go. At these times, trying to clear my throat or coughing was like a full time occupation. Sometimes it would clear successfully, and I could carry on, at least for a while. Other times it did not.

21/10/01 as I woke up, I could hear a beautiful female voice singing, rather like opera, and certainly that calibre of voice. I would be very surprised if it was not Maria's voice. The sound faded as I became fully conscious, but served to encourage me to persevere with my singing lessons.

I was intrigued when I discovered that some of the sounds that Maria had made through me in Hawaii, turned out to be similar to some of Felicity's warming up exercises, namely the "slides", or "portamentos", as I later discovered they are called.

At this stage, I was trying to practise a little every day when I could fit it in, hoping that this would strengthen my voice, as well as educate me, so that I would become a better channel for my new friend Maria.

29/10/01 was the day of my third lesson. I was particularly croaky throughout, making producing a beautiful sound more or less impossible in spite of numerous attempts to clear my throat. Then the miracle happened. For the last round of the last song, "Viva viva la Musica", Maria came through and sang it for me. She was not totally in my body, but just enough to change the nature of the sound. How does she do it so beautifully without even having to clear my throat first? I asked myself. I shared this with Felicity who had heard the change in my voice. She suggested that maybe the lady who sang it for me was trying to show me that this was how it could be the whole time. Neither of us really knew. This was the first and only time that Maria came through when Felicity could hear it.

By the time I was ready to leave for France in November, I had received a total of five lessons. I was hoping to make music a part of the little one-day seminars I was expecting to lead, so I took copies of some of the words with me. More surprises were in store for me, as I will relate in the next chapter.

Chapter 3
Life Leads Me To France

I was very lukewarm about the prospect of going to France. In fact, totally disinterested is perhaps closer to the truth. So how did this happen? It was Marguerite Vidal, the translator of my third book into the French language, who invited me to come to Alsace for a book promotion tour. After considerable hesitation, for I do not like to leave my horse, house, and garden too often, or for too long, I decided, that as all three of my completed books were now available in the French language, this would be a good moment to do this, and perhaps it was a necessary part of my pathway. It was more a sense of duty, than anything connected with pleasure.

I had no more than five or six days away from home in mind, and was fairly horrified when I learnt from Marguerite's e-mails that it had somehow been extended to cover thirteen days including my travelling days. I was not happy. However, during the night, my guides managed to persuade me that this was the right thing for me to do. So reluctantly, I agreed.

There were certainly times when I managed to feel quite enthusiastic about it all, to the point of eventually knowing, that if it had to be cancelled, I would feel greatly disappointed, and other moments when I dwelt on the fact, that it would involve being shut away from Mother Nature in stuffy book shops waiting to see if anyone wanted me to sign a book for them or not. Lacking confidence, I consoled myself that at least I would need very little French to manage that part, as long as I could remember how to sign my own name. "Well that should not be too difficult", I said to myself. Then there was a conference that had been proposed to last about an hour and a half. As this was a long time to speak, I decided to meditate in the hopes of receiving some inspiration for it.

My Meditation

This time, as guides, I saw a robed figure holding a cross with a circle around the top of it, who I felt must be Jesus, and a beautiful lady dressed in a red sari, with a little red mark on her forehead. I had not seen her before. She was stroking a little lamb, giving it loving caring nurturing energy. (I interpreted this as a sign that new life, or a new type of adventure was coming into my life.) Taking my arm, she gently guided me to where we needed to be. On the way there, we paused to observe people sitting and resting on the grass, watching children playing joyfully on a slide and some swings. Beyond all that, I saw a brightly shining guiding star in the sky, and from it came a white dove with a message in its beak. "Sing a song!" I read. This was quickly followed by seeing many whales in the ocean, who were singing their songs and calling for attention. Some dolphin energy was there too, but mostly the whale calls.

Around the shores of the ocean I saw many different species of animals gathering, who were fascinated by the whale songs. Physically they could not leave the land, but I observed how their out-of-body experiences allowed them to connect with the cetacean energies, thus picking up some of the wisdom and knowing, that these mammals come to remind us of now.

This vision made me aware of how all of us can connect with their very special consciousness, even if time and money do not permit foreign travel to meet them in the water physically. It can happen both in our sleep state, as well as in meditation. At a later date, this lady told me that I would be helped with the music, especially singing, during my trip. I imagined that it would be this lady who was going to help me. Little did I know concerning who was really coming! Read on.

In spite of this guidance, I still found ninety minutes of talking a daunting task. In my mind, I tried to convince myself it would not be as hard as I thought. After all, as Marguerite was willing to translate, everything would need to be said twice, once in each language, which would surely

20

reduce it to three quarters of an hour. I could further reduce the number of words necessary by playing whale song, and then singing a little. By now, I had calculated that all this would reduce it to half an hour of talking, which did not seem too difficult. After all, I had managed that much before in Barcelona.

My Preparations

At my request, Captain Roger Maier, who works for Bottom Time Adventures, and lives in Florida, sent me an excellent recording he had made himself of whale song. Then there were those five singing lessons I had had, so that I would be able to sing. It is interesting to note that Felicity had chosen to teach me songs that were like prayers for the Earth. This, I thought, would be very useful, as I had seen in a second meditation concerning what I should do in France, that part of it would involve helping the Earth.

Having observed on the programme, which Marguerite put together for me, how three one-day seminars were planned for me to lead, I spent quite a lot of time playing music on CDs I already had, and buying new ones, that I thought could possibly help with any meditations I might lead.

How the seminars came to be included is a story in itself. As I had never really understood the difference in usage of the words, conference, seminar, and workshop, (though I understood the latter) I unwittingly referred to the conference with the wrong word, namely seminar, in my correspondence with Marguerite. The result was that she asked me if I would like to give seminars (workshops) as well as the conference and the book signing. At first I was rather confused, due to my lack of understanding of my own language, but when I had sorted this out with Marguerite's help, and discovered that she was willing to organise workshops for me as well, I agreed, noting that their inclusion in the programme had considerably raised my enthusiasm level for the trip.

Thinking I would spend most of my evenings alone in what I wrongly supposed was a self-contained flat on the first floor, I also included two new CDs for my personal pleasure. These were both opera, something I had become extremely interested in since I made the acquaintance of

Maria, the one who sings. I just hoped that Marguerite would have a spare CD player I could borrow, and that if I kept the volume low, it would not disturb either her, or Richard, her partner, with whom she lived, presumably on the ground floor.

The fact that I would have a little kitchenette on the first floor, or so I believed, and would therefore be able to prepare all my own meals was a great relief, because my diet was very restricted. I felt that these arrangements would avoid making the lives of Richard and Marguerite unpleasant or difficult, especially if we were not happy together. For me, it would be like a safe haven to retire to when there was time, and I needed my own space. Secondly, I would be there for twelve nights, and this, I thought, would be a long time for Richard and Marguerite to share their personal space with me. So thinking that we would not have to be together all the time is what put my mind at rest.

I was accustomed to living alone in my own house. It might seem strange that I should concern myself so much with this issue, but I still remembered vividly, how in the past I had so often found myself trying to live alongside people who deeply resented my presence, or my lifestyle. I did not want to experience that again.

In between contemplating my fears and reservations, along with the fact that I did not want to be away from Starlight, my enthusiasm for the whole trip continued to increase. By the time I left England, I knew that if it had to be cancelled, I would be bitterly disappointed. So much time and effort had gone into preparing myself by then, that I did not want my trouble to be wasted. Being too busy to read a French book to help my French, I had even practised thinking in my limited French when I was alone. I knew I was being helped with it during the night, as several times, when I awoke in the morning, I discovered that my head was full of French thoughts. "I must try and speak at least a little bit of French when I get out there", I instructed myself.

My adventure began as I loaded my car with my luggage, and set off for Manchester airport on 14th. November 2001. I felt extremely stressed and concerned that if the airport was very full, or there was more traffic than usual, perhaps I would miss my flights. I had only travelled about a mile, when my guides showed me a vision of a rainbow. I accepted that as a sign that all would go well, and stopped worrying about my flights. I remembered how I had even seen a rainbow with my physical eyes, when out in the hills two days previously.

I arrived in good time at Manchester, and the journey continued to go well. Marguerite and Richard met me in Strasbourg, and drove me to the little village of Elsenheim where they live in Alsace. I was shown the first floor, which seemed to have everything I could wish for except the kitchen! A wave of inner panic swept through my veins. Having thought I was taking total responsibility for my own food, I had not given Marguerite any advance warning of the nature of my dietary needs, beyond the necessity of access to a health food shop. I would be staying with them for so long, and how would we manage to put up with each other? "Will this totally ruin an otherwise promising friendship?" I asked myself. At that point, I had completely forgotten about the rainbows. (In my mind they are good omens.)

That first evening, I was well fed by Marguerite, and having decided to put aside my other concerns as much as I could, I went upstairs to enjoy a lovely hot bath, and thankfully retired to bed. To make a short story of it, living in the same house as Richard and Marguerite, did not destroy the friendship.

This French experience consisted of one surprise after another, which made it all very exciting. The first one was that Marguerite had greeted me in French, not English as I had expected, when we met in the airport. I had rashly assumed that as she was obviously much more fluent in English than I was in French, we would speak English together. I had planned speaking some French when signing books, because, after all, I would not need to say very much, and it would be a nice informal way to practise the language and learn a little.

For my seminars, and the conference, English would be a must. I did not concern myself about my limited French, because I thought that Marguerite was going to translate every syllable that came out of my mouth. I was expecting to need some French for Richard, as I had had a partly intuitive feeling that he would not understand English, which turned out to be true.

Marguerite's help with my French was invaluable, but to my astonishment, I found myself guided to speak French all the time, except for most of my channelling. (There is more to be said about channelling later.) Suffice to say, it was the best opportunity of my life to improve my linguistic ability with the French language.

On the first day, we went to a bookshop in Mulhouse for book signing. As we were leaving, I observed the name of a little cafe in the street, "L'Arc-en-Ciel", "The Rainbow". This was my third rainbow, and an encouraging sign concerning things to come.

The second day was the day of my conference in Colmar. It was only after I had started to speak, that I realised that I was about to do the whole thing in French. It was partly because I could not decide at what point I was going to start speaking English again, something I had not done since I left Manchester. Of course I did not know all of the words, but found both Marguerite and my audience of approximately fifty people all very helpful each time I was in difficulties.

I did all of the things that I had been instructed to do when meditating before leaving, and that included standing there in front of all of them and singing "Donna Nobis Pacem" (Give us Peace) as a solo. Afterwards, when I wondered how on Earth I had found the courage to sing alone before so many people, I remembered that Maria was working with me, and knew that somehow she had helped. This was the first time I had sung before so many people successfully, without faltering or forgetting my words, since I was about twelve years old. My voice was a little husky, as I had just been speaking for the best part of an hour and a half at least. I commented half to myself, and half to the people, "C'etait mieux avant de parler". (I meant it was better before I had had to speak.) How was this received? They clapped! I heard myself say. "Merci" several times emphatically in expressive tones of deeply felt gratitude for their applause and love, in a way that I did not know I was capable of.

Later I understood that it had been Maria's energy coming through me with her thanks as well as mine. In my case it was perhaps more a sense of relief more than anything else to be well received. At the time, I was not really aware of how much help Maria was giving me. That realisation came later, for at this stage I did not understand what was happening.

The whale song CD was enjoyed, as I observed how some of the people closed their eyes while they listened to it, in order to feel the vibrations it brought more keenly. (No, they were not sleeping!) The questions started quite early in the evening, because without the need of a French translation, my prepared material had not lasted very long. The audience, with their inquiring minds, were an enormous help to me, frequently reminding me of things I had forgotten to say. Often, I answered their inquiries with a story. I felt that they guided me to share the things that were of most interest to them, which was exactly what I most wanted to do.

Perhaps it was this that made it so difficult to stop at the end of ninety minutes. We had been told that the doors of the building would be locked for the night at a set time, but it was still quite a struggle to convince everyone that we really had to stop and go home before we were locked in for the night. We managed to finish after approximately two hours.

I was happy, because I felt it had gone well. The whole experience had greatly enhanced my confidence, as well as allowing me to enjoy my audience. Enhanced confidence was something I would really need for the experiences coming to me during the rest of my trip. I observed that there is a part of me that thrives, when I am the centre of attention. What a blessing for me this was, and what a positive way had been shown to me to use this facet of my personality for the common good.

My First Seminars

Here is a really brief account of my first seminars, so that you can see where Maria fitted into them. I was really worried about giving these. I still lacked a lot of confidence in my own ability, including concerns about managing a full day of it. Whereas I already knew that I could not even contemplate the prospect of giving a seminar without including music, it would be a full eighteen months before I would fully understand to what extent this was a beginning of my adventures in the use of sound. The wonderful meditations I carefully noted down about the fairies and so on, belong in another book, but the musical aspects of them relate to my work and Maria more than I would ever have guessed.

Part of my preparation for these had consisted of leading little meditations in French for Marguerite and Richard in the mornings or evenings or both. I do not think Marguerite had been aware, that I had never led more than one person at a time, before my arrival at her house. I did not keep this a secret, and it was her idea even before I told her this, that it would be a good way for me to become accustomed to guiding people in the French language to practise with the three of us.

After each of these meditations, she was able to help me correct my French in places where I had used the wrong word, or mispronounced something. This did help both my confidence, and French considerably. I practised leading toning on these occasions as a preparation for the meditating. The feedback from Marguerite and Richard helped me to feel that there would be something special that I could give people in my seminars, even if this was totally non-definable in words.

During one of these tonings, I saw how the sound was causing the energies around my body to expand. I saw the angels in the room, (I gathered from my host and hostess that they were residents of the house), and also the nature spirits starting to arrive, which I found particularly encouraging, as part of the promised agenda for the seminars was to be a contact with nature. They, it seems, also respond to sound.

The morning of the first seminar arrived. One participant was expected, someone who had signed on after he had attended the conference the previous evening. I had been more than a little anxious about how I would keep one person happy and entertained for a whole day on his own, although it occurred to me that if Richard and Marguerite took part as well, it would feel like a group, and that is what I had prepared myself for. Luckily it was revealed over breakfast that they had the same idea.

I began the day with chanting OM, allowing everyone complete freedom of melodic line. All three of them obligingly joined in with me. I later used music on CDs for dancing as well as an aid to meditation. These things along with group sharings filled the morning.

When I discovered at lunchtime, that the one man who had come to join us was an experienced seminar leader, I was heartily relieved that I had not known that before I started, as it might have really unnerved me. He was so easy and helpful to lead, that by this time, I was happy enough in my work not to mind who or what he was. It was great to have him there. After lunch, it was time to go outside for exercise, fresh air, and the advertised "contact with nature".

We returned to the house, where, to my great delight a beautiful wood fire was lit, for all of us were cold. We drank herbal tea, ate a little something, and thus fortified continued with the workshop.

We shared the fruits we had received during our meditations outside with nature. To finish the day, I led a fourth meditation, using Hemi-Sync music, something I had discovered in Joan Ocean's workshops. It was developed by the Monroe Institute in the States, and, very simply put, it helps to organise the brainwaves in a manner that is conducive to the state required for meditation.

By the end of the day, I was well pleased with the results. Everybody had sung, danced, and meditated, and I had lived through it!

Officially, the second workshop was run under the same title as the first, namely "The Spiritual Journey", but I knew before I started, that I must stay open to inspiration throughout, and thus adjust it to the needs of those present. Having survived the previous day, I definitely had more confidence. Today we would be five people, Richard and Marguerite, a man and a woman coming together, whom I had never met before, and myself.

Different people coming together meant a change in the group energies, as well as introducing other interests. So it was, that during the tea break, the subject of dolphins was brought up by Mira (not her real name), so I followed the inspiration to play part of Roger's "Whale Song" CD to assist us in our meditation, which was particularly appreciated by her. To go along with this, I used whale, dolphin, and angel guides to help show us our spiritual pathways.

After lunch we enjoyed our outdoor contact with nature, in spite of the freezing cold temperatures, and shared our meditations in front of the fire on our return after some hot tea.

Instead of a final meditation, with this group, I felt we needed more music. So we finished the day singing "Viva viva la Musica", which roughly translates as "Long live Music!" followed by "Donna nobis Pacem". I invited people to join in with me as well as they could, and knowing that the pitch might be unattainable for the men, I told them to sing what ever notes they wanted. It was the words, with the meaning "Give us Peace" that were important. Some of the harmonies were beautiful!

The importance of including "Viva viva la Musica" was clear to me. Many years ago in meditation, I had learnt that one of the first things, which I had discovered about the needs of Planet Earth before my first incarnation on it, was that the planet needed music, so singing something that meant "Long live music!" was about celebrating one of the best aids to the well-being of the planet that I knew of.

After the visitors had left, Marguerite commented, "Your voice was stronger today". My speaking voice had had to be stronger, so that Martin, (not his real name), a slightly deaf participant in the group, could hear it, but I felt that she meant my singing. As we know, Maria helps from time to time with that, and although I had not sounded like an opera singer, I felt that she had been present quite often, helping in suitable quantities as the occasion demanded.

Chapter 4

The Most Surprising Revelation of All

It was soon after the second seminar, that Marguerite had asked me if someone was singing through me. I wanted to know why she was asking, and she replied, "Because it is not your voice when you sing". I confirmed that she was right, and told her about Maria, and how since I was aware of Maria's wish to sing through me, I had sung more often to try and train my voice, and now had had five singing lessons from Felicity. Marguerite commented that she doubted anyone could learn to sing as I sang after only five lessons, and was obviously very interested, for she must have thought about it a lot overnight.

In the interests of accuracy, I must add that although the sound may have been better than most people can manage without any proper training, it was still full of imperfections. Nonetheless, it was undoubtedly of a superior quality to anything I could ever have hoped to achieve if Maria had not been present doing at least some of it for me.

So it came to pass, that on the morning of 20th. November, while I was having breakfast that I thought to myself, "I think I have woken up just enough to tolerate, or even enjoy a little music." A few seconds later, I heard music. Marguerite had just started playing one of her CDs. It was not the opera that I would have chosen, but I decided that it was pleasing enough for me to appreciate it, and after all, this was not my house, and I must be willing to welcome others listening to music of their own choice, not just the things that I wanted to hear.

While I was eating Marguerite asked if I minded if she measured my vibrations. There are various ways of measuring them, and the system she used called them the "angstrom", or "aengstroem". (I saw two different spellings of it in books). A pendulum was used over the palm of my hand in this case. To put things in perspective, I will state a few facts here.

One angstrom = one millionth of a millimetre.

The vibrational length of red waves is 6,5000

The previous normal rate for a human being was around 6,500 to 8,000

Up to 10,000 is the measurement of the physical body

10,000 - 13,000, the etheric body

13,500 - 18,000 spiritual body.

It is probably a fair statement to say that the whole truth about the figures is not yet fully revealed, although very interesting research is taking place now, and all the time we are in a process of change as we evolve, and move closer to the Light, the Source from which we came. So many people are now well above what was previously considered normal.

I was measured. "The same as me!" said Marguerite excitedly, "150,000". Her next request was would I come and sing, channelling the voice of Maria. I said I was not ready, as I wanted to finish washing up the things I had used for my breakfast, and so on. Then I would come. I do not like to be rushed.

Still only half way through these mundane tasks, I heard the CD Marguerite was listening to start to play a setting for flute of Gounod's "Ave Maria". At this point, I felt Maria's vibrations so strongly, that I knew I must stop everything else immediately, and I walked hurriedly into the other room, stopping close to the CD player, and began to sing, adjusting the volume to my liking.

Marguerite said afterwards, that she had thought I would surely come at the right moment if it was meant to be, and I had. Maria sang. Marguerite also told me that she had almost cried when she heard it, and I myself felt very moved by the experience, to the point where I was not really sure what to do with myself, or where to go next, when the song finished.

I commented that she (the one who sings through me) liked the song, because Maria was her name. No doubt, I thought to myself, it made her feel welcome when I sang it. (Marguerite told me later that the words "Ave Maria" meant something like "I salute you Maria".) I remember embracing Marguerite, and full of emotion at that moment telling her "I did it for her! I did it for her!" (Maria). I was referring to the practise I had put in at home, and the singing lessons I had had, in short, my humble attempts to prepare my vocal chords for a better singer than myself to use them.

As I was trying to decide which I wanted to do most, walk in the sunshine, or drink cups of tea, both of us realised that Maria was still strongly present, and had not finished. We returned to the sitting room, and I asked Marguerite if she would tone with me. This was agreed, and it was recorded.

I started the sound coming out of my mouth, and almost immediately, Maria took over, as the sound started to soar upwards. At the time, I was not aware when Marguerite stopped singing, and also with my eyes closed, I had no idea of where she was, or what she was doing. To me the whole thing was amazing! Sounds came out of my mouth that had never come out of it before. Maria was moving my body as she sang in a way that was totally uncharacteristic for me. On the higher notes, there were what sounded to me like trills, where I could feel movements in my throat that were completely new to me. It would stop while Maria took another breath, and start again, sometimes from exactly where she had left off. The pitch varied. Sometimes I would feel and hear it descending to a level I personally felt more comfortable with, only to ascend again.

Finally, as the pitch came down really low, I heard Maria's voice fading, as she ceased singing. There was silence at last. I opened my eyes, and there was Marguerite just in front of me with her hands on the floor. When I asked her what she had been doing, she explained that after she had stopped singing herself, she had used some energy work to assist Maria to come through, and at the end, she was making sure that I was really grounded again.

Maria had never come through with so much power before. I could not possibly doubt that another being was working through me. After all, how could I possibly have known how to make sounds like that? There had been great determination on Maria's part to get through, and she had succeeded. I could feel the force of her will. Marguerite had really helped her, and I for my part had let go of any control I might have had in order to make it possible. I had given my full permission.

For me, the experience was overwhelming. I knew, that whereas it definitely had happened, I needed time to really believe and accept that something so powerful had taken place, and it really had happened to me.

When we listened to the recording of it together, we both laughed, in my case because these sounds were not something I was accustomed to hearing everyday. Also, I laugh at times when I am relaxing. In addition, it was so comical the way it would stop and start again, almost unexpectedly. I do not wish to exaggerate this story, lest someone hearing it at a later date be bitterly disappointed that it is not more impressive than it is, but what I have written is an account of my true feelings and reactions when it happened. It had felt like a very long time, but actually, this first recording of Maria's unaccompanied voice alone lasted only three and a half minutes. She did not sound as she would have done in her own physical body, but it was undoubtedly not something I would have been capable of doing without her, even if I had understood what she wanted.

Maria had finished, and Marguerite wanted to measure the angstrom while she was still there. Maria knew this, and waited patiently in my body looking around at the physical environment with wide-open big eyes. (She used her own eyes, not mine.) The measurement had increased from 150,000 (my personal normal) to somewhere between 275,000 and 280.000, which Marguerite told me confirmed that another entity was present.

At last I was free to go out in the sunshine, and walk for a while, with a hand drawn map of Elsenheim showing the bakery, and the mission of coming back with a loaf of bread, something I achieved.

An Astonishing Revelation

That evening, we played the recording of Maria to Richard. Then Marguerite wanted to make another recording of her. I agreed. While I was upstairs in the bathroom beforehand, I heard the words, "You should go downstairs and sing with Maria Callas". I knew that I had her voice on two of the CDs, which I had brought with me, so I decided to choose something sung by her for the Maria who sings through me to join in with.

I arrived downstairs, and Marguerite had a question for me. "Is it Maria Callas who sings through you?" Although surprised by her question, I remembered clearly, how when I was in Hawaii, a member of Joan's group, had asked me exactly the same question. Naturally I had dismissed such a possibility immediately. I felt sure that the lady who sang through me was someone who knew how to sing, whose life had been music, but who was not well known, although I felt she had sung opera on stage, maybe in a small theatre somewhere and probably not very often, or for only a short period of her life.

I had felt convinced that the possibility of a soprano with the ability of Maria Callas would never even dream about coming close to somebody as untalented as I am with my croaky, worn out, untrained, squeaky contralto voice, and who was rather old for starting such things in my own opinion. After all, singers should study at a music academy from an early age, while the vocal chords are elastic and trainable. I had done none of that. Instead, I had spent much of my life shouting to make myself heard in windy fields or horse-riding riding arenas, until I was so hoarse, I would have to beckon to my pupils to come over to me, so that with what little voice I had left, I could give them the next set of spoken instructions.

However, Marguerite was the second person to ask if it could be Callas, so the coincidence was too much for me to ignore it, especially as I would later understand the true significance of the words, "You should go downstairs and sing with Maria Callas", which I had just heard in the bathroom. That would give me three reasons to believe this remote possibility. At last, I would be fully ready to accept the unlikely truth, that, yes, it was indeed MARIA CALLAS.

Later on during the evening, Marguerite admitted that she had been certain it was Maria Callas who came through me, even before she asked the question. Therefore she must have asked me just to find out if I knew who it was, and I did not. Marguerite's next question was would I be willing to allow Maria Callas to speak through me? I gave her an affirmative, on the condition that she helped Maria and I with the process of letting her come.

An Initiation for Maria and me

I chose a track on my CD with her voice on it, and after dancing and moving around a bit to warm myself up, and loosen the physical body, I started to try and channel her voice, singing to the selected aria.

Marguerite and Richard were both present to assist us, and it was being recorded. Maria and I were there together, but it seemed to me at the time that it was my decision when it was not going very well to stop it, and try something else.

When I played the recording after I arrived home, on hearing my voice explaining this in English with a slight accent, as if I was not really completely familiar with my own language, to Marguerite, to whom I usually spoke French, I understood that I must have been at least half absent, and also, that it was Maria influencing my words. (I changed back to using my French, when Marguerite replied to me in French.)

It was at this point, that I grasped the significance of the instructions to sing with Maria in the bathroom, i.e. that it meant letting her sing through me, as opposed to singing along with her voice on a CD. It was only after my return home, while researching some of Maria's life, that I discovered she had been known to stop the orchestra in the middle of a recording, if she felt the quality of a note was not good enough, and then try again. So this behaviour was characteristic for her.

Following Marguerite's suggestion, we chose the recording of Ave Maria with the flute playing the melody, and no voice on it again, so that the only voice on our recording would be the combined efforts of Maria and myself. It was noticeable that the singing was mostly far more relaxed than in the morning. Marguerite observed this first, stating that it was probably because she knew that she was going to be allowed to talk afterwards.

However, it did not escape my own musical ear that the top B flat was slightly flat, a painful experience for me to listen to, but at the time, I did not know that this recording was all pitched a semitone higher than most sopranos sing it, so it was actually a B natural that was flat! My vocal chords had never been trained to sing any high notes. Therefore this little 'flaw' in the end result was disappointing, but not really surprising to me. Although Maria's own vocal chords had been capable of greater things than that, I dare to assume, that there must some limitations, when one has to sing using the body of someone whose conviction it is, that only a lower range of notes are available. This must be especially true, when it is someone who firmly believes on that day, he or she cannot do it, and therefore the sound will be awful! Apart from that, I was comforted to feel a warmth in her voice as she sang.

I remembered channelling an extraterrestrial entity in 1998 during Rhea Power's Light Worker Training, just for a few minutes. Apart from that, I had frequently relayed the information, as in the animal messages of my previous books, writing down all that I had been told afterwards, but I had not actually channelled entities in the way that allows them to enter my body sufficiently to speak directly to an audience again. Channelling the singing was the nearest I had come to that, and I found this a relatively non-threatening way for me to begin, as I did not have to worry about whether or not the right words were coming out of my mouth at the time.

Therefore I was quite relieved when channelling Maria's spoken voice, to hear a voice coming through me that I was certain did not belong to me. It was really necessary for Maria to bring through as much of her previous personality as she could, in order to convince me that it was really she coming through, and not I, who was making it all up. At the time, I knew almost nothing about her, so I could not consciously reinvent her personality for her. I know that many mediums have doubted the authenticity of their own channelling, and as I am no exception to that, I need a lot of evidence and convincing, before I can accept that these things really do happen.

Of course I know that it may be tinged with little bits of me here and there, but I did my best to keep myself enough out of the way to make the communication as pure as possible. In between singing and speaking, Marguerite played more music for my preparation, so I used it to dance and do some spinning. Meanwhile, Richard and Marguerite were supporting me energetically.

Maria's communication was delivered as though she were standing on a stage playing some famous Shakespearean role in my opinion. She used by body and arms freely to add expression to her words, and when I came to type them into my computer at home, I found myself wanting to write it like a musical score, putting words like fortissimo, piano, crescendo, pianissimo and writing in the pauses she had made for extra dramatic effect. I feel that she was standing behind me as I typed it all, carefully overseeing this latest creation of hers.

Here is a transcription of the words spoken. The words from the tape are all written in italics, and little editors notes added by me when I transcribed it are in ordinary print. I have chosen not to edit anything she said, so you will see how she uses repetition to make her points, and no doubt to add dramatic effect to her performance. Marguerite, who I had never previously heard speaking English, asked the questions. Thank goodness she knew English. M.V. = Marguerite Vidal, and M. = Maria.

M. V. "Maria, could we speak with you?"

M. "*Yes, of course my dear*"

M.V. "Um, can you also understand French? I know you knew many languages"

M. "*Yes, I understand French*"

M.V. "Do you prefer English?"

M. "*It is easier for the instrument*" (Note. Maria must have found this word "instrument" for medium or channel in my head, as in the past, I have frequently heard it used this way in England.)

M.V. "OK. Would you like to sit down? Or is it... good like... when you are standing?"

M. "*I, I* (slight stutter here. I do not know which of us was the cause of it.) *can sit if there is a chair*"

M.V. "Just a moment. I take the chair. It is here." (Pause while Marguerite put a chair just behind me).

M. V. "Thank you. Thank you for coming, and thank you for the instrument, I would like to know, what is the purpose of your coming here, and your work with the instrument?"

M. "*It is spiritual. It's very spiritual. There are many things in my lifetime that I did not achieve, but now I have a second chance. This instrument is very willing. I thank her for the permission to come. And it is my contribution to the evolution of the planet, to the evolution, to the changes in the planet, to assist in the ascension of the planet.*

I have always loved music very dearly. It is something very close to my heart. I bring this music, I bring this music to the Earth. I bring it with all the warmth and the love that my soul can give.

I have many regrets about my life on the Earth. This is my chance to give something to a planet, which gave me a great deal. I have been very privileged since I left the Earth. I have been shown many many things in other realms. I have seen many things I knew nothing about. I have seen the Light. I have felt the grace of God. I have a wish in my heart stronger than you can imagine, to bring that grace, to bring that Light, to bring these things to this planet, this planet at this time, which has so much need of all this. I can use sound to bring it. I can sing, I still know how to sing. It is the most powerful tool that I have, it is more powerful than words. I bring it to you with all the love in my heart.

I also bring joy. You may not hear it in my voice just now, but I bring joy. I understand how joy can heal. I understand, how when people laugh, they become happier. I understand how laughter heals. And when I hear your laughter, it is also a great upliftment for myself.

This instrument, she loves the music so much. She has a natural understanding of sound. I wish to help her use this sound in her spiritual work. It is my wish to inspire her, for I know many things that she can do. She is not alone, she is never alone, she was never alone! She thought she was alone. She thought she was different. She thought there was no one on the Earth who could understand her. She did not understand herself. When I saw this, and when I saw how her life had gone, how her life had begun... when I saw her failures, when I saw her disappoint-ments, and when I saw also the love in her heart, it was my strongest desire to come.

I wanted... I will heal it, if she will allow me to heal her, I will heal her. I need her permission. I would never touch her without her permission. I would never do anything to hurt her. She does not always trust. I would not hurt her voice. I would not hurt her physical body. I recognise it is the temple of her soul. I recognise her physical self is a creation of the great creator. I respect that. I respect that fully with my whole heart, and I wish so much she would recognise that more fully, and not wonder if I would harm her. I would never harm her. I love this dear soul with all my heart. I would never ever harm her. I only come to heal. I only come to give joy. It is my wish that she should know all this. I will never ever ever harm her. I will only help. I am here to heal, and I am so happy that she has the wish to allow me to heal through her, to heal others through her. This is for all of us a great blessing.

You have questions?"

M.V. "Thank you for all these blessings. The question for her would be... I think...she thinks it is good for her to take lessons with Felicity. What do you think of that?"

M. *"Yes, it is good that she does this. For the moment it is good that she does this, but she must know, that that is not the end. It is just a part of her preparation to help her. It is just something to give her confidence.*

She already can do everything, but working in this way... with Felicity, whose soul I also know, this will help her. This is a preparation for things to come. It is good that she takes these lessons. I wanted it, because I knew that (as) hard as I might try to show her how to sing, to tell her how to sing, to give her the confidence, she needed someone in a body also to support all the things that I tell her, to support all the things that I show her, to explain to her that she can trust what I say.

Sometimes she has the information first from me, and then from Felicity, sometimes it is the other way round. It is not important. When she hears it from two sources, she begins to believe. Her trust grows. This is what we want. I say "we", because we are many where I live.

We are many, and I am so blessed, for I am so often with the angels now. I do not always understand myself why they forgive me so much the things I did not do so well. I have almost forgiven myself what I did, and I feel ready to move forward now.

And Helena, Helena, she is so kind, she is so kind, and if she will allow me, I would love to use her, more and more for the mutual benefit of all."

M.V. "I think she will understand. Could you tell us something about the place where you are living now?"

M. "*It is full of Light... There are places here where music is very important. I am often there. I study the consequences of sound. It is sound in these realms that has healed my broken heart, for it was broken. It broke when my voice left me, before my death. I depended upon my voice, and it left. The disappointment was bitter. I was still in a low state, when I passed over to these realms.*

I was taken gently by the hand, at the right time by the angels, to this place where there is heavenly music. It was the music that healed my soul. One does not argue with music. One hears it, one absorbs it, one loves it dearly. I was so impressed by the healing I received myself, (that) I wanted to give it to others. I wanted to give it to others through the use of sound.

I spent a great deal of time wondering how could I give it to those who needed it, when I am here, and those I wanted to give it to, those who needed it the most, who could not access it here for themselves, they were still in bodies on the Earth, so what could I do, and the angels told me one day. They took me to a place on the Earth to witness someone channelling another entity. It was a surprise to me to see this. I saw the vibrations change. I saw that it could be done. And when I was asked, "Maria, would you like to do this? This is how you could help. This could be your work if you wish it." I was so grateful. It fulfilled the wishes of my heart.

And then, I began to study how this could be done. I watched many events on the Earth, where other entities came through an instrument, and, then the preparation began... I chose Helena, because I knew that she could understand how it was for me when my voice left me, and I knew how much she would appreciate it, if a beautiful sound could come through her, and I wanted so much to give her that. I knew that the wish in her heart had always been there to sing the high notes, and I knew, alone, she had never managed this. But I could do it for her. I could help her learn. Couldn't I give her this gift? I asked the beings of Light who were with me.

They told me, "Not yet, Maria. Not yet Maria. You have to wait. She is not ready." (As in many other places, she delivers this next bit quite dramatically with her passion.) And I waited, and I waited, and I waited, and I waited, and then at last I saw her vibrations, they were coming closer to mine, and I saw the preparation, and I saw the group of people she was with, and I saw how they loved her. I saw how they gave her love. I saw how they gave her healing, I saw how she opened like a flower in this atmosphere of love, like a pure white flower, and then, the beings of Light, the disincarnate ones, they came too. They also loved this atmosphere, that you beings had created upon the Earth in that place. They came, and the preparation for the first time was made.

Yes, she was coughing. She had coughed a great deal, but that served, because it brought her the compassion of all those who were there. It also made it very convincing when I sang, that it was not her. And it was important that she knew this, because only then could she accept my help.

I knew she had wished that one-day, someone would sing through her. For a long long time, she believed it was her only hope.

Well of course there were other ways this could have happened, but this was a good way for it, and I was so ready, and she was so happy, and this was the most wonderful way to start something that is not finished. She will see. She will see."

M.V. "Could you give her some advice for the future encounters?"

M. *"She will be guided. She will be guided. She will know. She will know in her heart. I will be there often, quite often. I know that I touch her heart, as she touches mine. For the moment, that is enough. Her story unfolds. Her path unfolds. She only needs to know what to do now. The guidance will come. The day after the guidance will come. She will always know where to go, and what to do, and how. I will show her that in her visions. She must trust. She does trust now, much more than she ever did before. She is beginning to understand."*

M.V. "Could you tell us something about the power of the sounds, because, we also worked with a group, and each person sang her personal sound, and all together, we noticed it was very powerful. Could you explain something about this to us?"

M. *"That type of music is a vibrational expression of those present. When it comes from people who walk their pathway, even when they know it not, the coming together is, in this way with sound is part of the unification of consciousness. Do not underrate the importance of this work. This is something you can do so easily. You just have to trust, that even when you cannot see the result, there is one, and it is good, and it is Light, and it raises and changes the vibrations, and this is very good."*

M.V. "Thank you".

M. *"It was not only me, for I have my personal guide beside me, and he has helped me with these answers, because, where I am, although I remember the words, we do not use them. To speak as I do now, I find the words in my instrument. She has the ability for clear thought, and this makes it much easier for me, than if I speak, or were to try to speak with someone, who, how can I say, has a head that is in a muddle."*

M.V. "Thank you."

M. "*It is my privilege and pleasure. It is my great pleasure.*"

M.V. "Well..."

M. "*I wish to say something*"

M.V. "Yes"

M. "*I speak good English don't you think?*" (Here her accent gets stronger, and she seems to be 'playing' with it for our amusement, and no doubt her own as well.)

M.V. "Yes"

M. "*Yes, I think so too, because it was not really my language.*" (Actually, I believe she had spoken very good English in her lifetime, but maybe she was feeling rather 'Greek' when she said this. Or, as I felt, playing with the words a little.)

M.V. "Um hum"

M. "*I think I have done very well, to speak.*"

M.V. "Yes, and..."

M. "*It is the first time I have spoken with a human voice for some time.*"

M.V. "And what impression do you have?"

M. "*I think it is good fun. It is very good fun. Yes.*"

M.V. "Well, I have no more questions. Do you have something else to tell us, or to tell our group of three here?"

M. "*Well, I am aware that both of you have done a great deal to help Helena, and you have helped me to come, and I am very, how you say? Reconnaissante?*" (Grateful, thankful)

M.V. "Yes" (Marguerite was starting to sound amused at this point, so one could say that Maria's efforts to entertain us were working!)

M. "*Et je peux parler un peu français de temps en temps. C'est pas trop difficile. Si je ne sais...si je ne sais pas les mots, oui, je peux parler en anglais, mais oui, je parle français un petit peu, et je crois, je crois, j'ai dit assez pour ce soir, n'est-ce-pas?*"

M.V. "Oui. Très bien. C'est parfait pour une première fois."

M. "*Merci*"

M.V. "Merveilleux. Merci beaucoup d'être venue et d'avoir accepté de nous parler, et... à une autre fois. Nous vous remercions infiniment, et remercions tous vos guides, et saluez de notre part tous ceux qui sont là-haut, dans vos sphères, et nous vous remercions infiniment."

M. "*Oui. Nous partons maintenant.*"

M.V. "Entendu. Je vous remercie. Et nous vous disons à la prochaine fois"

M. "*Merci tout le monde, tout est dit, merci.*"

M.V. "Et nous demandons à Helena de revenir complètement dans son canal."

(Helena) "Oui, je n'ai pas vraiment quitté." (I laughed, having stayed close enough to hear all of the words spoken, even though there were gaps in my memory afterwards, until I heard the recording.)

M.V. "Oui. Je sais. Alors, c'était le Mardi, 20 novembre, 2001, a Elsenheim, en Alsace."

(Helena) "Oui"

M.V. "Alors, voila!"

For the benefit of non-French speakers, the above French section consists of Maria joking about the quality of her French, and Marguerite and Maria thanking each other for everything. Then Marguerite asked me to return to my body, which happened very easily, for I announce that I had never really left. It would seem a shame to edit either the French or the English more than can be helped in this first transmission, for I find it all so touching just as it stands.

Showing the French part in its original state is of interest, because from the research point of view, it demonstrates that however much or little French Maria spoke in her lifetime, when speaking through me in a semi-trance state, she was limited by the words she could find already installed in my head. Therefore the French has whatever mistakes I would have made myself, had I chosen to speak it. This part of it, I see as a game. She was having fun, and entertaining her listeners. The serious 'work' was already achieved. The whole of this spoken transmission had lasted only twenty-three minutes.

All that I have described in this chapter had taken place in the short time of one day. There was a lot for me to take in. Oh my! Over dinner, we talked about Maria. All that I knew about her up to this point was as follows. She had been a soprano. Of the degree of her fame I had no idea. I had once heard someone say, "Yes, she was a soprano, but not a very nice one." I was not given the reason why she was not liked by some, and had insufficient interest to try and find out, but that statement somehow stuck in my mind.

I had brought the only tape I had of Maria with me to France, because after I had learnt that a singer wanted to come through me, a mild curiosity for opera began to emerge. I therefore managed to find the only recording I already owned of a woman singing operatic arias, and by coincidence, it had Maria's voice on it. I had only played it a few times before, and then lost interest in it. There was a picture of Maria on the front, but I had never really looked at it before this day in France. I had bought this cassette years ago when I temporally became interested in vocal works, having bought a number of recordings of Lieder sung by

Kathleen Ferrier, the famous contralto much admired by my father at one time, and a recording of "*Der Rosenkavalier*", because I had a horse in my care with that name. I forget who the soloists were. Later, I acquired some works by Mahler. That was in the early 1980s, and since then, I had almost abandoned classical music altogether.

Marguerite fetched a large encyclopaedia, which showed another picture of Maria. This was the first time I had really looked at her. "Oh, but she is beautiful!" I exclaimed. She was described in this book as having a lot of temperament. I was later to find out more about that, when I started to research her life.

Had I known at the time what a temper she is reported to have had, I would have been too afraid of her to want to risk channelling her, in case she took charge, had a tantrum in Marguerite's house, perhaps going completely wild, and damaging some precious object. This has never happened, either then or since. I thought that would have upset the peace of the place!

Here is what Marguerite had to say in an email received 1st February 2005 about this first visit of mine to Elsenheim.

"I marvel at the way it was possible that all this could happen... It's just crazy and almost incredible... There must be a plan! No human could have organized this. To make it as short as possible, I was in contact with Sarah Diane Pomerleau who was the link. She was your publisher; she was my teacher and "sister". She couldn't find her usual translator, so she offered me the job of translating your third book. It was really a present. That was already an initiation for me! I knew nothing about communication with animals for instance...

Well, after having translated the book, a compelling idea came to invite you in France for conferences and a workshop. I found it a little crazy too. I knew you never did that, and I was aware it was a challenge for you to do so for the first time... in French! But I followed my intuition and trusted that if it had to happen, it would, in spite of all barriers my intellect could raise. I felt there was something else behind the proposal I was led to express. This was confirmed by your acceptance, in spite of your own hesitations. How wise we were!

Yes, it turned out that the real purpose of your visit was... the development of this channelling and the changes, the awareness, the developments it would bring. I remember that, before we began the real conscious step towards Maria, I noticed that it was not you singing during the meditations, and that you were channelling a voice which was much more powerful and very different from yours. It was so amazing from a person who sometimes talked with such a small girl's voice. But you didn't say anything about it, nor did I. I waited for you to be ready to talk about that. When I heard this other voice, I knew "That's why she had to come. We'll probably work on that and develop it." I was so excited by the idea! I had to wait for you to be ready. When I help people I always feel like a midwife helping the mother to give birth, guiding her. It was the same with you. For this birth I had to wait for the right moment for you...

One morning I felt a strong push to play a CD where, at the end of it, there is a flute rendition of an "Ave Maria", only the music, no voice. I was in a peculiar state, as when I am preparing to channel. I sat down on the sofa in the sitting room, and just felt the energies there. I hoped you would feel this change of vibrations, I knew it was for you, but you were busy in the kitchen and noticed nothing.

So, a few minutes later, I stood up to tell you that I felt an energy favourable for something, although I cannot remember exactly how I put it.... I was surprised by your answer... "Later, when..." I realised I was in front of the human Helena, who was fully occupied with material actions, planning her timetable and controlling things, seemingly disconnected from her real self.

The inner call and the energies were so strong that I didn't mind and went back to the sofa, sitting there and going on with the channelling of energies. I had done my human part by speaking words, which had no effect on you, now I was consciously and fully serving something potent, surrounded and supported by the beings who usually help, and some others as well. The love that was present is indescribable. I wondered how long you would need to do all the things you had planned before being ready..."

Then came the "*Ave Maria*" at the end of the CD. I was at that moment so full of the being to whom this song was addressed, that it almost shocked me when you came out of the kitchen and rushed into the sitting room, standing in front of the CD player and began to sing. I had to be more present and, with my earthly presence and body, help the being coming to sing through you. You know what happened then.

During this first stay, I observed that you were amazed by all that, and this was totally normal. I also observed that you expressed much enthusiasm, astonishment and wonder at being able to sing such high notes which you never could before. All parts of you, the human with the ego as well, were touched by this experience. I could see the dance between your different aspects: sometimes it was the little girl there, sometimes the lost human in this world, sometimes the master, sometimes the judge, sometimes the other kingdoms lover etc. We all have such many and different aspects...

You would need some time to find a balance between these aspects, to calm some of them, to accept all this without mental barriers, to develop confidence not only in you, but in this being and in the divine plan which had made all this possible. Of course it was not the time to tell anyone about that during the workshops or the conferences..."

Chapter 5
Maria's Spoken Words

Two days later, when I was out for a walk on my own, I pondered over these experiences with Maria. This was definitely a new phase of my spiritual life. There were two main items here, the channelling of the spoken word, and the reality that it was Maria Callas who had come, as opposed to someone that none of us had heard of before. I began to understand why, for example, one evening when I had been singing to a CD, she had assisted me more with the sound each time Richard came into the room, or within sight, than she did when he was not there. She needed an audience, and she was interested in men.

When I arrived home after this trip, and read a book about her life, I discovered that these things were characteristic of her behaviour during her lifetime. All this was being enacted to give me more and more evidence that it was really her who came. Also, knowing full well what was happening, there had been a moment just before Richard entered, when she winked at me, and then she turned the volume up 'for him', just until he left the room again. With the wink had come the unspoken words, "Now, just you watch this!"

The more facets of her previous earthly personality she could show me, the easier it would be for me to continue believing it was her, and not some trip of my ego. I could add, that I sing best myself, when I am confident that nobody is around to hear me! So this was opposite behaviour to my own.

It occurred to me, that had she come through with her full power during my singing lessons, and had Felicity and I known who she was, were I in Felicity's place, I would have found it very undermining to my confidence as a teacher. After all, how could one compete or add anything to the knowledge of someone who had been such a legend in her lifetime? I began to realise that there was much more happening of importance during my French trip than I had ever dreamed of.

Maria and Gabriel

During the course of the evening meal on 23rd, as we discussed channelling Maria, I was aware that there would probably be another entity to follow her called Gabriel. I remembered this name of an angel called Gabriel being given to me in Hawaii, during Joan's workshop in July, and also how I have been shown a connection with an angel that would relate to this French trip when meditating before I left home. So I decided to warn Marguerite and Richard, that the next time, there might be someone else wanting to speak.

The following morning, I channelled Maria singing again. Just as the music was starting, having looked at a picture of Maria in a book of Marguerite's, it was easy to recognise her when she showed me herself clairvoyantly for the first time. (Previously, when I thought I saw her, it was actually Felicity she was showing me.) She stood just behind me, and reached around the right side of me to show me exactly how best to adjust the volume for the recording we were making.

I followed her instructions precisely, but when I tried to sing to it, I felt I wanted it a little louder, so that I could hear it more easily when we (she and I) were singing. I did what I thought was right, and regretted it later, when I noticed how it sounded too loud for the best effect on the recording. Maria had been right. Very interesting! How could she tell, when she no longer had a physical body?

There was another point worthy of mention concerning this little event. When she had shown me how much to adjust the volume, I was very struck by how elegant, sophisticated and poised she was. Every detail about her appeared to be perfect. (This was an aspect of her former self that was to be confirmed for me during my research after my return home.) The top B occurs twice in this particular arrangement of Gounod's *Ave Maria*. The first time, "we" hit it accurately, but the second time it was flat again, and painful to my ear.

The music finished, and for a moment all was quiet. Then Marguerite spoke.

"Thank you Maria. If you want to train with this instrument, you can do it, or if you prefer to sit down and speak, as you like?"

M. "*I will sit.*"

M.V. "Don't move. Here is the chair."

M. "*Thank you*"

M.V. "Thank you for your visit."

M. "*It is my pleasure to sing for you. Sometimes I feel limited with a body that is not mine, but it is still a pleasure to be allowed to come to do the best I can, for I know how much this child on the Earth enjoys the sound when she hears it. I know she has not learnt to do this alone. Yes, she asked me if she could sing first, and I was so happy to bring this.*

I wish to bring the joy of the birds, the song of the birds, all the beautiful things. I wish to bring them to the Earth. I wish to bring the Light, for I have been greatly honoured since I left the Earth. I have visited planes full of Light. I have visited marvellous realms that I never dreamt could exist in any place. And when I saw these things, and I thought of the people on the Earth, and how there was much sadness, how much my heart yearned to bring this Light, to bring it to the Earth, to give it to the people who were sad. How much I longed to uplift the vibrations on the Earth.

When I was still Maria Callas, when I still had the human form, my music uplifted people. I was not always aware how much it helped. And then I left, and I felt I was nobody, and there was nothing I could do. Yes, I sang in the other realms, for there are many who sing there, and I learnt to do it better and better, still better than I had ever sung on the Earth. But still I thought so often of the people on the Earth, especially when I felt pain in my heart, and I thought of the healing that is necessary on the Earth.

And it is my wish, when others are present, to sing through this channel. It is almost the only means I have to bring these vibrations through. To speak also is very good, and I am very grateful for that, because it is a way of giving evidence. My song, when I sing through this person, my song is also evidence that I STILL AM! I did not die, when I left my physical body. I still was, I still am, I always will be. There are so many who doubt this, and using the means of singing before I speak is a wonderful way of giving evidence.

We all know Helena never learnt to sing as I did, even though, it was from time to time, a deep wish and longing in her heart. And by being able to show that much is possible, even though, together, we still have difficulty sometimes with the very highest notes, I can nonetheless produce a sound she cannot produce alone.

This is so valuable, for those who doubt, if they hear her ever try to sing, if they perceive the fear she has, when she is alone, that someone might hear the notes she makes, and if they see, how when I come, her confidence is augmented, and how she is able to know each time she thinks the next note is too high, and then suddenly it happens, because I am there, and I produce it, and the sound, I believe you would say, it is very beautiful. And then, she feels transported, and I am so happy to see that. I know she knows she needs me to produce that sound, but it is something we do together, for she also remains present.

It is easier for her when she knows the music already, but still sometimes, when she is a little lost and unsure of the next note, I can help. I can put the note in her head first, and then she knows where WE, she and I, are going next. She knows, she allows, and I produce the sound. I make the best use I can of her vocal chords. Little by little they become stronger. Little by little it becomes easier for me.

But also I must say that her natural musical appreciation, the music that is already in her, is a great help to me, because she understands the sounds, she understands the expression. And therefore it is not so strange for her. It is just that this is something she has not done alone. Are there questions you wish to ask?"

M.V. "Yes. I would like to... for you to express the regrets you have concerning your life on Earth, and if you can heal them now."

M. *"Yes. Yes, I have many regrets. My values were not always spiritual. I was fond of diamonds, and riches on the planet Earth. I loved anything that sparkled... very much. (At this point, Maria was showing me a picture of a man presenting her with diamonds; I could not see exactly what it was, but maybe a necklace of some kind.)*

I feel it is particularly around the subject of men that I have regrets. They came so easily, and often I used them. Often, I did not love them, although they were strongly attracted to me. At the same time I must say, I needed the attention, I have always had a very strong need for people to listen to me, and for people to want to hear me.

And although, it seems a long time since I was Maria Callas, part of her lives on in me, and... yes, so I still have that need, although it is my belief that I have become more spiritually orientated, yes, much more, much more for I have seen the Light. I saw the Light. The angels took me by the hand, as I have already told you the first time I spoke. And when I saw the Light, and I saw how beautiful it was, I knew that, no matter how much I loved the diamonds, the Light was more than this. Yes there is Light in diamonds, for they come from the mineral kingdom. There is Light in all things on the Earth. All the beauties on the Earth, they carry the Light, the Light that is from the Source, as do the humans, although so rarely is this fully expressed. And that is sad, for there is much there to express...Yes...

So now, I have found a positive way to use this desire that I had as Maria to be listened to, to be noticed. I wish to be heard, and to be noticed, because I wish to bring these good things to the Earth. <u>I AM bringing them to the Earth. I know when I come, I bring the Light that now comes through me, which I did not carry fully when I was in human form, but now I have it. And what I need is the chance to be here, to be here on this planet, to use a physical form to bring it.</u> (The underlined part was all expressed with great passion. Then she seemed to gradually calm down again for a while.)

And Helena, oh bless her, she is willing. She had the same desire. She wishes to bring the Light. She also understands the need to be noticed, the need to be recognised, and she has noticed also, I must say, that if I am there, and someone is listening, I help her, and very often, if the somebody leaves the room, I am not interested any more. But, this is also evidence for her. I do not do that out of unkindness, because, she is the opposite to me when she sings.

When she sings, it is often her hope that no one will hear. Then she notices exactly the opposite is happening, and then she understands, I am there, even if I am not very powerful at the moment. Yes, that is interesting for her, and helps her. It is a way I can work, it is a way I can show her. Yes, yes, it is.

So my regrets, yes, yes... I remember also taking alcohol sometimes. And I am not sure I always used that well. Yes, I remember the glasses of red wine. I remember the men. I remember feeling self-disgust. I tried not to feel it. I tried to block it out, but in my heart, I knew my behaviour did not make me such a beautiful woman as my physical form, and my voice.

Yes... when I left this planet, I did so without love for myself. Then, in the other spheres, I received healing. I received so much healing. And the beings, they told me: "Maria! Maria! Do not lose hope! There is important work for you to do. It is really important, and the life you have just led has given you enormous insights into the state of humanity. Because you have led this life, you understand so well what it is that needs to be healed to make the people whole. If you had led another life, you would have learnt something else. But this life, as Maria Callas, has taught you exactly the lessons you need to learn to help others to understand how it is... for you yourself to understand how it is on the Earth... for others, who also do not love themselves enough, to understand that it was a choice of the soul to be how they are, to understand that there is a purpose, to learn not to judge themselves and the things they have done."

Now is the time for all of us to heal ourselves. Now is the time for us to understand the greater love of our souls that has allowed us to experience the darkness, so that we may know the Light. So that we may help others who dwell in darkness, be it in the realms invisible to the human people, or the realms that are visible, the third dimension, as you call it, the dimension I often thought was the only dimension that existed, but, as we all know, that is not so.

So I ask all of you who regret the things that you've done, perhaps earlier in your lives, not to look back and think how terrible I was, or even how terrible I am, for some of you still think that, but to think, how wonderful! I went through all that! That, all those things that happened were so perfect. They were part of the big plan that the creator has, so that we may learn, so that we know how much better the Light is than the shadow, how much more joy there is in the Light, than in the shadows.

Yes... you see, if we have never experienced these things, and I say, "we", because we have all, all those incarnate, have experienced something, where perhaps they feel regret, "I did the wrong thing", etcetera. Yes, if one needed this. We needed it. How could we know the difference between the shadows, the darkness, and the Light, if we have only ever dwelt in the Light? We have to visit the shadow, the darkness to experience separation. How could we know what separation was from the Light, if we had never been separated?

Of course, it is not an eternal hell in the darkness. Oh no! It is a visit for the lessons of the soul. And when we have learnt these things, and most of us have learnt a lot through our numerous incarnations, and all the experience we have had, then, it is time to return to the Light. For those who hear my words, for those present in the room now, and for those who hear them at other times, it is time to return to the Light. This is so important. I cannot say it enough times. It is time to return to the Light!

Focus on the Light, and regret nothing you have done before. There is a reason why people who incarnate on this planet pass, pass first through, what my instrument calls, the Mists of Forgetfulness. If we did not do that,(pass through them) to visit the shadows, the dark places would be impossible, because we would always remember the Light. We would know where it was. We would know how it was. We would know how important it was. But if first, as we incarnate, we detach ourselves from the Light, so that we arrive completely ignorant, of course, this is not always the case, but very often, and all we can do is learn from our parents, our environment, and very often that teaches us very little about the Light for many people, then it is possible to experience darkness, for we do not know that there is something else.

But so many people have done this so many times since the Earth began and people inhabited the Earth! We don't have to go on, and on, and on repeating the lesson. We have learnt it. Now is the time to pierce that mist, to draw it aside like opening the curtains and allowing the sun to enter a room. It is in this way that the Light floods and fills our being, and it is not difficult. Then, as we become more an' more, more and more immersed in the Light, this Light radiates out from us. This Light reminds others.

And yes, I was not far away last night, when you were... the three of you here present were in the Light. I heard the channelling. I heard, I felt the messages, and yet it is true, in fact, if you visit a place of relative darkness, not complete darkness, it is not necessary to say anything, Just be there, and your Light will shine, I could say, automatically. And it will radiate out, just like the sun when the clouds do not block it. It will reach everywhere, but unlike the sun, which is a little limited by a tree which blocks its light, for this light, nothing can block it. It just floooooooooooooooooows out, like water. (She used sound on the word "flows" to illustrate her meaning). If you pour water through the air of your third dimension, which of course I have not forgotten, into a glass, it floooooooooooooows automatically down into the glass. Nothing makes it go this way, or that way. Of course, if there is wind, yes, it moves a little, but it still, it still descends. It still goes somewhere with the moisture.

The Light, this Light, that you are now reconnecting with, it comes out, it goooes (she made the word 'goes' last extra long to convey the sense of movement with the sound) somewhere. And each time it touches whatever is there, be it a human, be it an animal, be it a plant, be it the mineral kingdom, be it even the devas, they are not less of course. No way. I would be clear about that, but I am trying to communicate to you, that (with) all consciousness on the Earth, when the Light comes, some of that Mist of Forgetfulness is removed.

This is the gift that you have. This is your reason for being here now. This is how the work is done. Even other languages are not necessary, even if you, none of you could speak at all, all you would have to do to spread the Light would be to wish it to radiate out, but maybe not even that, for I know that if you are, and all those who hear my voice are, it happens automatically without any effort. Now, I think, if you think about these words, you will agree that nothing could be easier. What is there on the Earth that is easier to do when you are on the Earth that just..."

M.V. "Be"

M. "*Be? Yes, yes, yes. Thank you my friend. That was the word I needed. Thank you. I think I have finished.*"

M.V. "Um hum. Thank you, just a question,"

M. "*Yes*"

M.V. "We know we go often in places to radiate (Light), but how it is that yesterday, I was so tired in the evening?"

M. "*Yes. Yes, yes I did see that. I did see that. (This was said with real compassion in her voice.) Yes. It has something to do with the vibrations. Also the events on the Earth.* (During Maria's hesitations here, I could see her guides around her, and I felt that some of the time when she was saying "yes", she was biding her time whilst receiving the answers for this line of questioning from them. Then she confirmed what she has shown me for Richard and Marguerite in words.)

Understand that as Maria I do not know everything, but I am asking for the information, and it is coming, and I see the vibrations, they are very steady, and then, (sound like 'fwit' made with her breath to convey the meaning of descending energy) but then comes up, ah, ah oui, ah, I know. (Here, she was showing me a picture like a line of Light on a graph to show how first the vibrations were maintained at a certain level, and then suddenly there was a deep fall like a trough, before they gradually rose up again to their former level. This no doubt is what the 'comes up' part of her prose refers to. The little sounds which were coming out of her, "ah, ah oui, ah, I know" just before this next bit, seem to have been part of her dialogue with her own guides. She continued.)

Sometimes, when you go to a place, where there is perhaps less Light than you are accustomed to, and there is a great need, these good energies leave you a little quickly, and for a while you feel low. But, ask for help. Were you not given help in the channelling, when the energies of Jesus were present, for I know that my instrument felt a great healing in that after a difficult day? It was not easy for her either. But, yes, that is the reason. There was a great hunger for Light where you went, and just for a while, yes, it lowers the energies, but then they come back up. It is not so serious. Um, you do not need to be so worried.

What you did in the evening was very good, for that has helped greatly to give, to give you the spiritual nourishment that you need, and yes, there are two angels behind me, and they say that you should not be concerned about this. Just accept... Yes, and sometimes take time for yourself, for you need that, as many do."

M.V. "Yes"

M."*I am Maria, I am still here, but I myself am now channelling for the information, and passing it to Helena to express, because you ask questions, where I have to look for the answers, as they do not directly concern myself. Is there anything else? I feel there...is another energy, who could speak more directly with you than I can. This energy now is wishing... to enter. I Maria, I say adieu for the moment."*

M.V. "Thank you Maria."

M. "*Um.*"

M.V. " Thank you very much."

Gabriel's Transmission

(Here, there is a noticeable change in the tone of the voice coming through. It is a softer gentler sound, and began quite hesitantly, as though looking for the words. The countless "ers" have been edited out to make it easier to read.)

G. "*Oh, yes. Yes I have come, because, yes, yes, yes, there are some things that you would like me to express for you. And also, there are two of you here to listen, and I would like to help Richard. To make this easy for my instrument, I ask that she continue to use English, and I ask that you translate the answers for Richard, because like that it is... is easier for her not to live too much in her head.*"

M.V. "*OK. I will translate for you*" (That last sentence was said in French, and addressed to Richard.)

G. "*Um.*" (Here Marguerite tells Richard that another identity has come through to do something for him.) "*If the French comes easily, ça va, mais si non, she will speak English.*" (Meaning it would be fine for me to speak French if it came to me, but otherwise I would speak English. To make it easy to read, I will omit the translations, and translate anything else that was said in French into English.)

M.V. "It's no problem. I can translate."

G. " *Thank you. Thank you so much. Does he have a question?*"

R. "Who are you?"

G. " *I am an angel.*"

M.V. "And what is the message you have to tell him?"

G. "*I am waiting for his questions. But if he does not have questions, I can say something.*

I see that you, you Richard, you are a being of Light. Um. And we, the angels, we love you very much, and you are very precious to us. We acknowledge the progress you have made in this life as Richard. Yes, and we acknowledge your courage to choose this pathway, and it is without doubt the best possible pathway for you. Yes, yes, trust. Your heart will be very deeply touched. This is the best possible initiation into the Light that you could possibly wish for. You will always be helped and supported, both by the incarnate, and by the discarnate.

Yes, yes, and I wish to tell you, that although you have already travelled a very very long way on your spiritual pathway, you can enjoy knowing that there is still a beautiful pathway for you to follow, and the further you go, the more joy and Light will fill your being. You will never ever regret the effort that you make now, and the beings around you will love you greatly in a spiritual way, both the discarnate, and the incarnate. Do not be afraid of this. Just accept it, accept the love. And I feel, I would like to say without ceasing again and again, the words, do not be afraid! It is not necessary to fear. Do not allow your fear to block the precious gifts in your life. Do not block with your fear."

R. "I have a question"

G. "*Yes*"

M.V. (Translates) "He has still some resistance when he says during the channelling, who he is, and speaking with 'tu' or 'vous', because 'vous' is a distance he still maintains." (As a channel for Jesus, he refers to the distance he felt he should maintain between Jesus and himself is what I thought he meant. Long after my return home, Marguerite informed me that what he actually wanted to ask was slightly different. When people came to him for a channelling session, he was afraid of allowing Jesus to say "tu" to them. Therefore he did not allow the "tu" to go through. However, as Marguerite pointed out, Gabriel had completely understood the question, and gave exactly the right answer.

For the benefit of non-French speakers, I will explain that "vous" is the formal polite form of "you", and "tu" is the familiar version of it for friends and children.)

G. "*Yes, yes, yes, um, um. Ask yourself, "Why am I afraid to reveal the identity of the being, that comes through me?" We do not ask you to say, "I, Richard, am Jesus", but if you love him, why not perform this service for him? It is a sign of your adoration of the Divine, of your desire to be in the Light, and by the beings, by Jesus and the angels, this desire you*

59

have to serve is accepted as a great gift for them. It is also the best possible way you could find for the evolution of your own soul. And what reason could you possibly have to channel something that was less than God.

Ask yourself that. Always aim for the highest, the purest Light. Yes, because this is the fastest possible path for you, Richard, to reach the Light in your own full glory. Never think, "I am not good enough, I am not worthy", because that is a limitation. You are a creation of the Divine! Accept this truth. If you accept this truth, then, you will see why it is your natural inheritance to have a strong connection with the Light and beings such as Jesus. This belongs to you.

On the subject of "tu" and "vous", this "vous" has something to do with the beliefs that you have acquired on planet Earth. If, for example, Jesus is really a being full of love, why should he require this distance with the word, "vous"? Does he not have enough love to enter directly into the hearts of those he would touch? Of course we know you know how much love he carries.

But if you allow him to use the word "tu", that will help to change the outmoded beliefs of the people who think of God as something very distant from themselves. If God is an essence, who is already in the heart of someone, this essence, this divine energy, is already as close as is possible, therefore, there is no need to create a distance with "vous". Using "tu" will help to put people in touch with the enormous love of Jesus. He is not afraid of people, as some of us are. I could say, Helena, sometimes. No. He is not afraid. He is not afraid to come close. He has no fear. Therefore he does not need "vous" to maintain a distance.

But we also understand enough of your culture to know that you have also used "vous" to be polite, and because you do not wish to offend the people for whom you are channelling. We ask, we ask, and this is very important, that you do not regret that until now, you have used "vous". Because we know, we, the angelic realm, and also Jesus, you have always given the best that you could at the time. For that reason, we accept with pleasure all the times you have used "vous". It was not wrong at that time. Do not regret it. Just understand, that was one step of your journey. Now it is time to take the next step up, and we, in the angelic realms, are there to assist you. Anything else?"

R. "I have the impression that with the change from "vous" to "tu", there is a change of vibrations".

G. "*Yes, yes, it becomes more intimate, and the vibrations carry much more Light, and this makes the channelling more powerful.*"

R. "At the moment the word "vous" is so easy and fluent, but now I will get myself used to saying "Tu".

G. "*We thank you for understanding, and accepting this, and if it takes a little time to change the habit, we understand that also. For we have great love for you, and we thank you very much for listening to the words that we give you through Helena this morning.*"

R. "I thank, I thank you".

G. "*I understand.*" (Said in French, although the tenses were mixed up!)

M. "Could one ask which angel is speaking, if it is necessary?"

G. "*Gabriel.*"

M. "Is Gabriel going to accompany Helena?"

G. "*Yes, more and more often.*"

M. "Very good. Do you wish to express something else?"

G. "*Yes. Yes, there is a reason why I am coming closer to Helena more often. I have visited her many times in her life, especially when her spirits were low, because I knew, that not only did I love this soul, but that one day, she would have very important spiritual work to do upon this planet, and for that reason, I, and other angels, and many other beings from other dimensions have always watched over her to protect her well being. Yes, she needed to experience pain, and she has, but we were always there to lift her up when necessary.*

We were always there to help her maintain life in her spiritual body. (I feel that the word should have been physical, not spiritual here, for I remember understanding the sense behind this message as it came through me.) This is why you find her still living in a spi.. physical body on the Earth today. Sometimes, it was difficult. She seemed so ready to leave.

Somehow we had to develop her will to stay, and we are very thankful for the courage she has shown to endure all, and be here, to give the service to others, to all of creation that is physical, which, as we have explained to Richard and his work, will augment and raise the vibrations, and the evolution of her own soul, which is so ready to live in the Light. She has a very deep connection with the Light, and because the time has come for her to be more present, for her soul to be more present on the Earth for this work, than it ever was before, we will be close to her more and more frequently. That is why, although my name has been brought to her attention before, ..." (At this point the tape ran out, so the remaining little bit was not recorded. However, I know that the reference to Gabriel's name having been brought to my attention before, refers both to the meditation in Hawaii, when I was with Joan, and to the occasion years previously in London, when it was given to me by the trance medium, Linda Waldron, along with that of Michael.)

Chapter 6

Maria Speaks For the Third Time

The 25th November was to be my last day in France, and we had planned that I would give my third one-day long seminar then. Strangely, in spite of the interest in my work shown at the two conferences I had given, we had no participants. So it did not happen. It was all part of the divine plan, as you will see.

Instead of giving this seminar, I knew, when the morning came, that I was going to channel Maria again. I felt it would be with the spoken word. Marguerite and Richard were both present.

Prompted by Marguerite, I first danced a little to loosen my physical body, and then did some preparation for my vocal chords, just as Felicity had taught me. I knew that Maria was present, for even the warming up had been easier than usual. I asked her if we could sing together before she spoke. I could see her face clearly, as she smiled an affirmative. We sang "*Ave Maria*" again.

The music stopped, and the voice of Marguerite began the conversation.

M.V. "Hello Maria. Are you here?"

M. "*Oh yes, I'm here.*"

M.V. "Do you want to speak?"

M. "*I would like a chair.*"

M.V. "Yes. (M.V. placed a chair behind Maria.) You can sit down."

M. "*Thank you.*"

M.V. "What would you like to share with us today?"

M. "*I would like to tell you, it is true, what you have thought. Yes, it is a partnership, a partnership with Helena. I am always thankful she is willing, even though it is difficult sometimes to convince her, that I am right, and that she has heard, and that she has seen exactly that which I have sent to her. Um, yes, yes, and little by little, I find I am allowed more freedom. I have not come through with my full force, not yet. Perhaps one day I will be able to do that.*"

M.V. "What is it, the purpose?"

M. "*I am trying to ask myself that question, but I can tell you from my heart, that I have the wish to serve. I have the wish to serve. I have the wish to stir the energies. Yes, to make the energies in Helena go faster. Yes, I give her pictures now to make that clear. I am working also with her lower chakras, because they do not move enough. I have learnt these things also.*

To keep her interested, and to convince her I am here, it is perhaps not strictly necessary, but it is a great learning lesson for both of us to sing. I know how much she loves to sing, and this touches, this touches my heart. When I feel the appreciation, and how she feels my voice transports her to Heaven, this touches my heart; this helps me on my pathway.

She must know that this is an exchange. We are helping each other. Yes, although I live on another plane, to express it, I would say that I reap afterwards when I see the joy, when I see, how even though, she thinks she cannot sing without me, when this happens because we are both there, how her heart expands, how her heart fills with joy, and how she is also ready to give credit to those around her who help.

But it is also my wish, that she should take a little more credit for herself, because I can see a big effort that comes from her, a big desire to learn to trust, a big desire to allow me to come. I have seen, that much as she loves the music, this is not easy for her, even though she wants it so much.

But I am helping. I am doing what I can when I come, to show her it can be easy. Yes, and you are right, Marguerite, she needs to believe that it is easy. It is easy, when she lets go, when she trusts, it is not so hard.

At the same time, it is also my great pleasure to show her what can be done by discarnate beings on the Earth, what they can understand and perceive, how much of that (is) for her education, and also for the education of others, for I know that she will pass on the wisdom that she receives. Yes, yes, um. (I had the impression that many of these ums and yeses, were addressed not to Marguerite and Richard, but to her own guides again, and sometimes even as though she was addressing herself, whilst contemplating the words already spoken and her next move.)

Of course, I am willing to share with the people here the knowledge that I have. Each day, though we have no days here, I... I learn a little more of things in other spheres. As I explained yesterday, there is still a great deal that I do not know. However, if you have any questions that I am able to answer concerning life on my side, yes, I will do my best."

M.V. "Is it a choice of yours that you stay in those areas, and not incarnate again?"

M. "*At the moment, yes, I choose it. Yes, I choose it. It would not be wise for me to reincarnate now. It is not the right time, for there is much for me to learn here, that is easier for me to learn here than on the Earth. I still have the lessons of the life of Maria Callas very close to me. I am not ready for another life on Earth.*"

M.V. "OK. There is also something that surprised me, because I thought that when somebody died, he loses his personality, and apparently you haven't? So before another incarnation, people keep their personalities?"

M. "*There are many issues that I have experienced on Earth, that I still need to work with. When I have completed that work, it will be possible for me to incarnate if I wish. It will be without the personality of Maria. It would be in another place, possibly even another planet, for I see a place where I may go, where the vibrations are much less dense than the*

Earth. And there I will not be Maria Callas, for I will have other lessons to learn."

M.V. "Just to help us to bring Light and understanding on the Earth."

M. "*I see the three of you, and I see that you are walking pathways of Light. And I see, that as you expand, and evolve, you obtain the capacity to carry and channel more and more Light. And if the three of you are faithful to your inner guidance, this will always continue. You will walk your pathway in the best way possible, and you cannot do more than that. It is not necessary to be concerned with whether or not you are doing the right thing. If everyday, you tune in to your inner guidance, and every moment, you are ready to change your ideas about what you think you should do, and when, and all that, then you will not falter, but you will continue to evolve, and you will be a part of the greatest healing that the Earth, and all the beings on the Earth, including yourselves could ever hope to receive. And although there may be sadness at times, for the most part, you will receive great great joy.*

And when, eventually, you cease to be as humans incarnated on the Earth, as it is at the moment, for the Earth also will have changed much, you will find your reception in the higher realms, in the Light, overwhelming. Not too overwhelming, but more Light, and more joy, more appreciation from others and from yourselves to yourselves of all that you have accomplished for the evolution of creation... (At this point, the tape was turned over, so we lost a word or two perhaps, but Marguerite repeated her question, so we do have all of that.)

M.V. "Could you give some advice for Helena when she returns home for the work with you?"

M. "*When it is necessary to advise her, I will be there. I have chosen to support her for the time being on her pathway. Of course, I am not the only one. She knows she has many guides at the moment. Many of them more evolved than I, but I understand well the affairs of the Earth, and I understand well human feeling. I understand human emotion. I see Helena with her highs, when she is full of joy, and I also see her low moments. I see her when she is tired, I see her when she feels empty, I see*

*her when she is full of sadness. I understand all this. I felt these things
also.*

*It is my wish to be able to lift her up into the Light, when she needs it,
and I know, that this gift she has, that enables us to sing together is a
simple and easy way to do this.*

*As I have heard you say, she has many characteristics in common with
me. Even though in other ways she is very different, there is so much that
we share, and it is this that makes it easy for us to understand each other.
I am often touched by her love, her gentleness. Yes, and being near (to
her) that helps me. But, I do not come just for help, I come to give also. I
come to love and be loved in return. This is not a selfish wish, for the
giving of love is a service, and when she gives her love to me, which
begins to be more, she serves herself. It raises her vibrations, and mine
also.*

*Meanwhile, I wish that she knows she is like a precious jewel in my heart.
And also, I forgive her all her mistakes, as she calls them. I forgive her
all her doubts. I understand that for Helena, this is a learning process,
and when I see her run to the kitchen to make more and more and more
and more and more cups of tea, I laugh! And I also think this is one of the
most harmless addictions and escapes I have ever seen. And I also wish
her great joy with her tea, whenever she wishes it. We all laugh here
when we see this, for the angels are often with me. We think "Oh! We
have lost her again! She has gone for another cup of tea! And now, she
has gone to the bathroom!"* (I, Helena, would say that the latter was not
such a serious problem for them, because I have noticed that they tend to
follow me there! I would also like to mention that this tea I was drinking
was either herbal, or very often a weak solution of organic green jasmine,
not the strong black variety.")

*But then, when she feels me she knows she has something else to do, and
we are very thankful that she comes and does the work also. But, um, it is
of course important that, well, if I say important, it becomes too serious
for her, but, I would like her to experience it all more as joy, and not as
the very serious work, that she is afraid she will get wrong. Yes. She is
beginning to understand this, and all of us here are here to help,*

especially Gabriel, the angel. Gabriel for his/her part is there to help Helena to reconnect more and more with the joy of her inner child, to allow the inner child to play. We laugh when we see, how much like a child she is, how her attitude to anything like work is so like a little child, who prefers to play; but somehow we wish her to understand, that as in our realms, as in our realms, working is a pleasure, not something painful to be avoided. Yes, and I am guided very much in my words by Gabriel, who is very close just now. This angel is full of golden Light. This angel, this Gabriel, delights in the magic what you would call, that I would have called in my lifetime, magic. Yes. Do you have other questions?"

M.V. "Er..."

M. *"Yes? When I have come these times, I have seen the energy of Mary in you. And I have seen how you care, how you care for this child through whom I come, who at the moment, is undergoing a new birth. She is undergoing an initiation. She is passing from one vibration to another. At the moment, it is a great assistance and help to her, that she is living in-between the vibrations of you, Marguerite, and Mary, and of you, Richard, and Jesus. This mix is very balanced. It is exactly right for Helena during her time in France. When she has a need, if one of you cannot fulfil it for her, always the other one can.*

This is greatly accelerating her progress on her spiritual path. When she returns to her home, when she will not know herself, and it will be necessary for her to change the vibrations in her own house. The devas, who assist in the garden with the flowers will be overjoyed when they see this. They will welcome her with open arms, even if the weather does not permit her to spend much time in the garden. This is what the devas, all the little beings, the little people in the garden have wanted from her.

These changes in her vibration will greatly increase the contact that is possible between her, and, I like the expression, the little people, for they are little beings. Each has a purpose for being there, and they have also a wonderful simplicity along with, I would say, an amazing facility to understand much of the human condition. They carry Light, and with the changes in Helena, the amount of Light in her little domain, the house and the garden, will greatly increase, and it will also flood beyond the physical boundaries, and this will greatly assist those in the neighbourhood, who also desire a connection with the Light.

Living close to her is a loving mother, supported of course by her man. Like me, her name is Maria, and we have seen a little boy, her son. One day, he will do great things, and it is good that he will feel, and the parents also, the overflow of love and Light that is able to be channelled to that place on the Earth through Helena's presence there. This is an automatic service that is rendered by all beings who carry Light. It is the same as when two of you visited Dijon, and the Light that you brought passed through the physical boundaries, and brought Light to an area in need.

Helena will always be guided. This lifts a burden from her shoulders. She has no need to concern herself with, "What do I do next? What do I do next year? What should I do the year after that?' We will always tell her when action is necessary. When I say, "we", I speak for all her guides now, for it is, it is like a team, a team of beings around her. There are some who are almost always there to care for her, and some, like myself, who come and go, depending on the work necessary at the time.

And yes, while she was sleeping last night, I did as requested, I came, and while she slept, when she was free in another realm, we held hands, we danced together, I embraced her. It was so wonderful to have her in my realm. We discussed the work we would do together, although all is not to be revealed at the same time, and yes, I did give her advice.

It is not necessary to remind her of these things, because they will come into her mind, as and when they are needed. This way, it is not necessary for her to try and remember everything, and by this means, it is easier for her to keep her head clear, and remain receptive to the inspiration from above. She has asked for this. It is her choice. It is not a command. It is her choice, for in the centre of her soul, in the part of her which knows, she understands that this is the best way, and in the highest interest of all of creation, for all of creation."

M.V. "Could you explain to her what she didn't understand yesterday night, when Maria told her about the work inside the Earth, and not only with above, and I feel what you told before about lower chakras has a connection with that? Could you explain to her?"

M. "*Um. About the lower chakras, it is good, if sometimes she sings the low notes, because they resonate with the lower chakras. This will assist her. Also, it would help the Earth, and Helena, if she were to make a conscious effort sometime, to attune herself to the beings who live in the Earth.*

Of course, we know, that space is an illusion, but there is work that she could do out of her body to help the energies in the planet. This does not mean losing her connection with the things that you say are outside the planet. Not at all, because it is necessary that every part of creation remain connected with the Source.

But when I say these words, I know that in one sense, they are all nonsense, because, space as you think of it, is something that is only perceptible in your own, although it is not yours, but you are there sometimes, in your own dimension, the third dimension. When one moves up the different dimensions, and up is not the right word either, because space does not exist, there is no difference. Everything exists. It just exists. Nothing is further away from other things than everything else. It is all together. It is all separate.

The planet Earth is a planet of polarities, and with this it carries many illusions. One of them is the concept of space. On Planet Earth, and other physical planets, which are also polarities, there has been a separation of that which is, and it is this that creates the illusion of space.

When all that is, the Light, shadow, everything, when all that is comes together, this illusion will diminish to the point where in the higher dimensions, you will find that you are in the Source, in the Light, at the Light, and also that nothing else exists, only the Light, only the created energy. That is the only thing that there is. All other things are contained within it.

70

Words are not sufficient to describe it, but helped by the words from my own incarnation, and given the concepts that I have learnt from my guides, and helped by the words in Helena's head, I am giving you the closest idea that I can of how things are, not how they were, not how they will be, but how they are.

For time also does not exist, even though with, as Helena calls it, a little brain, it is difficult to conceive how this can be. The understanding with the little brain is not necessary. Just know that there is something, maybe beyond your comprehension, that it is nonetheless there. It is not necessary to be able to describe it with accuracy in words, for to know it is to experience it, not to use words to describe it. To know it is to have the inner knowing. To know it, it is not necessary to be master of any language, just to be in touch with your inner knowing, that these things are as they are."

M.V. "... if you have something else to say?"

M. "*No. It is time for me to withdraw, if there is nothing urgent just now, but I wish to say again, that with this transmission, I have been much helped by my own guides, especially my own guides, and also the presence of Gabriel to give you the information as well as I can.*

But there is one little thing about myself I wish to express, and that is the enormous lessons of humility that I am having to learn, the discovery of how little I know. But also combined with the love present here, that heals, yes, in a sense my broken heart, and helps me on my journey, my spiritual journey.

I thank you very much, all three of you, er, for your assistance. I acknowledge Richard for his presence, that has assisted greatly with the energy. And I acknowledge Marguerite, who has asked the questions, who has listened to her inner guidance in order that this transmission could take place, and of course Helena for being willing to let go of the reins, to let go..."

At this point the tape ran out, but I know to what this last part was referring. Earlier on in one of the channellings of Maria, she had shown me a picture of Marguerite and I sitting side by side on a little cart drawn by a horse. The reins were in my hands. Then I saw myself handing the reins over to Marguerite. I understood that these were my instructions from Maria. So the last sentence, which I have long forgotten, may well have finished "(to let go) *of the controls, and surrender to the guidance of Marguerite*".

This was a hard thing for me to do, as I like to have the initiative in my own hands at almost all times, but I was willing to do this to please and help Maria. I think it made the channelling easier, and relieved me of some of the responsibility that I was choosing to carry myself. It put me into a more passive state.

After this channelling, the three of us had lunch together, and then I spent about two and a half hours walking in the countryside around Elsenheim, absorbing the experiences of the morning, and arriving back at dusk.

Chapter 7

Reflections and Research

I had flown home from France in really high spirits. I knew it would take time to absorb the amazing experiences I had had there, for they had been very profound.

I was still waking in the mornings with the sound of music in my ears, especially Gounod's *Ave Maria*, and I particularly wanted to know more about my connection with Maria Callas.

While still in France, I had really been too well occupied to consider questioning the material that had come through me during my channelling of her, but the more I thought about it later, the more anxious I became that I should only have channelled truth. I began to wonder how much of it had been a part of me strongly influenced by my preconceived ideas about Maria, (although, as I had known almost nothing at all about her beforehand, there was only a minimal danger of that happening in this case) and also that it could have been influenced by my own beliefs about spiritual philosophy. So mostly to put my mind at ease concerning the accuracy of this channelling, if that was possible, and partly for interest, I decided that some serious research on her life was necessary.

It took me until about the second week in January, roughly six weeks in fact, before I had the insight, that if I was really just the transmitter, whether or not the information was true was not my responsibility. Perhaps making it my business to supervise, and/or censor the information being given could cause me to remain too present in my physical body for the best results, and inhibit the efforts of those trying to speak through me? I was not aware of having censored anything, but those were my thoughts about it. If Maria, instead of speaking the truth, as she had, prefered to give us only lies, that was up to her, and nothing to do with me, I told myself. I would of course retain the freedom to disbelief it all afterwards, if I wished. I would not, however, be a worse channel for having let her relate her own version of events.

Two days after my return in November, before I had drawn these conclusions, and was still very concerned that I had perhaps made most of it up, or coloured the truth vividly with my own thoughts, there were a few things I felt really desperate to check up on. What bothered me most, having channelled that she had lost her voice, was the possibility that she had never lost it during her lifetime, but only at the moment of death. Then there was the question of diamonds. Had men, or even just one man ever given her diamonds? Did she really like that sort of thing? I had to find out.

I felt inspired to go shopping. I wanted to try to see if there was a CD album dedicated solely to her, and preferably with the words, so that I could sing the music with her more easily. I also wanted to read about her life, so I stopped first at the bookshop to order a biography, and bought a cassette recorder with the intention of being able to record her voice.

On arrival at the music shop, I went straight to the back of it as I knew that that was where both the jazz, and more importantly to me, the classical music was to be found. As far as I could remember, the type of album that I was hoping to find would be at the very back on a shelf a little to the right.

Before getting that far, I felt moved to stop and glance at the CDs to my left. The first title I read was *Romantic Callas*. There it was with her picture on the front. Some of the recordings do not include the words, and one often cannot tell if they are included, until after purchase when one opens the case. I was informed by the shop assistant, that this was the only collection of her work that they had in stock, so I decided to take a risk that the words might not be there, and bought it.

When I arrived home, the first thing I did was to open it and find out what I had bought myself. There were two CDs, a small book with a brief history of her life, and the words with about five of the recordings in

French, another wish of mine. This experience took me right back to the time at the beginning of my spiritual development at the end of the 1970s, when Winston Churchill was in touch with me, and I was led in the same manner to discover the information about him that I needed to know.

Reading the brief account of her life helped me to see that Maria and I had more in common with each other than I had ever dreamed of. She was described as being increasingly overweight as a young woman, awkward, and gauche, tormented by numerous pimples on her face, and overshadowed by her elder sister. All of this applied to me, even though I never became as fat as she did. I remember thinking I looked pretty awful, and my mother constantly told me so. Therefore I felt I would never be really loved while I had spots on my face, and was overweight. My sister was two years younger than I was, but at school she was much more successful than I with the academic work, for which reason I was constantly compared with her. "Your sister works hard, and she has scored 80% this week, whereas you are barely over 40%, and sometimes even less than that. Now why? If she can do it at her age, then why can't you?" Tormented thus, it was not surprising that I often wished she had been sent to a different school. I felt hopelessly inadequate by comparison.

Then I had read that it was quite a while before Maria had really learnt to fully experience herself as a woman. Although my history with men was very different from hers, I had experienced some aspects of not knowing what it was to be a woman long into adulthood.

At a time when her weight was seriously threatening her career, in the space of just a few months, she had managed to loose weight, and transform herself into the person that the public like to call "La Divina". It was then that she became elegant and beautiful and began to attract the men more.

I too had managed to loose weight, and had found that it greatly increased my confidence, as I no longer had to worry about whether or not I was looking too fat, although I did from time to time, and still do, concern myself with not becoming fat. It was better for my career with the horses as well, as I could then ride the smaller ones without overburdening them. Had my attitude to overweight been different, no doubt less weight loss for most of the horses would have sufficed, but following my upbringing, I had this deeply instilled belief that fat I was unlovable.

I too did not like what I saw when I looked at myself in the mirror. If I dare to believe what I have read about her, Maria had had a similar experience in her formative years, and therefore later maintained a very slender figure for the best part of fifteen years.

On a video I was later to acquire, she says how important the words were to her, and what they meant. I am the same. Earlier in the day when listening to the CD, as soon as I heard a really wonderful love-song, a duet, the first thing I wanted to know about it, was what were the words. It was in Italian, but the translation told me it concerned going into the Light after death, which is a very important subject for me. No wonder I felt such a strong attraction to that duet, and had felt Maria's vibrations very close when I was listening to it.

Another discovery was the correctness of my observation about Maria's big eyes. The many pictures I found of her did indeed confirm that she had lovely expressive big dark eyes.

On 1/12/01 after breakfast, I telephoned a shop in Chester to see if they had a video I had seen advertised in my CD booklet about her, that I thought might give me more information about her life. It was in stock.

Also, other points about the channelling in France were still bothering me. The first words she had spoken with my body were so deep in pitch. Surely this could not be the voice of a soprano? Was it possible she had deliberately dropped to a lower voice just to make it easy for me, or what was going on there? Also she had at times spoken with an accent that was not my own, but as I can be quite clever with that sort of thing at times myself, I wondered if subconsciously I had supplied her with an accent that was not hers just to convince the world that my channelling was genuine. Then an incoming telephone call from the bookshop told me that the book about her life, which I was hoping would also include her death, had arrived. With two things to pick up, I changed my plan for the morning, and walked into Chester to collect them. When I inquired if they had any other videos in the shop about Maria, I learnt that only the one that I wanted and needed was in stock.

On my arrival home with the book and the video, I could not bring myself to go and ride Starlight before I had read enough of the last chapter in the biography to discover the information so vital to me, that she had indeed lost her voice before the end of her life. I was greatly relieved, because that confirmed for me that at least that part of the channelling was genuine.

After riding my horse and eating some lunch, I sat down to watch the video. To my astonishment, in the very first interview with her, she spoke in a deeper voice than I had expected, not unlike the one she had used when she first came through me. The whole video was full of revelations that helped me to understand why I of all people had been chosen. There were so many parallels in our lives, little similarities on a human level that enabled me to empathise with her difficulties as a person, even though in many ways, she and I are so totally different in temperament, tastes and culture.

I began to find the channelling more and more genuine the more I thought about it, and the more I learnt about her. Her obsession in the first recording with me to sing that top A again and again with a sort of desperation about it, and how she had performed a slide from this top A down a full octave with me one day.

At the end of her life, my research told me, she had had a difficulty with that note, and when she finally made it, the quality was really poor, so she had used the opportunity to slide down an octave giving a wonderful artistic effect to the music, just as she had done with me, when we had sung unaccompanied in France.

In her prime, according to some accounts, the E above top C had been her highest note on a good day, whereas even a top C had cracked one day on stage towards the end of her career. It was thought (I read) that the short duration of her voice was due to the fact that she had overworked it, which is exactly what I had done to mine as a child.

Lacking in proper training, I did not understand the dangers involved in singing too loudly, and forcing it or bellowing. Felicity had contributed the useful information that when a singer is lacking in confidence, there is often a tendency to sing too loudly. Not only had I done this many times in childhood with my middle range, but I still found it almost impossible to sing my top notes as softly as one should be able to. I had tried to force them before my lessons started, with a sort of grim determination to get them out somehow, and let go of my fear of how awful they might sound, which I now know is very bad for the voice.

A fellow artist on the video described Maria as tightening up more and more as her confidence left her, when she knew that she was about to sing the top notes she was having trouble with towards the end of her life. I could equate with this so easily. This is exactly what I had experienced when channelling her voice, apart from the one time when she sang the top B with me wonderfully well. It was probably caused by my throat tightening up, as I am always a little present, and very attentive when channelling. Therefore it could have been caused my me, not Maria, but it is equally possible that she allowed that to happen as part of the genuine evidence she constantly provided that she was really there.

I would also like to point out, that many of the notes that had come easily, with her singing through me, were far beyond the range I had grown up regarding as my limitation.

Two days later, I started reading Maria's biography again. This time I began at the beginning. Every word held a fascination for me. There was so much more that she had experienced and felt, that I had either lived through, or could easily empathise with, even though the Hawley household, into which I was born, had been much more harmonious than hers, something for which I am eternally grateful.

When I discovered that many times she had been given diamonds, and how much she loved them, I heaved another huge sigh of relief. I had not invented the bit about men giving her diamonds after all!

When I read how she began her career at ten singing Gounod's *Ave Maria*, I rushed into my kitchen to find out if that was the one she had been singing with me. It was. Then I wanted to know about the other work she had sung so early on in her career, Bizet's *Habanera* from *Carmen*.

I went through my CDs and cassettes, and discovered that I had two recordings of her singing *Habanera* in my house, but to hear *Ave Maria*, a CD with another soloist, Kiri, was needed. When I played *Habanera*, I discovered that it was one of my favourite arias from *Carmen*. I was attracted not only to the beautiful melody, but also the words, rythm and the slightly rebellious mood of it. For my pleasure, I decided to sing with it, as I was searching for something that was easier for my vocal chords than Ave Maria. I sang all of the notes with ease. I had done nothing to warm up first, but the sound was rich, full, and above all, on that occasion, effortless. It came to an end much too quickly for me, so I decided to sing it again.

This time all my usual problems arose. My voice was croaking, weak, and had nothing of the beautiful sound I had just heard coming out of my mouth. I stopped the music quickly, and was silent again. I understood. Maria had sung it with me the first time, but stayed well out of the way the second time. This was so interesting, as it left me certain that when she is really present, she sings beautifully, even with my voice. It is also worth noting that my untrained voice seldom lasts very long, as it has been so little used over the greater part of my life. Sometimes I had wondered if it was wishful thinking that she helped in spite of all the evidence I had been given. For the time being, I was sure. The difference with her and without her was striking.

In early January, I was still busy typing the events of my French Book Tour into my computer. Weary of typing, and in need of fresh air, I went out for a walk near my house. I felt really low, and wondered if transcribing the channelling of Maria was partly to blame. I had heard the pain in her voice. I realised that whatever healing she had received since her death, she still had a long way to go with the healing of her emotions. Was her sharing this with incarnate beings a part of her healing? I felt it was.

If it left me feeling so low myself, was I really willing to do this with her? The insight came to me that in order to really heal another soul, it is necessary to descend to whatever level they are at to feel it, empathise, and understand, before it is possible to lift him or her up out of it. Did I mind doing this? I asked myself. No, I did not. For one thing, one can rise up again oneself, and for another, I knew that I was happy to allow others to serve me in this way, so helping another was very acceptable to me.

Since then, I have changed my opinion slightly, as I feel that whereas empathy is of the utmost importance, one needs to maintain one's own position of emotional balance, to hold one's own space, and then to reach out a hand to help another soul to rise. This seems to me a much healthier way to do it. I mused over the fact that I did not yet know why such powerful characters as Winston Churchill, Albert Brandl, a strong character who was the director of a large State owned riding centre in Germany and gifted trainer of horses, (see Book One for these stories) and now Maria Callas were interested in using me as a channel, for I do not possess the same power and influence as they had, and I am not well known.

In fact, this association with Maria provoked many thoughts, which arose in my quieter moments. For example, a week or two later I thought how hard it must have been for such a perfectionist to agree to sing with such an imperfect vehicle as myself, and produce a very imperfect result with her name attached to it.

The next day in early January while going for a short walk, I remembered reading in the book about Maria's life, how she had made the acquaintance of Churchill on board the luxury yacht of Onnassis. Furthermore, at the time when Winston was connecting with me, which was the late seventies or early eighties approximately, it was already after the death of Maria, so it was not impossible that Churchill had led her to me.

One day when I was discussing Maria with Patrick on the telephone, he channelled that Maria knew that I was not quite ready to do the channelling we had done in France, but had decided she wanted to have a go anyway. There is a part of me which is willing to take the plunge a little early as well, so I can see why on a soul level, I had agreed to it.

More evidence followed in January. Maria showed me a picture of herself, and said, "I want you to love me". A few days later, I read in a book, that in spite of a sometimes nonchalant manner, other people's appreciation and love for her had always been very important to her.

Having wondered about channelling that "English was not really my language", or words to that effect, I read that she once told the press that whereas she always counted in English, having learnt arithmetic in that tongue, she actually thought in Greek. I also read that in spite of the time she spent growing up in New York, later in her life when she had not been using English much, it became rather disjointed. (I imagine she had been speaking mostly Greek or Italian while living abroad.)

I continued researching everything about her, finding countless little details to support the evidence she continually gave me to convince me this was more than my imagination. I would spend hours reflecting on my findings. There would be times of doubt, of wondering if this was just a make-believe ego trip, and a way of deluding myself that some dream world I preferred to believe in was real, and other moments when I felt sure it was her, even if I still did not understand why we were doing it all. For example, when singing in the car on 4/2/02, Maria was there, and I found myself channelling her words to me as we sang. I answered her, although I am not certain if it was with her voice or mine. When I reached a point on the road, where I knew I needed to concentrate on where I was going, and prepare myself mentally for two horse clients I was about to help, she withdrew, and the last three notes contained the familiar croakiness of my own voice. However, I felt that the timing for finishing was perfect. Later I had to stop singing in the car, because I found it took too much of my attention away from my driving, and where I was going. It was too easy to miss the right turning! Then on 8th. February, I read about an incident in Maria's lifetime, when she sang her words to someone, instead of speaking them.

Another thing happened. I was copying some pages from a book about her, following the list of page numbers I had written out for myself to copy, when one of the numbers mysteriously changed itself in my head. While I was copying the "wrong" page, I felt Maria's energies and had visual images of her very close to me. When I discovered afterwards what had happened, I realised that she had changed the page number I was thinking of, so that I would find the bit about her treasured painting of the Madonna, a little picture which she took with her everywhere. This made her choice to be interviewed by Marguerite, who channells the Madonna, so natural.

At this point, it is really worthwhile mentioning the points that not long after my return home, Marguerite had expressed to me in an email concerning the experience of interviewing Maria. I have written what she wrote mostly in her words, but with one or two little changes in my own words to make the meaning clearer. I found it very interesting feed-back. "From the first time Maria spoke through you, I realised that it was not only something special for the three of us, but that it was also a healing and an initiation for her, in fact more than that.

As you may know, I work with Sarah's (Sarah Diane Pomerleau) method of the conscious exploration of the passages. Therefore I have some experience of these transitions or journeys of the soul after death, and my ideas were conditioned by personal experience and other things I had heard or read. Through these encounters with a discarnate soul whose incarnation is not so far away, nevertheless a generation or more, (at the time, just over twenty-four years) I experienced something new for me: having a normal conversation (spoken out loud on both sides, not how I usually work relying on telepathy from the soul concerned) with a former human being. I did not think for a moment that I was speaking to a dead woman, but to a soul who is continuing to evolve. It is interesting to hear her former points of view, and now to have a small idea of how she lives, and what she learns, etc...I think the most impressive part of it for me was that she had not lost the ardent temperament for which she was so well known. I thought that after death a soul had less emotions, but that is not true. Maria still has all of her passion. She is still so passionate, but her determination and will are no longer directed at attracting the attention to herself, like a child who has whims, but is aimed at helping the Earth and other humans, so that they will not have the same illusions as she did. (Even if she still likes to have an audience when she helps you to sing!)

I am conscious that she is evolving, because she said that she still had regrets and that she is learning to love herself. In one of the three channellings, when she stepped aside to let Gabriel talk to Richard, Gabriel said to him that he should not regret or think what he had done before was wrong, because we all do our best at the moment we do it. It seems Maria has to understand this as well in order to love herself unconditionally. So living here, or living in other realms, we never rest. We always evolve. It would be a good thing for the many people who do not like living here on the Earth to know that!

Moreover, I was very conscious, that when I spoke to her and asked questions, it was a little as if I was having a session with a human. For example, when I asked her to tell us which things in her previous life she regretted, I thought that if she could talk about them, that would be part of a healing for her, and help the understanding of all humans. I am fully aware of the fact that she and we were all receiving greater healing, or healing at a much more extended level. I will try to explain what I feel: now she is on what we call "other levels". Her guides help her with the teachings and healings. OK. That is fine, but now something else occurs: she is also healing directly, through your channelling and our talk, through the vibrations and perfume she left on earth as well as healing the Earth itself, because she recognises aloud what was, what is, etc. These types of denser vibration that a voice gives bring healing on this earthly density. The work we did and we do is like an anchor, and the Earth hears it as well as many other realms. This repercussion on the Earth appears to me as a completion, and may greatly help the Earth to renew herself. That is also brotherhood with the Earth. WE have the density of the Earth, and are also part of the great movement, supporting it and acting as anchors.

I think this is part of the conscious new partnership we are discovering and living (between incarnated and discarnated, between the different realms etc.) part of the discovery of the non-separation of all that is."

Both Marguerite and I shared the feeling that we would one day meet again to work with Maria. We did, but we had to wait a while. Other things needed to happen first. There were still lessons I needed to learn before I was ready to take things further. The following chapters will illustrate some of them, but before that, there are still a few little incidents which belong here in this chapter.

In early March, 2002, when I explained to Patrick Kempe how Maria seemed to be teaching me to sing by demonstrating with my voice what she wanted me to do, so that I could feel it, and then try to imitate it on my own, he thought this was so wonderful, that I must keep on working at it.

The following day, I had the insight that this was indeed a good way to teach someone, as it overcomes the problem of trying to put a feeling, or bodily sensation into words, which means everything has to go through the intellect, and might have made it impossible for me to understand or do it, as I would not have known how the muscles would feel, or what exactly was meant. Having thought of being helped by a discarnate being as a handicap up until this point, I now saw that certain aspects of it could be an enormous advantage both for Maria and myself. Maria had a teaching aid at her disposal that was denied her during her lifetime, namely that of giving me the experience in my own body, something wonderful that defies any spoken language. Also, I did not have to travel to somewhere else, or find a small fortune with which to pay a very famous teacher for lessons!

Sometimes when practising, I was really aware of Maria with me. Her plan was not to do it all for me, but to listen and advise. Sometimes she would demonstrate something to help me. Often this would happen as we approached one of the slightly higher pitched passages. I would feel her energy coming into my body, and she would carry the sound over the "difficult" bit, and then withdraw, leaving me to finish it. Other times, she left it me to manage the whole thing as well as I could, perhaps to see if I had succeeded in learning anything, and certainly to give me the chance to acquire the skill for myself. Clearly, she was trying to train me, but it would only be in 2003 that I would really understand that this was what it was about, as I will explain later. For the time being, I thought it was learning to channel her sound that was really the only thing that mattered, and my practises were just to keep my vocal chords in training for her.

Chapter 8
Success, A Tough Lesson

In early February 2002, I started to prepare myself for a trip to the Dominican Republic, where I was to join one of Joan's Humpback Whale Seminars. We were to board a large live-aboard boat called "Bottom Time", and make the trip out to Silver Banks, a calm area about 60 miles off shore where we could moor the big boat, stay for a week, and make two excursions in small boats to watch and swim with the whales each day. I had signed on for two weeks, so with just one night on the mainland in between trips, I would be going out there twice. That, of course, was a wonderful experience, but for me it was not only about whales and ETS, but also Maria. I wondered if she would come with me, and if she did, would I be able to channel her voice. Only time would tell. On 12th February, the last day before my departure, something happened which gave me a clue. I had not expected to have time for a singing practise, but somehow I spontaneously started to sing along with a CD, and soon after starting "Ave Maria", I felt Maria's voice start to come through, and assist me with the high notes. I took it as reassurance that she did indeed intend to be with me at some point during my trip away, so I felt comforted.

Before she left, she showed me a picture, in which I saw her pick me up by the scruff of the neck to put me down somewhere else in the limelight. Maybe changes to my lifestyle lay ahead. It also dawned on me that many people who had known her during her lifetime, or even just enjoyed her music, could well find her connection with me very interesting.

My first adventure with her on the boat took place on 19th February. Joan was suffering from a cold with a bad throat, so she asked me if I would mind leading some toning with the group, and if Maria would come to sing with us. I replied that I would welcome her if she came, and agreed to lead the toning for the group, having first explained to them what we were going to do, and how.

All of this seemed to go smoothly, as far as I could tell. While I was talking to the group before we sang, twice I saw Maria asking me to take my glasses off. This reminded me of how, during her lifetime, she had always removed her glasses before going on stage, in spite of being very shortsighted. I knew that it was not really necessary to remove mine, in order to channel her voice, but took it as a sign from her to let me know that she was really present, and would help me sing. Just in case she did not sing, I decided to wait until afterwards to tell the group that someone had been singing through me. Nonetheless, seeing her before we started had helped my confidence.

I began the sound with a suitably low-pitched starting note to encourage everyone to join in. Continuing as well as I could, hoping for inspiration and help, I heard a voice, probably Maria's, saying, "Just sit back and relax!" I did, and from that instant Maria sang freely taking the sound upwards. Had I been able to maintain this degree of non-involvement, and relaxation, the quality would have been much better throughout.

Notwithstanding my personal imperfections, when I opened my eyes at the end of the toning, I could see that several faces had been lit up by the sound of Maria's voice. At the same time, with my inner eye, I perceived Maria acknowledging the silent appreciation from the group.

Then she came over to me, and gave me a pink rose. Wanting to present her with a gift, following some deliberation concerning the most suitable colour, I handed her a white rose, fully open, and with creamy coloured tips to its petals. (I felt that she added some sparkles to it, just to remind me of how she loved things that shone and glistened.) Touched by her love for me, during the short silence that followed the toning, I embraced her clairvoyantly, my head resting on her shoulder for a moment or two, almost weeping with emotion and happiness, and all this behaviour was completely spontaneous.

Then I explained to the group, how someone else had been singing through me, and how I had seen her in a bright red dress with her long dark hair. That much I shared with them, whilst declining to mention that she had been wearing beautiful diamonds around her neck, for the simple reason, that I could not decide if I had seen them accurately, or just imagined them. However the following morning, before we boarded the little boats to swim with the whales, she made a point of showing me the diamonds again, so that I would know I really had seen them the previous evening.

Returning to the evening, Kaiwi gave me the feedback that he had really noticed how the sound was being channelled through me as it started to ascend, which must have been just after Maria had told me to sit back and relax. He had also observed how the sound of the whole group produced a spiral of many colours, which he felt had descended into him through his crown chakra during the following meditation about the whales.

Other feedback came from Brianna, whose heart had been touched. The emotion was very visible in her face, for she was almost crying. Then there was Allison, who commented, "That was high soprano!" and Joan, who added, that Maria has a wonderful sense of humour, and brings with her joy as well as the Light when she comes.

The "success" of the evening no doubt enhanced my confidence, as when Joan led some toning before we boarded the little boats to go and swim with the whales, I was able to let Maria through again in a more relaxed way, which produced a better quality of sound.

There were only a few occasions when Joan chose to use toning with her group. Each time Maria had been coming through, and all that I was aware of was the fact that her "supporters" wanted to hear her, and looked forward each time to her coming. I thought I was sharing the limelight with her as a star.

Maria was such a big thing in my life, that my thoughts were frequently centred on her. I often practised, with the help of a Walkman, one or more items from my small but growing repertoire of classical music arias. So each day I would wonder, "Will Joan have toning before the meditations today? Will I be able to channel Maria's voice?" My happiness level often seemed to revolve around this.

The very few times that we did tone, and Maria came through, it seemed to me that her voice was admired and appreciated, but unknown to me, it was causing Joan some trouble with her group. I was in for a shock. One morning a warning came my way, which showed me just how un-tuned in I really was. This was the beginning of a tough lesson.

It was not those in the unseen realms I was failing to check in with, but some of the people around me in Joan's group. Something was worrying Joan. She came over to me quietly, and explained how some of the group were not happy with Maria. She wondered if I could consider singing very softly at least this once, so that the other people could actually hear themselves sing and enjoy the harmonies they were making. "Maria has such a strong voice", as Joan put it.

No one could have explained this brewing problem within the group to me in a kinder or more loving way than Joan did. Nonetheless I was crestfallen! I reacted by feeling really hurt, and also disappointed with myself that I had not seen this coming. Maybe my ego was experiencing a huge blow, or perhaps it was just bitter disappointment.

Either way, I did not blame Joan. She had a group to keep happy, and I had not been helping. This was the beginning of a tough lesson, in which I was to learn over time the importance of channelling when it was appropriate, and making sure that recipients of Maria's sounds were open to receiving this gift. I sang in a whisper that morning using my own weak voice, and as softly as I could without actually refraining from singing altogether. Dear sweet Joan came and thanked me for it. She even had to ask me if I had actually been singing or not, because I was so quiet, she had not been able to hear it.

In following trips with Joan I was much warier. I still made mistakes now and then, but tried to remember that this was someone else's seminar, and I must respect both the wishes of the group present, and its leader. The other point I would have to learn was that there might almost always be someone who resented Maria's strong voice, especially if he or she felt they had not been consulted first, or did not know that Joan had actually asked me to channel Maria.

This warning concerning my misjudgement about the appropriateness of my channelling was a really tough lesson, but one I had to learn. It would not be easy, and this would not be the last time someone would be offended by the channelled sounds. Sometimes my judgement was to be tested, and other times the lesson was learning to cope with the objections of those who did not really understand the benefits they could reap from it, or had no knowledge of the fact that Joan had just told me Maria was welcome. There would be other things of this nature for me to learn to cope with as well. For the time being, I just weathered this painful experience as well as I could.

The moment of joy did come, however, on the very last night of the second of my two weeks on board the boat. It was a group sharing and closing meeting. No one was in a hurry to go to bed, as the following morning we could sleep late while Bottom Time was sailing back to Puerto Plata. Therefore I knew that it would be all right to use more than two words to get my point across, at least within reason!

After giving a shortened version of how my friendship with Maria Callas had begun, I chose to recount in full a brief event that had taken place in my cabin just two days previously.

After breakfast, I had gone downstairs to practise my singing as I often did. I was trying to improve my personal rendition of Gounod's "Ave Maria". I was managing it, but not with any great brilliance. As I approached the latter part of it containing the higher notes, which worried me, for the third attempt that morning, I wondered if I would manage that top B flat or not. Would it be a flat B flat, a screechy failure I would regret in case someone heard it and it hurt his or her sensitive ears, or what?

So many times my personal fears of not managing it had caused my throat to tighten, thus completely eliminating the possibility of anything beautiful coming out of it in the higher registers. Shortly before this looming difficulty, I felt goose bumps, and the energy of Maria descending through my crown chakra. As I heard her strong rich voice coming through me, I began to relax with pleasure surging through my veins. Soon, a perfect, effortless and beautiful top B flat came ringing out of my mouth! "We" finished the aria with me in a very high state of excitement. Never had it been as good as that before!

I was standing there, clutching the towel rail for balance with my left hand, for the boat was moving as it always did, holding the Walkman in my right hand, and shaking more violently than I can ever remember in my life before. It was from pure elation and joyful excitement. Somehow, I managed not to drop the Walkman. It felt like the realisation of one of my wildest dreams that such a sound should come through me. It was the first time that I felt Maria had really been able to show the full beauty of her voice in this dimension as a soprano! If it was possible once, then surely it could happen a second time, and then again, if I cared for my vocal chords.

Two big realisations had dawned on me. 1) Top B flat does not have to be difficult if Maria is really there. 2) The smaller voice, which sang the first mostly lower part of "Ave Maria", was not only quite pleasant to listen to, but it was surely mine! Therefore I must have made some progress with my own singing voice as well.

I told Joan's group how I had experienced a desperate need to share this event with someone. How I had rushed upstairs, and been lucky enough to find somebody there who already knew the "Maria" story, and after she (Camilla) had finished talking to someone else, she had been kind enough to listen to me.

Relieved and delighted to have finally had the chance to share so much of it all with every one, I sat down again.

The group had been spellbound while I recounted all this, and I later realised that I must have been channelling, not in a deep trance, but enough for every word and physical move that I made to be inspired. I suspected Maria to be responsible for a lot of it, because when I had demonstrated a few easy notes from "Ave Maria", the sound had come out with a full and rich voice.

Joan came to me later and thanked me for entertaining the group, who, she pointed out, had all enjoyed it. I appreciated this acknowledgement very much, but knew that alone, I could not have done it. Perhaps the opportunity Joan had given me during the first week to introduce and lead the toning when her throat was bad, and this little informal talk to Joan's group about Maria, though it cannot have lasted more than about ten minutes, was a taste of the limelight that Maria intended to be a part of my life at some stage.

The following day as Bottom Time started its voyage back to the mainland, Joan told me of an instance where she had known another medium, who channelled someone else, and ended up writing a whole book about him. This man had died before he had finished what he came to earth to do, and resolved the situation by coming through someone else, as Maria was inclined to do with me. "Maria could be a whole book", Joan said.

Certainly, this could happen, as I seem to get more and more information about her, or rather experience with her. I decided to keep my mind open. More important than this, Joan, who did not know that Maria had already told me, added that Maria would always make sure that I was in the right place at the right time for our purposes. I would not need to worry about that.

Another thing that Joan felt moved to tell me was that whereas it was good that I wrote books, really I should be on stage, as I was a natural. She was referring to my sharing with the group of my connections with Maria. "You stood up, and you were on stage!" she commented. I knew exactly what she meant, as she continued to state that although my humour does come through a little in my books, it is much better when I am present.

My own conception of this, as I have already explained, is that it was not really me who spoke. Also neither the tone of voice used, nor the timing, nor, for that matter, the facial expressions and body language can be shown in the written text. The "script" which I could never have managed to write myself seemed to have been given to me, or channelled word by word as I spoke, as well as having a wonderful feeling of being connected and responding to the audience.

There is one last point concerning Maria that had taken place during this trip, which is important to mention before closing the chapter. During one of Joan's led meditations, feeling that perhaps after all I needed my own programme rather than trying to stay with Joan's words too precisely, I allowed myself to drift into an alpha state, where I found myself sandwiched between Maria Callas and the angel Gabriel.

They showed me a pathway of Light, on which was written, "Helena's Spiritual Pathway". It was not straight, but ran in quite a wiggly line like a meandering river, and there was rich vegetation on either side of it. Escorted by these two companions, I had a wonderful time with some ETS and so on, but what I did not realise was that I was being shown that Maria was to act as one of my guides. If she had told me, I would not have believed her, not then. It took a very much longer time before I could accept that this was part of her role in my life. You will see as the story unfolds.

Chapter 9

Singling Tips and More Experience in Hawaii

My next trip away from home was to Hawaii. I was due to leave home on17/7/02. Summer is always busy, so it is not surprising that I had not been singing. In spite of this, during the days preceding my departure, I noticed that Maria was around me more than usual, so I made a few attempts to sing in my house, hoping as usual, that no one could hear it. In spite of the weeks of disuse, I found my upper register still accessible, and these tops notes, which require a lot more effort, were even in tune, as far as I could tell. So I left for Hawaii with big expectations of what I might do with Maria, and how her lovely strong voice would come through me.

In many ways I was bitterly disappointed. Channelling Maria gave me such pleasure, and there were very few suitable openings for her during this trip. Chris James was co-leading the seminar with Joan. I must say that he is a wonderfully talented man, very musical, with an excellent ear for pitch, and that there must be little he does not know about singing. One can add to this that he has an understanding of many spiritual gifts, one of them being using sound for healing.

At the time I had little interest in the latter, and felt very frustrated when I found that I had to keep my voice so very quiet all the time, apart from once, when he asked me to sing out more, but that day I could not find the voice! I think it was partly my fear of being told I was doing it wrong that made my throat too tight, combined with the fact that my voice was already tired that day.

The workshop was excellent, but I was not. Joan had warned me that I would have to sing quietly months beforehand, but I had been unable to let go of the fond hopes that Maria would be able to come through as well at some point. If not, then why was she standing just behind me with her hands on my shoulders, the very first evening that we met with Chris, all of us poised and ready to sing with him?

Maria had appeared dressed in pink, a flower in her hair, which was still long and flowing, and handed me a red rose just before the end of that session. It was a good feeling to know that she was supporting me, but if I could not bring her through, then why, oh why was she there? I would have to wait until May 2003 for the answer to that.

If I looked at the trip as a whole, rather than my frustration during the seminar, then I could see that I profited from other aspects. For example, the contact with Joan, the things that happened in the ocean with the dolphins, the meditations that Joan had led, and various other little gems that came my way from time to time.

I felt so strongly that I could not possibly have been called to Hawaii in order to learn from Chris's seminar, which I quickly labelled as very good, but as unsuitable for me as it was good. It seemed more likely I was present for something special taking place outside the seminar. I was right about the latter point, but not about the unsuitability of Chris's workshop. I will explain why in due course.

Whereas I never channelled Maria during Chris's sessions with us, I had allowed Maria to sing during the toning on two of the boat trips. (Chris was always on another boat, so I felt I could let this happen without offending him.) When I had finished the first time, one of the group members turned to me and asked about "my voice", which she had noticed. When I explained that the lady who sang through me was called Maria, she exclaimed, "Oh! Maria Callas?" without any hesitation or time to think about it.

It should have come to me as no surprise that a seminar with singing as its theme would attract singers, and some of them very knowledgeable. These kind people were willing to share what they knew with me, and gave me some useful feedback in two instances after channelling Maria on the boat.

Simona was a professional singer, so when it came from her that one of Maria's top notes was "pretty impressive" on the second boat trip three days after the first one, it started a conversation I welcomed. When I told her how these high notes resonated right in the top of my mouth, instead of lower down, where I felt the others sounding, she explained that this was something commonly known amongst singers.

She went on to say that many singers like to bend down slightly to sing high notes, as they must be brought down, not reached up for. For example, one could try moving the body as though sweeping the floor. Quite apart from anything else, any distraction that prevents one from thinking too much about the high note will help it.

I could understand that, as my best high notes have often occurred, either when I was not expecting to sing high, or when I had no idea how high up I was going. That kept away any preconceived ideas about such and such a pitch not being possible for me. Other tips on expressing the meaning of a song were also explained to me by her. It sounded a little like being a good actress to me, and really living the part.

There is more about this second boat trip channelling, which really has to be mentioned, even though certain aspects of it cannot be proven. As I have already stated, I had kept my urge to channel well in check in the seminar room, but when Jack asked me to lead some toning on the boat, as leader, I felt that it was up to me how this was to be done. It was surely an invitation for Maria to come. After all, she could do it so much better than I could.

As usual, I could not feel sure in advance that Maria would actually come, but was delighted to feel her moving into my body. The notes became clearer and more confident. It was during this singing that the note, which had impressed Simone so much, came ringing out from the top of my mouth, and with greater volume than ever before. Maria, who was thankful for the feedback Simone gave me, presented her with a pink rose, a message I naturally passed on.

Along with these wonderful things, a lady from England had no hesitation in expressing how much she had disliked it all. She complained bitterly that the "noise" had disturbed her, and robbed her of the wonderful quiet state she had achieved during the preceding meditation, which Jack had led. "If you had just sung "OO" quietly as the rest of us did, that would have been all right."

Either way, I felt mortified. It was another tough lesson, and emotionally, I seemed to be dealing with it really badly. (If someone had told me what an awful horse I had, and how badly he went for me just after Starlight had given his best ever performance, I might have found that very tough and hurtful as well, ending up with similar emotions.) No doubt part of me wanted to defend Maria. Someone had just criticised a good friend of mine, namely her, even if she had not known whom she was referring to. The biggest help with this came to me while we were swimming in the ocean just after the chanting. Another group member swam over to me, because she had something she really wanted to share. She said that the sounds which came out of my mouth were very similar to those made by two people who channelled the Hathor. These people had been part of an ancient civilisation who left the planet rather as the Atlanteans had. They may even have ascended. Later, some of them returned, mostly to Egypt, she thought, where they made their healing sounds in the temples there.

She seemed emphatic that I should hear these channellings, and said that two other people doing this work were starting to move around more now. I have never heard them to my knowledge, but feel that this may be a good thing, as not having heard them prevents any tendency to try and mimic someone else from getting into my own channelling.

Along with all this, Henriette told me about a very loud bang that had occurred at the back of the boat close to where she and I were sitting. It was so loud, that the captain thought it necessary to get into the water and check the underneath of the boat, as he thought we might have hit a rock he had not seen, but there were no rocks. He said nothing, but later Joan told me that one of the two batteries on the boat had exploded.

No matter to whom I spoke about it, each one of the others seemed to have heard that bang. So why had not I heard it? I think that either I was being protected in some way from the noise that might not have shocked me too much in my altered state when Maria was still in my body, or it happened just as Maria was leaving, but I had not fully re-entered my body. Therefore, I could easily have missed sounds very audible to others.

If Maria's voice had shattered glass during her lifetime, it could well have been the result of that high note that shattered this battery. Another hypothesis is that she came with an enormous amount of love, and that as it pushed the negative energies out of the way, for there was no room for them, their departure exploded the battery. I chose not to discuss this with the captain, in case I got banned from his boat!

Going back to the complaints of the English lady, I must say that they did have their positive consequences. I began to see more clearly, that it was important that those present should know a little more about what was coming in advance. This would have given the lady a chance to move herself further away from Maria's strong voice.

Also I must be sure that it is a legitimate moment for Maria to be brought through. This is particularly important when I am not leading my own workshop, and those present might be unaware that perhaps on some level, they need to hear what Maria could offer them. Even with this perception, getting over the feelings of sadness and rejection was not easy for me. Someone rejecting Maria felt just the same as someone rejecting me. It would not be the last time I would have to deal with things of this nature.

I cannot leave the subject of Chris's seminar without mentioning the help that I was given by Chris himself, which I was later able to use when working away at my singing at home. He commented that I had a tendency to screw up my face and twist my jaw, in particular when singing the high notes. Although he did not tell me so directly, I think his accurate ear noticed that the high notes were frequently out of tune in my case, for he said something about many professional sopranos having difficulty with that.

Thinking back to my violin playing days, I remembered how much harder the intonation was higher up than lower down, because the intervals between the notes are much closer together. Therefore one had to be far more accurate, both with the fingers, and with one's ear. Looked at like this, it was easy for me to understand why the top notes are more difficult to get in tune when singing.

Whether it be with or without Maria, I have a lot of vibrato in my higher notes, and the effort of stopping that, as Chris rightly did not like it the context of his work, tended to make me so tight, that my voice became strained in the upper register. I later read in a book about singing, that whereas soloists may do as they wish, there is no place for vibrato in individual choir members. It can spoil the purity of the harmonies.

All this may seem rather technical to those who do not sing, but it was part of my training for what was to come, and not least the toning of each other's chakras that we did with Chris working in pairs. This was something completely new to me, and whereas I was disinterested in it at the time, I would have been fascinated, had I known how closely this would relate to some of the work that Maria would do with me later. His comments on my poor deportment were also very helpful. So you see, when I had overcome the disappointment of no channelling, I was able to appreciate the help and knowledge Chris imparted to us, and know that actually, I was in exactly the right workshop.

After Joan's and Chris James's Seminar

I did not return to England immediately, but stayed a few more nights on the island to enjoy myself. It was during this time that Joan invited me to visit the Ranch, so that I could meditate with her. It was mainly a meditation about ETS and workshops, and the planned Portal seminar for August 2003.

Maria, who seldom wastes an opportunity, showed me during the first one how she now had a mentor in the spirit realms. He was dressed in white, wore a tall headdress, and reminded me of someone from ancient Egypt. It was he who was guiding her musical studies at the time. I spent that night at Sky Ranch.

The following morning, I was just about to leave the Ranch, when a voice said, "Hi Helena!" I was putting the last things into my car at the time, looked up, and not far away I saw Rose, who I had not seen for a year. I walked over to greet her. She asked me about my singing. She had heard me practising the previous evening, even though she was some distance away from Joan's house, and I was completely out of sight. Rose had mistaken me for an opera singer who lives on the island.

When she spoke to Joan about it, Joan told her it was I without adding any more than that. So Rose, assuming I was a professional singer, wanted me to tell her about my career singing opera. When I told her that actually I worked with horses and had never sung opera anywhere, or had the usual formal training for this art, at least not from an incarnate being, she was amazed.

I explained that Maria Callas had helped me, but only sporadically, as I did not have the time to study as music students do, and that I had never tried to sing seriously, as I had neither the voice, nor the talent, nor the time. Rose told me that her brother was a professional opera singer, a tenor.

As we chatted about it together, it eventually entered my mind that Maria, having died at the age of 54, was now wishing to work as a discarnate entity through me to assist with the production of sounds to help and heal our planet. She had chosen, as many others from the spirit realms have, to employ her gifts for this cause. Although this "theory" was easy for me to understand intellectually, I realised later that I had not really known then if it was true or not, and consequently took very little notice of it.

Rose felt that my work with Maria had a lot to do with healing and love. She asked me if I would be willing to visit the Ranch again before I left the island, as she wanted to spend some time with Maria. However, as she fell ill the following day, and I left before she was well, that never happened. I think it was as well, because I had a sort of gut feeling that I might not be ready or able to live up to her expectations.

Rose loved music, and shared some of her CDs with me. Like Joan, she was really keen to go out and buy herself some recordings of Maria singing in her lifetime. When I told her that I still had my beloved violin, even though I did not play any more, she was convinced that not only did I have work to do singing, but that if I took up playing my violin again, that it would go really well, and I would be amazed.

More about the Exploding Battery

It often happens that when I do not completely understand something at first, insights arrive in my quiet moments as to the true meaning of events at a later date. Therefore it is not surprising that after my return home, when by myself walking quietly in the hills on 6th September, at last I began to feel I understood more about the probable cause and purpose of the loud bang on the boat after channelling Maria's sounds in Hawaii.

I had recently been reading *Le Coeur d'un Couple*, (The Heart of a couple") about the loving relationship of Colette and Paul-Émile Victor, both during their time together on Earth, and after Paul-Émile had died. There is a story in it, which goes roughly like this:

One day, at a time in her life when she was working on learning and practising forgiveness, because she understood that this was necessary in order to serve love, Colette was expecting a young woman to visit her for lunch, who particularly irritated her in many ways. With a strong feeling of resentment, she began to lay the table. She put out four large whisky glasses. All four of them exploded! She fetched four more glasses, and each of these exploded as soon as she put them down. To avoid getting hurt, she protected her face with a plastic bag, as, trembling, she put a ninth glass on the table, and that followed the other eight. She used the word "explode", because all that was left was dust.

After the explosion of the thirteenth glass, she stopped to think about it. She felt there was a link between the very strong negative emotions she felt towards this woman and the explosions. So she repeated to herself that she forgave her, rather more mechanically than with any real conviction. As she continued to put the last remaining glasses from her cupboard on the table, each one exploded as the others had done.

Then in panic, as she knelt on the floor, not to comply with forgiveness, but using all of her fervour in an attempt to make it real. Suddenly, she broke into tears, as she became aware that her visitor was a damaged child. Behind her apparent coldness lay the need to be loved. Colette was now able to send her genuine loving thoughts, and this enabled her to feel serene again. Then everything returned to normal, and no more glasses were broken. Following this, the two women were able to form a sincere friendship.

Colette understood that negative emotions of intolerance, antipathy, etc., when emitted by the means of thought, were enormously powerful weapons of destruction. She knew that future events could be influenced by the negative or positive emotions that we emit today and, as I understand it, love is the other side of the negative coin.

After reading that, I understood that the battery exploding at the back of the boat was not broken by the volume of the channelled sound of Maria's voice in this case, but much more likely by the anger of someone, or several people, who did not like her coming through. Also, the love that Maria brings with her voice could well have pushed out anger relating to other issues lingering in our psyches, at least from those ready to release it. This would explain why the explosion took place after the sound had been omitted, and not when the sound was made. It deffinitely occurred before the English lady had aired her views to me.

It was really important for me to understand this, because otherwise I might have worried about channelling her in her full force in the future, in case she destroyed something else. She had not damaged anything. That had more to do with us. So Maria was innocent.

The above discovery made it possible for me to receive another very important insight. I had hurt my back and, unable to ride my horse, I had gone for a half-day hike over easy terrain in a desperate attempt to get out of the house and into the fresh air. Alone with my thoughts, it was easy for my guides to contact me. I remembered how in Maria's lifetime, she preferred to be among friends, as in spite of her genius, she had not always been well recieved.

Now the first time she came through me, as far as I know, all present were thrilled to hear her, even though I did not know who she was then, and neither did they. Her coming was a complete surprise to all of us.

On the boat when the battery exploded, I know for certain that the lady sitting next to me objected quite strongly, and although some of the group expressed their pleasure and wonder at what had happened, there may have been others who stayed silent, yet regretted the whole thing. This could have contributed to the negativity, which ruined the battery, and explain how it could happen after the sound had stopped.

Having got this far with my realisations, a really important lesson that I was to learn became clear to me. The first time that Maria came through, I was taken unawares, and therefore that was perfectly in order. Following that, I never warned anyone that she might come, no matter where I was, because I thought it would be so disappointing if she stayed away and nothing happened, not to mention a blow to my ego! What a nuisance! Oh well, never mind the size of my ego, what was it I must learn? Simply this. Before giving Maria permission to come through, I must first tell all of those present what might happen if I allowed it, even if I did not choose to mention her name, and then ask all of those present, if they would like her to come.

This was a very important part of my education, as I felt that in the future my work with people would increase. Finally I understood at least some of the lessons I had been privileged to receive, as part of my personal preparation for the future.

Chapter 10

Tempestuous Times

It was the evening of 9th September 2002, following a quiet walk in some nearby hills. I started to look for a suitable CD to sing along with for my singing practice. I had contemplated sitting down to rest for a bit first, but being under the impression that Maria did not want to wait, I decided to start straight away. I thought I would work on one or two of the lower pitched and easier arias, because I am really not a soprano, and felt that these very high notes were really hard on my voice. I hesitated. Could this really be what I was supposed to be working on tonight?

Frequently during the day I had heard the harder arias being sung in my head, even though it was just little bits of them. Why had it not been the more suitable works for my voice instead? Should I after all risk the welfare of my vocal chords, and try something harder against my own judgement?

"Well, what did you think I have been loosening you up for all day?" chimed in the slightly indignant voice of Maria. Frankly, I had not realised she was standing so close to me. I recalled how I had sung for a short while without difficulty in my car, and no doubt due to this distraction, had taken a wrong turning. I also understood that Maria had been working on my vocal chords on a subtle level, even when I was silent, which was almost all of the rest of the day, for I had been roaming the hills alone.

So I dived straight into *Casta Diva* without any further warm up. I was really surprised at how well I was able to sing it. I could feel Maria's musicality coming through me. I was left with the conviction that it was right to continue working at becoming more of a soprano, at least as long as Maria was close to me guiding me that way.

Meanwhile, I was left with something to laugh about. It was the irate way in which she had said, "Well, what did you think I had been loosening you up for all day?" This was the second time she had made me laugh. The first was some months previously when I was practising singing softly to save my voice and spare the neighbours the sound, and she unexpectedly said, "What is the matter with you? Are you afraid of the noise, or something?" How good of her to agree to work with a quiet reserved English lady!

The next little incident occurred on 15th. September. My voice did not feel very strong, and I doubted I could manage many high notes. Some days, they just are not there. Nonetheless, I decided to try the "Ave Maria" from Verdi's opera, "Othello". It stays reasonably low pitched until near the end, when "Ave" is sung on an ascending arpeggio ending on top A flat. Although that is not so very far up, it is plenty high enough to give me trouble if my throat is not co-operating. Just before the first note of that arpeggio, I felt goose bumps all over, and Maria did it for me perfectly! When I repeated it, she left me to do it on my own, but her help had given my confidence a boost, and it was so nice to know that she was really there. I continued to sing higher things without too much difficulty. Later in the day, I observed that in every quiet moment, in my head, I could hear the voices of others talking about Maria on a video I have about her life and art. I realised that there must be a reason why Maria or someone wanted me to listen to it again. So I sat down in front of my television, and watched all 77 minutes of it as attentively as I could.

Shortly before the end, I knew why. I had never seen the significance of it before, or even managed to remember what di Stefano had said. In an interview, he talks about how she would use her finger to point at things when she was in good form and telling everybody else how they should sing. It was not the words he used as much as his physical demonstration of how she did it that suddenly made me understand why I had been asked to watch this video yet again. Many times, when I have been practising singing "on my own", I have seen Maria making signs with her forefinger, but usually considered that it was just my mind interpreting what I should do next, and not necessarily coming from her. Now I knew it was her.

Before recounting any more little episodes between Maria and me, I must stress that as by this time I had read a number of different accounts of her lifetime, this knowledge of how she was, or may have been, could well have coloured my assessment of her intentions and emotions. Readers are advised to use their own judgement, even though I write these things with as much accuracy and honesty as I can muster.

Eleven days later, (20th) I decided to write a postcard to Julia Day, my English publisher. No sooner had I written, "Maria Callas is still trying to teach me to sing", than her voice chipped in to say, "I am not trying to teach you to sing. I am teaching you to sing. I am succeeding! How dare you write, "trying", as if I could not do it?" This was so typical of her. As is often the case, I had not realised she was "in earshot" before she spoke expressing herself in her usual direct way. So far so good.

Then, having neglected to open my emails for a few days, when I did, I found one from a friend, which said, "You DO know, I presume, that today, Monday September 16th, is rather a special day. Maria C. died exactly 25 years ago. I am so curious to know whether she is still with you and if she commented on her "anniversary" in any way! It is so strange, ever since you told me about Maria's presence I keep coming across her, documentaries on the radio, lots of her singing and people mentioning her often! One lady, she is English by birth but has lived here for a very long time, she is a singer too, said that when she had seen Maria perform in the theatre that it was the most profound experience she had ever had!"

The same day, I wrote back to her, admitted I had not noticed the date, and quoted something that Maria had said which I had laughed about a little. I had never intended to hurt Maria's feelings, or upset her in any way, but upset she was, or so it seemed to me.

That evening I decided to have a little singing practise in my kitchen. Maria was definitely present, and advising me on how to do it. Her energy felt completely different. It seemed to have a certain urgency in it, and a lot of tension. Suddenly, she was much stricter, and more demanding of effort on my part than I had previously felt her to be. It was a bit like singing inside a very tight corset. I must hold myself exactly "so", etcetera.

Only months later did I realise that this could have been her most determined effort so far to help me with my singing. Everything she was doing with my body was necessary to make the best possible use of my voice. One day, I would have to start doing this for myself, regardless of whether or not Maria was around, if I seriously wanted to sing well.

I completed the practise, had a hot bath, and went to bed thinking no more about it. I never questioned why she was different. The following day I was dedicating to a full-length hike, so I was to be by myself with my thoughts peacefully wandering about, as I love to do, especially in the good weather we were enjoying.

I was happy to be going and felt at peace with the world, and all that is in it. I had only walked a short distance, when all of this changed. This story illustrates some of the most intense emotional experiences I had had with her at the time.

I became aware that Maria and I had had some kind of discordant time together during my sleep. I could feel the aftermath of it painfully lodged in my solar plexus. When I questioned the cause of it, Maria was there. It was about this one particular story that I had shared about her in an email to Julia Day, and worse than that to at least one other person as well, shortly before I sang the previous evening, that had deeply disturbed her.

"Don't you see what a difficult position that puts me in?" she stormed, still angry with me. I knew then that I must have debated this issue all night with her. Thus the state of my solar plexus, even though I had no memory of any words spoken by either of us. She was referring to my having quoted her as saying that she was not "trying" to teach me, as I had written at first, but "succeeding" in teaching me.

Whether this was a misquote of her thoughts, or simply something she had said for my ears only, I perhaps will never know. It seemed that there could be many reasons for her minding that I had passed it on. It might have been that if word of this got around, then due to the weaknesses in what I see as a very inadequate singing performance on my part, in spite of her help, that all that we had done together so far would be questioned, including the identity of Maria herself.

106

It could have been that she felt her own reputation as an accomplished teacher was about to be ruined, when someone heard how badly I sang. After all, no one would know how much less I knew, or how much less I could do before she came into my life.

Maybe it was the possibility of the press finding out that bothered her. It was as though I had told the whole world. I was astonished! It had never occurred to me that something like that could bother someone no longer living in this dimension. She had been gone for twenty-five years now. Evidently, for some reason, it had upset her unbelievably deeply. I had never intended that, and thought how little I understood both about life after death, and especially about her. No wonder I felt so miserable about it all.

As I walked through the beautiful hills, and sat down at around five o'clock in the afternoon, in a wonderful sunlit valley on a comfortable rock to eat my last sandwich surveying the lovely scenery around me, I noted that my inner peace was still seriously disrupted. "Had Maria decided to leave me? Did it matter if she had? Could I cope with someone who had such a tempestuous temperament in my close vicinity? I had always been very afraid of people with a temper.

If she was leaving me for someone more suitable, then why had she sung with me the previous evening after the email had been sent? Why was she still venting her feelings concerning my actions when I set out on my walk in the morning? Would not it have been simpler to just depart?" I found myself wishing for life how it was before I met her. I wanted to return to a time when it was just the horses, the mountains, my garden, and a little writing or channelling of the ETS from time to time.

I pondered over how thoughtless and clumsy I can be in my dealings with people, and how lucky I was that I still had some friends in spite of this. The events of the night had another effect. I realised more clearly than ever, that Maria was not some miscellaneous journey of my imagination. She was very, very, real. The experience was like a relationship with an incarnated person. It was as intense as that. I had never been so convinced of her presence as I was now. My imagination could never make me feel like this.

I tried to communicate with her a little as I traversed still more beautiful countryside, wondering if enough time had passed for her to have simmered down enough to be able to listen to me expressing myself.

Before I went to bed, I gave myself a very short singing practise, just to see if she was still with me or not, and she was. As I lay down in bed that night, I decided to try once more to talk to her about it. I spoke softly out loud, as sometimes I think it is heard more clearly than my thoughts, even by the discarnate. I do not remember the exact words I used, but I recall some of the sentiments expressed by me in my bewildered state. It was something like this:

"I never meant to cause you any pain or embarrassment. I am truly sorry. I had no idea that what I was doing would upset you. I admit to my thoughtlessness. I have treated others in a similar manner before now, and am therefore lucky that I still have some friends. That is how I am.

I understand nothing of what exactly our relationship is supposed to be. Do I need your approval, as though you were my mother? Does it matter, or is it unimportant? Who is helping whom in this? I have no idea. I am very sorry that you are so upset by my behaviour. I never intended that. I did not foresee it. Is this the end? Or do we carry on? Is there something I need to do to put things right? Or is it too late?

Maria, you have no idea how hard all this is for me. I have simply been trusting that our time together is right, without any conception of why we do it, or what exactly the big purpose of it is, if there is one. You are still a perfectionist. I have that in me as well, but choose to put many things into my life, because it feels right, and therefore I cannot dedicate myself to music now as you once did.

If only I knew why we were doing these things together, or what exactly we were aiming for, it would be so much easier to understand you and how you feel, and perhaps even manage not to make so many mistakes. If you know the answers to these things better than I, could not you tell me please?

108

No doubt the part of me you communicate with at night when I am sleeping already has the answers, but my conscious self is still longing and needing to know, if it is timely. Part of me wants to walk away from you to a safer place, where I could have my peace back, but I know that I cannot go back to the comfortable place where I was before you arrived in my life, for I have changed through it, and the work that we have done together so far would seem to be such a waste of time and energy if it led nowhere. I do love you really, but it is hard for me at the moment. I wish you goodnight."

I felt her presence in the room, and perceived that I had been heard, and she seemed to be calmer. Well, I had done my best to make my peace with her, and felt content to drift away into sleep.

The following morning, I was relieved to observe that my solar plexus felt comfortable again. I supposed that Maria was also calm now. Probably I had irritated her in a number of ways, and this last time had been the last straw that broke the camel's back. "I must try and learn more about diplomacy," I instructed myself. Did nobody warn her that I was like this before she decided to work with me? I wonder? It was certainly an intense learning process for both of us.

It was the 22nd September, when I decided to answer Joan Ocean's emails, and found that Maria was present. I obliged her by sending Joan her love. I shared with Joan how many questions I had about Maria and myself, but not the story I have just related. No sooner had I switched the computer off, than Maria gave me a loving little message for Joan, but it was time to leave the house and see to Starlight, so that had to wait. This horse would want to get his exercise with me, so that he could have his lunch!

Later in the day, I decided to send Joan Maria's message. I asked Maria to watch carefully while I typed it in, so that I would not get any of it wrong and upset her again. At the end, she asked me to sign her name for her. I was really worried. Could this just be an idea of mine? Would Maria be furious if I did that? "Maria, do you really want me to sign your name at the bottom? Tell me!" First, she just pointed to herself, which was not clear enough in meaning for me.

I sat there waiting for instructions from her, which I could be certain I had understood correctly. Her telepathic messages had little effect, for I seriously doubted my ability to get it right. Eventually she put her hands together, as though in prayer to me, almost pleading with me to write her name as the sender. Eventually, I yielded, now sure that what I was doing was in keeping with her wishes. That done, I felt her love so clearly, that I was almost in tears, and certain that we were at complete peace with each other again.

Now that we seemed to have worked through this difficult time, I began to count the gifts it had brought with it. First of all, her presence was so tangible to me through these emotions, both the negative and the positive, that I was even more certain than before that it was really her, and nothing imaginary.

Secondly, I recalled having read in one of the books written about her life on Earth, that on one occasion, when she was very annoyed by the behaviour of one of the other soloists in an opera she was performing, while she was on stage, she had been extremely professional and kept her temper under strict control. At the end, after the final curtain, she really let him have it, and expressed her rage fully.

Please bear in mind that many authors and the press may have grossly exaggerated the stories concerning her temperament, as that way, they made more sensational reading. So perhaps this was merely inspired by truth, and not fair to her.

However, that is exactly what I had just experienced. When she sang with me in the evening after I had sent the email she did not like, she had kept herself very controlled, but clearly, after I was asleep, caution seems to have been thrown to the wind. If the state of shock that I was feeling the following morning is anything to go by, this might be true. If so, then she had given me invaluable evidence of her identity.

I knew it had been an honest exchange on her side. Any anger had been clean anger. I could sense that by the nature of the energy that I was still carrying around in me in the morning. On my side, I was sure I had said something, but was probably so surprised and taken back by this, that I doubt I managed to explain myself very well. That had had to wait until the following evening when I was in bed, just as I have already recounted. It often takes me time to think things out clearly in situations such as this.

Another good thing that had come out of it would appear to be, that having noticed that I was capable of putting her words in an email when she did not want me to, Maria could now ask me to transmit the messages that she did want to convey to others. Thus the few words from her for Joan, and her insistence that I sign her name at the end.

Chapter 11

Love and Forgiveness

It was 24/9/02. I had noticed that since these rather painful and troubling interactions between Maria and myself, my singing practices had intensified and were, at least for the time being, more frequent. I found that the time and energy required was quite draining. Now if this was all in a good cause, within reason, it did not matter. If, on the other hand, it was just an obsession, whether it be Maria's or mine, then it did matter, and my life needed rebalancing. If it were a pointless craze just to satisfy the emotional needs of Maria or myself, it was poor use of precious time indeed.

It brought back memories to me. I recalled how many years ago, I had almost forced myself to learn German from books and tapes in the evenings after work when I was tired, even though my logic told me that my need of the language was just for a few words, and in no way justified such intensive study. Yet I worked on, convinced that something outside myself was driving me, and that there was a good reason for it, even though I did not know what that reason was.

Many times since, I have reaped the rewards of that effort when walking my spiritual pathway. Could it be the same with the singing? I was unable to rule out the possibility that it might, which is what had brought me as far into it as I had already gone, but could it be Maria resisting life in the other realms, and trying to live an earthly life through me, instead of moving forward herself? Was she "stuck", for lack of a better way of putting it? I did not know.

As soon as I had switched the video off, I decided to try and ask Maria for more answers to my questions. She was present. At first, I thought I was looking at a spider's web between the two of us, but when she punched it with her fist, it shattered in a way that only glass can. I heard the noise, saw splinters of glass glinting in the light, and observed quite a large hole in the centre of this sheet of glass that existed between Maria and myself.

She came towards me, and reached through the hole she had made with her right hand. On her ring finger, she wore a beautiful ring, which appeared to be of gold with a large ruby set in diamonds. I was unsure whether I wanted to take the hand offered me or not. The memory of her "rage", as I thought of it, was still so fresh in my mind. "What are you trying to do?", I asked suspiciously. "I am trying to reach you", she replied. Those were the only words that I got from her all evening.

Nonetheless, I hesitantly reached out for the hand she offered me, and allowed her to lead me by the hand through the hole she had made in the glass to a small upright piano, with one of those piano stools in front of it designed to seat two comfortably. I sat down beside her on her right side. With her left hand, she was pointing out things in a music score that had one of the corners of the page bent back at the top to make turning the page easy if one was playing the piano, and placed her right arm loosely around my waist.

She was certainly interested in teaching me, although not offering me any reasons for wanting to do it. I looked anxiously back at the hole in the glass we had walked through, wondering if this was really right. Was it a good thing to spend so much time in her astral realm, if that is what it was? Should not I be living my earthly life and having friendships with incarnated people in my own dimension instead? I had no answer, but it seemed strange to me.

Maria knew exactly how I was feeling, and that I was tired. She showed me a picture of her walking up the stairs of my house with her arm comfortingly around my back, as she suggested without words that it was time for me to go to bed. She was right. I sat quietly another two minutes thinking things over, and then followed her good advice with the thought that surely it cannot be bad to associated with someone capable of treating me so kindly.

When I awoke the next morning, I noticed my mother's brother, David, standing beside my bed in the smart uniform he had worn in his lifetime. (He died aged 22, having drowned at sea). I had never known him, but he had appeared to me many years previously, when my mother and one of my aunts were able to confirm the details about him that I gave them, and showed me photographs that matched my vision.

There were no words from him, but this was his third recent appearance, and I understood that he was there to give me help and support in my dealings with this very strong woman, Maria. I was extremely grateful to know that someone else was there. It gave me the spiritual strength to continue. I now had the knowledge that if things went wrong again, I would not be alone with it, and unsure how to cope. I felt much safer. David was helping both of us by making me feel safe enough to chance being close to Maria.

I had many thoughts through the day. At first, I was very relieved to be doing "normal" things, such as riding my horse, tending the garden and talking to incarnate beings, instead of the discarnate ones dwelling in other realms. Later, I started to consider how it would be for Maria, if I chose to stop working with her. I saw that it would be very unforgiving of me, and would show no love on my part.

Supposing Starlight had refused to work with me after I got things so very wrong for him near the beginning of our partnership, when I barely understood him at all? He had allowed me to persevere and gain his trust, yet always knowing that he could not count on my getting things it for him. Could not I perhaps manage to adopt a kinder attitude towards Maria?

She, in her turn, must have decided to forgive me for getting her so annoyed, and not even realising that she did not like what I was doing, or how much my approach to matters irritated her. She could have walked away from me, or borne a grudge against me for months, but she never left my side, angry or hurt as she may have felt.

Furthermore, I was allowed to feel the force of her genuine love only two days later, when I obliged her by sending Joan her message. In my opinion, our partnership could not be easy for Maria either. I decided to meet her half way, in spite of knowing that she could well become at least as vexed with me again from time to time, and I might never find it easy to deal with. It was a part of her previous character that she seemed to have retained. The evening singing practise, however, went well, and I ended the day feeling much more at peace about things.

On 26th September, I went for a walk in the mountains. This time alone has the enormous advantage that insights I might find really useful will sometimes flood into my relatively quiet mind. This time it was about Maria. I began to understand what she had been trying to communicate in the vision where she had smashed the sheet of glass between us with her fist, and told me as she offered me her hand, that she was trying to reach me. I had thought that this fell far short of an adequate answer to my countless questions, but actually, had I realised the full implications of her words, I would have learnt a lot from them.

She meant that she was trying to reach my heart. I could now see how perfectly this interpretation fitted in with the friendly way she had led me over to the piano, put her arm around me, taken pains to show me little points about the music and later, knowing how tired and bewildered I felt after the recent events with her, escorting me tenderly up the stairs to suggest I might like to go to bed.

She really did want to teach me how to sing, but also to have an open trusting friendship with me. I knew that I had never really trusted her, and not only her, for I seldom trusted other friendships. They were always too good to be true, and I could never believe that anyone would really be able to love me for long at a stretch. I thought of other friends, and wondered if they had been equally frustrated with me without expressing it, when they found in me someone they wanted to befriend, but who was incapable of long term trust, no matter how much love I was shown.

Dimly aware that I had never really mastered this aspect of life, I had thought that my only hope would be if I formed a proper partnership with an incarnated man. Instead, I had an offer from a determined discarnate woman. "Oh well," I thought to myself, "At least if I manage to love her deeply, she cannot upset me by dying on me, because she has already done that." (I meant that I could not suffer bereavement from her physical death, and lose someone I had come to love that way.)

With an incarnated man, it would have been so easy to dismiss his love by telling myself that he only treats me in a loving way because he wants sex from time to time (like the last one some years back). If I refused him that, he would surely leave to "love" someone else instead.

Maria was not after sex, and I was no longer capable of thinking that I was merely a chosen channel for her, so that she could work through me with her voice in some way, regardless of what she thought about me as a person. I had seen myself as a tool in her hands, thinking maybe I was nothing more than that to her. I am sure she is well aware that I, like the other mortals on the planet, have many imperfections, but she still wanted to love and help me.

The big advantage of her offer of friendship was that she seemed to find time to spend with me frequently, and consistently, both in my waking hours and during the night. Most of the incarnate have so many worldly things to see to, that to spend that much time with one person is impossible.

As I walked on through the hills, enjoying the wind blowing through my untidy bits of hair, which had escaped from the hair tie that held the rest of it in place, and thinking how wonderful it was that my appearance was totally unimportant in this situation, I became aware of Maria again. She was hovering about round my head with a pair of scissors in her hand. She wanted to cut my hair. I looked to see what she would to do with it, had she been able, and saw she although she cut it, it was not really too short, but nicely arranged with the ends turned up just clear of my shoulders.

"It looks pretty like that," I thought, "but I imagine it would require a lot more maintenance than it does now, especially if I cram a riding hat down on top of it, or go for a walk in the wind!" The loving caring thoughts that came from Maria with this attention were not wasted on me. I did not know if I would ever alter my hair, but at this moment, having realised what her message, "I am trying to reach you" really meant, I was moved, and open to her sweet love. I felt whole. Something in me had really changed and healed.

The following day, I discovered that I had been sent an email about Venus, the planet of love. It must have arrived while I was out on the hills. Part of it read,

"26 September 2002
The planet Venus reaches its greatest brilliancy today. At visual magnitude -4.6, Venus outshines Sirius by a factor of 18; only the Sun and Moon are brighter."

I felt that the vibrations of Venus were assisting the developing love between Maria and myself, and that Maria had been aware of this opportunity, even though I only learnt about it later when I read the email.

The following day, curious about the spiritual significance of the ring with the ruby that Maria had been wearing when she reached out towards me with her hand through the hole in the glass, I wandered into Chester library to look for a book on gemstones. I felt Maria just behind me. I found a little book in which it said, that rubies are the stones representing the fire of passion. Its colour symbolises daring, charity, and divine love. It is a jewel representing both religious and secular power.

Personally at this time, I was definitely experiencing love, and therefore feel I had been successful in forgiving Maria any emotional discomfort I had felt with her, although I do not think I ever blamed her, as I had put the problems down to my insensitivity to her feelings. She for her part had no problem expressing her love for me, and it was exactly this, which helped to open my heart to her.

Where Music Comes From, 28/9/02

The following day after I had lain down in bed, a true communication with Maria commenced. I had been thinking about how much I loved her. This was still fairly new for me, as I had not dared to really feel this much love for her before. She was beside me, this time without a piano, but carefully showing me things in a music score. I was able to read some of the words from "Vissi d'arte", and took it as an instruction from her that this was a time to go back to that aria for further study in my next singing practise. (We were using opera arias to train me.)

The next event was really special. As we studied various aspects of the music together, we drifted away into a dimension where music exists. It was a place where music comes from, the source of music. I have known for some time, that music is not of this earthly dimension, but comes from somewhere else, and that the Earth needs it for her healing. I was able to see how the sounds carried the vibrations to heal the cells of the human body.

In this special place, I was privileged to move freely independently of Maria. I was in the music of the spheres. I could see it in the form of particles like little light-cells or bubbles of varying colours. I could feel it all around me, and how it penetrated every part of all my subtle bodies cleansing, healing and transforming them. When I heard it softly ringing in my ears, I knew that I was there to fill myself completely with the music on all levels, and bring it into my physical body and conscious mind to pass it on. "We absorb the music here, and then bring it back to the Earth to heal souls", Maria said to me.

I learnt how most talented musicians come here in their sleep state for food to feed their art, even if they are not aware of it. Maria had in her lifetime. They are in the service of music. This source of music is what Maria had been referring to when she told me during the seminar at Sky Ranch in 2001, that since her death she had studied heavenly music, and that she wanted to bring it to the third (physical) dimension. I had understood then that this was part of the purpose of she and I coming together. Joan Ocean's suggestion that I was a part of the original soul who had incarnated as Maria Callas all made sense. Otherwise, I would seem to be a very odd choice as a vessel to work through.

Maria's Tapestry and a Blue Sapphire

On 1/10/02, I felt that my voice had been particularly weak, and wondered where I had gone wrong. Perhaps I had done too much, and strained my vocal chords a little. They could be tired. How did Maria feel about this? I had not sensed her very much while I had been singing, which worried me as well. Perhaps she had been busy with something else.

Seeking some answers, I decided to try and contact her later in the evening, when I was sitting quietly in my chair. Contact was made. Maria showed me herself with a tapestry in her hands. I understood that it represented the project that she and I were working on together.

The background of the design was beige, and I could see a number of little pink roses, some of them still in bud. Maria was busy sowing it as I watched, working on the background at that particular moment. Although much was accomplished, there was quite a large area still to be filled in. She drew my attention to a patch of bare canvass in the middle, and showed me that this was to be a beautiful large red flower. I could not see if it would be a rose or not, but knew it represented something we had not yet done together.

"The best bit is still to come", she told me, referring to the unsown flower. Not knowing to what event in our future Maria was referring did not bother me. This knowledge that something good was still to come answered all of my most pressing questions well enough, and gave me the reassurance and peace of mind that I had been hoping for.

In addition to the above-mentioned tapestry, she showed me a blue sapphire. I searched for its significance in the library book, and learnt that it belongs to the same mineral family as the ruby, and is known as the celestial stone. It is emblematic of immortality and chastity, representing the spiritual values of humanity, and has always stood for the mystery of the celestial. In various religions, it stands for the Light of God, a stone of justice and truth, and the powers of Heaven.

The bit about immortality was interesting to me, in view of Maria's present situation. I myself had no doubts that she still lived, and wondered if this was included to demonstrate the integrity of our communication, or possibly for the benefit of others, who would later read these words.

Voice Problems Again

13/10/02 I was having a singing practise as usual. The quality of the sound coming out of my mouth was worse than usual. My throat was so husky, and the high notes were barely there. I kept on and on trying; hoping that I would be able to sing through it, and my throat would eventually clear. Sometimes, instead of just giving up, I have been able to sing my way through this type of problem. I did my best to sing softly, so that I would not damage anything, but little seemed to improve. I could not feel Maria's presence, but thought I should persevere whether she was there or not. I was learning the music, so singing somehow did seem to have a point to it.

After quite a while, I thought I would complete the session with Gounod's *Ave Maria*. Maria chose not to keep quiet any longer. "Your poor voice!" she exclaimed, having read my thoughts. I should have made use of her good judgement, and stopped torturing my vocal chords immediately. Alas, I had already made my mind up concerning what I wanted to do, but I did take a little notice of her, as I decided to sing even more softly, hoping I would not do myself any further damage. It was awful, although useful for reminding myself of the Latin words and the music.

After this, I spent the rest of the evening wondering where I had gone wrong. Had I failed to hear words of advise from Maria that might have caused me to rest my voice instead of working it? She had tried to tell me. How often did she speak to me, and due to lack of psychic talent, I did not hear her? It must be exasperating for her, if she found herself communicating with someone deaf and blind, as I must be to her sometimes. How many times did I hear her and see her pictures, but dismiss it all as imagination, and take no notice of her?

Working with a discarnate being has many advantages, but how difficult it seemed to be just now for both of us. I felt really sorry that I could not do better for her. I work willingly for those whom I love, but at this moment I could be letting both of us down.

Gloomily I sat in my chair wondering where Maria was. I felt her around my head. She seemed to be sympathetically running her fingers through my hair in a comforting way, but rather than believe it, I thought perhaps it was just wishful thinking that I had her sympathy. Secondly, I did not wish to become an emotional burden to her, so that she found herself trying to pick up the pieces every time something upset me. I wanted to be useful to her, and a good student. After all, how many professional singers would have longed to be in my place? Surely I was very privileged.

After I lay down in bed, I felt I really must try to tell her how I felt about things, and find out how she was. "You have no idea how hard it is for me, when so often I am not in the right state to manage to hear or see you, even if you are trying desperately hard to make your presence known to me! I do not even know how many times you have been totally ignored by me, because I cannot see or hear you. Another problem is still not knowing why we are doing all this. If I did know, I might be able to see in which direction I should go with it all. I am truly sorry for any pain I may cause you, and say these words out loud in the hopes that they will be even clearer to you, than if I just thought them. Please put some answers into my head, while I am sleeping, so that I might know and understand more about these things when I awake tomorrow."

With that, I told her that I loved her, and I fell silent. I was aware of her comforting me by running her fingers gently through my hair again. This time, I believed the experience, felt the love, and was so grateful for the compassion and love that she was showing me.

For those who think I must be abnormally stupid not to have some idea of why she and I were working together, in spite of the fact much light had been shed on it, I will explain why I could not really accept that it had something to do with healing when I finally did reach a point where I could believe it in a later chapter.

Chapter 12

Maria is Given
Some Healing

The following day, I was mostly busy with other more mundane matters, until the evening, which found me in the house. I wondered if I should sing again, but saw pictures of Maria with her finger over her mouth, and waving it from side to side a little, as though warning me that it was not a good idea. I accepted that my voice needed a couple of days to recover before working again. Maria gave me love and comfort caressing my head. I felt this love all around me, as insights into at least one reason for the two of us being together began to fall into place.

I had read many accounts of Maria's life, and although her love of Onassis was frequently mentioned, her real ability to love other people only seldom. I recalled how right at the beginning of this, when I had asked her what she wanted from me, yes, all those months ago, she had replied quite clearly, "I want you to love me." I told her, "Well, I cannot love to order, my love has to be earned, or so it seems to me. I am not yet evolved enough to manage it any other way."

However, I did love her now, sometimes intensely, and sometimes less so. I already knew for certain that I must write a book about her, and now I saw how an honest account of our friendship, just as it happened, would go a long way towards redressing the balance of her reputation.

Her weaknesses, it is well known, were frequently exaggerated by the press. Her artistic abilities were renowned, but the off stage real person, who she was, remained to some extent a stranger. Her many biographers had no doubt done their best, but how could they inform others of her strengths in areas where they themselves had had little or no personal experience?

I was having a direct emotional contact with her. I knew she still had some temperament, but it was an honest one. She just expressed how she felt. I had no desire to hide that, but recorded all that took place between us with integrity. I thought about how unsatisfactory I would find it to die and be unjustly judged by the world, both when and after I had left it. Would not my soul be crying out in pain for lack of recognition of at least a little more good in me than was generally acknowledged?

After all, Maria had given so much to the world. To be acclaimed as "La Divina" on stage, to be acknowledged as having changed opera for all time, would not have put right for me the need to loved for myself, and not for the achievements of my lifetime, had I been born Maria. So I was really pleased to see that there was a real service I could render for her. I could put the records straight for her, not by dissecting her earthly life as many had already done, but by recounting the simple tale of her time with me. This would be the truth I had personally experienced, and not something I had read in someone else's book, or been told by a previous friend/acquaintance of hers.

Few had spoken of the inner purity of her soul. No wonder I had so often seen with my inner eye that she was once in touch with the innocence of childhood. It was when I saw her looking out through those young infant eyes with the distant gaze of a visionary, the same expression I had sometimes seen in my own eyes when still a small child, that I felt so very similar to her.

Since then, of course, I have lived a very different kind of life, and am of a contrasting disposition to her, being of other parentage. I loved her, and wished to serve. She was being wonderfully understanding about my musical imperfections, which are many. I thought of how she must have suffered at the end of her life, when her voice was in decline. No wonder she was capable of such compassion when I had just had a bad session.

The morning after typing in this last story, I decided to share it with Joan Ocean. A moment or two before I clicked on the "send" icon of my computer, I saw Maria looking rather anxious, her right hand up by her face, as though she were about to bite her nails. (She did not). She must have been thinking something like, "Oh dear! What is Helena going to do now?" Unfortunately, I did not interpret the implications of her expression quickly enough to avoid sending it.

After the email had left my computer for Hawaii, I found myself registering a lot of anxiety coming from her. I realised that I should never have sent it, because she did not feel ready to share herself so freely and openly. Maybe the wounds of her earthly life were still so fresh and open that this made her feel too vulnerable.

Wanting to put things right for her, I frantically sent more emails to Joan, explaining briefly what was upsetting Maria, and requesting that after she had read it, she deleted it from her computer, so that no one else would see it. Then I noticed discomfort in my solar plexus, and my logic told me, that if mine hurts, probably so does Maria's. Therefore I first apologised to her, and then offered her the reassurance that Joan was a truly loving being, and that she was safe with Joan. Somehow, I felt that I still had not done enough, and I must communicate more with her at a deeper level.

So I went downstairs, and sitting in my favourite chair, I asked the angels to help me do something to make her feel more comfortable. I did not know what would follow, but found myself in Maria's realm, using my spiritual healer hands to smooth out the tissues of her auric field, especially around the area of her solar plexus, where I believed most of the trouble to lie.

Guided and assisted by the inspiration of the angels along with a certain inner knowing, I worked around all sides of her, my fingers combing the fabric of her energy into place with a soft golden light, occasionally tinged with a luminous pale blue. When the work was finished, I sat back to survey her. To my delight, she took off a red robe she had been wearing over a long cream coloured dress, and let it fall to the ground.

I understood the spiritual implications of this. She felt safe enough to shed a part of her "armour", or her mask, one could call it. She had the courage to trust and reveal more of herself, thus making it possible for her to become more vulnerable, for healing had really taken place.

124

I was very pleased, when I saw this, and noted how tranquil she felt just then. Satisfied that I had done all I could for her, just before I turned my mind to other things, I had the pleasant surprise of discovering that healing Maria (with the assistance, and by the grace of the angels) had healed me. I was no longer sore, or concerned about what I had done. I felt at peace.

That evening, as I lay in a lovely hot bath before going to bed, Maria appeared. She wanted to let me know that she was well. In pictures and words, she communicated, "Fingers crossed, I'm OK now." The next morning, I delighted in sending Joan the good news that Maria was smiling again. When I added a little personal message from her to Joan, the smile grew from generous to radiant, so I knew that all was well.

Fascinated by the nature of the material that I found myself typing into my computer so often about this "working friendship" between Maria and me, I wondered how she was going to feel about everything being made available to all who chose to buy a copy of the book I had in mind. "It will be good", she said. I felt that the healing to help her with being vulnerable was a useful preparation for this.

Although Joan had only been informed about parts of my interaction with Maria, she felt it right on 18th. October, to reply to one of my e-mails in this way:

"Dear Helena,
Thank you for all the updates and fascinating information. The experience of healing Maria is so special and a good reminder that no matter where (in which dimension) our friends and soul mates are, we can still help them and interact with them." Then further on she wrote, "Always remember that YOU are in charge of your life and your body and your ideas, no one else. Your role will be -- to be firm with Maria and not let her make decisions for you. This seems to be a very important spiritual preparation for you for what is coming. To be discerning and to follow your own direction regardless of what beautiful Light Beings may suggest otherwise. No one, no Being, no ET is more important than YOU are. You rule! :-)"

This reminder that I rule, caused me to sit back and take a good look at my life and how I was living it. I saw how a number of times in the past, in spite of having the belief about myself that I am a rather self-centred selfish person, I have thrown myself headlong into the service of other beings, regardless of whether they have had two legs or four, without considering my own needs or desires. Sometimes, on these occasions, I have quite simply thought that that was my own need or desire, but looking back I realised that there has almost always been the price to pay for lack of attention to myself, or to my own real interests.

It is not that these experiences have not given me a great deal, for they have, and especially the present one with Maria, where I have already learned an enormous amount, and only a part of it about music. So I tried to see what was getting neglected in my life now that needed attention, and what did I really want to do myself. Book Four was getting very little work done on it, and I felt that as winter approached, and my garden needed less time for its care, it was the golden opportunity to spend more time putting this fourth book together. The material for it was there in abundance in my computer, and I would never have time to work on this book once spring arrived.

Then there was what did I really want to do? I reflected on how in my late teens, I had had to choose, which of my three talents or loves out of horses, art and music, I wanted to indulge in for my career. I had chosen horses, but always hoping I would somehow find time for the other two as well.

The love of art had manifested itself in my paintings for my books, but as far as music was concerned, there was nothing. I felt that my innate talent lay more in the use of the voice, than playing my much loved but very neglected violin, or the piano.

However, there were problems here. Firstly, my throat condition. It gets congested, especially in winter, and at such times I cannot sing until it clears. That eliminated any possibility of being a professional. For that, I would have needed a more reliable voice. I would have loved so much to be a soprano as Maria has been, but although since she came into my life, I had definitely acquired some new notes, and much more confidence, I did not have her range.

Yet the music was in me, and somehow, I would love to use it in service, but how? I did not want to sing anything less than classical, or opera. Channelled sound for healing was another interesting option. Nothing less than one or both of those would satisfy me, bearing in mind that anything too easy I lose interest in very quickly.

I had never had a satisfactory reply from Maria concerning where our work together was supposed to be leading us, even though I had asked many times. I was beginning to wonder if she knew. (With hindsight, I would surmise that she did know, or at least knew more of the plan than I did.) What on Earth could I do? I decided to remember what I wanted, and see what doors might open to me.

After Joan's email and these thoughts, she seemed to back away from me a bit. Her absence was actually helpful, as it made it easier for me to tune into my own thoughts. She had not left, however, and I did not mean her to, as I considered it was still an incomplete experience with her. I felt her one night as I lay down in bed, present in a comforting way, for she was quietly working on the tension I wanted to let go of in my shoulders, a gift I accepted gratefully. This helped me to drift off to sleep.

One of the things she had managed to teach me, was that when there are two persons involved, in this case, she and I, then one must consult or at least talk to the other one, rather than just carry on making one's own decisions as though no one else was there. Maria was my friend. Therefore I was not intending to simply walk away from her, but try yet again to find out what it was she hoped to get out of this.

So one afternoon, rather than sing, I sat down comfortably, called her, and asked her what she wanted. I know that I was heard and that she came, for she spoke to me, not just in thoughts and pictures as was often the case, but with the same speaking voice that she had had when incarnated. Having heard this on video, it was easy for me to recognise it. We spoke together for about ten minutes. She answered me very directly with the words, "I want to speak through you". I paused, and told her that I was willing to do that for her when the right place, time and people came together, as had been the case in France nearly a year ago. It occurred to me that there must be a lot she might usefully share about life after death, and all speaking from her own experiences. What ever it was, if it would help either her or those who heard her words, I was willing. I could see that this would serve my own spiritual development as well.

The next topic was music. This was definitely a shared love. However, I did not feel it was going as well as it should at the time, or that she was really that interested. "But it's fun, isn't it?" she asked me.

I had my doubts, as I had let it all get so serious lately. Then, remembering my own interests and desires needed to be catered for as well, and taking into account that I can only sing for short periods of time, so it does not take much out of my day, I determined to give myself this gift. Whether or not she was present was her choice when I sang, and I would just do what I could for my personal pleasure, even if none of it ever helped anyone else. (It occurred to me that thinking I could sing well enough to give pleasure to others might well be a trip of my ego, wanting to be more in the limelight.)

I knew after this conversation with her that I had already forgotten much of it, but the point that I heard her own voice throughout stayed with me, convincing me it had been real. I spent quite a lot of time reassessing how I would tackle the singing differently. I would cease thinking I had to be able to sing higher than I could without strain, select the arias accordingly, and take it from there.

I found, however, that I could not let go of my desire to sing "Casta Diva", and some others of equally high pitch, because the degree of difficulty gave them such a strong attraction. I came up with a plan for those as well. If I learned them very thoroughly, then I would be able to manage without a CD to accompany me, and I could pitch them about three semitones lower, which would put them comfortably within my vocal range. When learning them, instead of straining my poor voice, I could either drop an octave on the highest passages, or memorise it all so well, that I would be able to do it all properly at my chosen pitch later.

As I lay in bed that night, Maria chose to visit me. She seemed delighted with my own ideas, and was clapping her hands to celebrate them. When I sang the following evening, I found her with me. I could tell, as the sound is so much richer when she is there, and providing I did not try to sing outside my Maria-assisted range, it sounded incredibly like her voice on the CD. Perhaps a blend of hers and mine would describe it best.

This does not happen when she is absent, and my range is smaller. I finished feeling much happier about it all. It occurred to me later that often she had sacrificed her own interests for others, that is, given herself away, as she did with Onassis. I felt that frequently when I had looked to her for guidance, she had actually held back a bit, as she wanted me to learn to take more of the initiative myself, something I had been slow to comprehend.

Joan's email had been the little bit of help necessary to make this next step.

Chapter 13

I Buy A Piano!

26/1/03

By this time, I had temporarily stopped singing. I knew that I always had difficulties with my throat in the winter, so the poor quality of the sound that came out depressed me greatly, and I had chosen to wait until the summer. My energy levels were often low. I was putting it down to age and the climate, until after I had followed the advice of a builder. It was he who kindly told me that the problem I had with fumes from the gas boiler in my kitchen, which heats the water and radiators in my house, could be resolved with a more modern boiler.

This would be an expensive change to make, but the symptoms of gas poisoning were severe enough for me to justify spending the money. Now I understood why so often I felt unwell. I would start wondering if I should go back to bed, because of the drowsiness the fumes were causing, along with a slight headache, low energy, and almost a loss of the ability to think. These were clearly linked to the time that I spent in my house, especially in the kitchen near the boiler.

Going outside would improve how I felt quite quickly. I always smelt gas when the boiler lit up, but far worse than that were the carbon monoxide fumes that cannot be smelt. I had not realised how bad they were, in spite of an instinctive desire to keep opening the windows, because the cold air rushing in was preferable to the airlessness of the house. It took nearly a month before I could get this new boiler installed, but the money was well spent. Little by little I began to feel better, and more like doing things, even writing my books.

During this period of time when I did not sing, I often thought about Maria, and sometimes she would get my attention one way or another.

For example, after I came home with a bunch of flowers given to me by the garage as a present for buying a new car, I found her strutting about the room as though she wanted to arrange them, just as I had seen her perfecting the flower arrangements in her own house on a video. There was one red rose, which I put in the centre. I knew that she had always enjoyed red roses.

Three weeks later, by which time I had removed the rose (it died first) and one or two other dead ones, the vase of flowers was still there. I was sitting in my chair reading something, when I became aware of Maria saying, "Isn't it time you threw away those dead flowers?", or words to that effect. I went over to look at them, and sure enough, most of them had died quietly without my noticing. I threw them away.

Meanwhile, as my interest in singing was still alive, I had bought myself a book on how to sing. Certainly Maria had taught me quite a lot about technique, but there were so many questions I wanted to ask, and even if Maria had already answered them, I needed to know if I had heard and felt her correctly.

The confirmation of all these things was in the book. I was fascinated. Even the time she had been so very particular about how I was holding myself to sing, supporting my ribcage in such a way that I had to use my breath and diaphragm correctly, turned out to be described in great detail in this book. Maria had it right, or should I say that the author of the book was correct!

Then I started one of James Twyman's courses, which I had downloaded from the Internet. This seemed to open me further, giving me more energy. As I sat in my chair one morning, having read some of this, Maria appeared. I had often wondered how she felt about my not singing. Was she still with me? Was she disappointed?

Well there she was, and I felt that she understood my vocal silence, and maybe it was timely. She looked wonderful! She was wearing a long rich red dress, with a low enough neckline to display a beautiful diamond necklace. I could not take my eyes off those diamonds. They shone, glistened, and gave out a lot of Light. She was showing me her rings. One had diamonds, and the other a large red ruby. She offered me a ring with a blue sapphire, knowing that I loved blue, but somehow I felt more attracted to the diamonds, which she also wanted to give me, and the ruby.

Then the unexpected happened. Instead of her entering my body as one might have expected, I was first shown her heart, which I saw as pure and white, the kind of soft white that tells me it has been tempered by earthly experiences. Next, having observed the Light around her, I found that I felt very comfortable in her presence. This was the preparation I needed for the really unexpected part.

Involuntarily, yet with the option to stop it if I chose to, part of my consciousness drifted out of my own body into hers. I was surveying things through her eyes. She was on a really spiritual level. I felt none of the temperament that she was renowned for in her earthly existence as Maria Callas. She was in a place where Light abounded. I stayed to feel the energies there for a little while, before Maria showed me her watch. I did not know what time it said, but understood that this was the moment for our communication to cease.

As I lingered where I was, watching her walk away from me a little, much of the good energy stayed with me. I felt very quiet and peaceful, having been in quite an aggressive mood beforehand.

The 6th February brought another change. I had been resting my singing voice since Christmas, and felt too discouraged by my personal shortcomings to even want to listen to the beautiful recordings of Maria's voice on CDs. Several that I had bought lay unopened on the shelf. Hearing her sing so beautifully reminded me painfully of what I would love to be able to do, but did not have the vocal equipment for.

Now, for some strange reason, having just finished reading a book about singing technique, which had confirmed for me so many of the things that Maria had taught or shown me, I looked at the recording of Macbeth, an opera I did not know, and decided to open the little package. Busy preparing a meal for myself, I did not consult the libretto, so I had no idea which part Maria would be singing, and anyway, did not understand the Italian.

After a bit, I heard a woman's speaking voice. "It has a higher pitch than Maria's", I thought to myself, and listened entranced as the lady then began to sing with a wonderful rich full-bodied voice at what I considered to be a contralto pitch. It was so beautiful, that I decided to find out whom the contralto might be. It turned out that all this was Maria! Later in the opera, she sings a top D, and covers an enormous range in the part of Lady Macbeth. I read in the little booklet that came with the music, that Maria had deliberately raised the normal pitch of her speaking voice, so that it would blend and join smoothly with the following sung lines. Thus my confusion about her identity.

In the afternoon, I decided to go shopping for one or two small items of food, and so on. As I put my hat and coat on, Maria was beside me, telling me what coloured scarf would look best with my outfit. Her advice was good, but I did not have one in that shade of red, so I could not oblige her.

I suppose I might have guessed that her presence that day had a reason, but I had not realised she planned to come with me. Oh what a surprise! Instead of the health-food shop, I went straight to a music shop!

I had been thinking how useful it would be if I could find a tiny little keyboard on which to play some of the recommended warm-up and other vocal exercises I had seen in the book called, "How to Sing", as my vocal sight-reading is not very good. Something spanning about three or four octaves would surely do the trick. I could put it away in a drawer when out of use, and plug it into an electric socket, having sat it down on a table, when I wanted it. It would be much quicker and easier than having to tune up and play musical passages I wanted to sing on my long neglected violin. Traditional pianos were out of the question. The grand pianos were far too big and expensive to fit inside my tiny house, and even an upright piano would take up more space than I could spare, and a decent one would be dear.

So I looked at the electronic digital keyboards, or digital pianos, as some were described. Every reason for not buying anything at all was going through my head. "When the novelty wears off, you will probably never play it. You take on too many projects that you have not got time for, and then see none of them through. What a waste of money! That big thing over there would take up too much space, and only be useful if you practise regularly, which is very unlikely. Look at the fate of that beautiful violin! It lies idle collecting dust on top of a cupboard. This keyboard thing will just add to the clutter and spoil the look of the house." Well, that was the advice, which I gave myself.

Then came the thoughts: "It would be so much easier than using the pitch pipes, which are only designed for single notes. A small keyboard would not take up much space. Perhaps the cheapest one would not cost too much. The fact that they plug into an electric socket means that they take up much less room than a traditional piano." I was getting far too interested.

I could not resist the temptation to ask the salesman a question or two. I had recently watched a programme about sales techniques on the television, so I knew that I must not take more than a very little of his time, or I would end up buying something I did not really want. It was hopeless! The more he told me, the more I wanted to know about these modern electronic instruments, that I had never even dreamt existed in such an advanced form, not to mention the amazing things that could be done with them.

I was convinced when I entered the shop that the sound would be horrible, but I discovered that if I avoided the cheaper models, they really were not that bad. Furthermore, there were "things" on them, which I knew would help me. I left the shop with a leaflet about one of the more expensive ones (still much cheaper than a proper piano, I told myself) in my shopping bag to think it over.

By now, I knew in my heart that I was already committed. I started measuring up the little spaces in my house to see if one could be fitted in. It could. I began to recognise how often, and how much in my heart, I had longed for access to a piano over the years, even though I knew I was much better suited by nature to the violin than the piano.

Why had I denied myself this treasure? Clearly I still harboured the belief that I must not spend too much money, and particularly not on myself.

Happiness does not come from material riches. This is true. I recognised that for me this theory needs to be balanced by the understanding that although we are spiritual beings, we live in a material world, and that there are times when it is appropriate for some of us to own a few things in order to assist in anchoring Light and the God-given gifts that we are born with on this planet.

Feelings of "I do not deserve to have...." which I got from my poor dear mother are not appropriate. Maria is helping me bring in more of the personality that I inherit from my father. Although he never wasted money, he had no trouble with this issue. I could say that my parents balanced each other very well.

As I had walked back from the town, Maria had helped me by dancing around me delighted that I would eventually buy one, saying, "But it is not a proper music house without a piano!" Her joy was infectious, and I arrived home full of it.

The following day, I went to buy this digital piano, and a stand to fix it to. I realised that my table was not the right height to put it on. With the stand in one cardboard box, and the piano in another, I drove home with it in my little Renault Clio.

A conventional piano would have been far to big too transport that way, especially the best possible enormous grand piano that I might have chosen to dream about. Thanks to a temporary back injury, I was able to dedicate the necessary time to unpack it, work out from a book of instructions how to put it together, and begin the process of learning how to play the accompaniment of Gounod's *Ave Maria*.

I had long ago bought the music score for that, because although I never had any intention of buying a piano or playing it, I had needed it in order to find out what the Latin words were. Besides, Maria had consistently shown more interest in my singing this song with her than the other vocal work, which I loved. The piano part was astonishingly simple, even if rather fast.

However, modern technology even has a way around that little problem. I discovered from the piano's book of instructions, that not only could anything I wanted to play be painlessly transposed to the pitch of my choice, but it could also be recorded, and the tempo of the recording altered without changing the pitch. Therefore I would not have to run out of breath while waiting for my fingers to find their way to the notes, and would not have to try and play and sing at once.

The more I discovered about this machine, the more I saw how Maria had helped me to choose something that was far more useful to me than either a grand piano, or a tiny keyboard such as I had had in mind. I was so grateful to her when I found all this out afterwards. No wonder she was so wild with joy when she knew I had made the right choice.

For my part, as I sat down and started to play, having not touched a keyboard for over thirty years, I could not believe the pleasure it gave me, even though there was nothing I remembered well enough to play fluently. This was a wish of mine that I had held in almost total denial. Again I was thankful that Maria had helped lead me there.

Perhaps at last, I was allowing myself more self love, which could in turn lead to more ways of giving love out to the world. I pondered the countless possibilities this could give me. I would have to do a lot of work, but I felt it could lead somewhere, and that the things I had learnt about music, both in my childhood and then later with Maria, could be put to good use. Could I fulfil a dream, and use my musical talents in service? I certainly had the best possible musical guide anyone could wish for standing beside me. Only time would give me the answers, but this piano was a breakthrough!

About four days later, in spite of having spent much of my time playing it, I still could not really believe that I owned a piano, and there it was in my house. Having always known that of the two instruments I had studied in my youth, I far preferred the violin, and only turned to a piano more reluctantly. I had kept the violin just in case I ever felt motivated by something to start playing it again later in life, but had long ago relinquished any hope or desire of ever reviving my piano skills.

Encouraged by my progress with my piano, I decided to try and start singing again. Clearly my voice was in a weak state, but I thought that perhaps, if I was very gentle with it, it would recover. About the second or third day, it was so bad, that I felt I was not even capable of singing a nursery rhyme. I went to bed feeling very depressed about it.

Were my vocal chords ruined beyond repair? Was it this persistent problem I had with my throat, which never seemed to be clear enough to sing freely? Was I living in dreamland when I sat down at the piano painstakingly learning the accompaniment for "Ave Maria", so that I would later be able to sing to it? If I was really so deluded, then why did Maria encourage me to play? Was she just trying to find an alternative outlet for my musical expression? If that was the case, then why learn accompaniments? Would not it be better to play sonatas? It did not make sense, unless she could see that somehow my voice and throat were going to recover.

The previous summer, I had tried to get a music score of "*La Paloma*", because I was having difficulty finding the words of it with a CD. I was interested in this work, because Maria had sung it early on in her career. The music shop assistant in Chester told me that it was unavailable. I had thought of just using this song to sing "la" to in the absence of the words, but Maria told me clearly, "Oh no, you should learn the words." I found some of them with one of the CDs, but had to manage without the rest of them, and without the score.

As it was one of the easier songs to learn by listening, this did not seem to matter too much at the time. With this new possibility of accompanying myself on the piano, I decided to try again. I was in luck! The first shop in Chester, which I tried, told me they could order it quite easily. This was a pointer to the fact that in spite of all, I was really intended to sing had occurred in the morning.

As I lay in bed that night, I asked Maria's advice. She suggested praying to the Madonna, not surprising really, as that is what she would have done in her lifetime I thought. So I did, as well as the angels, and any other entity out there who might be able to help me get over my throat and voice problems. I also asked for guidance from the divine wisdom that lives within me.

The next morning, Valentine's Day, I had an appointment with a therapist who had agreed to treat my back with the Bowen Technique. Not knowing whether or not that could somehow help my throat or not, I told her about my problem, and why I minded so much. She suggested visiting a herbalist she knew of, telling me what the possible cause of my troubles might be, and that it was probably treatable. This was very encouraging. I resolved to visit the herbalist. As it happened, the herbalist was away, so I would have to wait for that, but meanwhile I was still in need of more Bowen technique for other parts of my body.

So on 27th. February, I went back for more. After my pelvis and a few other bits had been treated, this helpful lady set to work to see what she could do that might help my singing. As she sang in a choir herself, she understood the needs of a singer very well. During the treatment, I observed quite dramatic changes in my chest and throat. I was curious to see if this would help in spite of the congestion I so frequently experienced when I wanted to sing.

That evening, as I lay in a special position on my back on the floor to aid circulation and healing for the bits of me, which had been treated by the therapist according to her instructions, I tried to sing. I had done the same thing the previous evening, and been almost completely unable to produce the notes, so I had given up very quickly. This time, however, it was different. The sound came out. I was excited.

The following evening, standing up in my kitchen, busy doing other things, I had Maria singing on a CD. When I joined in with some of the easier bits, I found a big difference. My lungs were freer. It was as though they were larger and more elastic. It had freed up the whole of my chest. Even better than that, I could open my throat more easily, and make more space for the sound to come out of it.

Delighted, I decided it was time to play a recording of "Ave Maria", and sing along to the easier parts. Some of it, as I may have already mentioned, is rather high for me. To my astonishment, I discovered that I could sing all of the notes again, even the top B flat. (Luckily there is only one of those.) I sang it several times, and then Maria, whose presence I could feel, advised me to stop.

I sang a little more, but wisely, I feel, resisted the temptation to try any more top B flats. (When the singing is going well, I have a lot of difficulty stopping myself from doing more than is wise. I am like that with the other things in my life as well.) I did, however, manage to remind myself that Maria is much better than I am at knowing when to stop.

I knew that my vocal chords were weak, and that I could only sing for very short periods of time if I did not want to strain them. This was, however, the biggest ray of hope I had had for some time that I might be able to learn to sing in spite of my physical shortcomings. Maria's optimism, which she demonstrated by staying with me, and her encouragement with the piano, had puzzled me greatly.

I had often wondered if there was something in the future she could see from where she was, which I could not. Surely there must be a reason for all this? Looked at from an intellectual point of view, the whole thing was totally illogical.

Anyway, she was usually there when I practised the piano. She would give little words of advice, which I found very helpful. One day when I tried to sing at the same time as playing, she said, "Try it a little faster. You will find it easier." It was easier. I thought it would have been more difficult, but Maria knew.

Another time she told me to stop playing, because if I carried on, my fingers would get too tired. Thinking it might be just my own lazy thoughts, I determinedly carried on, but what Maria had warned me about is exactly what happened! So I had to rest my hands completely as far as playing the piano was concerned the following day. They ached with stiff muscles.

One evening, when I was thinking about her, and wondering how it was for her communicating with someone in another dimension, namely mine, she showed me a picture. I saw myself on a stage performing and learning things, while Maria stood slightly behind me with a hand on my shoulder, teaching and guiding me in my part. I and my reality all looked faint and faded, whereas Maria looked solid, wore white with a rich red robe over her shoulders, and her long dark hair was hanging down her back.

I understood that for her, it was as though she experienced a window in time. She lived in her post incarnation present, but interacted with the present day rather as I might look at another age past or present through a time portal.

I frequently wondered if her coming to me had something to do with my learning not to accept my limitations, but to seek the way through them, to transcend the boundaries, but in a realistic manner. This would have an enormous positive mind-opening impact on the rest of my spiritual life.

On 1st March 2003, another strange thing happened. I switched my computer on, and went away to another room while it was booting up. When I came back, there were pictures of Maria Callas being shown in sequence from her website. That had never happened before. I was expecting to see either the desktop, a blank screen, or the possible "wallpaper" pictures of mountains etc. that had been installed as the "screen saver", if it is left on without being used for too long a time.

I had only visited this page of her website once, and that was some time ago before my computer was wiped clean, taken to bits, and a new motherboard (what ever that may be) installed in it. When I clicked on it, the pictures of her disappeared, and the previously expected desktop appeared in their place. I was not connected to the Internet either before or after this happened.

I took this incident as confirmation that she was still around me, and that it was time to type the most recent evidence of her presence and our interaction into this document, which I have now done. I needed this evidence both for myself and to share with others, as sometimes it was hard to tell if her words were not hers, but some trip of the ego, whilst Maria was actually far away somewhere else.

I also knew, that she does not belong to me. I mean that she is a free spirit just as much as I am. I must accept the gifts she brings me, and also that she has the right to leave me when she wishes, and to serve others on this earth at any time. In other words, there is no place for possessiveness or jealousy. Although these emotions most likely come from a sense of insecurity, to feel that way would be an unkindness on my part towards her in my opinion.

It was easy to see this when I imagined how I would feel about these things were I in her place. Only the ego wants to own things. The higher self always chooses to let go, or rather never hold onto things, thus giving others the freedom it has itself. I knew I was still to some extent possessive, and so wished I was not, because I saw it as a failing on my part, and an unkindness to Maria, even if she understood the reasons why better than I did.

On 4th March, she showed me a picture of myself on the stage, and her standing slightly behind me with her right hand resting gently on my left shoulder. There was an area towards one of the corners of the stage, where I could see a brilliant light. She was in a sense guiding me towards this light, and told me we could walk the journey to the Light together. I was delighted. It seemed to be so much more fun to go with someone than on one's own. I stepped forward gladly. I felt that this must all be relevant to the In-breath of God, the returning to the Source from which we came.

This last vision is one that I never forget. It seems to have been indelibly imprinted onto my consciousness, even though there have been many times when I have wrongly doubted the truth of it. It was and is so beautiful!

Chapter 14

My Preparations For France

On 19th March, Patrick Kempe mentioned on the telephone, that "The conversation must go as planned". This was channelled, and neither of us knew what it could possibly be about. I watched my conversations with various people throughout the day, and nothing seemed to connect with it. In the evening, I had reason to telephone Marguerite Vidal about something. I did not normally telephone her, but my email to her would not agree to leave my computer, and neither could her fax machine receive faxes just then, so the telephone seemed the best quick solution.

It seemed a fairly harmless little chat with her, until I observed myself agreeing that I would go to France again this year. I never meant to let myself into another visit abroad so soon, because I felt very behind with my writing I needed and wanted to spend the time, which I had not already planned to spend away here, to write Book Four, look after my garden, and train my horse. ("Book Four" was to be about everything other than Maria.)

As I put the telephone down, I began to wonder how I had allowed myself to agree so easily to something I did not want to do. Then I remembered the channelled words of Patrick Kempe, and realised that this was meant to be. This knowledge helped me to accept it all, and prevented me from thinking I was just a rather weak person who could easily be talked into anything. Equally interesting is the fact that in an email sent to me in 2005, Marguerite wrote,

"It was during a telephone conversation with you that I was inspired, without having planned it beforehand, to suggest coming here again to you."

So the planning did not come from either of us!

Further reflections on my own feelings about it helped me to see that I did not dislike going to France, or to other places where I might travel, but I loved being at home, and this was the main reason for my resistance. I saw that I was very lucky to enjoy my home so much, and having understood myself better, could now start to feel enthusiastic about a visit to Marguerite's house again.

The following morning, I was well rewarded for my willingness to go there by Maria, who sang the whole of *Ave Maria* through me during a singing practise.

This feeling of joyous anticipation gradually grew. I watched how my life was unfolding. I saw how I was being led in the right direction to get the help that I needed with my body. It had started when I strained my back, and sought the help from the Bowen Technique practitioner, as I related in the previous chapter. The herbalist, who had been recommended to me, was first away on holiday, and then on her return, so busy that I had to wait several weeks before she could see me.

When I finally managed to meet her for my appointment, although I had only asked for help with my throat she asked me many questions about my general health, going right back to my childhood, in order to get a grasp of my condition, and to make an accurate diagnoses.

Then she diagnosed internal candida, which, she explained, might well be part of the cause of the congestion and singing difficulties. I was also sensitive to "mixed moulds", as she called them. This is why my throat was so much worse in the dampness of winter. A homeopathic remedy sorted that out, but the candida, caused not by my present diet, but whatever I had eaten in the past, was very deep rooted and took a long while to clear.

There were, however some more immediate results, which I was overjoyed about. My ability to ride my horse correctly had been inhibited by the state of my skin, which bled with increasing regularity when I sat in the saddle. In spite of the pain, I had persevered, because it meant so much to me to be able to train Starlight. Not long after I started taking the herbal remedy for candida, the skin began to heal. Riding became a great pleasure again.

When I returned to the therapist at a later date, I was treated for laryngitis, and then much later helped with spasms occurring in my gut with inhibited any sort of effort in life.

I had to thank not just the therapist, but also Maria for this, as without her encouragement in my musical life, I would never have bothered to try and sort out my throat problems, and therefore never discovered what was wrong with the rest of me, or treated these ailments properly. I wanted so much to be a better instrument for Maria to come through. She had been the source of my motivation to improve my health.

Furthermore, she had stayed with me, comforting me in my non-singing periods, and I felt a genuine love for her now. This was something she had asked for so early on in our friendship, but I knew that I could not force my emotions. She had won my love with her constant attentions to me, even when I felt I was failing to understand or manage my part in this unusual partnership.

I had told Marguerite that my visit could either be the beginning or the end of May. If these dates were unsuitable, then I would need to wait until the autumn. The beginning of May was not convenient for her, so I carried on with my life and Starlight's training. As I had received no confirmation that the end of May was any good either, when time passed, I drew the conclusion nothing further would happen before the autumn.

A Sudden Change of Plan

On the morning of 3rd. May, after a very demanding three-day dressage course with a visiting exceptionally talented trainer from abroad to help me with Starlight, I checked my emails, and found one from Marguerite. She was waiting for me to confirm my visit at the end of May, having forgotten to tell me I was wanted, which I subsequently pointed out to her. We spoke on the telephone, and I flew into action to book my flights etc.

144

Actually, all of this was PERFECT! Had I known before or during that intensive training with Starlight that I was going to France, it would have been much harder to channel my attention into the training, instead of concerning myself with preparations for France. I was not meant to know even one day earlier that I was going away so soon. (26th May)

Somehow, I never doubted that I would be able to have a seat on the aeroplane, but I was astonished at how easily I obtained one. The direct flight to Basel was the cheapest and also the one I preferred. There was plenty of space on the aircraft, and the travel agency did not keep me waiting, but gave me all the help I wanted as soon as I entered their shop. When I returned to collect the tickets sometime later, it was the same. There was a queue of other people waiting for attention, but as soon as they saw me, and I absentmindedly walked straight up to an assistant, she decided that I should not have to wait, as she could help me straight away, and it would not take too long. Nobody complained about this! The others just sat there waiting their turn for help patiently. I had the same success buying myself some euros. No delays, and wonderful help. I never remembered making my travel arrangements being so easy before.

With great enthusiasm, I hurled myself into the preparations at home training my voice, playing the piano, and thinking about the seminars I was going to give. I had not wanted to give any more seminars, but it seems that they went with the rest of the deal. At least they might help cover some of my expenses.

A pulled muscle in my ribs made focusing myself so wholeheartedly on the music easier. I was not sure how I had managed to injure myself, but found riding Starlight painful, so I decided to wait a few days, while it healed, before getting on him again. Then, just as I was considering another ride, Starlight cut his heel and was lame, so still no riding. Off course I missed my riding and Starlight very much, but the relative ease of centring my life on the French visit did not escape my notice. All of this was meant to be.

On May 9th, I heard Maria say, "I will give you evidence that you cannot possibly refute." Now refute is not a word I use myself, so I knew this could not be one of my own thoughts or fantasies. This knowledge added more fuel to the fire of my enthusiasm.

Later, as I walked the streets of Chester to collect my air tickets, and buy myself some Euros, I heard her say, "I would like you to get out more, and enjoy yourself". I managed to respond to this shortly afterwards by inviting a friend, Margot, to wander down to some "Tea Rooms" in Chester with me one Sunday morning for tea and a snack, after which we strolled around one of the town parks, walking back beside the River Dee. This brought me joy and relaxation, as well as gain from the mutual sharing that took place between us.

The preparation for my French trip became more and more intense, and the ideas, which I felt I should follow up, more and more ambitious, which is perhaps why I was getting so very tired mentally.

In view of this, it is not surprising that when I tried to type another fairy story into my computer, I found myself making more and more typing errors. I struggled to regain my focus for a while, but continued to deteriorate so rapidly, that I decided I must go out for a breath of fresh air, using my wish to post a letter as an additional purpose for a short walk. Normally, I always close the computer down before going out to save electricity, but this time, thinking I would only be going out for a few minutes, I left it on.

Once out of the house, it was such a relief not to be trying to type any more, that I selected one of the more distant letter boxes in which to post my letter, and then took the long way round to walk back to my house. So the planned outing of ten minutes took me fifty minutes.

As I came in through my front door, I heard the faint sound of music playing. "Oh, one of the neighbours must be listening to music!" I thought to myself. "I wonder who it is?" Then as I was taking my outdoor shoes off, I began to wonder if the sound could be coming from upstairs in my own house. Still with hat and coat on, I started to climb the little staircase, and about half way up, I recognised the voice of Maria singing. This was really a mystery, because I had not played any music all day, so I could not possibly have left anything playing before I went out, and I had not played anything upstairs for at least a month.

On entering my office at the top of the stairs, I realised it was coming from my computer. When I left the house earlier, the fairy story with all of my typing mistakes   was covering the screen. Now it was mostly red with pictures of Maria flashing in various corners, and her voice singing an aria. Now, as you will know, something like this had happened once before when I left the computer switched on, but that time there was no sound. I sat down in front of it, thinking I had better listen to the end of the aria just in case there was a message in it for me somewhere. However, it seemed to be the longest aria I had ever heard, as it went on and on and on....

I had much still to fit into my day, and wondered how long I must sit there. Also, I wanted to warm myself up with some of the lovely tea I had made earlier, which I had left ready for myself in a flask downstairs. Time passed. By now, I had thrown my hat off onto the floor, but still wore my coat. Then the sweetest gentlest little voice said softly into my left ear, "I'm so sorry! I did not mean to hold you up." It was Maria standing behind my left shoulder! That told me that she was responsible for this, and shortly afterwards, I understood why the aria had no end. She had taken all this from the net, where it had been edited to have no beginning and no end, but would play indefinitely!

This evidence had a strong impact on me, for I had been wondering yet again, how much of what I believed to be her voice speaking to me was really just part of my own thoughts, and how much was actually her. The effect on the music practise I had later that day was dramatic. I took much more notice of the voice in my ear, following her instructions as closely as I could.

I worried about my lack of technique making it hard to play and sing the notes in a musical way, and getting the balance between voice and piano right. There is such a wide gap between playing the notes in the right order at the correct moment, and putting the feeling and music into it. "Don't worry! I will help look after that", she told me. Suddenly I observed that I had started to play a passage I normally execute quite loudly very softly. I looked up at the music score, and saw that it was marked "pianissimo" (means play very quietly). What more evidence could I require to convince me that this was really happening?

Two days before my departure, Maria sang "*Ave Maria*" through me when I played the piano. Although some of it was my voice, I could feel her very strongly. By this time, I had modified my ambitions regarding how much I could manage to achieve in the remaining time before my departure to France. Marguerite had told me in an email that I was ready, and I did not need to prepare myself any more. She knew I was getting very stressed by it, and as the following chapter will illustrate, she turned out to be right. I was feeling very tired, but I did the best I could.

By the day before my departure, I felt desperate for a mental break. Even trying to sort the garden out before I left was becoming too much for me. So I took a complete break from all my preparations, and gave myself the present of a three-hour ramble in some nearby hills.

I pondered over the fact that my work with Maria with the main inhibiter of my progress with Book Four. I was resenting this, a state of affairs that would persist until much later, when I eventually managed to see that putting her book first was not just something for her, but in my own best interests as well.

My gift to me of the walk was perfect. I felt very good about having done it instead of other unfinished tasks. I was at peace. I thought of Patrick's words, "When you feel you need inspiration, that is the time to go in the mountains" I went because I needed a break.

That night, being unable to fall asleep easily, I lay awake in bed thinking about things. It worried me that an entity outside myself, Maria in this case, seemed to be ruling and organising my life for me according to her wishes, not mine. Surely I should be ruling my life? I felt I needed to keep my own interests in sight, not just hers. I could see that everything that had happened so far was very valuable experience for me, but maybe I needed more balance in my life. At the same time, I wanted to find ways of helping Maria, and felt sure that to totally abandon her would be wrong and unthinkable. Somehow we must work together.

Chapter 15

My Second Stay In Elsenheim Begins

As the time drew closer to my departure, although I did not know what would happen in France with Maria, I could sense her excitement as well as my own, and felt a joyous anticipation about it. I was glad that there would be several days in France before the two-day seminar, as this would give me time to get used to speaking French again, recover from the exertion of all the preparation I had put in, and most important of all, there would be the things that Marguerite, Richard, and I would do together, and sometimes with Maria? Could it even be often with Maria? Surely that would have to be part of it, and probably the reason for her excitement about it all. It was certainly my overriding reason for wanting to go there.

There was so much more for me to find out concerning this friendship with Maria Callas. I still did not really know what it was for. I had so many doubts about the wisdom of it all. Was she trying to finish an incomplete life of her own through me? Was that at the expense of my true mission here? Should I be telling her very firmly that I had other things to do, and would she please either be on her way into the Light, or help a potential opera singer, something I still insisted I was not?

Even if the ability was latent in me, my life this time was not to do as Maria had done in hers. A "normal" career singing opera was not for me. Even if I could do it, the dedication required would exclude all else, and I was certain that it would be a huge mistake. Anyway, it would never work for me, and would just be a short cut to sorrow and frustration.

Maria had told me many times about her spiritual motivation, but I had so little trust. Was she saying this, because she knew that it was the only reason I would be willing to work with her? Or could it actually be the truth? Also, I had heard stories of other channels being slightly abused by the so-called "high entities" they channelled. There were documented cases of such beings wanting to enjoy themselves consuming foods or drink, which the medium they came through was allergic to, and thus damaging the person's health. With so many doubts, suspicions and fears, it was amazing Maria was still with me.

When my mind was not full of all this, I enjoyed her presence enormously. It had been a wonderful excuse to play the piano, and bring music into my life again. Then there was the sound of her voice. When she did come through, I was in heaven! She knew that. I had to find out more. I felt I could not do it alone, but Marguerite, strongly supported by Richard, would help me. France was quite simply "obligatory".

On 26/5/03, I arrived in Elsenheim, Alsace, hoping to find answers for at least some of my questions. The following morning, it fell to me to lead a meditation. As I had not been in the country long enough to have many French words on the tip of my tongue at that point, I decided to use toning more than anything else, as that way few words would be necessary.

Maria was present and sang through me. I felt the vibrations in the room change as her voice rang out, and followed the toning with a period of silence to allow us time to feel the changes, and to let the energies settle. During this silent meditation, I saw Maria. She looked very restless. I watched her walking this way and that way through our little circle of three, (four people counting her) and stopping to examine the red candle, which Marguerite had placed in the center. I thought she wanted it extinguished, but could not understand why. Red was her favourite colour during her previous incarnation, (she was even wearing a red skirt now) and candles are spiritual things.

You can imagine how my suspicions about her motivation for being with me were growing, not decreasing at that point. Disturbed by her constant movement, and my lack of comprehension about her reason for wanting to put the candle out, I asked her to sit still, explaining that I wanted to respect the wishes of the other people present. She sat down quietly on the floor opposite me. I was relieved.

Several days later, when I was having trouble singing close to some incense that was irritating my throat quite badly, Maria managed to get me to understand that she had been concerned that the candle so close to me would make the air too dry for my throat, and therefore it would be harder to sing.

A Private Session

At 3.0pm on my first afternoon there, Gabrielle arrived for a private session with me. I had no idea how I was going to help her beforehand, having decided that the best thing would be to follow my inner guidance after I had found out why she had come. Having listened to her first, I used several different tools during the session. For example, some of the time, it was clairvoyance. The part that intrigued me the most, however, was when I had her lying down on the bed, and felt guided to use sound. I did not know what guides were with me, and was ready to try just with my own intuition, thinking, "Well, I cannot do her any harm, and maybe toning her chakras would help."

I began with deep notes close to her feet, and noticed how the pitch changed as I worked my way slowly upward towards her head, and higher chakras. It was very apparent that I was indeed channeling, for I did not choose the notes myself, and the voice coming through was beautiful. "We must not frighten the lady", I said silently to the source of the sound. "I could never have done this without Maria's training first," I told myself, "although I have no indication that it is she who sings. To whomever it is stepping in to help me, I am deeply grateful".

I carried on, now aware that the sounds were aimed at the chakras situated above Gabrielle's head. The pitch began to descend, as I moved towards her feet again, and yet not as I had expected back through the same series of notes, which had been sung on the way up, but at a higher pitch. I understood later that these notes were aimed at the more subtle levels of the auric field, thus the higher register, though nonetheless continuing to descend until they were aimed at the chakras below the feet.

One thing that really helped me to avoid controlling the sound myself was the simple fact that I saw visions at the same time as singing, which kept my mind occupied elsewhere, and stopped it from interfering. There were angels around us, but the point that really stuck in my mind, was seeing a little black dog bouncing around the table as we worked. It occurred to me that perhaps Gabrielle had, or had had a dog of that description, but lacking confidence in my clairvoyance, I conveniently forgot to mention it. A good thing as it turned out later. I had to wait to find out who the dog was, and why it was there. When I reach that stage in my adventures, I will tell you. For the time being, I had to wait. Meanwhile, I thought no more about it.This private session gave me much more confidence, and made at least some of the singing I had been working so very hard at before I left home make sense.

Channelling Maria, the Fourth Interview

That evening, Marguerite suggested that perhaps the three of us could do something together. The plan was to contact Maria, and to let her come through. First I danced to the music of Enya, and felt her in my body enjoying being in touch with the physical movement. Then I chose to sing "Ave Maria", thinking that she would like to install herself more by singing that through me. As it turned out, not only were the first few notes rather wobbly and nervous sounding, but also I ended up doing the whole of it mostly, but not entirely, on my own. It lacked life, and sounded altogether uninspired without her voice and passion to illumine it.

Undaunted, I sat down in a circle with Richard and Marguerite to see what we could for Maria. I had wondered if she needed help, and wanted to find out. We recorded it. Whilst taking great care to preserve the meaning as well as I could, I have done a little light editing to the following transcript, just to make it slightly easier to read. As much as possible is exactly how it was spoken. As usual, I have put M.V. for Marguerite Vidal, R. for Richard and M. for Maria.

M. "*It is very kind of you to invite me.*"

M.V. "Is there something we can do together to help you? Or have you something to tell the three of us?"

M. "*I have wanted to speak, when I am here with you, for a long time. I am still very much in love with music, sound, and all the possibilities that go with this. At the moment the colour amber is very important for me, like the amber colour in the room where Helena sleeps.*

Sometimes it is really hard for me to come. Sometimes it is easier just to stay in other realms, and not to make the effort. I did not really wish to sing Ave Maria tonight, but I did assist a little. The movement was good. I enjoyed the movement. I was able to be there, and feel the movement of the physical body, that Helena and I shared together before the song. I am thankful for that, but it was right to stop." (I had stopped the music tape before the end of the track, because I felt I should.)

M.V. "Can you tell us about what you are experiencing in the realms where you are, when you are not here?"

M. "*It is sounds, vibrations like silver. It is hard to put my finger on exactly what it is there. There is something in these sounds, which always fascinates me. I still feel there is something I wish to give to Planet Earth. Even to me it is not yet clear exactly how, but I know it cannot be as it was before, when I was incarnated here. That I have understood, and also (that) my motivation must now be different. For this reason, when I helped Helena with the session earlier* (the one with Gabriella), *I kept my identity a little bit of a secret at the time, for I did not do it to push my own name. She did not mention me, and that was good also, but I was there. I was delighted to be able to watch, for I could see the energies change with the sound. That is one possibility for me, though it comes but rarely.*

I have tried also to understand the problems in Helena's life, and her difficulties trying to comprehend why I am really with her, what it is we have to do, if it is for her, if it is for me. I would say it is for both of us."

M.V. "Isn't it also for more people than both of you?"

M. "*In a sense, yes. Yes. It was a big difference for me, when I brought the sound through Helena, much more powerfully than I have just done, during the afternoon, while I was working without my name, and I was not looking for applause.*"

M.V. "Can you tell us about the changes you noticed, when singing the sounds, in the chakras and the vibrations?"

M. "*Yes. I watched the life come into them. They began to resonate and vibrate faster. The auras of both Helena and the lady expanded. The colours became vibrant, and especially with the lady who was lying down, the chakra system began to come into balance. It was good that Helena allowed me to control the pitch, because I was able to see the effect, and it was far easier for me than for her to know where the sound should go. The aura became freer,* (I speak of the lady now) *more vibrant, more expansive, and certain energies, of which she had no need, left. Therefore it was cleaner and more useful to her afterwards. Little things in the physical body began to heal, little things even the lady didn't know about, although she certainly felt something.*

My reward was seeing these changes, although I did not do it for that. I did it because I was searching for another way to work. I do thank all three of you in the room, for having given me this opportunity. I have worked very hard in the other realms amassing knowledge. Although it is not hard work in the sense that work is considered work on the Earth. One absorbs it energetically. The whole process contains much more pleasure, but this little outlet, and it was the right time, was a possibility for me to give this gift to others. To make it useful, I needed it myself first. Then I could give it away, and yet I still have it. That was good."

M.V. "You know Helena had some physical trouble in the last days. (During the last few days I spent at home before coming to France. Virus etc.) Can you help her with the sound, or anything?"

M. "*Yes, and actually she did use sound a little for her own healing, just a very little, she did, the sounds that she made herself, and it did help,*

154

although that had no comparison with what happened this afternoon. Yes, it is a possibility for self-healing. The sound can be used to remove blocks on all levels, when it is harmonious."

M.V. "Can you do something for her now?"

M. "*For her?*"

M.V. "For her body."

M. "*If she would stand, I will bring some sounds through.*"

M.V. "Do you want to stand up?"

M. "*Yes*"

(M.V. assisted Maria to stand up.)

M. "*Thank you.*"

After a brief pause, Maria began to produce sounds. (Sing). They started low, sliding from one place to another. After considerable variation in pitch, from top A to as low as D flat below middle C, and with the last part reminiscent of the end of "Casta Diva", the whole thing took about seven minutes. Then Maria sat down with Marguerite's assistance.

"*I would like to speak a little about that.*"

M.V. "Yes. We listen to you."

M. "*You will have heard how I use the slides, a little piece up, down, up and down. This assists with the connections between the chakras. First I did some to clear and clean especially the lower chakras. Then I did some to connect each one to the next, sometimes moving just one chakra up, other times going more directly from one to another, and then back up again, so that the whole of the chakra canal was clear. And then with Helena helping me with her body, for she knew what to do, and I told her when to do it, I was able to bring out the higher notes. Next, and I will tell you it was for pleasure, and for the pleasure of those present, I sang a few notes more familiar to her, as after the preparation, it became so much easier to bring out clear sound. Also the body was relaxed. The last slide down was just to bring the energies down a little into the body. Also during this work, at the request of Helena, I produced sounds, not only for her, but for all three of you."*

M.V. "Thank you"

M. *"It was my pleasure to do that."*

M.V. "We would like to know, if there is anything that we can do for you, to help you. If you need some healing, we could help you with it."

M. *"The greatest healer is your love. I am aware that it is not the love of others that I should search for. It is better to focus my energies on what I can give, but even just to find myself in a loving energy field on the Earth, where this quality is not always present, is a healing for my past. There was so much then that I did not understand about life and all that is, even though deep in my heart, I knew something was missing. It was of course love, and I searched for ways of finding it. I had to sing for it. That is why I felt sad when singing Ave Maria tonight. But, the other things we did, the movement, and singing for the chakras; those things, they did not make me sad.*

I sang Ave Maria with Helena of my own will before she came (to France), *because I felt that the reassurance of my presence in her body, which is where I put myself, would help with her confidence. I know it fails her sometimes, this question of confidence, and I wanted to assist her with that, and I believe that I did. I know that I did. Yes."*

M.V. "Is it part of your work with her, these sounds for healing chakras with other persons?"

M. *"Yes, and not only with other persons. It can be used to heal nature outside. I would love to see in her seminar the group gathered around a large tree. All can tone according to their own guidance for that experience. I would like Helena to arrange this for us, for nature, for the planet. Then, at her invitation, with her permission, for I understand that my respect for her is very important, her and her physical body, and all that she is, I would like to be invited to produce these sounds through her. But I would say, and I mean this really powerfully, that the work Helena has done at home, with me, with the piano, which both of us enjoy, with her voice, her study, her interest, her efforts to bring her health up to a good level, the following she has made of her guidance to receive help with her throat, and everything that is involved producing sound, all that is meant to be. All this has been so valuable, also for our, my friendship with her, our partnership together, that of she and I. Yes, because we have used this time to learn to listen to each other. For yes, I do listen to her and her needs as well. Sometimes it is very difficult, and I certainly had my anxieties before I came out here.*

I think it is partly being in the aura of Helena that gives me the anxieties. Now I do not blame her, for I understand what it is to be on the Earth, and I hold myself responsible for being where I am. I do not blame her, and I wish to comfort her, least she think she is in any way blamed, but, just as she receives qualities from me, I receive qualities from her, and I have my own not so desirable qualities sometimes, and I knew that I was a little anxious about this. Would the opening be there? Would I have the chance to speak and explain as I am doing now.

I knew that both of you, in particular, Marguerite, would be open to assist me, but it is still a great relief to me that it all comes together, for I really did wish to do as I am doing now, to express myself on this planet to beings in bodies. I see it happening again in the future, for I love both of you very much. I would say to you and Richard, so I wish to try and speak using Helena's knowledge of the French language. (At this point, she began speaking French, not fluently, as she may have done in her lifetime, but more as I would speak it. The following translation of both Maria's and Marguerites questions, which were also in French, is therefore my own.)

I apologise if sometimes I have difficulty finding the French words in Helena's head before I can use them to speak to you, but I wish to tell both of you that you are perfect for people like Helena and me. As you have already noticed Marguerite, we both have the same problem,

Helena and I, the problem of a real connection, friendly and pleasant with love with people. In my case, I have my little dog, a bitch. She was with me this afternoon in the room upstairs. Helena observed her, but she thought it was a dog belonging to the lady who was lying on the bed. Luckily, Helena said nothing, because she (the dog) was with me. Yes. She was with me when I was incarnate on Earth as well. I have a dog, and Helena? She has a horse.

During my lifetime, I loved my dog. With Helena, there is love between her and the horses, but I want to say that it is not possible to really love the animals fully, if one has not learnt how to give the same sort of love, real love to all of creation. That means loving everything on the Earth, all of the other realities, the other dimensions, for the extraterrestrials, the angels, the fairies, all the other kingdoms, and for all that exists.

It is the same thing as having a love for God, for the force which is behind all things that are, for everything. This explains the need to be able to love people. Yes, it is that. Many people believe that if one loves the animals, it is enough, but it is not. It is much better than not loving anything at all. One must say that. However, without love for all things, there is always a part that remains blocked.

It is necessary to have love for people one loves, and also the people one does not like very much, because without love, one cannot help them. If one has not love for someone, and compassion, there is always a little void in one's own heart, where love is not present. One must fill it with love, which exists everywhere. This is the point I want to make. It is the reason why I am working with Helena at the moment. For you see, we can work very well together, and we have the same needs, the same lessons to learn on the Earth.

In addition, I wish to reply to a question, which was in Helena's head before she left England. She was interested in knowing, if I had wanted to live on the Earth for longer to do things, for I was only fifty-three years old when I died. When I left, there were some things that I had not really accomplished as a human being. This is true, but, for the most important lessons, it was necessary for me to change my environment. I was on the Earth amongst people, who one could say were kind, and all that. I was not living without friends, but I needed more than that in order to achieve the progress necessary for my soul.

Yes, I am really happy to have found Helena now. With her, we can work together on the same problems. We make a very good team. It is worthwhile for her to continue to sing in her home, and play the violin, and listen to music. I would be very happy if she could think of that as a pleasure, not as work she must do. All the same, when she does these things, it helps us greatly to improve our connection. I am happy to give her the little bits of advice about the music, etcetera. That is my pleasure, and something I can give to her. I want to help this way from time to time. I would like to say, I have understood the problems with the time for Helena, and I would like to say, that it will not spoil our friendship, if she cannot find time for these things, because she needs to do other things as well. I understand that, but it is very good that she did everything that she has done to prepare herself before she came here. I respect that very much, yes."

M.V. "For you and your confidence as well?"

M. *"Yes, and I have some qualities I can give, as you have already noticed. Also the combination of Helena's qualities and mine is very very good, and it produces an excellent balance, yes. You have some questions?"*

M.V. "Yes, about the suggestion made about having a healing around a tree. Simply, I would like to say, that with our vibrations, we try to heal the memories which are in the Earth, where in past times there was conflict, because here we are in Alsace, and we have had many wars, and I think that we could not only do a healing for a tree, but also for the memories deep in the Earth at the same time with our sounds?"

M. *"Yes, it is not necessary to visit a place in order to heal it. It is not necessary to be in the forest for that. One can do it here in this room. It is possible like that, as you wish."*

M.V. "Yes, as it will happen."

M. "*Yes, it is good. It is important to know why one is singing. This way, one can send the vibrations to heal the Earth, or a place that is beneath the surface, and so on with ones thoughts. The desire alone is all that is needed when singing.*"

M.V. "We have been doing that, but without sounds, and now we are going to do it with sounds."

M. "*Yes, yes!! (said with obvious joy and enthusiasm) Of course! Yes, of course. Yes, and if you wish, to finish this session, and I have noticed we are four, you, Richard, and I, and the spirit of Helena, and to complete we could do something for a place, wherever you would like to send healing.*"

M.V. "Perhaps to Algeria, where there has been an earthquake?"

M. "*Yes, yes, that would do well. Are there any other questions, or shall we do the sounds together?*"

M.V. "No, that is enough for today."

M. "*One could…*" (Here, she made a gesture with her hands and arms to complete this sentence.)

M.V. "We stand up now?"

M. "*Yes, and at the end, there will not be a problem for me to leave Helena's body. But before starting, and before we finish speaking, I would like to thank you both very much for this invitation, (to come here) which you have given me. I am so happy. I am touched deeply in my heart, and I will think of you during the night. I would like to visit all three of you during the night, while you are sleeping. We can work together in another dimension without you being conscious of it, if you wish. Would you like that?*"

M.V. "Yes."

M. "*And Richard?*"

R. "Yes".

M. *"Thank you"*.

M.V. " and Richard, thank you".

M. " *For Algeria*."

At this point the singing started. There are only about two minutes of it on the tape, but that may have been almost all of it. The part that is on the tape finishes with a dramatic slide down, although the tape stops before the slide has reached its destination.

During this session, Marguerite had assisted Maria physically with her standing up and sitting down.

It was decided later after discussing it with Marguerite, not to channel Maria in the French language again during my stay, as it seems to take away much of the fluency of the transmission, and was making it extra hard for me to keep out of Maria's way. For example, when I channeled "bitch" for her, I worried greatly over the possibility that I should have perhaps said "dog" instead. I never did manage to find out the sex of Maria's poodles.

It is my hope that maybe one day, I will be able to go into a deep enough trance, that other entities could be successfully channeled in languages I know nothing of. It would take a higher level of trust than I have at the moment.

Another difficulty with channeling is that if I already have a strong conviction about something, which is incorrect, it is possible that even a personality as strong as Maria may not be able to override this.

Before going to bed that night, I was able to watch the first half of a DVD which I had bought in Chester, even though I did not possess a DVD player, and neither did I know anyone who had one. "One day I might buy myself one," I told myself, "and then I will have the means of seeing this interesting DVD about Maria Callas." It then occurred to me, as I packed my suitcases for France, that Marguerite and Richard were more into the latest technological developments then I was, so maybe they had one. I put the DVD into my bag just incase. I was lucky!

The first half of this was a concert she had given in Hamburg in 1959. It was obvious she was not happy. The cold was having a tightening effect on her vocal chords, and making the top notes very difficult. To be able to hear and see this made me realize how well she must understand how I feel about it on days when I have a similar problem. It also gave me more insight into why it is not always equally easy.

As I was too tired to want to sit through the second half, and knowing I would be able to look at that another evening, I went to bed.

Chapter 16

Healing Sessions and Maria's Fifth Interview

Our Healing Sessions

After breakfast on the Wednesday morning, Marguerite came to me, and asked me if I would like to do something with her and Richard. When I asked what she had in mind, she said she thought it would be fun to give each other healing sessions. One of us could lie on the table, while the other two did the healing.

I had the pleasure of being healed first. I noted that Maria was taking a keen interest in all of it, although not participating. With my third eye, I viewed an ET ship above the house, and without using my physical body or conscious choice, I automatically started waving my arms at them to show them where we were, and guide them in. It was as though I was standing at the end of a runway. The ship stopped immediately overhead, and quite a few of its passengers descended, and came into the house.

It is my belief, that as they gathered around the healing table, they were helping to guide Richard, in particular with his work. One of them indicated a place in my abdomen on the left side. I wondered what they had seen there, and why they found it of interest. After the session, I found out. Although I had said nothing about this, Richard told me that I had just had a psychic operation, indicating the exact spot, which the ETS had shown me. He said he had lifted out some grey matter from there, demonstrating with his hands as he spoke. For quite a long period of time following this healing, I had less trouble with my digestion, and the frequency of abdominal pain that had been slowly increasing, greatly diminished, so that I felt much more comfortable.

The next one on the table was Marguerite. I had never worked with Richard before, so I followed my inspiration, and found myself guided to channel sound. This time I knew it was Maria. She was not alone, however, for the ETS were guiding me as well. I had some difficulties with my throat, because of the incense, which adversely affected the quality of the sound, although it did not prevent me from singing.

After lunch, it was Richard's turn to be healed. Both Maria and the ETs were to be my guides. I mentioned the problem with the incense to Marguerite before we started. She told me that if it caused a problem, it could be moved. I surmised she considered I was just a little nervous, and that really the incense would be fine where it was, close to me. So I said no more.

When I tried to channel sound for Richard, it was really hard, because the incense was in my throat, causing me to cough, so I had to stop and try to clear it repeatedly. However, I was too engrossed in what I was doing to think of moving away from the incense, or taking the incense out of the room. Marguerite moved quickly behind me, and must have taken it away for me. I never looked to see if it had gone or not, until later, as I chose to work with my eyes shut. My throat cleared, and I had no further trouble bringing the sound through. I knew that Richard was open to being worked on this way, because he said before the session started, "You can sing for me if you wish, Helena."

The sounds were amazing! This time it was really Maria who was in charge of the sounds. She was clearly delighted to have an opportunity to work this way with Richard. I was channeling her in complete ignorance of what was required, or where. Maria, on the other hand, knew exactly where to go, and produced a great variety of different sound effects. I was overjoyed to find her so happy. At last, it seemed she was doing something she really wanted to do. Evidently, this is what she had been training for since the demise of her physical body. All that she had gone through to gain my trust, and to prepare me physically and mentally, had ripened into delicious fruits for her.

It was this experience that really answered my questions concerning "Why are we doing this?" and so on. Now I was certain that all of my worries about her motivation, and her spiritual well-being, such as, "was she wandering about lost in the astral, or trying to live a life through me, when it would be better for her to go to the Light", were unfounded.

This discovery brought an enormous sense of relief, and a peace to my soul. This led to sleeping better at night, instead of wondering if I had lost my way, and allowed Maria to lead in me a direction, which was not right for my spiritual pathway, even though I felt compelled to follow it blindly. It marked a new beginning. Maria and I were a team, or more accurately, working together as part of a larger team, some of its members discarnate, and others still living their earthly incarnations as I was.

That evening, we watched the second half of the DVD. This was a joy! What a contrast! Maria had chosen her repertoire wisely, with nothing too high for her changing voice, and sang with obvious enjoyment. It was a concert given in 1962 at Covent Garden.

Maria's Fifth Interview with Marguerite.

First of all, for my own pleasure, I decided to sing "*Casta Diva*" to a CD I had brought with me of Maria singing it. I sang merrily to myself as I descended the stairs, explained to Marguerite that this was going to be just for my personal pleasure, and we did not need to record it. I replied, when asked, that it made no difference to me if Marguerite was there and listening or not. She left the room, but was not far away as I started to sing.

Maria sang through me for all of it. The performance was not perfect, because I was responsible for a few things as well, but in another sense it was perfection, because it made me so happy. Near the end, where I had already planned to miss out the highest notes on the grounds they were too difficult, I heard Maria say, "Go on! You know you can get up there." I tried, and with her help I succeeded. The top B flat is the highest note I can manage with any quality, and that only on a good day. I was delighted.

Without the need to sing anything else, I called Marguerite, and we recorded all that followed in English.

M.V. "Hello. Are you willing to talk about something special, such as the yesterday's experiences with the sounds and healing?"

M. *"Yes. I was extremely happy about that, as Helena knows. I am much...I am extremely grateful, thankful, not only to Helena, but to all those who have made this possible, for there are many. Those who have helped Helena with her throat in England, Joan Ocean, who welcomed me the first time I came, the first time I was able to produce sound through Helena, all the people there in that group in Hawaii, who gave me their love, who made it more comfortable for me to come and to help Helena. Then later Marguerite, there was you. You have been especially helpful to me, and your knowledge of the English language is an enormous help in this instance. Your willingness to assist does not go unnoticed.*

We, and I say "we", for we are many here also, give you our thanks, our love, our blessing, and we shine Light upon you Marguerite. For you see, when I speak as Maria. I would have you know that I am not alone in other realms, but, as Helena knows, I have studied, although "studied" is not the best word to use over here, (in the realm where she lives now) though people understand it, with not only one mentor, but several.

I have been given gifts here, which I did not possess as an incarnated human being. It is these gifts, which enable me to work as I did with enormous joy during the healing session. It took time for Helena and I to really reach a point, which truly started during this stay, gently at first, with Gabrielle.

Helena, who did not know who came, for I withheld my name, asked me when she allowed the channelling, to be careful, and not to frighten the lady. I was indeed careful, but also grateful that Helena allowed the sound to come through, allowed me to inspire her, gave me the chance to work in a simple way, that was neither frightening to the lady, who enjoyed it, or alarming or worrying for Helena. It was also right for me that day, because I have not worked with sound in this way through other incarnated beings. I waited a long time for this. I thank Helena for the time she has put in, which has enabled her to understand so many things, and (helped me) to form a friendship with her.

Being in a human body puts me strongly in touch with emotion. I wish to control (the emotions she was feeling, for tears were very close at times) just enough to be able to tell you how touched I am, how happy I am, that at last, after many months of doubt, Helena trusts me. There is still a little way to go, but now we have begun. This will come. I understand the sensitivity level of each person with whom I am privileged to work through Helena. I know exactly what to do.

I was overjoyed, particularly in the afternoon, when I found Helena's confidence level had risen considerably, and she gave me complete trust, which made me so happy, and free to do these things which I knew how to do now, to use the gifts which I have been given over here in the place that is so far, and yet so close and the same place as where you are. It is wonderful! I would say it has whetted my appetite for more. It is the trust between Helena and I that I now appreciate. It took so long. I am thankful."

M.V. "How is it with your emotions now?"

M. "*Sometimes, it is a little hard to be clear, because I am also in touch with the emotions of Helena, but I would say that in this life I am living now, I feel joy, love, compassion, peace. I was also a little anxious about coming here. It was not necessary, but as time passes, in the earthly sense, I find more and more ways of reaching Helena. She only needs to understand, and when I am able to make her understand, to enable her to understand, then her cooperation level helps me greatly. Does that answer your question?*"

M.V. "Yes, I just wanted to know, isn't it also a possibility for you to heal the earthly level of your life, when you come here?"

M. "*Yes. Yes.*"

M.V. "So that the part of you which was hurt receives some healing, so that when you one day will come back with another body, this life (as Maria Callas) does not disturb you any more?"

M. "*Who says I am coming back?*" (Very suddenly Maria had sat bolt upright in the chair, and reacted with tones of mock indignation. Marguerite laughed a little, adding,
"*One day, I said.*"

M. "*I will let that pass.*" (Immediate forgiveness. Maria was not angry, it was just a reaction she had had, and had made a joke out of it.)

M.V. "Yes, but this may be an chance to heal the wounds you had here and took with you, maybe I..." Maria interrupts,

"*It is true. My heart was in a very damaged state. There was so much that I needed to learn, and as I tried to convey to you, when I came before this week, I have realised that it is easier for me to make a breakthrough here, than it would have been, if I had stayed in that body for longer. If it were necessary to come again in human form, if I strongly desired it, then of course I would do it; but at the moment, when I think what I would lose, for example all the work that I have done with Helena, and that she has done with me, and that you have done with me, you are not forgotten Marguerite.*

Never forget! (The voice starts to sound emotional again here for while.) *In fact when I think of you, and what you have done for me, and Helena, for both of us, I am truly deeply touched, very deeply. Never ever think that you are taken for granted Marguerite, for you are not. It is your guides who have helped to bring us together, not only yours, not only the angels around you, and the blessed energy of "Marie", (Mary) as you call her, but also mine, and Helena's. For at that level we all know that we are one, and we all work for the same purpose.*

So yes, at the moment, although it would be possible in a certain sense to have many other lives in different places, different planets, other realities all at the same time, and it is even possible that parts of my soul are doing that, in fact I feel that they are, but the bit of me who identifies still

168

with Maria, although I know that I was not Maria, because that was the identity of that lifetime, and my soul is something much bigger than that, that part of me would lose this possibility to serve in a way that would not be possible in physical form. Supposing that I were in physical form, and I wanted to do this work, the only way I see it could happen would be for somebody with the knowledge I now have, to be there, and to be channelled through me.

But I have the knowledge, when I am here, and I wish to use it through Helena. You see, it is a divine knowledge. To some extent I can give it to Helena, but when in human form, the easiest way for her to do this work that I wish to do, is to close her intellect down, not completely, but mostly, and thus allow me to do it through her. Now I would have you know this is not something to boost my ego. I have long realised that that is a complete waste of energy.

Think what this brings! Of course I have thoughts for myself, for it brings me a great deal. As you have pointed out, it is part of healing my earth life. Think of what it brings Helena! Have you not seen how happy she was after she understood what her life was to be about?"

M.V. "Yes, but you bring more than Helena too. You bring me, you bring Richard, and you bring the hearts of all people, because we are one. I thank you for it. I am also very moved." (I did not know what Marguerite meant by this, so after my return home, I emailed her for an explanation. After I read her reply, I understood that she wanted to point out that the work Maria and I are doing together had a far greater reaching effect than the gifts, which I am receiving from it personally, such as happiness, and healing. She was referring to the benefits that others receive, such as Richard, and her, as well as the gifts that will be brought to the hearts of every person who hears the channelled sounds, and also to the world through the transmission of the vibrations. She wrote, "I already knew about that part of your great work (for both of you) in spite of the fact that the workshop had still not taken place. I mean it is a great gift for you, but not only for you, for the world.")

M. *"Then we are both very moved. It is so wonderful that you see this. So wonderful!* (Both Maria and Marguerite sounded close to tears here) *Marguerite you are a ray of sunlight."*

169

M.V. "Thank you. When I saw you on the movie, which Helena brought, (my DVD) and I think I never saw you before, and I was touched by your smile."

M. "*I kept that bit. I still have it, even if I now have to do it with Helena's face! When I am in the other worlds, when I am in form, for I am not always in complete form there you know, because it is not necessary to have complete form, as you have so much on the Earth, then I still smile. And we laugh here, and there is joy here, and there is Light here, and although I use the word when I speak through Helena, for ease of expression, I would like to eliminate two words from all the languages. The first is "difficult", and the second is "work".*"

M.V. "Yes, I agree."

M. "*Nothing is work! Did I not play yesterday when, with great delight, I came through with Helena's permission, when she was assisting with Richard's healing?* (When Marguerite and I were working together.) *I know, and I will say this for her, Helena felt a little bit...she wished that she had been able to give the same experience to you, but we were still preparing at that time.*"

M.V. "No problem."

M. "*Thank you, thank you. We did try. We gave you what we could, Helena and I. Helena allowed me to do...*"   (Marguerite interrupts here.)

M.V. "I know. Everything is perfect"

M. "*Thank you. Thank you.*"

M.V. "I thank you."

M. "*For Helena and I it was perfect, because we had to move to where we were with Richard step by step. You were one of the steps. So my sweet.*"

M.V. "Thank you for everything. Thank you so much."

170

M. "*Yes, it is so, the whole thing is so moving! Yes, and when you organised this wonderful little ceremony you had on top of the hill,* (yesterday evening) *I was there, but I gave Helena a sign,* (she put her finger across her lips, and Marguerite laughed.)"

M.V. "Well. I thought she would sing, or you, or both of you would sing, but nothing came."

M. "*I was there, and I enjoyed it, but I chose to let Helena sing quietly. We wanted, if you like, to give you the chance to do this little thing in a way that was right for you. Also, the air at that moment was a little dry, and I knew we had done a great deal already. So, for me it was perfect. I was also asking Helena not to ask me to come through just then, and to be honest, she was a little relieved, because she was having doubts she could manage it at that moment. It was part of developing our partnership, that of Helena and I.*

When she asks me not to come, I respect it. It can work the other way too, for sometimes I can see when a moment is not right, because I can feel what is happening with the people round her better than she can. Then I can advise her. This way, we will not be in danger of imposing these sounds on those who do not wish to see (hear) them.

Now I am not saying it would have upset you and Richard last night, but as I have explained, it was not quite the right moment, and Helena and I benefited from the possibility of listening to the wishes of each other. It was that. Yes."

M.V. "And we must also learn to live and to act on our own, without always being helped, although we always appreciate help."

M. "*Oh yes! Well! Yes, and Helena thought that she was going to sing alone this morning, but, there was a little doubt in her mind, which she did not express to you. However,*" (Marguerite interrupts here)

"It is human though."

M. "*However, however, I wasted no time!*" (Both laugh).

171

M.V. "Waste is also a word we can take out of our vocabulary. All things are useful. Every experience."

M. "*Yes. When I sang with her this morning...I had been asking her to sing that you know! I was telling her yesterday, and I told her again this morning, and then again, and then again, and then again, until she chose at last not to ignore me, that she should sing this. At last she realised that the desire in her heart was so strong, that it would not bring her any happiness to resist it. Then, with a little technical help from me, it was arranged, and Helena and I enjoyed ourselves together. So, thank you for permitting and assisting with this.*" (Marguerite helped me insert the CD, and start it playing on the right track to sing along to.)

M.V. "I enjoyed it too. I knew this song, but I did not know what it was called, although I knew it, and I think I am going to buy it one day, I think so, yes."

M. "*Yes, yes. It is a favourite of mine, and I know that Helena loves it too. It is also a perfect balance for* "Ave Maria", *because there you have something very Christian, and something very Pagan.* "Ave Maria" *was the perfect beginning for Helena, because it was something not too hard to get her voice around.* "Casta Diva" *is also fairly simple, but it has been a challenge for her, to which she has risen, and is still rising.*

There is something she and I have in common. The wish always to push away the limitations, to look at a bigger mountain, never to think, this is enough, but umm, well, what more could we do to get up? What she and I are starting to do now is wonderful, but this will go further. Ah! She did not know that! But I tell you now, and I tell her also, this will go further. But, like all things, we take it step by step. Sometimes, I can't resist a bit of a leap, just so irresistible! Sometimes, if I take her by surprise, she does things she did not think she could do, because she has not got time to work out that it is too, terrible word coming up, difficult. Yes, yes, and you, Marguerite, sometimes you use the same technique with her. (Marguerite laughs) *That is something you and I have in common.*"

M.V. "Yes, but it is always easier to help someone else than oneself."

172

M. *"Yes, that is the blessing about helping each other in this, er...Ah! Words escape me! For, any word I choose to use has limitation. Shall I say "in creation?"*

M.V. "Yes. When Helena talked about "*Casta Diva*", and how the energies were Celtic energies. It was also like a light that lightens, because, as you said yesterday, the ceremony was about the fusion of the different energies, which are not different, but men, humankind, have divided all. I found it was a sign that she sang, or you sang this, this morning. Thank you."

M. *"Shall we say, Helena and I sang together."*

M.V. "Yes."

M. *"The biggest thing I can do for her is to give her confidence. She grew up so shy, so timid, so afraid to be heard. I have not got that!"* (Marguerite laughs.)

M.V. "Yes, and she is losing that too."

M. *"Yes. That is what we give to each other, I say we give to each other, because each time she lets a little bit of that go, it is a gift to me, because it is...well I do not do this for reward, but in simple terms, I see the fruits of my presence. Ah! This little tiny candle is becoming a huge fire! Of course that makes me happy. When I see her, and her name means "Light" you know, when I see this Light expand, when I see how she moves towards being what she always has been, what she is, how this part of her becomes more present, becomes more anchored, shall we say, in physical form! Of course no words are adequate, but if one must describe things, that is how I would put it. It is not the words themselves, that are important, but understanding the concept behind the words. Of course, you of all people are aware of that."*

M.V. "Yes, words are limited."

M. *"Yes, and it is part of my plan, for now we have in Helena's little repertoire a Christian song in Latin, another one, the druid song, in*

Italian. There is a Spanish one. She will learn to play that eventually. Yes, she has seen the music, and she used that terrible word "difficult", when she glanced at it. It won't be once she has learnt it. Spanish! This is furthering everything that she and I do together, is outside race and creed. Then wherever our work is taken, even if her repertoire is not sounded, she will carry the energies of all these diversities. It is part of that. And she will sing in French, yes, she will sing in French.

But I would tell you, at the moment, it takes her, in earth terms, a long time to really learn these things, to get her fingers round it on the piano, but in our terms, it does not take too long, and it will give her great pleasure. The day she bought the piano, I was, er, how can I say, hugely happy. When I saw the pleasure she had, while touching the keyboard again, that made me happy too.

It was not an easy road for her, and yet, she knew there was a purpose in this, even though she could not have told you what that purpose was. This was the motivation, which caused her to put in almost more work, another bad word, than I thought she would ever manage. But understand, however, and I speak to you Marguerite, because Helena (already) knows, it will be necessary sometimes to balance life carefully, but that is something she and I will work out."

M.V. "Only to make use of the opportunity while you are here, if you want, if you wish, to give healing to the hearts of the people living here on Earth, and yours."

M. *"That of course is what my work is about. It is more healing the whole being that interests me, not one specific area."*

M.V. "Well you can do whatever you wish. What is necessary though?"

M. *"Is that a question?"* (She meant, "Is that a request?")

M.V. "No. I offer you the possibility to do it now for the Earth, and people living on it. What do you feel?"

(Maria accepted the invitation, and rose to her feet with some help. She made sounds for five minutes. Again, there were a great variety of different ones. The tonal range went from top B (3 times), to the G below middle C. When I checked out the pitch later with my pipes, I was amazed to discover that it went above top B flat, as I considered that my limit with her.)

M. "*It is finished.*"

M.V. "Thank you."

M. "*Will you help me find the chair?*" (Marguerite assisted.)

M.V. "It is right here." (Maria sat down.)

M. "*Thank you. I will speak to you again. I am also here now to answer any questions you have about the sound.*"

M.V. "Yes. When you were producing sounds, I was thinking about the sounds produced by the animals, and I thought they are doing the same, and we are not aware of it. We think it is barking, it's this or that, but some animals, not all, produce the exact sounds the world needs. I think this now. I am aware of that."

M. "*This is very true. The cetaceans are a good example, and wolves, also owls. There are many. Few are aware of that.*"

M. V. "I just realised it (for the first time) when you produced the sounds now."

M. "*Yes, for with my sound, I reached out to all the kingdoms of the Earth, not just the planet itself, or the people on it, but all of it, every kingdom. For all is part of creation.*"

M.V. "Thank you for making me more aware."

M. "*You are making Helena more aware as well.*"

M.V. "Now I have no other questions at the moment. Yes, I sometimes use sounds as well, but they are very different from these I have heard, but I think they produce also something. I do not know what, but…"

M. "*I heard your sounds. I knew about them before, for I have seen he who comes through with you for that. Marguerite they are beautiful! They produce wonderful work. Yes they are different, but there are many ways to heal. Your pathway is special for you. Give great thanks for it. It is perfect. It helps and touches those around you.*"

M.V. "Yes, sometimes I am aware of it, and sometimes I have also lack of confidence."

M. "*Ah ha. Well, yes. It may be a while since I had a body, but I cannot forget that. I have tried many times, but it is completely impossible,* (said light-heartedly, and then more seriously) *and you know, it is actually something you can be thankful for, this lack of confidence. How could you understand other people's lack of confidence, if you had never had it? Would that not be difficult? When I come, I still have some characteristics that I had before. I feel it when I start telling you what to do. Well, you may as well know who I was, but do not take it too seriously!*"

M.V. "Thank you for who you are. I have no more questions. "

M. "*Thank you Marguerite for being a part of that, which brings peace to my soul.*"

M.V. "I am honoured to be part of this part. Well."

M. "*And for facilitating this opening for me. For I am truly present, and there is something I would like to do. It is very human. While I am still here in Helena's body, as Maria, although in a sense the name is meaningless now, I would like to gently embrace your physical form.*"

M.V. "I thought of that too."

M. "*Help me to my feet...*" Here the tape finished, but as Marguerite was assisting her to stand, or it may have been when she sat again with more help at the end, I remember her saying,

"*Thank you. It is a little tricky in someone else's body, especially when one has not done it for a long time.*" At the times when Maria asked for help like this, I was aware that my legs were very weak, and that there was little balance in my body, and at one point, neither Maria nor I seemed to have any idea where to find the chair.

It was very clear that Maria had no intention of saying "Goodbye" at the end of this conversation. Still sitting on the chair, I exclaimed suddenly, "She's gone!" She had jumped out in an instant of her own will, and I had found myself immediately fully reinstalled in my body. I was amazed at the speed of this transfer, as usually, it is more gradual. So that was her fourth interview with Marguerite.

One of the things that struck me, as I transcribed this last recording, was the variety of different emotions, which are so audible on the tape. It ranges from a very serious tone of voice, to humour and gaiety; heart felt love at the times when tears flowed down the cheeks of one or both of us, enormous confidence and conviction, compassion, and kindness. There were times when the accent Maria sometimes had when speaking English would come through, and other times, when the words were pronounced as I would pronounce them.

Afterwards, I could still feel Maria's love with great peace and calm. When I mentioned that to Marguerite, she said she had felt that as well.

Chapter 17

Maria's Seminar

The Preparations

Friday 30th May was the day before my first ever seminar as long as two days. Although it was my seminar in theory, in practise, Maria was such a big part of it that I could not resist choosing the title I have chosen for this chapter. It felt like her seminar to me, and I was delighted about that.

I spent the morning peacefully enough, catching up with one or two of my own things, and taking myself for a walk in the sunshine. In the afternoon, the three of us went shopping. Seven people were expected from outside, and then there would be the three of us, so food for ten persons had to be bought.

It was my request to be taken to a flower shop, because I wanted to make the group room look as beautiful as possible, and thought it would be nice to buy Maria some roses, knowing how much she had loved these flowers during her lifetime. When I asked her what colour they should be, she had shown me red, and then pink, and I thought I saw white or pale yellow as well. I took this to be the order of her preferences. So we set out in search of deep red roses. The colour existed, but it was only in the third shop that we thought the quality was good enough. I ended up buying four dark red, three pink, three slightly smaller creamy-white ones with green ferns and some small tiny white flowers that florists often use as fillers in almost any arrangement.

By this time I was feeling so grateful to Maria for doing this wonderful work with me, that I felt it was impossible to spend too much money in her honour. Marguerite and the florist, on the other hand, were both clearly rather surprised to discover how much money I was willing to spend. The latter asked me if it was someone's birthday, or an anniversary. I replied that it was not for that, but the flowers were a "thank you" for a very kind friend who had helped me a lot recently. For this reason, she put a little note on the completed bouquet, which read, "Thank you". It was perfect. We had ten roses, and there would be ten of us in the room.

In the evening, Marguerite helped me find a vase in which to put them, and we placed them in the centre of the group room. I hid the little thank you note in the middle of them, as none of the group would know that I channelled Maria Callas, and I did not feel like revealing so much at the beginning should someone see it, and ask me, "Who are the flowers for?" Some of my books were put on display just outside the door, and we added further decorations to the room to represent both Christian and Pagan energies, plus anything else we could find to make it look pretty. Marguerite added a sweetly scented dark red rose from her garden as her personal contribution for Maria. I had seen the little rose bush in her garden the previous evening, and thought that one of the blooms would be exactly right for Maria, but as it was the only rose bush like that, I did not ask, because I thought they might be too precious to pick.

A Cat Coming?

I had been told at lunchtime that a lady who was bringing her cat wanted a private session with me. I had felt uneasy about the cat coming, as soon as I had heard that there would be one, provided I did not mind. I was told it was a calm cat, that it could stay in the bedroom all day, and therefore would not disturb the group in any way. I said I did not mind, but I am not sure how honest of me this really was, because I feared that the cat's owner would want me to talk to it, and I would not be able to help in this way.

I strongly recommended that the cat stay in the bedroom, because I remembered how when I was still in my teens, and played the violin, every time I started to practise, the cat that often shared the room with me, would leave in a hurry. So I knew that cats had very sensitive ears, and therefore Maria singing full blast might make it miserable.

I simply could not believe that someone would bring a cat, without the expectation that I might somehow be persuaded to talk to it. I could not even converse freely with my own horse, and communication with other animals had not always been successful either. I thought I could work my way round things by saying, "Well the cat might not want to talk, in which case I can not force it." That would be honest. Had there been no cat, I still would not have been happy about giving a private session during the workshop, because I was already wondering if I had enough stamina to manage a two-day one, even without a private session. In fact, most of my worries stemmed from a personal lack of confidence.

Reluctantly, I agreed to give a half-hour session before starting with the rest of the group. My worries turned out to be unfounded, but as the story of the cat and the consequences continued even after my return home, I will write first about the seminar, and the other events that took place in France before I left the country.

The Seminar Begins

As I looked at my calendar on the day I was finally ready to type the stories of the Seminar into my computer, I saw that exactly four weeks had elapsed since the day that the seminar began. I had made no notes while still in France regarding what had happened, but felt that the most salient and important points had remained in my mind, even if my memory of the exact wording of things, and the correct order of events had faded a little. My spiritual guides were around me as I wrote, and I knew that they agreed with these thoughts of mine. Nothing was lost that should be shared in this book. Therefore I wrote about it as inspired.

Having completed the private session with Dany and Nina, her cat, I sat down in our circle of ten people to start the seminar. Although I had so often been faced with more than ten people at a time in the riding lessons I had given for so much of my life, as I looked around the circle counting the people, I thought to myself, "There are an awful lot of them! How am I going to cope with so many for two whole days?" Knowing, however, that a journey of a thousand miles begins with a single step, I began.

We did many things together. One of them was dancing. For ten people there was enough space to dance as freely as one wished. I had brought more music than I needed, but chose to use one with Enya's songs on it. I remembered how Maria had liked her music when I danced to it earlier in the week, and thought that she would approve. With a cassette, especially one I had not played right through for a long time, it would have been difficult to select a particular track as one easily can with a CD, so I just played pieces from it in the order they came from time to time over the weekend.

Sometimes I sang along with it as I moved, and often, I felt that Maria was singing softly with me, especially the song, "How can I keep from singing". At the end of the second morning, I used the aria, "*Je veux vivre*", in this instance sung by Renee Fleming. This was lively, and suitably in French, so I felt everyone enjoyed moving around to that. (For non-French speakers, the title means, "*I want to live*".)

Marguerite contributed her angel cards and fairy cards, and I invited everyone to pick one from each of the two packs, so that we would all have a personal theme for the two days. On the first of the two cards I chose for myself, it said "energy". This seemed very appropriate, as I was concerned about having enough of it to see me through the two days. On the second was written, "dance and song". This was advice I needed to follow. Most of the time I did, but as you will shortly hear, on one occasion, I needed prompting by Marguerite to remind me of this.

I have forgotten what it was I had in mind for the second half of this first morning, but whatever it was, we did not do it. I began according to my own ideas. It seemed to me that as I obviously had a musical guide, and much of this workshop would probably be about sound, I must explain to the group something about it. I had brought printed out information concerning how low notes help the root chakra and the throat chakra, and these ultimately assist all the other chakras to work better.

I read this information to the group (in French), and then left it out on the table for them to look at, as some of them were having trouble with my accent. Now I was trying to tell the story of how Maria came into my life, without actually mentioning her name, which I thought might be too much for some of them to believe at this stage. Of course, it was rather a long story, so as I was getting rather lost in it, after a while, Marguerite interrupted to say that she was being told I have spoken enough, and please would I sing for them.

I thought of singing one of my carefully learnt pieces, or singing along with something, and went over to the CD player in an attempt to select an aria. Marguerite spoke again. "Just sing!", which I understood to mean without the use of a CD. I responded with something like, "What? Now?" "Yes" she replied. So I wandered into the centre of the group who were seated, and realised that this was the time for me to channel Maria.

I stood still while she found her way into my body. I knew she was there, and felt quite confident I would shortly begin. Marguerite, thinking I was stuck, I suppose, decided to try and help me by toning. By now, Maria was installed, and she signalled with her hand to Marguerite to be quiet. There was silence in the room.

Maria started to sing her healing sounds. I was present enough to help with any necessary physical movement, able to partially open my eyes to avoid bumping into anything, or anyone throughout. Turning her body around, I felt her wish to direct the sounds to each member of the group in turn.

We moved over to the first person, where Maria spent a minute or two toning the energy centres of her body, and as far as I can remember, uttered a word or two in English to her before moving on.

One by one, they received her help as she moved slowly around the circle. Marguerite very helpfully made this easier, by going behind someone, and asking her to stand up for her turn. After this, Maria took each person by the hands, led him or her forward a step or two, so that she could easily move around him or her, and then when she moved on to the next one, whoever it was would sit down again.

The atmosphere in the room reminded me strongly of the feeling I remembered when participating in energy work led by other seminar leaders. It had a sort of mystical feel about it.

By the time Maria and I were half way round the group, I seemed to have been channelling her voice for a very long time, and I was feeling pretty tired. Through my half open eyes, I observed about four or five more people still to be toned. I wondered how I would manage it. Would my vocal chords stand up to it? "Oh well," I thought to myself, "Maria was used to pushing herself beyond that which is easy in her previous life, and I can do that as well when it is necessary", so I asked her to keep going. I could have stopped it, with the intention of doing the rest later, but I knew how it might feel to be a member of a group still waiting for a turn that might never come, if we took a break.

Although the sounds coming out of my mouth were not mine, I was conscious enough to have some control over how much time each individual received, providing Maria was willing. Therefore, I took great care to see that Maria would not move on to the next person too quickly, in order to save our energy. I thought as I came to the end, that everyone had received about the same. Discussing it over lunch, at least two people had noticed that the last ones had received more of our time than the first ones, which was definitely the result of trying not to give them less than the rest.

Following this, I gave the group quiet time with gentle music just to absorb what had happened to them, before we went to lunch.

I was very tired. It was the only occasion I found myself with little voice for speaking after singing. My vocal chords had been working without a break for more than an hour, something they never normally have to do. Feeling exhausted, I thankfully took advantage of Marguerite's kindness in allowing me to make tea for myself whenever I wished, as I stood in the corner of her very busy small kitchen, trying not to get in the way. I needed to be away from the group for a little while to recover my energies. Still weak, I made my way to join everyone else at lunch.

Luckily, the majority were content talking to each other for most of the time, so I did not make the effort to talk very much. However, when someone asked me, "How long have you been channelling La Callas?" I was more than a little surprised. I had not meant to reveal that so soon. "Oh! You knew! How did you find out?" I wondered if Marguerite had said something. The lady responded that she did not know. The words just slipped out of her mouth. It also came out later in the day, that when Marguerite had asked me to stop talking, and sing, Maria was behind this. I was probably too occupied with my thoughts, and what I should say to the group next, for her to reach me, so she spoke to Marguerite, asking her to tell me to stop talking. "She has already said enough! Tell her to sing!" Marguerite's awareness of Maria's presence had been good from the beginning, even back in 2001.

The Afternoon Session

While I was in the kitchen at lunchtime, Marguerite asked me if I would like to take the group to the same hill we had walked up two days previously, where we had done the little healing ceremony bringing the energies of the world's different religions into harmony. I was delighted with this idea. Thus, I was able to give the group a chance to wander off separately in silence, with instructions to take time for a little meditation somewhere. It could be with a tree, a rock, the devic kingdom, or what ever they chose. So I gave them many ideas to choose from, advising them to take pen and notepad to write down the results.

No sooner had I set foot on the mountain terrain, than my full energy returned, as I had predicted it would. I walked swiftly up the hill well ahead of the group, and soon had my own space. The physical movement brought joy to my soul. I had been yearning for this. (Those in the group who did not like walking, had been told they could find themselves a tree or something near the bottom of it, so that no one would have to go further than he or she wanted.) I set out down the far side of the hill, until I was quite near the bottom of it, before looking at my watch, and thinking it was time to head back up again before descending down to the car park.

As I was returning to the summit, it occurred to me that I still had not meditated. I was trying to follow my inner guidance, and had not seen any tree or rock that I felt a particular attraction to. Then, quite close to the top, I spotted a rock that was beautifully shaped like a chair, so I sat down on it, and took out my notebook and pen. I asked for something to share with the group, without naming any specific kingdom to communicate with me. This is what happened.

Maria appeared holding a posy of sweet-scented pink, white, and light blue flowers. She spoke.

184

"They come from somewhere else, but I wish to give them to you. You can receive their essence in your soul, just as I accept the gift of flowers, which you bought for me yesterday. I return this love you gave to me, and more besides. We are opening doors for each other, in perfect accord with our divine destiny, as is best for all creation. We love and trust each other more and more as Earthly time passes by. We knew each other well before our incarnations, and all was planned with care. We will go far together, but not alone, for many join together in consciousness now, thus playing a part in uniting all that is, and healing the wounds of separation with love and joy."

At this point, she gave me a fragrant cream-coloured rose, and planted jewels of various colours made from light and energy in my chakras. Next, she placed a hand gently on the centre of my back to guide me towards the group.

As I walked back, I received more insights from her, mostly about her previous incarnation. It had been necessary for her life to make a big impact on the world, so that she would not be forgotten. This would make her work with me now more meaningful, as people would know whom she had been.

Also she had had an important mission of her own, namely to change opera for all time. For this, the temperament of a sensitive and tempestuous headstrong woman as Maria Callas was necessary, to contain the qualities needed for her work. This, combined with an enormous natural spiritual force, gave her the power to fulfil all that was necessary in that life. Her early death was part of the plan as well.

This allowed her time to prepare herself, with much help from the other dimensions, for the work she would have to do with me when I was mature enough and ready. We are very compatible, she and I, as well as being a good balance for each other. This was partly because we both came from the same root-soul, as Joan Ocean once observed. Our lives, personalities, background and so on, have extremely little in common on the surface of things. It is perhaps partly this that helps create a balance, even though Maria no longer holds on to the temperament she once had.

I realised that all of us were a little weary as we returned for tea and cakes beautifully organised by Marguerite, and it was getting quite late in the day, so rather than organising sharing or toning in the group room, I suggested than those who might be interested could watch the second half of my DVD, so that they could see the beautiful face and hear the lovely voice that Maria, who had given them so much with her sounds in the morning, had had during her lifetime.

Of the three who were not staying in Marguerite's house, only one chose not to stay and watch it. With great honesty, and very nicely, she explained that she had never liked "La Callas", and also she was staying locally with relatives she seldom saw, and wanted to spend the evening relaxing with them. By the time she reappeared for the second day, I had a little message for her from Maria. Namely, that Maria respected her honesty and integrity, and wanted her to know that she loved her. This was accepted by the lady in good spirit.

The rest of us, apart from Richard and Marguerite who had already seen it, and had other things to do, sat down eagerly to watch it. While this was going on, Dany, sitting next to me, said, "Maria has a voice just like yours."

On Sunday morning, I gave a private session to Geneviève, one of the group. This was also interesting for me. I did not sing in this one, but channelled several different entities I did not know, each one coming to help with a question appropriate to their knowledge. Marguerite suggested later, that perhaps I was channelling Geneviève's guides, which I think is quite possible.

Shortly after half past nine, the group gathered for our second day. I decided to start with dancing to Enya's music. It was so obvious to me that Maria was already very present, as she sang along with the music, and enjoyed the movement. Now I had planned a group sharing next, but with Maria ready and waiting, I decided to change the plan. She had a very good reason for wanting to step in earlier. She had seen how fatigued I had been at the end of the toning she and I had done together the previous day at the end of the morning. Therefore she thought it would be easier for me to work with her earlier in the day, while I was still fresh. So I told the group that Maria had already arrived, and proposed that I ask her to sing for the birds, because they had sung so beautifully for us outside the window, and it was also a request from Marguerite.

I stood in the centre of the seated group with my eyes closed, (their chairs were arranged in a circle as usual) as Maria and I began.

Everything seemed to be going well for quite a while, but when instead of something, which I could easily understand related to birds, it changed into much deeper sounds, rather like a gorilla and no longer had vibrations that I felt could possibly relate to any birds that I knew about, I became worried. I was even less confident, when the tone dropped still further, and the vibrations changed again.

I wondered if there could possibly be some rather large birds I knew nothing about on some distant continent I had not yet visited. I thought perhaps I had lost Maria somehow, and started to consider stopping the sound. If, without my noticing it, some other entity was interfering with our healing work, then he, she or it had no place in our seminar.

Maria could clearly feel me on the verge of seizing up, and her voice came through silently to me, "Do not resist! Do not resist!" I continued uneasily until it was finished. I was to find out what had happened after our morning tea break.

Maria did not leave when she stopped singing, for she wanted to speak to the group. They welcomed her. As she began talking, I was getting a vision of one of the red roses in the vase of flowers I had bought for her. She wanted to hold one, but this was not said out loud. I told her silently, "You can't have one of those, because if we take one out, the whole arrangement will fall apart." I had temporarily forgotten they were hers to do whatever she liked with.

Accepting my denial of her wish, she interrupted what ever it was she had been talking about to the group, and as though it was a command, said, "Someone here has brought me a flower. Bring it to me please!" I knew exactly which flower she meant, and so did Marguerite, who kindly

France - May 2003. Sunday morning break. *(Helena left and Marguerite)*

went and fetched the lovely dark red rose she had picked from her garden. Maria took it in her hands. No longer speaking, she dropped her head down, and buried her nose deep into the centre of the rose inhaling its fragrance. This seemed to go on for some time.

Eventually she lifted her head to express what pleasure it gave her to smell it by the means of my physical senses. She said it had been so long since she had had the pleasure of the scent of an "Earth" rose, as she called it. She continued talking, but not for long. "Excuse me," she said, but I need a little time for myself just now." This was followed by a further silence, as she plunged my nose into the centre of her flower again. When she thought she had had enough of it, and when she wanted her hands free, she dropped it down the front of the top I was wearing, because, as she pointed out, this was the closest she could get it to her spiritual heart as she dwelt inside my body. Marguerite was duly thanked. Maria told the group whatever it was she wanted to say, and then made herself available to answer questions from anyone in the group who had one. As far as I can remember, Marguerite helped decide whose turn it was, as I was only semi-present. This continued until there were no more questions, and Maria took her leave. I was feeling great, and still had plenty of energy.

After the tea break, I announced the promised sharing for the group. Each person had the chance to speak. This is when I found out what had happened when Maria was supposedly singing for the birds. While Maria was singing, Marguerite had seen a gorilla walk into the circle, so she asked Maria telepathically if she would sing for it, as it was there. Someone else had seen it as well. Next, Marguerite saw a buffalo arrive, so she asked, "Couldn't you sing for that as well?" This was when the sounds went even deeper. It was for the buffalo! I had not seen either of these animals.

In the Forest with Maria

All of the experiences with Maria were wonderful, but this next one was the most wonderful of all of them for me. It is the one that lingers in my mind more frequently than the rest.

It was Sunday afternoon, and it had been decided to visit a forest, located fairly close to Elsenheim, as we did not want our outing to take too long. (Some of the group were returning to their distant homes that evening.) I wanted to grant Maria her request she had made in the first recorded channelling with Richard and Marguerite, namely,

"I would love to see in her seminar the group gathered around a large tree. All can tone according to their own guidance for that experience. I would like Helena to arrange this for us, for nature, for the planet. Then, at her invitation, with her permission, for I understand that my respect for her is very important, her and her physical body, and all that she is, I would like to be invited to produce these sounds through her."

We parked the cars by the side of the road, and I briefed the group as follows. Today, we would not be going off separately, but meditating together. Requests having been made for contact with nature and the Council of Animals, all this was to be included. I strongly recommended as little conversation as possible walking out there, because they would get a greater value from the meditation if their minds had the chance to become quiet first.

I did not know this forest, apart from one path where I had been before. After I had lead the group down the lane between the trees to the place where this started, I was about to go down it, but Marguerite thought it was too difficult to follow, and dissuaded me. I knew that there were some lovely beech trees down there in a relatively open area, but as many of the group were not accustomed to walking in a forest, I agreed to continue down the lane, and look for another path. Further on, I found one. It did not look any easier, but I felt so strongly that I was supposed to find a tree somewhere to the left of the metalled lane, that I decided to try it.

There were some nettles, and quite a lot of other vegetation on the path, not to mention the possibility of biting insects, along with uneven ground. These were not things that would have bothered me much on my own, but as I was particularly anxious that the group should not be bitten, scratched, stung or lose their footing, I requested help from the unseen angels and beings around us for protection. I put out a direct

Leading the group into the forest to find a tree on Sunday afternoon.

communication to the insect kingdom, that during our meditation especially, they would leave us unbothered, for we were doing healing work that would benefit them also. All this was respected.

Meanwhile, I had no previous knowledge of the area to tell me if this path would lead us to a suitable tree or not. I had no map and no compass. Frequently I turned my head to see if I was walking slowly enough for the group to keep up with me, for my natural pace would have left them far behind. There they were, in single file following my tracks exactly in silence. I went extra slowly in order to give them time to see where the occasional nettles were, and not get stung.

"They are so trusting!" I thought to myself. "They think I know exactly where to find them a nice tree, when actually, I have no idea. I do not even know if there is a suitable tree within easy walking distance." In this state of complete ignorance, I saw only one solution. I must ask my guides to guide me, and at every step, I must be ready to listen to them for instructions about changes of direction, and where my eyes should be focused.

They gave me a picture of a fairly large tree with enough space around it for the group to stand in a circle, situated in dappled shade. It was an oak tree. I left the path, and moving in accordance with my inner guidance, I cautiously picked my way through the undergrowth, until I saw several quite large oak trees. One had a number of dead or dying branches on it, another was wonderfully large, but on one side there was no space to move around it, so it would not do.

Meanwhile, my eyes constantly returned to a tall oak in dappled shade with space around it for us. I walked over to it, touched it, and thought, "Yes, this is exactly the tree which my guides have been showing me."

Without words, I indicated to the group that they were to form a circle round it. I asked Maria what we should do; wondering if this was her solo time, or what? She said to me, "You must let them sing, or they will not develop." Maria led the toning, as without words, I indicated to the group that they were to sing with her.

Meanwhile, I watched with my inner eye to see what would take place. Gradually the council of Animals assembled. I even saw a large black beetle quite close to me. Maria's singing was beautiful. When the cetaceans arrived, the nature of her sound changed, as she tuned into them. They came after the other animals. The incarnated insects left us in peace as I had requested, and when Maria had started singing, a pleasant breeze arrived from nowhere, which kept us comfortable on this very warm day.

Although the breeze may have had something to do with it, Dany, who had kept her eyes open, noticed how, when Maria started to sing, the trees began to quiver. One in particular had moved gracefully to and fro to the sound. After all, this was for them as well, not just the animals and us.

About halfway through this, Maria's voice, beautifully accompanied by the harmonies sung by the group, lifted itself into the melody of "Silent night, holy night, All is calm, all is bright". Even though this was mid-afternoon, the unsung words, silent, holy, calm, and bright along with its beautiful melody seemed so perfect for setting the atmosphere for our healing work. I even heard at least one voice from the group sing with her at one point, for it was not pitched so very high.

When, later on, I heard someone else take a vocal risk, and allow her voice to soar upwards just once, I understood what Maria had meant about giving the group the chance to develop themselves, by letting them sing. They needed the space in which to experiment. Actually, this was not the first time they had sung. On one occasion, during a group toning in the house, Maria had chosen to sing with them, but softly. Her voice had still carried well enough to be clearly audible, but, as she had put it afterwards, "I wanted to give the stage to you", referring to the group. Of course I had recounted this message out loud to them.

The only animal I had seen with us in the forest, that I knew was still incarnate, was Dany's cat, which came and sat down at my feet during the singing. I made a plan to tell Dany later. Finally, this beauty came to an end, and quietly, I led the way back to the waiting cars. Everyone seemed very relaxed, as they strolled back down the lane behind me, with those at the back who wanted to, starting to talk softly amongst themselves when we came closer to the car park.

After refreshments, we had a group meeting on the lawn in the garden, and it was then that I asked Dany, if I could share something with her about her cat, a story I wish to tell in a separate chapter about Nina. In the same way, I am making a separate chapter about Romeo, Monique's cat, her private session with Maria and I, and the events that followed it.

Here is another exert from Marguerite's email in February 2005.

"We didn't plan any conference for this second stay. As far as I was concerned, I knew you came to go a step further in your alliance with Maria. I suppose that a part of you knew it as well. We had a lot of activities involving Maria before the workshop.

This seminar was not announced as having anything to do with Maria, but the moment came when you, the personality Helena, began to tell the participants your story with her. I could feel her loving presence vibrating, but you were busy with your intellect trying to tell this, and I saw how you began to feel awkward and uncomfortable, as if you did not know how to tell the story… the words you said did not seem to lead anywhere and the whole thing appeared uneasy to me. So I dared to do something I rarely do, especially because I know you don't like to be directed, but I felt I had to. I dared to interrupt your human talk and suggested you to channel Maria. I didn't know how you would react, but after a second of surprise, you seemed to be relieved. So we told the participants what was going on next and all was perfect, each one welcoming this unexpected part of the workshop."

I had lost track of where I was in the story, and being much more comfortable with sound than words, especially French words, it was the easy option to just channel Maria instead. I was surprised that Marguerite seemed to think I could just jump straight into it, but that is exactly how it happened. I was relieved.

Chapter 18

A Little Tea Story

"La Foire bio"

On June 2nd, on our way to Basel airport, Marguerite, Richard, and I were able to spend some time at "la foire". This was like a trade fair, set up with tents and trade stands for every imaginable type of organic and environmentally friendly product you can think of. It was a very hot day as we wandered around looking at everything, and sampling some of the wide selection of edible products on display. We had plenty of time, so there was no rush. I particularly enjoyed having no responsibility for anything or anyone other than me. I had had a wonderful time giving the seminar, but not to be carrying that responsibility for a while was very relaxing.

Eventually we reached a table on which were displayed a wonderful selection of organically grown beautiful teas, brought by the owners of my favourite teashop in France. I started trying to focus on what I wanted to buy, but realized I could no longer think clearly, and would shortly pass out from dehydration in the heat if I did not get water quickly. Richard was not far away carrying with him a bottle of water from which I drank thankfully.

The table with the teas on it was placed near the exit of a big marquee, so at least I was getting better air to breath standing there. The water revived me quickly, so I was able to set about the serious business of choosing myself some wonderful tea to take home. Needless to say, it was their most expensive tea that I was really interested in. It was a white tea, "Xue YA Jasmin" in French called, "Aiguilles d'argent au jasmin". It is made from the tender golden leaves growing at the tips of the young tea plants, blended with jasmine flowers.

By this time, France was using Euros. Whereas I knew that speciality teas were always more expensive than ordinary tea, I felt confident that I could buy myself as much as I wanted without spending too much money. I had no head for arithmetic, therefore when the assistant told me the price, I had no idea how much it cost in Sterling. Delighted to have found what I wanted, I asked for a large amount of it to take home with me. Hopefully it would be enough to last me for about a year.

By this time, Marguerite was at my side. She realized I had not managed to comprehend that I was spending a huge amount of money, and did her best to enlighten me several times. I just thought she did not realize that I already knew special teas cost a little more than the rest, and brushed aside her comments.

Shopping completed, we sat down together for a meal. I knew that Marguerite had been truly amazed at how money I was willing to spend on myself for good tea, but when we worked out together how much that was in Sterling, I was in for a big shock! It took me quite a long time to recover from that.

As we drove from La Foie to the airport, the subject of the cost of my tea came up again. Marguerite told me that she had felt sure that Maria did not want me to find out how expensive it was until afterwards, just in case I decided not to allow myself something so very good.

The story continued after I arrived home. I was still struggling with the issue of coming to terms with this expenditure just on tea, and worse still, apart from a small gift of some of it I made to Marguerite, all of this was money spent on myself had been for something that was unessential.

As I considered what Marguerite had told me concerning Maria not wanting me to know how much I was paying for the tea, I pondered over things such as "was I really strong enough to remain me, make my own decisions, and not be manipulated by Maria too much?" This fear of being controlled by another entity, who might steer my life off on a tangent to suit herself, thus taking me away from my spiritual pathway, and turning me into his or her "captive" was still strong in me. It was this feeling of being swept away by a current out of my own control, because

I was too weak to prevent it, which I felt I would eventually have to deal with. It would be another ten months, before I found a solution to this, as I will explain when the story gets that far in a later chapter, ("Miracles in Germany").

So it remained a repetitive source of conflict from time to time, which I wrestled with. I did not think Maria was not present whilst I was thinking about all these things, and on the other side of the coin, I was feeling abandoned by her. She had been so very close during my stay in France. I wondered how long it would be before I had the pleasure of hearing her beautiful voice coming out of me again. I was sad, but not for long.

As I lay in a lovely hot bath before going to bed, (the water was heated by the sun on the solar panels on my roof) I could not help thinking about the price of that white tea again. Eventually I began to feel happy enough to start laughing out loud, because it occurred to me that if those leaves can be used five or six times, that made it the cheapest tea in the shop! Furthermore, it meant that I did not give Marguerite a hundred grams of lovely tea, but five or six times that amount, depending on how many times she re-used the leaves. That was even better.

So, as I lay there chuckling about all this to myself, I heard Maria say, "I knew you would not mind!" The next step for me was to understand and accept that unconsciously I did not want to find out the real cost myself either! Maria had helped me to do exactly what I wanted without my having a guilty conscience. My trust and love for her came flooding back. Then I realised how helping me to receive this present from me for myself, was her gift to me.

Again I remembered how, when I bought her the gift of roses, I felt that nothing was too good for her, and completely ignored the price. She wanted me to be able to do the same for myself. It was so good to know that she was still around.

Chapter 19

Dany, Nina (La Chatte) & Maria

I can never think of Nina without the French words, "la chatte" coming into my mind. When I met Dany and Nina in her little cat cage for the first time the evening before the seminar, I pointed to this cat, and said, "Ah! The cat!" using the French masculine form of the word, "le chat". I was quickly corrected by Dany, who said with great emphasis, "Non, la chatte!" "Oh, a female cat", I thought to myself, and managed to call her "la chatte" from then on. I later learnt that Dany's profession was teaching English, so it was second nature to her to correct at least a little of my faulty French, so that I could improve it. Her English is so good, that later on we spoke mostly English to each other.

The private session for Nina was arranged for the following morning, to take place before the seminar as planned. So when I was ready, I made my way to Dany's bedroom to see what would happen, for I knew not in what manner I would be able to serve.

As soon as I saw Nina, I loved her. I had not expected to, but emotions such as love are spontaneous. She was curled up on the bed, and Dany and I were seated. After my worst fears were confirmed, namely that Dany was hoping I would be able to talk to her, and hear what she had to say, I said rather tentatively, "I think I have to sing to her. Would you mind?" I knew that it might be too much for Nina's ears, so as my eyes were going to be shut, I asked Dany to stop me, if Nina became too distressed by it.

Maria was there. The sound was slightly quieter than usual, thus adapted for Nina's needs, and hopefully, her ears as well.

When all was quiet again, I opened my eyes expecting to see Nina still contentedly curled up on the bed, but there was no sign of her. Dany searched the room, looking behind every bit of furniture in turn. Eventually Nina was discovered curled up peacefully under the duvet. We supposed that at times when she found the sound too strong for her, maybe when the toning was more for Dany than her, she had hidden herself there to protect her ears.

After Dany had found her, I decided to pass on the observations I had made during Maria's singing, and Dany wrote it all down, so that now, weeks later, I still have an accurate record for this book. This is what I told her.

"At the beginning and the end, I heard the sound for both of you. In the middle, it was definitely for Nina, whereas part of the end was more for you than her. When I came to the point where the sound was for Nina, it was quieter and gentler. It was as though I was moving in the direction of feline consciousness and needs. (When I said "I", I was really talking about "Maria", but had not revealed her identity to Dany at this stage, so described it more as though I had done it alone. Dany was told the full truth of what had happened later.)

The angels were present, and also the presence of another entity in my body. (Here was the first part of the truth coming out!) The notes just came. I kept my mind out of it. It began with her paws, then the chakra over her head, moving towards the tail, some notes for her digestive system, and one note in particular was especially for her tail. There followed other sounds. I felt that I was really moving into the feline species. At the end, the sound was stronger again, with seventy percent of it for you. There was something here, which was lifted up high into the Light, which had to be released. (I indicated the womb area of Dany's body, where I had seen a mass of grey debris, which obviously needed cleaning out, for it did not serve her.) Then I noticed that the atmosphere around you looked cleaner.

She (Nina) is part of divine essence, and so are you, as is everything else in creation. She is part of you. When it is time for her to go, it is natural for you not to wish to let this part of you depart, but your willingness to release her from physical life will be the strongest form of love that you could possibly show her. Even when she is gone, you will not really have lost her, for her spirit can remain close to you for as long as you both wish it. When you look at things, know that all is part of you."

So, although I had not been aware of Nina saying anything, I felt that the session had gone well, and hoped that both of them would have received some benefit from Maria's voice. I knew it was possible that Nina might decide to speak to me sometime during the seminar at a time chosen by herself, but did not concern myself with this. My mind was already on giving the first two-day seminar of my life. I was still concerned about how I was going to manage it, even though my trust level had been greatly assisted by the events with Maria, which had already taken place since my arrival in France.

It was in the course in this next story that Nina managed to speak to me. She had made the connection, when she came to join the Council of Animals during our group meditation around the tree on the Sunday afternoon. I knew I must pass on what she had shared to Dany. So, after the group was finished, we sat down together in the garden, and Dany wrote down all that I told her as before. Here it is.

"During the meditation around the tree, more and more animals of all kinds arrived. As you know, animals are better at making out-of-the-body trips than most humans. Nina came. It was definitely she. Sitting down on the ground close to my feet, I felt was her way of saying "Thank you" to me. (If she had not already done so, it may have been a way of thanking Maria as well, as the latter was present and singing through me when this happened.) Nina left after that, and I made the wrong assumption that her communication with me was finished.

She came back to see me again, when I was returning to Elsenheim in the car after the meditation. At first she was just beside me, but then she climbed onto my lap to sit on my knees. With her little front paws, she walked up my chest, and licked my face for a while, sometimes pausing to affectionately rub her head against my neck and the lower part of my face. She said, "Thank you so much for coming. You, with Maria, have managed to teach me things I did not know. I had learnt to trust Dany, but

I feared the others. Now there is an opening in my heart, which tells me that there are other people like you, Helena, out there. It will take time, but little by little I will learn to trust them more. I regret that I am not bolder with you when I am in my physical body, but I know that you are full of love, and that you understand I need time in which to adjust myself. Naturally, I thank Dany from the depths of my heart for bringing me here."

Dany told me later, after my return home, that Nina had not wanted to leave Elsenheim. Speaking of the seminar and Nina, she wrote, "My heart has opened up, as well as Nina's. She is different. Her soul sings and purrs and coos." Being the beginning of this adventure with sound and Maria, I found it very helpful to receive this encouraging feedback. Over time, through the medium of email, I learnt from Dany that Nina continued to improve. At first it was increased confidence, willingness to connect with people, and becoming more affectionate.

Dany told me how she would purr with pleasure when a postcard from me arrived, and enjoyed listening to CDs of Maria singing in her lifetime. Later, at the age of fourteen, when she played, she did so with such energy and enthusiasm, that no one could believe her age. Dany wrote, "The most spectacular change in her since she met Maria and you lies in her almost human communication. She doesn't mew but seems to speak at times: sentences, with sorts of definite syllables, especially when hungry or determined to get me to play. Nina does concentrate when she gives a kiss, and if I do so to her unexpectedly, she gives a sweet gurgling sound that comes from her belly. She is much more affectionate indeed."

Chapter 20

Romeo & Monique

On 29/1/03, I received an email from Alsace, France. It was Marguerite Vidal seeking help on behalf of a friend. This is part of it.

"I just received a call from a friend who is now in Africa in order to teach the population how to plant seeds and collect new seeds from the old ones without having to buy more... showing them how to feed themselves and be independent. Well, she received very bad news from her home in France about her beloved cat "Romeo". (It is Monique Schmidt who wanted to invite you to come and give a conference or seminar last year.) The veterinarian says he has the feline strain of AIDS, and now his hind legs are paralysed, and that there is nothing that can be done. She is very upset because she says he is not a cat like others, he is a master, and she wished she could be with him because all this seems strange to her. He is about 6 years old. She phoned me to help her and send energy to the cat and asked if I could ask you for help too. I told her I would ask you, in spite of the fact that she and I know, as we read in your books, you are reluctant to put your energy into such things. But if you have any message concerning this cat "Romeo", even if you don't try to contact him, thank you for giving it further attention. If nothing happens, it's also OK. I just wanted to let you know, as she asked me to do so. We don't want to bother you."

I felt moved to respond. I strongly recommended using Linda Tellington-Jones's TTEAM TOUCH. The reason I thought of this was having read in Linda's "news letter", that TTOUCH work had achieved miracles before on the paralysed hind legs of a cat or a dog. I did not know if any of these animals had had AIDS, and I explained that results were never guaranteed. I informed her that it was especially effective if the person giving the animal the TTouch was aware that he or she was waking up the divine spark of Light that already existed in the physical cells of the sick animal. This would activate the animal's own ability to heal itself. (This was my opinion.) Next I wrote,

"You are right in thinking that I do not choose to work as an animal healer or communicator. It is partly because I do not feel it is my mission to do so, and also, I am not very good at it, apart from one or two rare exceptions. I suggest that I am sent a photograph of Romeo as soon as possible. Then, in the very unlikely event of him trying to contact me of his own will, I will know it is he. Otherwise, it could be anybody's cat, and I would not know what to do with the message if he gave me one."

I completed my little message with the following words,

"As soon as I read your email, I felt the emotional distress, which could be Monique's. My heart went out to her. It is definitely not Romeo's emotional state that I picked up, for I have no contact with him at present. I am so familiar with this painful feeling, because of the times when one of my own animals has had a problem that I decided to respond tonight, not tomorrow. When it is me who is suffering this way, I am so very grateful if I can find someone to run to who will listen, even if whoever it is it turns out to be is completely unable to help in any way other than just listening, and understanding how I feel. Well, I hope that this little message from me will bring some cheer, even if not very much. Anyway, it comes with my love and compassion."

Quite soon after sending this, I felt strongly inspired to write a second answer.

"I do not know if what I am about to write will help Monique or not, but without having had any direct contact with the cat, I did pick something up.

The world needs masters, especially at this time. Should Romeo leave his physical body, he will not leave Monique. Actually, it would become even easier for him to be with her and inspire her, especially when she is away in Africa, than it is at present, when there is always the pull of his physical body to drag him back from time to time. I have no idea if he will pull through this aids illness or not. That information has not been given to me. I do know that he will never leave her in this lifetime if she needs him. He will always be there, with or without a physical body. May she have courage to face this situation, and recognise it for what it is. Romeo's love will always be there for her."

Marguerite replied with the following information on 2/2/03.

"Thank you so much for your answers. As it is very difficult to contact her directly, I sent love and vibrations to her, and I told her daughter in case she could speak with her mother, because two days ago the daughter waited for a decision from her mother about an euthanasia by the veterinarian or not, because Monique should not return home before March. So the daughter said to me: either the cat dies naturally himself, or my mother has to decide that it's better to help him die. But the daughter did not want to take the decision, for he is not her cat. Thank you so much for giving me this answer, I will phone right now to the daughter. When Monique hears that, if she calls, I'm sure it will help her. I THANK YOU VERY MUCH FOR HER."

Eventually, having thought no more about it, on 22/2/03, a photograph of Romeo arrived in the post, sent to me by Monique's daughter, Magali. Along with the picture was a letter, dated 18/2/03, which told me that Romeo had made some improvement over the last seven or eight days. There was now a little movement in his hind legs, but he was too weak to walk, and that for four or five days now he had had a fever. The cat's moral was good, even though he had spent the last four weeks in an animal hospital.

My first reaction was "Oh no! Not something else to do! I already have too many different projects in my life." I felt really low and dragged down by the prospect of more demands being made on me, even though it had been my own suggestion that a photograph be sent to me. I managed to work through these emotions as the day wore on, and Romeo, having seen his opportunity, chose to make contact. I wrote the following email to Monique's daughter.

204

"Dear Magali Schmidt,

The photograph and your letter arrived today. It is helpful that I can see his eyes. I did not ask for communication with him, as I knew he could reach me if he wanted to.

Very soon after I saw his picture, he said with great emphasis, "I am a cat!" It was obvious to me that he was very proud and pleased to be a cat. He added, "Always remember that!" I feel there is some deep significance behind these words, which perhaps you will understand if it is necessary, but do not forget what he said.

He is not ready to die yet. He wants to have a look around at a few more things while still in his physical body. He would like to be able to move his back legs again. I feel strongly that Linda Tellington-Jones's "TTEAM TOUCH" work would help him to regain more awareness and movement in his back legs. You can do no harm by trying it. Linda's web sites are easy to find if you type in her name to your search machine on your computer. She has made videos to help people who cannot attend her clinics. So you could buy one to show you how to do it.

I understand that at the moment, Romeo's soul is not well enough anchored in his body. It seems to dwell mostly in his front end where he still has movement. I feel that some of this may be connected with his being a master. He likes to spend so much time out of his body, which is great, but he must remember to return fully afterwards. He most probably knows this. Sometimes slipping back into the physical form is a little tricky, especially when he likes to keep at least one paw somewhere else. (I do not mean that in a literal sense.) He tells me that he also needs help and healing around the main part of his body behind his front legs. This will assist in drawing more of his energy towards his back legs. You could help his body awareness with TTEAM TOUCH there as well. Do try it. It would really help him, even if you yourself cannot see the result. Well that is all the help that I can give you at the moment. I see Romeo looking content with this message that I am sending you. He is lying down, licking his front paws, and does not need to say any more."

Whereas I knew that TTOUCH would probably help Romeo, it became evident that Monique was unlikely to manage to do this herself, even though she continued as time went on to ask for more information about it. The information was always freely given, but in some way, Monique had a problem with it, which she chose not to express to me clearly.

Meanwhile, Marguerite sent healing energy to Romeo, who responded well, was no longer paralysed, and seemed to have improved health in every way. I received this news at the end of March, and then the story of Romeo ceased to be part of my life for a while.

Romeo takes a Turn for the Worse

Before I departed to France again at the end of June, I heard from Marguerite that Romeo was unwell again. Secondly, that Monique had chosen to attend my two-day seminar at the weekend. I wondered what would follow.

It was the Saturday evening when Monique chose to ask me for a private session in which she could talk to me about Romeo. I knew intuitively that it would be more than listening to her, but agreed for this to take place on the Sunday evening after the seminar was finished.

She told me how Romeo was unwell, eating very little and unable to move freely. She mentioned the cats' AIDS virus, and that the vet had told her that nothing could be done. She added that he no longer liked to be touched. "Speak to him! What does he want to say?" She presented me with another photograph. I told her that I was not receiving any direct communication from Romeo, but with her permission, I would like to channel Maria's healing sounds, as they would undoubtedly help him on some level, even if he never recovered his physical health. Maybe, they would bring peace to his soul. I did not know. I felt there was nothing to lose, and maybe something to gain.

This was the only occasion during this trip, when I really had trouble bringing Maria's voice through. Although my vocal chords were not tired, I did nothing but cough and try to clear my throat unsuccessfully. I do not give up easily, and neither does Maria. Eventually she said to me "Move your body a bit". I was already standing up, but as there was very little space for movement in between my chair and the roses I had bought for Maria, I walked over to another part of the room where I could move, and tried again.

Shortly after I began moving, Maria's voice came through crystal clear, and I had no further problems with my throat until after the singing had finished. As I listened to the singing, I found some of it to be the saddest sounds I had ever heard. It was not all like that. As Monique observed afterwards, at times, Maria seemed to be talking what Monique referred to as "cat language". It sounded so much like "meow", the sound that cats so often make.

I had thought beforehand, that this might help Romeo, because even though he was not physically present, the vibrations of the music could be sent by the power of thought directly to him. Actually, nothing had to be sent anywhere, because the music seemed to reach him automatically, and he arrived in the room in astral form. As I continued to channel the sound, I perceived him sitting on the floor in front of me slightly to my left.

Romeo explained his dilemma by the means of pictures. He was very unsure what to do. He turned his head alternately to look at an inviting exit to the physical world on his left-hand side, and then towards his earthly existence and surroundings where he was. He was sitting so close to this ascending tunnel of Light that led to the Light, and would enable him to be rid of his sick decrepit physical body. He wanted to leave, but like many of us, Monique was finding it so very hard to release him to a new and happier life. Her desire to keep him physically with her was holding him here, even though he was ready and wanting to depart. I saw countless other cats who had already departed this earthly life, and were ready to escort Romeo to another world. They were calling him, but he did not feel he could go.

Romeo looked up at Maria, who full of compassion, took his astral form into her loving arms, and held him close to her breast. She caressed him gently as she sang. He was not happy. He kept looking over first one shoulder, then another at the ground, and obviously was afraid of falling. Aware of his insecurity, Maria, still singing, moved to a chair, so that she could hold him on her lap, where he might feel safer. This, however, did not stop him from continuing to peer anxiously at the floor over his shoulders, as a further demonstration of his persistent fear of falling. I understood later that this was his way of telling us how he experienced life in his physical form.

When I related this story to Monique, she was able to confirm that Romeo was indeed afraid of falling. He never used to be, but now it was sometimes necessary to lift him down from places, where previously, he would have jumped. As I came to understand more and more clearly afterwards, how it was Monique's difficulty letting him go that was holding him back, I spoke about that to Marguerite the following day, gladly accepting her offer to pass on the things I had not explained fully to Monique already. (I was under the impression that Monique did not understand English, which she later informed me was not the case. It is just that she usually declines to speak it.)

I thought once again that the communication had finished after this session, but I was wrong. The next part took place in Basel airport. I had gone to the "Ladies", (les toilettes). I was sitting down quite relaxed in there, when I was shown another vision. I had not asked for this either. I was seeing the time of Romeo's death, whenever that might take place.

I saw him find the courage to start his ascent up the tunnel to the Light. My spirit went with him to guide and assist him in this journey. The higher we went, the more like a fluffy young kitten Romeo appeared. At the foot of the tunnel, I saw his empty emaciated physical form left behind him, and as he reached the top, he emerged into the Light to be with the other cats, his little hind legs full of strength, his body perfect, as he leapt around in happiness, at last free from the pain, discomfort, and fear of falling that he had felt in his previous body. He continued his journey into the Light with other cats around him, and I returned, as was right for me, to my physical body in the "Ladies" in Basil airport.

I realised I would not have to know when he was dying. Having made this connection with him, I would be there for him at the right moment, even if I were sleeping in bed.

At home again in England, on 21/6/03, I received another email from Marguerite. When I read it, I gave an enormous sigh of relief, both for Monique and Romeo. In it she wrote,

"Yesterday I telephoned Dany (the one who came with her cat) and, what a surprise, she told me that Monique was with her. I then spoke to Monique directly, who told me her cat had died three hours before she took the train to Paris. She had recently asked him not to die when she would not be at home, and not to hide when he was ready to leave. Her wishes were fulfilled, and she spent some hours with him in her arms until he died. It's a great thing for her, and she told me, "I did it alone and didn't ask for help from anyone". Her husband was not at home either. So, as Romeo made the journey out of the physical dimension, she had made the important shift from being unready and unwilling to release him from this dimension, to being able to support him in his departure... So, I leave you with this now. End of a chapter!"

As I reread this message about Monique's courage to face up to everything, and do the most loving act possible to help her beloved Romeo, it brings tears to my eyes. Certainly, it had taken her a little while to reach a point where she could do this, but she had done it! The difficulty Monique experienced in letting Romeo go is normal! With her permission, this story is here to help the countless number of other people out there trying to face a similar situation. It might be with an animal, or a human, in fact with anything, even a place one has to leave. It makes no difference.

Samarpan wrote the following words to me in an email, nearly a year afterwards. (There is more about Samarpan in some later chapters of this book).

"Enjoy each moment totally, because everything in this world passes, and we can't hold on to anything or anybody."

Chapter 21

June 2003 & A Rose For Maria

This trip to France with Maria was life changing. It marked the beginning of a new phase in my spiritual development and work. Before I left, I already knew that it did not matter it was nearly the end of May, and still no one had asked me to teach them how to ride. Now I took that a stage further. I realized, that should someone ask for help with his or her horse, I must say very firmly "No". That is exactly what I did when a potential horse client telephoned me, asking if I would be willing to teach his daughter to ride. I had other work to do now, and that era of my life was finished.

Starlight, on the other hand, was staying. He was more than a luxury. I had endured the two months without a horse after Wilderness died in a state of misery. Happiness returned when Starlight entered my life. Yes, he was definitely meant to be with me, for which I was truly grateful. Without the necessity to drive all over the place teaching horse riding, I would be freer to concentrate on my spiritual enterprises.

I surveyed my garden, and thought how beautiful it was. It had colour everywhere. The foxgloves were particularly magnificent this year. Like the aquilegias, they had a wonderful range of colours, and had self seeded all over the place. I wanted to speak to the fairies about weeds. There were not very many, but someone had told me the fairies could help suppress their growth, so I decided to ask.

I was sitting on the grass at the bottom of my garden at the time. They knew I was speaking to them. They had been working busily in the flowerbeds, but came out onto the lawn to listen to me. After I had made my requests, with such an audience, what could be more natural than singing to them. I sang softly for a little, and then decided that I could help more with the sound, if I was indoors, and not concerned about disturbing the neighbours. The fairies would still receive it all. I sat indoors near the window, and channelled Maria's sounds to help and delight them. For my part, it was a way of saying thank you, and giving them something. It went well. Maria sang, and I thought it was all very beautiful.

This opened my mind to other possibilities. I had heard from Julia Day, that she was still having problems at Auton Farm with all sorts of things, which made it less than a pleasure to be there for her. Although she was receiving help from many people, I decided that I would like to offer her something. My love and compassion was going out to her.

As it seemed that Maria was so willing to help, even when I was not with a group of other people to augment the energies for her to come through, I found an empty tape, and decided to see if I could channel her onto it. It worked! The tape was duly put into the post with an explanatory postcard. I did so hope it would help.

That evening, I telephoned Joan Ocean. She had been there at the very beginning of the Maria story, and I was bursting with glad tidings of great joy. I could not wait to share it all. No doubt it was a beautiful Hawaiian morning, and Joan was at home. After I had spoken for some time about the nature of my work with Maria, Joan told me how much she longed to hear Maria's voice again.

That gave me another idea. Why not see if Maria was willing to sing down the telephone? "This is an experiment", I announced. "I am going to see if I can manage to channel her voice down the telephone. Would you like that?" "Oh yes, I'd love it. May the other people here listen as well?" "Yes, of course! But no results are guaranteed."

Maria came through easily. For me it was just the same as channelling her voice for the group in France had been. Then the unexpected happened. When the singing stopped, I became aware that Maria wanted to speak directly to Joan. I had not mentioned this possibility to Joan

The rose for Maria in the foreground

beforehand, but when Maria started with the words, "Would it be all right to speak with you?" (This was not recorded, but I think that is what she said.) Joan understood immediately without being told that this was Maria's voice, not mine, and gave her an affirmative.

Maria both spoke and listened to Joan for quite a while, or so it seemed to me. I knew at the time what Maria was saying, but Joan's voice went very faint, and seemed to be far away. I could not really focus on it, as I was not truly in my body. As I remember it, towards the end, Maria explained this to Joan. She used the expression that Joan's voice was "very distant to Helena", and explained that she needed to withdraw before Joan could talk to me directly again. This was done. She slipped out gradually, and I returned.

Unlike me, Joan had noticed when Maria made dolphin sounds, and told me how the cat, who was outside, recognised them, having lived near the ocean for so long, and began to meow in response.

Later, in an email, she mentioned having undergone many clearings lately, especially on the night before I phoned, and stated what a good idea it was for Maria to follow them up by sounding Joan's nervous system, as it had rearranged her brain, and re-wove her patterns. At first, she had felt a little disorientated, but then all her left-brain debris fell out, and her bodies' wave forms became harmonious again. This feedback was invaluable to me. It helped me to understand more about the nature of the work, which Maria and I were doing together.

The Rose

As I began to understand more about how many possibilities there might be for this work with Maria, the telephone, cassettes sent through the post, private sessions, seminars, channelling for the other realms as well as the physical, and maybe much more that I had not yet thought of; it occurred to me, that I could do none of this without Maria. How very blessed I was that she chose to work with me. It needed both of us, but what a team! I was so pleased and delighted, that I decided to place a strongly scented, disease resistant dark red rose on my patio.

I had very few roses in my garden, partly because of the disease factor, and mostly because of my dislike of anything with thorns. Someone told me about an excellent rose nursery nearby, where I might find such a rose, and kindly lent me a catalogue. There seemed to be one that might be suitable, so I set off in my car to buy it. Unfortunately, I was told that this particular rose could not survive for more than three years in a pot on my patio. Nonetheless, I bought it, because there was nothing else there with all of the other qualities I was looking for.

As I drove home with the rose beside me in a little pot, I wondered if it was really true that it could not be kept happy with enough compost and water on my patio. The rose answered my question. It showed me, with a picture, how much it wanted to get its roots deep down into the earth. So I knew it really did need a place in one of my flowerbeds.

I thought of putting it in my heart shaped bed beside the Irish Yew. It would get plenty of sunshine there, but this site was rather windy, especially in winter. So I asked the rose if it would mind the winter gales, when it was dormant. I felt it shiver, with a picture of winter's icy blast racing past it. Finally, I thought of another place. If I cleared a little of my heather back, I could make a space for it in full sun, away from the roots of the Yew tree, where there would be enough moisture, and well sheltered from the north west wind that is so prevalent here in the winter. My sweetly scented yellow rose grew close to the spot, and seemed to do well there.

With great enthusiasm, I set about planting Maria's rose, thinking how the average man in the street would most probably refer me to a psychiatrist for being so much in love with, and so grateful towards a discarnate entity, who was not a blood relation, and whom I had never met during her lifetime. No matter, this was my life for me to live as seemed fit.

I planted it most carefully, following the instructions that were printed on the little label attached to it very precisely, and taking the added precaution of filling the hole with water to allow the surrounding soil to absorb some of it before I added the rose. It was June, and the ground was dry. With the rose, soil, and compost all in place, it was time to communicate with both the rose, and the nature spirits.

214

I started with the rose. I squatted down in front of it, for it was only small, no more than a foot tall. I channelled Light and love and energy through my crown chakra, and out again through my heart to the rose. After a while, the fairies instructed me, "Back off a bit now, will you!" So I did, not sure if my energy work was too much for the rose, or it was simply that the fairies wanted to take over with the very special work of their own. Standing back a little, upright now, I asked for their assistance with the welfare and care of the rose, telling them that it was there in honour of Maria, the entity who had sung through me for them. Then I called in the "red rose devas", as this was the only red rose in the garden, and I thought that they might not be already present. As a final touch, I asked all of the other plants in the garden to welcome the rose, so that "she", for by this time I was sure that this rose carried more feminine energy than anything else, would be happy and feel at home in the garden. Later in the day, when I walked past the rose, I saw at least a dozen or more, tiny little "red rose" devas working busily around her.

Pleased with what I had done for Maria, it dawned on me that I had chosen a colour that would be lovely in my garden, but was not the colour I would have selected had I been shopping just for myself. I would have liked lilac or purple, which would have looked wonderful with the foxgloves. Secondly, I was still lacking a rose for the patio, so I went shopping again, and came back with a lilac patio rose, and a purple rose to place near the foxgloves in the border.

Now I was giving myself love, as well as Maria and my garden. I chose these two roses for myself by the simple method of telling the lady selling them what colour and qualities I was looking for in the roses, and then letting her tell me which two she recommended. What a coincidence, that the two I took home were the two in the catalogue with the most suitable names. The patio lilac rose was called "Dream Lover", and the other one, which was purple, "New Age". Actually, contrary to what I had been told, the purple one turned out to be dark red, another Maria-coloured rose!

Although I had managed to make time to plant my roses, there was so much to do on my return that I had to sacrifice many of the things I would have like to have done. Music was one of them. It seemed more important to get the material into my computer for Maria's book than to sing, if I had to choose.

Another important thing for me was to read another book about Maria. There had been this hesitancy when channelling her in French, as to whether Toy was a dog or a bitch, and I wanted to find out. This information was not given in the book I found in the library. It turned out to be written without compassion for the troubles at the end of her life, but I found myself reading about tantrums on a scale and frequency that I had not been so aware of before. These accounts may have been exaggerated and inaccurate, but supposing at least some of it were true?

I thought to myself again, of how I would have been so very afraid, if not terrified of her temper, had I ever met her in physical form. She seemed so very different from the loving spirit who works with me now.

I realised that it was important that I fully accept all of her, not just the bits of her I liked. This meant I needed to embrace everything she was as Maria Callas, and not just what she is now. "How?" I asked myself. The answer came from Maria herself, for I heard it clearly in my head. "You must first look at your own life, and totally love yourself, even the parts of you, you find so undesirable, and the things you regret having done to yourself or others. Only then will you be able to accept the parts of me you do not like at present."

When I followed this advice, and looked at times when I had lost my temper, or done things I found to be unkind or cruel, it led me to try and understand why I had been like that, and "misbehaved" so badly. I considered my emotional state at the time of these incidents, and the events leading up to these scenes from my past, which I preferred to forget about. Sometimes I had been very tired, other times I had felt unsupported or unrecognised by others, and just frustrated out of my mind when I could not get, or do what I wanted. I had certainly known anger, and I knew only too well how it had felt. It never brought me any pleasure, and the burning sensation in my solar plexus, the tension, the misery that can go with it were awful.

216

So if Maria's rages were as bad as people say they were, then how she must have suffered, and how many regrets she must have had at the end of her life, and beforehand. Seen this way, I could only feel compassion for her. On another level, that of a researcher, the changes in her temperament since she left her physical body, and is now so much more of what she really is, rather than the personality and physical being she was in her lifetime, and yet still holds the knowledge and learning of that life is very interesting.

It was during this time after my French trip, that having read she had two poodles at the same time, Tea and Toy, I began to wonder what colour the other one was. Toy, the one she took everywhere with her when possible, was the black one. In my head I kept seeing a much lighter coloured second poodle, but was this my imagination? I read of a third poodle, Djedda that I think came later, and may have been one of the two, which she had at the end.

It was Dany who helpfully, and as far as I know completely unwittingly, supplied me with this necessary information. When she sent me the information I had dictated to her about her cat, in case it was of interest, she included an old copy of "Paris Match", which had been devoted to Maria. It must have been published fairly soon after her death in 1977, and the pages had already turned rather yellow with age.

There was a résumé of her life, and a picture of her with two poodles on her lap, which she is said to have taken for the same walk around the block every day towards the end of her life in Paris. There were other pictures as well, but this was the important one for me. The second poodle was white. Until then, I had been thinking my clairvoyance was wrong when Maria showed me the lighter coloured one!

Chapter 22

Azores June 2003

I had a number of reasons for going on this trip. The main one was that I felt it would be very helpful to connect with Joan again before going to Hawaii to assist with her Portal 2003 seminar. Secondly, having chosen not to have a whale-swimming holiday at Silver Banks this year, I could not see anything that was just pure holiday in my diary, apart from four and a half days after the coming Portal Seminar in August for my relaxation. Thirdly, I felt such a strong desire for new adventure. I had never visited the Azores before, so this would provide me with something new. Fourthly, there would be whales and dolphins to swim with there, which meant fun and delight to be had by those who chose it.

While working in my garden two days before I was due to leave, I heard beautiful operatic arias being played by one of my neighbours. She must have turned the volume fairly high, as by standing as close to the boundary hedge as possible, I was able to start singing along with it, and felt Maria's vibrations come quite strongly into my body. It finished all too soon. So feeling inspired, I decided to take a break from the garden work, and ran into my house, where I first closed the doors and windows, before putting on one of my own CDs to sing along with.

I understood that this encouragement from Maria meant that although I had barely sung at all since my French trip, she intended to come with me to Joan's workshop, for there would be something for us to do there.

"Maria's Sounds for the Group, the Whales and the Dolphins"

When Joan's group met in the afternoon of 20th July in the hotel, it was very warm in there. After spending the morning out on the boat, I felt readier to go to sleep than take in the content of a talk, or remain conscious through a meditation. No doubt others felt the same way, as Joan decided we should move outside to do some toning. The physical movement of the very short walk to a suitable location would be good for all of us. Also Joan told me later that she had felt we should not make too much noise in the hotel.

Actually, nothing was said about toning until after we arrived there. It was a beautiful spot on the coast with a mixture of sun and shade, so that we could choose which we wanted to be in. I chose the sunshine, and sat down on a rocky ledge next to Joan. She turned to me, and asked me how I was feeling. Much revived by the warmth of the sun, for I had felt cold on the boat and in the water during the morning, I announced, "I am feeling great, thank you."

It then came to me as a complete surprise, when she asked me if I would like to do something with Maria for the group. I felt that I was being offered a wonderful opportunity to step into an opening that had been prepared for us. I agreed, on the condition that Joan had a word with them first about it. So Joan said a few words to them about what I was going to do.

I was sitting on the higher side of the slope. To address the group looking down at them did not feel right, so I moved to the lower side of the circle, standing up to speak with my back to the ocean, and the group in front of me. As Joan had said very little, it seemed right to explain in my own words how I had a musical guide called Maria, and to tell them the story of how she had come through me the first time in 2001 in Hawaii. I instructed them briefly on the art of toning together, and then we began. They had agreed it would be nice to sing for all of creation, and more specifically the unification of the group, dolphins, whales, and ETS etc.

Maria definitely did come through, but I had not felt her vibes as clearly as usual, so when it was complete, I asked her, "Maria! Are you there?"

She showed me herself with a keyboard, pointing at something on a music score. Reading the question in my mind, she said, "That was just a warm up". I took this to mean that we would get another opportunity later in the week.

Meanwhile, something was happening in the group, which I did not know how to deal with. The singing was supposed to have stopped, but one member of the group was singing on and on and on. I was concerned on two accounts. Firstly, it appeared that I had lost control of the group, which is something that always bothers me. Secondly, after being trusted and privileged to do something with them for just a little while, it now seemed it was running well over the allocated time. Joan would surely want to start her meditation. Having waited for a while, I said gently, "Finish when you are ready". This seemed to have no effect, so I looked across at Joan, the experienced seminar leader, with the question written in my eyes, "What do I do about this?" Joan put her finger across her lips, so that I understood all I had to do was wait.

Eventually there was silence again. I learnt later that the lady, who did not stop singing with the rest of us, had announced prior to starting, that she was not going to sing a note! Anyway, she did finish eventually, and Joan was finally able to lead her meditation.

At the end of it, and with only the words, "Let's sing for the dolphins now!" Joan started to lead more chanting. Feeling that Maria was still very welcome, I continued to channel her voice. Joan having taken back the responsibility for the group, and knowing that Maria was being so well received, I was much more relaxed.

Therefore the sound was freer, and my throat more open to let it out. From sounds similar to singing, it moved to something else. Sounds, which do not occur in opera to my knowledge, were starting to come through. Maria sang her way through a rich variety of them. Even after everyone else had fallen silent, as it felt right to me, I was happy to allow Maria to continue until she had finished. To complete her solo, she was emphatic as the pitch descended, that I place my hands palms down upon the earth, so that we could touch and bless it, as well as grounding the energies there.

Standing up again slowly, I opened my eyes, and saw that those of the group closest to me had gathered around with smiling open faces to thank me. With Maria still strongly present, and longing to say something to the whole group, I was barely capable of acknowledging these thanks, as it was so urgent to make Joan understand that Maria still had a few words to say.

Eventually the desired permission from Joan was given, and Maria was able to deliver her short speech. It was done quite solemnly, as she acknowledged the love of the group, and thanked them very sincerely, and especially Joan, for making this work possible for her. Finally she bowed very deeply to honour everyone in a very authentic and loving way. Then I could turn my attention to those around me with their appreciation and extremely valuable feedback.

Joan told me that she had heard the calls of all the different types of whale and dolphin she knew. There was quite a long list of them. My own experience of their sounds is relatively so limited, that I had not even realised this had happened. Thinking back, I could recall some deep sounds that must have been the humpback whale songs, but that was the only part I could recognise.

It was also commented on, that there had been a lot of activity amongst the birds near the water's edge, and our group. That surprised me less, as I had several times before been aware of a connection between cetacean and bird energies.

A certain high note, the highest that had ever come out of my mouth, produced more feedback. I remembered hearing this note. It was effortless and sung softly, the hardest thing to do with a high note. It had amazed me! That was something I could never have done without Maria. Both Joan and Jean-Luc perceived that it had opened a communication portal.

That evening, Harriet, with whom I was sharing a room, told me that she had noticed how much closer the group had become with each other since the singing. The aim to unify the group had been successful.

An Over-dinner Conversation with Joan

Walk-ins

This was really important for me. Joan asked me if I thought I was a walk-in. (That means an entity who was not born here, but had an agreement with another soul that at the right time, the entity or soul who was already living a life in a physical body would agree to leave by walking out, thus leaving the physical form vacant for the other entity/soul to walk into it.)

Joan and I discussed this possibility. It is nowhere near as rare as one might think. The physical body does not die, so the life of the person concerned appears to be continuing as normal. Joan seemed to feel that I was one, or at least that another aspect of my soul had entered my body. I had considered this possibility long ago, when probably nothing more than an increased amount of the soul already inhabiting the body had entered to provide greater spiritual strength, and help prepare my mind for the present time.

Joan started me thinking about it again, and caused me to try and recall anything that might be relevant. I remembered a time when I had viewed a powerful white light coming my way. Well, it could have been an indication that Maria was starting to come closer, or even more of my own soul and power was approaching. It is equally possible that another entity was taking a look to see how I was getting on, and to remind me subconsciously of an agreement we had made long ago, that I would shortly be leaving this body, as the other soul entered to come and start its spiritual work on the Earth in human form. I remembered how, when I had viewed this light, I had felt rather threatened by it, but at the same time recognised it as something good.

Now I began to wonder if it really was that very light which had finally entered my body, and lived in me in place of the former soul occupying my body. If so, it explains why the "Helena" inhabiting my body at the time felt these mixed emotions of being threatened, and yet knowing it was something good for her. Her physical life was nearing its end, but the move to life on the other side of death, and the entity taking over the body were both positive things to look forward to.

This topic had come up after I told Joan that I had chosen to terminate my career as a professional horse woman, and how strange it felt not to be professional any more. I shared with her how I felt I had laid down a burden I had carried for a long time, because it no longer served me, and how free and easy I found life without it. I recalled the vision I had had, in which I climbed up to the top of a mountain carrying a backpack. On reaching the summit, I had seen myself take off the backpack, laying it down on the ground, and walking away happily without it, never even looking back.

Joan shared with me how it had been for her after she had walked in. As the new entity living in her body, she could not get over how brilliant and beautiful the colours were on Earth. She told me how she had noticed a great change in herself, especially regarding how she felt towards her relatives, and about her own life. For this reason, she made certain changes in what she was doing.

Joan asked me if I knew at what point I had walked in. She explained to me that it sometimes happened during channelling. Instead of the "old me" returning to my body, the "walk-in" me would have entered it instead. Other times it happens while one is unconscious during an operation, or during one's sleep state.

I thought about it, and recalled how it was after France that I had decided to give up my career with horses. As I flew back to England, I had definitely felt different. My attitudes had changed in a number of ways. Therefore it was very likely this had taken place after channelling, or during one of my nights in Alsace.

The following morning, with my mind still full of these things, as I walked towards the harbour to board the boat, I remembered how one morning at home shortly after my French trip, I had noticed how brilliant and wonderful the colours around me were. Even those of my very ordinary clothes looked so wonderful. I had found it a curious thing, that I had never noticed or perceived colours in this way before. When I went outside that day, this phenomenon continued, so much so that I wondered if I was wearing different glasses from usual. No, they were exactly what I normally wore.

I realised that there were countless little personality traits, which were leaving me, or had already left. These evidently belonged to the pre-walk-in me, and no longer served any purpose. As I thought about my work with Maria, it dawned on me that perhaps she had requested the opportunity to work with a walk-in. This latter thought gave me goose bumps all over, which seemed to stay with me for ages, in spite of the warmth of the sunshine. I realised that I had hit upon the truth. I came to understand that this was what she had wanted. This way, she would be able to get on with her work a great deal faster, than if she were still working with the old me, hampered by so many personality traits, which tended to get in the way of what we were doing together. Especially my beliefs about my limitations needed to go. Nonetheless, Maria had now worked diligently with the old me before this had happened, so that the way was well prepared for the walk-in I am now. The life being lived in Helena's body would have continuity.

When I told Joan about my experiences with the colours, she said, "I thought you might remember that." When I asked Joan what had made her suspect I had walked in, she said it was the telephone conversation she had had with me before I left England. I had been so different that it was like talking to another person. For one thing, I sounded much more confidant. That made me think of something Julia Day had commented after I had channelled Maria's voice onto a tape for her. "What happened to the shy Helena?" Admittedly it was not my own voice, but Maria's on the tape, but she must have felt that the shy Helena would not have been ready to share this with her. Not having understood what had happened myself at the time, I dismissed it with the comment, "Oh that was Maria, not me!"

I have told this walk-in story in full, because of its relevance to my mission with Maria. However, I am well aware that it is not something I can share with everyone. At the time I was on cloud nine about it, but later realised that as every identity is part of the illusion we all live in our incarnated state, I should not make it food for the ego, or some kind of spiritual one-upmanship. It is simply a part of the reality I am living. For those who read this, it can be accepted or rejected. It can be equally well described as an increase in my spiritual awareness, which has helped my partnership with Maria.

Maria in Sonia's Garden

The hotel, which we were staying in, was owned by Antonio and Sonia. I had first met Sonia one evening, when I found her gazing into the goldfish pond in the hotel garden. I mistook her for one of the other hotel guests. For some reason, I had to say hello to this lady. Presumably she was as curious to look at everything as I was. We had not spoken very long, before she revealed to me that she was the gardener, and also Antonio's wife. I told her that I loved gardening as well, and said a few words about my own garden. Sonia explained that she was manageress of the hotel, and that she was referred to as the "Fairy Queen" by Antonio. I revealed a strong interest in fairies myself, and no doubt on account of our mutual interest, she invited me to visit her private garden, which was just a short walk away, if I was interested and had the time.

So it was Tuesday evening when I arrived at Sonia's gate. I had no difficulty spotting her doing some weeding quite close to the driveway. Her garden was beautiful! She called it "The Secret Garden", because, as she explained, not everybody was taken there. Mother Nature had done a wonderful job for her, thus rewarding the many hours of care she gave it. It was a mixture of splendid mature trees, and a large variety of both flowers and foliage plants growing amongst them interspersed with plenty of stones and rocks. The colour scheme was impressive. There was a marvellous atmosphere, which I can best describe as sacred, not to mention a prolific variety of fairy life in all directions.

After we had wandered quietly through the trees along some lovely little paths, we sat down to chat. I found myself talking to her about Maria. I told her a bit about the nature of channelling, and also briefly of the events with Maria and the group. At least part of the time, most probably when she could follow what I was saying, I felt an intense interest coming from her. So I offered to channel Maria. I asked Sonia if she would like me to sing for the fairies and plants in her garden. Sonia replied that really she would like some help for herself, as she felt that her needs were greater than those of her garden, which was doing better than she felt she was. I agreed.

Maria and I began to sing. Sonia had her little dog, Malinka, (whose name means "Tiny" in Czech,) beside her. Malinka was intensely curious at first, and came over to my feet to investigate. Then, as the pitch ascended and the volume increased, she became afraid, and began to bark. Probably she had never heard anything like it before. Therefore I stopped channelling, and asked Sonia if I should continue or not. Sonia took Malinka into her arms, saying that she would be all right, and bade me to carry on.

Maria and I continued, but at a softer volume, and avoided the highest notes in order to prevent Malinka becoming upset again. I felt love and compassion coming through the sound more strongly than before. I feel sure it was Malinka who had brought about this reaction of more tenderness in Maria and me. It helped all present greatly in my opinion. Maria finished at a low pitch, with soft gentle notes, thus grounding Sonia, and some notes especially for Malinka, who received them well. To complete it, Maria touched and blessed the earth with my hands.

I stood up slowly with open eyes, and looked at Sonia, wondering what effect this would have had on her. "That was amazing!" she said. "Have you studied music? Do you teach it or something?" "No". "Then how did you learn to let your voice ring out like that?" I explained again, how it was not me who sang, but Maria, for I could never produce sound like that without her help.

Looking around the garden from the rock where we were standing, I saw fairies of all kinds and sizes. They revealed themselves as larger and stronger than most I have seen, so they went very well together with the flourishing well-grown plants. They were standing around gazing at us with an air of surprise and appreciation. It was as though the rock on which we stood was a stage, and the slopes below showed me the fairies in the audience. Behind us, higher up, were those in this outdoor theatre gallery, and the dress circle. On the slopes just in front of us was the grave of Billy Boy, a much-loved dog. I asked if Billy Boy had some brown colouring on him, which she affirmed. I had just seen Billy Boy's spirit, standing near his grave, and looking cheerfully up at us with his tail wagging. He then bounded up the slope, and danced around Sonia to express his love for her.

Next, we walked on together through the garden to Sonia's car. As I had made myself rather late with the channelling, she offered me a welcome lift in it. We followed the path around her garden to a place where Sonia stopped the car to show me her goldfish pond. This seemed so appropriate, as we had first met beside a goldfish pond, not this one, but the one in the hotel garden. Later, I explained to Sonia that the sounds had worked to open up communication channels between the fairy kingdom and ours. The veil between the two was thinner now. All Sonia need do was to be open to all of this.

After Sonia had driven me back to the hotel, I discovered that the boat with the rest of the group on it was later back than expected, so with no group meeting to attend, I settled down in my room to write about the afternoon's experiences. As I came towards the end of this account, I observed Malinka in an out-of-the-body state, gazing at me with wide-open eyes, and an expression of wonder in them. Instructions came from her to tell Sonia that she had visited me in this way, which I duly did.

At dinner that evening, I spoke to Joan, and she told me how when she returned from the boat to the hotel, she had been wildly excited, because the dolphins had given them such a good time that afternoon. Malinka, who was with Sonia in the hotel reception, began to bark and get upset, so Joan quietened down, and the little dog came over to say hello. Sonia said that this was very unusual. Normally she did not go near other people, as Sonia had not had her very long, and she was very wary of those she did not know.

This made me think about Malinka's behaviour with me in Sonia's car as she drove me back to the hotel. She had shown a preference for my lap rather than Sonia's, and climbed all over me, wanting to lick my face and neck. I was not too keen on having my face licked, so I restrained her gently. Seeing this, Sonia took her back onto her own lap.

Hearing Joan's story, I seriously began to wonder if Maria's singing had opened her more towards people, providing they were quiet with her. The intention had never been to sing for the dog, but she had needed it. Maria had become aware of this, and responded with notes for her. My silent request to Maria had merely been, "Please go gently, and try not to frighten the dog", for it distressed me to see her upset. It was surely this, which had brought Maria's love through.

In-between Trips, and the Walk-in Experience

When I returned home afterwards, I experienced a great deal of stress caused by my big suitcase failing to get as far as Heathrow when I did, although it may have simply gone to the wrong terminal. Either way, I had to travel on to Manchester, and then home without it, and wait until the evening before I was due to fly to Hawaii for it to be delivered to my doorstep. It contained everything I would need for snorkelling with dolphins, and a number of other equally precious items. Therefore during the hectic few days at home from the 26th. -31st. July, when I was to leave early in the morning, I spent a lot of time on the telephone assisting and keeping up with the search for my highly valued possessions. Even more time was spent worrying about how best to cope if I did not get it back in time. I did manage to think of a provisional plan, which I luckily never needed to implement. I had other concerns as well, but in the interests of brevity, I will decline to go into those.

In spite of all this, I somehow found time to reflect on my life, and most of all the conversation I had had with Joan about walk-ins, and whether or not I was one. The more I considered this possibility, the more sense it made to conclude that Joan was right. I was a walk-in. Since I had walked in, there seemed to be so many spontaneous changes in my wishes and attitude to life. Giving up the horse work was just a start. My taste in colour and how I wanted my house to look had altered. I desired different colours around me, luckily not everywhere, but this seriously affected my choices for an area I had arranged to have re-decorated when I was next away.

Then I mused over the point that if someone walked in, the life walked into would appear to continue as normal, at least to most other people. The new entity would take over with a minimum of problems, because the memory would still be in place. This would contain knowledge such as who one was, Helena Hawley in my case, which house was mine, and where to find it, who everyone else was in my life, and how to carry on as

228

Helena with her previously learnt skills, but being able to add my own, and make any changes necessary for the purpose of my coming. My own personality would be present, and could be used in conjunction with the learnt knowledge of the physical brain for my mission as required.

The fact that I would be as someone born under the same star signs as the previous occupant of this body, is another thing that would contribute usefully to the continuity of the life and personality. I realise that I worked much of this out with my mind, and therefore is not information to be relied upon. However, the mind always likes to rationalise everything, even the things beyond its comprehension.

I looked around to see how I thought and felt about this new environment I had walked into. Most things seemed to be in good order. The unstoppable thought, "But the horse is perfect!" entered my head. This explains why, since I walked in, I have had a better relationship with Starlight than I had before. I assumed that he had not been chosen for the "old" Helena, but for me. She had bought him, very helpfully, having been guided to pick the right one for me, and there he was, exactly the type of animal I really wanted. The improvement was not so dramatic, but it was the beginning of progress and understanding between horse and rider at a faster rate than before I arrived. The old Helena had done her best with him, but I was able to do better, because as a different being, I was more suited than she had been to blend with this animal.

As Joan was later to point out to me, one is left with personality "residues" from the being that previously inhabited the body. Therefore many personality traits could remain, rather like an inheritance, or other goods thrown in with the deal, as I put it. Some of these might be useful, and others would need to be worked on, improved, or released. Perhaps it is these residues that not only help for the life to continue without many people noticing the changes, but also sometimes the reason why the concept of "walk-ins" is not accepted by all. Some just think of it as a spiritual awakening for the soul already present in the body. Actually, it does not really matter if one has walked in or not. The responsibilities for the life being led remain unchanged. The mind is bound to be interested, but it is not what has happened, but the present situation that counts.

In this instance, what makes this personal transformation I was experiencing as a walk-in so important is the positive reaction and delight, which I could feel from Maria about it.

To live a duet, one needs a good and suitable partner.

Chapter 23

Through the Portal With Maria

On 31/7/03 I left on schedule for Hawaii. The journey would take me two days as usual, but I knew I would find the night spent in the States on my way helpful for mind and body to start adjusting to the different time zones.

I was met in Kona airport by another member of the team who would be helping with this seminar of Joan's, and taken to Joan's house, where I thankfully completed my journey. I had agreed to be one of the helping team of people at Joan's request. Including her, there would be eight of us helping, and we were to number forty-five people in total. The other helpers all impressed me enormously. They were so willing, and managed to do and give so much! Enough said. I did my best, and found myself still alive at the end of it, having gained invaluable experience in many different areas, which would not have happened nearly so fully if I had not been on the helping team. Thank you Joan.

I was to start my stay at Joan's Ranch, sleeping in her house, as this would give me the best chance to rest. Then, before the group arrived, I had agreed to move out and install myself in a tent on the hillside paddock just above the house. I went up there the first evening to spend time beside this tent, and familiarise myself with my home to be. The view of the trees was beautiful. The tent, which had some bushes just behind it, looked out onto the grassy clearing backed by ohia trees. Nature had done a really artistic job designing these trees. Their shape and colouring appealed to me enormously.

I sat outside my tent gazing at this view. "What could be lovelier to see first thing in the morning when one got out of bed?" I asked myself. If I lived in an environment like this one, I would not need a cultivated garden around me, but only to keep the grass rough cut and pleasant to walk over, whilst allowing Nature to do the rest un-interfered with by me. Such an arrangement would release me from the hours of labour necessary to maintain the little patch I had at home in its present organised state. Perhaps such an arrangement as this could act as a major stress reducer in my life.

It is worth bearing in mind, however, that I only experience my garden as a burden when I cannot find the time to care for it properly, which is exactly what had happened between the Azores trip and this one. The rest of the year it is a highly valued source of pleasure, creativity, and means of reducing stress, as well as keeping me in close contact with Mother Earth, and the Fairy Kingdom.

Although I was weary that first evening, my time was still my own. As I was craving physical exercise, when the rain stopped at dusk, I decided to go for a walk. An ambitious route was not necessary, so long as I could move and breathe the fresh air. So I set off down the hill from Joan's driveway. An hour would be sufficient; therefore when I reached the main highway, I turned round to walk back up the road the way I had come.

I had not gone far on my way back, before I saw first one, and then a few more Kahunas in spirit form approaching me from either side of the narrow lane. The first lady to reach me placed a wreath of flowers around my neck. Incidentally, I was still wearing a similar necklace, which had been presented to me when I was met at the airport. The flowers in it were giving out a beautiful scent in the night air. Now I was adorned with two one these, one material, and one "invisible". The material one had yellow flowers, but this second one contained several other colours, a mixture of yellow, with light orange, shades of pink, and one or two that were quite red. The ladies were all what I would describe as typical Hawaiian body type, if there is such a thing, namely stocky and well covered.

As I had read somewhere that Kahunas were capable of using their powers in many ways, some more commendable than others, their presence made me uneasy. Wanting to handle things diplomatically, I explained to them that I was by nature a suspicious entity regarding things I was not familiar with, and that for that reason I was worried by their closeness to me. I added that I chose to love and bless both them and their island, regardless of what their intentions with me might be. They seemed to know all this about me already. I felt two things. Firstly, they had been expecting me to come, and wished to welcome me. Secondly, that I may have had a past life connection with the island.

They continued to walk with me up the hill, during which time I perceived only goodness and kindness coming from them. The lady who had approached me first, told me that I would be welcomed anywhere I felt guided to go on their island. As she spoke, she made a sweeping gesture with her left hand and arm, indicating an extensive area of this rocky volcanic land. Meanwhile, I had goose bumps all over me, even though the uphill walk was making me physically warm. I knew they were close. At a certain point, they all stopped, leaving me to continue walking back up to Joan's house without them.

Evidently they had reached the border of the piece of territory for which they were guardians. Aware that I was leaving them behind me now, my inner vision was drawn to myself again. I observed so many more flowers on my person. There were garlands round my wrists and ankles as well as around my neck. The energy of the Kahunas was in my body. This gave strength to my legs, and my walking speed increased.

After I had returned to Sky Ranch in the darkness of night, Joan remarked on how rested I looked. Then I realised that I had received the healing energy of the Kahunas, which was helping me to get over jet lag. They knew I had come to give service with little time to recover from my long journey first, so they chose to help me.

When I awoke the next morning, I spontaneously reconnected with them on their dimension. To their leaders, I handed some European flowers as gifts. There were daisies, a few roses and other flowers, but mostly daisies. This was my way of saying thank you.

Having helped with the seminar preparations as much as I could, which was not much, I accepted Joan's offer to go with her to a talk she was giving to someone else's group nearby. I spoke to one or two of the people there, and discovered an opera singer amongst them. The gift I received from our short conversation was the knowledge that "Helena" was a Greek name. Maria, with her Greek origins, must have known that, even though it was new information to me.

Channelling Maria

The first day of the seminar passed fairly uneventfully for me. It was on the second day that Maria was given her first opening with this group.

We were sitting outside in the sunshine at the Ranch, and I had listened with great interest as Elaine Thompson gave a wonderful talk on the healing effects of sound, and her very technical work with notes and her computer. As she finished, it dawned on me that this would be a wonderful preparation for the group to understand a little of what Maria's "noises" might be about. Surely I could just channel her without the need for more words first, now in this very instant? I put my hand up to get Joan's attention, and volunteered. "Well, if Maria is already here…" "Yes. She's here", I replied, noticing that it was mostly Maria's voice that spoke through me with these words. Permission was granted.

We were seated in a circle around a pile of magnificent crystals placed over the centre of the 2003 Portal opening. (More about that later.) I felt moved to rise from my chair, and place myself close to the Portal vortex and the crystals in the centre. As soon as I was there I began to feel these strong vibrations moving through and pulsating in my body. Maria and I found a lot of energy at our disposal. This was further augmented by the group energy around us. The two of us were like conduits for the Portal energy.

The sounds from Maria were, not surprisingly, powerful. Douglas Webster remarked afterwards, that it seemed to him that Maria was singing for or to the Portal. So that was how it started, with my physical body facing the crystals, and the group around us. In the second part, however, Maria and I faced outwards towards the people. There were too

234

many of them to tone each one of them separately, but by turning slowly as we sang, all were able to receive a share of healing sound. Maria then kissed the ground as she anchored these energies into the earth.

When all was silent again, she acknowledged each section of the group, turning my body slowly as she did so. Finally, placing herself directly facing Joan, she gave her a special bow, for Joan was the one who had supported her, and given her this opportunity to serve.

I was about to make my way back to my chair, when Joan asked me if I would be willing to give a little talk to the group about how Maria had come into my life, and what it was all about. I agreed. I was open about Maria's identity, and found a receptive audience.

Over the next few days, little by little feedback came my way. The most interesting thing was how people can still feel the effects of Maria's sounds in their bodies in the following days, or day, depending on the person. Many had really experienced them physically at the time.

In one of Joan's meditations on 5th August, I saw Maria with people I believe to have been her guides rather than mine. They were dressed in white, and mostly wearing tall hats, rather like the mentor she had shown me before.

Physical Changes

There is a strong connection between these and the Portal Opening. The latter helps to accelerate that which is already occurring in this physical reality. For those who choose it, this is a time for an excellent opportunity to evolve and mutate. We could move from having two strands of DNA operative back to the original twelve that we started out with at the beginning of human incarnations. During one of our meetings with Joan, we were invited to share anything we had personally experienced along the lines of physical changes.

A number of us had suffered from nausea and headaches, some more severely than others. One cannot rule out the possibility that this may have been caused by the "vog", the name given to the less good air that sometimes blows over on the wind from the volcano when it is active, and not from the portal energy as most of us thought. I had noticed this since arriving on the island. It usually occurred late evening, just as I was going to bed, and I would find that both sensations had left me when I awoke the following morning. The timing of these inconveniences was really very good, because it never interfered with my spiritual work, and mostly must have happened while I was sleeping.

The other thing, which intrigued me, was the strange sensations I had had in my legs. Both legs were reacting in exactly the same way, and I would only feel it when I arose in the mornings. By the time the group activities were underway each day, my legs felt normal again. Had these sensations started after my first swim, or following some unaccustomed physical activity, I would had put it down to that, but it began the very first morning, and continued throughout, and also for a while after my stay at the Ranch. It felt exactly the same in both legs. There was no pain or discomfort, just this odd sensation as though there were a piece of string attached to the inside of each knee running upwards still on the inside of each leg, but a little more towards the front than the rear of my thighs. I would be unaware of it while still lying in bed, but as soon as I started to move each morning, I would notice it. It was just as though I was being rewired, or undergoing some subtle change in my body's meridians.

Story Teller

Story Teller is not the name that this lady's parents gave her, but the name chosen to describe and refer to what is going on with the aid of this particular physical body now. (My words) Many people say that all of us have twelve aspects to our souls, never more, and never less than that. Whereas I do not know if this is so, I have no difficulty accepting that we could have twelve aspects. Story Teller definitely has. In her case, I quote:

"Story Teller" is the name and combined voice of a conscious collective of twelve unique beings, who are incarnated in harmony within one human body. Such a pattern of consciousness is known as Tsa'A'Densoul, which roughly translates as "souls who have aligned by the complimentarity of their matrix, bonding to one another in a complex geometry prior to incarnation, maintaining individual perspective, while releasing autonomy in physical form."

Story Teller is devoted to a spiritual path of Radical Truth, Radical Trust, Radical Personal Responsibility, and Radical Compassion."

The above information about her is something I copied from a little leaflet she makes available for those she meets and others. There is much more about her on the net, as she is supported by the Tsa'A'Densoul Project. In Story Teller's case, Joan told us that the twelve aspects had walked in at various different times since the birth of her physical body.

The first time I spoke to her, she had only just arrived at Joan's ranch, and was sitting down waiting for her breakfast at the table in Joan's house. My attraction to her was instant as I looked into her eyes while we spoke. On the subject of channelling, she asked me how it was for my physical body afterwards. What kind of effect did it have on it? Before I had managed to formulate an intelligible answer, her food arrived, and I was asked by the person who brought it to her to leave, so I did. Otherwise her food would have got cold. So I departed, having not found out in which direction this conversation was leading us, or why she was asking me this question.

Intuitively, I felt I had to pursue this further at the next suitable opportunity. So three days later, I was thankful to accept Story Teller's offer to speak to me for fifteen minutes privately. Before this, she had already helped me understand with more certainty my own situation as a walk-in. I put it to her that I felt the old Helena had left when the new me entered, but wanted to know if I had analysed things correctly. She confirmed with one word that I was right. This was what had happened. "Yes".

My Private Session with 'Story Teller'

This session, on 10th August, was very meaningful and important for me. It was to influence both my thinking and actions in the future and my present. It concerned the subject of my channelling. Story Teller was well equipped to make a fair assessment of it, as it was three days after my arrival, and she had heard me channelling Maria, at least two different ETs, one of whom had explained that he was not accustomed to communicating with words, and caused much amusement as he attempted to master some to speak through me, (the laughter, which the group hardly dared let out in case they were not supposed to be laughing, was gladly accepted by both the ET and myself), and she had also heard me share my clairvoyant viewings of ships and all else that I perceived going on as the group sat around the fire one evening.

Story Teller had the ability to perceive what was going on in my body during channelling far more accurately than I had. She explained to me that Maria's energy was rather hot for me, and that if she was allowed into my body too much, it would be damaging for my throat and vocal chords. Far better would be for her to train me to do the work myself, to teach me how to use my vocal chords, rather than allow her to do it all for me. The two of us should be working together as a team.

On hearing this, it was an easy step for me to see that this what exactly what Maria had been trying to do with me for a long time. To some extent she was succeeding, but I had a strong preconceived idea, that I was supposed to let her do all of it if I could. So every time I had channelled her, the further in she managed to come, the better I thought I had done it. Had she stopped coming in as much as she sometimes does, I might have been too disheartened to continue, for it was those moments of her very strong presence that kept me interested.

Maria probably knew this, and had deliberately withheld herself many times in order to keep my throat in good order. I knew she did this, and had often wondered why. I thought that either proper channelling took too much of her energy, or she thought it used too much of mine. Had she explained it to me as Story Teller now did, I would not have believed her, but thought I had heard wrongly, or that she was losing interest in working with me. I needed to get this information from a third party.

She also told me that Maria was a sorceress. I did not know what that meant, or even if it was a bad or a good thing. So when I returned home, I consulted the dictionary to find out. I learnt from that, that a sorceress was a wizard well versed in the magic arts. I perceived that in itself, sorcery was neither a good nor an evil thing. Like any other sort of power, it would depend on how it was used. This explained to me why so much good could be achieved with her help, which I presently would be unable to manage without her. The important thing was to keep it all on a loving vibration.

Story Teller told me that it was very important that I dictate exactly how close Maria, or any other eager entity that wanted to communicate through me was allowed to come. I suppose I did not need to point out how Maria had always shown me great respect, never trying to force her way into my body against my wishes.

Certainly she had always been accustomed to having centre stage during her lifetime, but although shadows of that former personality still remained, she had made it very clear to me on a number of occasions that she was changing. She was very consciously working for the good of others in this special way with me. However, I knew that when leading seminars, it was necessary to make sure that the participants had the chance to sing and be part of it as well. Otherwise, as Maria had already told me, they would not develop.

Story Teller made a very important point for my concept of what my life might be about just now, when she said that although Maria might be the first, she is certainly not the last one for me to channel. In her words, "Maria is not the end, but just the beginning for you." This statement made a deep impression on me. It left me feeling I should do more work on Maria's book, and that perhaps this was the time to bring it to its conclusion. Her story would never be finished, so if I waited for it to end, the book would never be finished either.

The necessity to use discretion, and know with whom I was dealing when channelling, is something I had heard others say, but perhaps it was time now for me to learn to do this. It made sense, as if I could learn not to channel too fully those with vibrations or energy that was incompatible with my own, then the physical vehicle would last for longer, in which case I could be of service in this way for a greater length of time.

That evening, as we sat around the fire in Joan's paddock, she led some toning, which gave me the perfect opportunity to practice what Story Teller had told me. So I did my best to make sure that it was me who governed how far Maria could come into my body. When dealing with an entity as respectful as Maria, the control was very easy. The harder task was discerning how much control to use. In other words, knowing how far in to invite her for the best results, and when to listen to her guidance concerning how to do things myself.

It was part of my good fortune that Story Teller was present that evening, so the following day she gave me some feedback. She said that the sound was much smoother, and she considered it far less jarring to my physical body. I agreed with her that it had felt much more comfortable, and I thought that the tone of it was rounder and softer. She told me that working this way together would be very helpful to me, and the effect on Maria would be that I would soften her a little, which would be good for her. That, I think, was going to take place anyhow, regardless of whether or not I learnt to discriminate more myself, just because we were in contact with each other. She, in her turn I had observed, was having a wonderful influence on my level of confidence.

The Portal

It is clear to me that Maria is very interested and involved with the transmutation of our planet. Therefore, it is appropriate here to explain a little about it. I speak of the 2003 August 12th Portal, that being the day when it would peak. I would have known nothing about it, had I not been with Joan.

She first told me that something exciting was going to happen a year beforehand. I had just participated in Chris James's seminar in 2002, which he co-led with Joan, and allowed myself a short holiday on the Big Island before going home. It was then that Joan invited me to spend some time with her on the Ranch. There was a special meditation, which she wanted us to do together. The ETs had instructed her to choose me for this, rather than anyone else. Maybe this was because they knew I was comfortable with them. The purpose was to look at what was going to happen on August 12th 2003, when it was expected that energetically, we would be passing through a portal. Joan explained to me how portals such as this one open every twenty years. Planet Earth has four biorhythm cycles which peak simultaneously once every twenty years. This has occurred on August 12, 1943, 1963 and 1983 and would again on August 12, 2003. Sky Ranch is a particularly good location for it, because in Joan's words,

"Sky Ranch is located on the slopes of the world's most massive and tallest single mountain, Mauna Kea, 35,000 feet high, when measured from its base far beneath the ocean surface. The latitude of the Ranch is at 19.5 degrees north. This relates to the geometric energy form, the Star Tetrahedron (also known as " Merkabah", implanted within the Earth.) This super-imposed Star Tetrahedron action produces a huge upwelling of energy at 19.5 degrees on most, if not all planets in this solar system. It is our geometric transportation vehicle to the stars as we move into the next evolutionary stage — from Duality to Complementarity, which is the geometric form of the dodecahedron. This powerful field of energy at Sky Ranch amplified our contacts with extraterrestrial civilizations."

Although some of these technicalities were beyond my comprehension, as we continued to talk about it, I sensed that the centre of its location would be somewhere very close to Joan's house. When the time came, this turned out to be true, for it was actually on her land. The day for this preview of it was 29.07.2002, which adds up to 22. My age at that time was 56, which makes 11. Both of these numbers are considered to be special numbers in Hawaii. Then we discovered that Joan's birth date contained the same numerology as mine, except that the numbers came in different places. So I would surmise that it makes it relatively easy for us to work together on the same wavelengths, thus creating harmony.

One of the reasons for this preview of events to come was to help us start getting accustomed to the changing energies. These new energies would be of a higher frequency. Joan told me of her plan to hold a two-week intensive ET workshop covering the time in which the portal would peak. I had seen it advertised in her seminar schedule, but decided it was not one I was interested in. I felt it would require a longer visit to Hawaii than I wished to make, and that my energy would never last for the full two weeks. This latter supposition was based on my memory of finding her one week long intensive in which I had participated in 2001 very demanding. I must, however, point out that it had brought me great spiritual rewards, and most exciting of all, was the occasion Maria had picked to sing through me for the first time.

Had Joan merely asked me if I would come and participate, I would have declined on the grounds of insufficient time and energy. Whereas when she requested I came and helped with it in return for a free place, as I was unable to avoid knowing that it was where I was meant to be, I agreed without hesitation. Only later did considerable doubts concerning my ability to cope with this task start to enter my mind, but by then I was committed. I have no regrets I accepted. It turned out to be wonderful.

The Meditation with Joan, 29/7/02

I did not expect Maria to make an appearance during this, even though the two of us were already acquainted. In this account of what happened, I wrote the events down in the order I remembered them, which may not be the exact order in which it all happened.

Maria came. She showed me a picture of her spiritual mentor, who, someone told me afterwards, may well be working along the same lines as the Hathor, or even have been one of them when incarnated. He was dressed in white, and portrayed himself wearing a very tall hat, rather like the one I had seen worn by the high priest in the opera "*Aida*".

This helped reinforce what she had already told me a year previously about wanting to bring heavenly music to the Earth for the benefit of mankind. No wonder one of the group had commented on this possible link to the Hathor, when I had channelled her sound one day during the seminar on the boat.

During this meditation, Joan was playing a chant called, "Kadosh, kadosh, kadosh". Maria chose to sing a beautiful descant to it, high above the notes of the melody, but in her own dimension, so that I could lie there in silence listening to her. When I shared these things with Joan afterwards, we realised that Maria having a mentor, such as she had shown me, would provide the stability that she had sometimes lacked in her previous incarnation.

In the meditation, there were dolphins around me as I became aware of seeing the portal high above me. In it was portrayed the symbol of an open eye, which Jean-Luc told me later often meant a gateway. In this case, it was a gateway to other frequencies, those of higher dimensions than the ones in which most of us currently existed. One could think of it as a gateway to the dimensional shift of the Earth. Clearly visible was a spaceship with quite a number of ETs spilling out of it onto our planet. I realised later that they were coming to work on Earth to help prepare both people and planet for the vibrational shift.

On either side of the portal entrance, I saw Joan and I positioned like ambassadors, with Joan on the right and me on the left. Joan's group members were passing between the two of us into the Light of the portal. It was as though we were holding the portal open, or in some way guiding them through it.

There was more, but this is all that related to the portal and Maria's future involvement. I never comprehended her intention to assist with it at the time, because I still had no real understanding of why she wanted to sing through me, or what exactly all this was in aid of. Telling me about heavenly music was just a theory to me then, not something I deeply believed. Secondly, I had little understanding of how such a thing could help.

PReparation for the Portal

Everything we did in this Portal Seminar was part of the preparation, even just being there in the energy field. The meditation and work with Joan in the group on August 10th 2003, was aimed to help us clear our energy fields of limitations and restrictions, and anything else that would not be useful for us to keep.

First of all, I tuned in to see what needed to be worked on in my case. I saw a very strong post stuck in some solid rock. I was tethered to this post by a thick piece of rope. I could see myself running around in circles attempting to get away from it, but always held back by the rope attached to the post. The more I struggled, the more the rope got twisted around the post, and the less freedom I had. When I tried to work out what this meant for me, I was not sure to begin with, if I should stay still and be centred beside the post, or be set free from it in some way. After some reflection, I felt I should become centred and stable in myself where I was, but free to run around, or move away from this post when I wanted to, like leaving the mother ship, and going out into the ocean.

During the meditation that followed, having first met my guides, I learnt that I was tethered to one place in my mind, because each time I had left the family home with my parents in it, something seemed to go wrong for me. For example persecution by other people, being left out, feeling unaccepted, unneeded and unwanted, along with the consequent feelings of insecurity, whereas I felt safe in the family home, and then later safe in my own house. I could see how I even felt safer in the ocean if I was not too far out, unless I was swimming from a boat when it did not bother me. Therefore I had developed this deep psychological belief that "Things always go wrong if I am away from the post", (which represents home and security). Of course I felt tethered to it! While all these insights were falling into place, I could see that the rope was weakening and fraying in the middle, until it broke. Then it was repeatedly shown to me how the chain around my waist to which the rope had been tied, was falling apart, and literally disintegrating. Finally, the post came out of the rock, withered and completely disintegrated, disappearing from my sight as it did so. I was free! I could venture forth when and where I liked, and return to my starting point when it suited me. Just watching these pictures passing before my inner eye was enough to work the magic.

I communicate with the ETs on my own.

The climax of the seminar was to be the evening ceremony of August 12th around the fire. This was to be our chance to go through the portal. It seemed more than likely that this would involve staying awake into the small hours, and I seriously doubted my ability to manage that. I had been finding the necessary self-discipline to get myself up early in the mornings to do the things I needed to do for myself, but was experiencing increasing difficulty as the days went by in staying awake for the evening sessions. Yet this was the reason for the whole seminar, being there physically present, and preferably awake to enter the portal at the right time. I felt distressed about it.

It was already the morning of 12th. I stood close to the fire, (which I had declined to enjoy the previous evening, due to my strong desire for bed,) warming myself, as the smouldering bed of ashes was still giving out heat. I wondered if the portal was still by the fire, the latest venue it had moved to, as Joan had been dowsing it the previous day. My body started to sway gently, as I concluded I was definitely in the best spot. Closing my eyes, I saw the connecting shaft of light, as I put the question out to the ETs, "Do you only work here at night, or do you come here in the daytime as well?" "We come when ever you like", they replied.

I began to perceive them around me in the whole of the clearing. They were moving about on the grass, installing their own energies and Light connections into the ground. This was part of the plan. I could see that it was extremely beneficial for most of us to spend as much time in their energy field as possible, so that we became more and more comfortable there, and familiar with it. This would be helpful preparation for mixing with them both in and out of the body, regardless of whether it was on or off one of their ships. In any case, I felt I belonged up there, just as much as down here.

Bringing their ships down to ground level, albeit still in another dimension, was a way of helping us to get to know and trust them, something that would be very necessary for our well being in days to come. It was another way of assisting us to overcome any fears or reservations we might have about going on one of their ships. If we were already in one of these ships, at the same time as sitting comfortably on a chair or the ground on planet Earth, then what on earth was there to be afraid of? It was a normal and comfortable thing to do. The question, "Am I brave enough to enter a ship?" would barely arise. Only one's intention as related to the deepest wishes of the soul would count. All would be smooth and perfect.

Meanwhile, I pondered yet again over my problem of staying awake in the evenings. Would it matter if I went to bed on this very special occasion of Portal night? Should my physical body still be up and out there adding my support to the group throughout the whole event? Thus supporting everything we had been working for? Would my absence be letting Joan down, as I had agreed to come out to Hawaii to offer her my help? Could I perhaps go to bed, and then the following morning ask the group if any of them had spotted me on a ship as part of the ET welcoming party? It was not such an unreasonable thought for someone who knows that she is currently living several parallel lives as an ET.

I saw pictures of myself helping the group to find their way onto a ship, leading them by the hand in keeping with their wishes, all this in my out-of-the-body state. I might not even be aware of it with my human mind. They would feel comfortable with me, because they knew me. Whether or not anyone would enter a ship physically was not revealed to me. I did not need to know, for what would be would be, and it was not for me to change things in this instance.

These thoughts gave me some peace of mind, as it seemed that if it was necessary for me to go to bed early, the ETs would understand, no matter what others thought, and I could just follow my inner guidance.

We enter the Portal.

It is worth pointing out, that as I experienced things, I entered the Portal by a gradual process during almost the whole of the time I was on the island. However, it definitely did have a climax. To my huge relief, it happened not late at night, while I was sleeping in my tent, but in the morning! It was an answer to my prayers! The ETs had heard me, and the Universe is so kind!

This is the story of the events that led up to it.

I went down from my tent to join the group as they were completing their breakfast, and noticed that Celeste, who had just arrived from her house, was clearly very distressed. There were a number of people round her, and she was tearful. In passing, I heard her saying something about blood and her darling little dog, the 14-year-old Babaji. I did not manage to get the whole story just then, but when the group met a few minutes later, Joan made the announcement that Celeste had something to tell us all.

Briefly recounted, it seemed that when she had woken in the morning, she had found blood all over the place in her house. It came from Babaji.

Every time he sneezed, it came pouring out of his nose. She feared for his life, and took him to the vet, who diagnosed cancer. Celeste has great spiritual maturity, and was completely ready to release him from this incarnation, if he chose to leave now. She was willing to support him in whatever decision he chose to make about life or death. She told us that he was not yet sure himself what exactly he wanted to do.

She left him with the vet, who had heavily sedated him, so that he would not move about and start sneezing, thus loosing more blood. The quantity of blood she had had to clean up in her home was great, and cleaning it up must have been a process that was both physically and emotionally exhausting, especially coming, as it did, on top of her very demanding schedule.

This story, which I have so far only told in part, recounted with such bravery, honesty and sincerity moved us all, leaving barely a dry eye in the room. Later, one of the men shared with us that he never normally cried, but this time he too had wet eyes, and it had opened his heart.

Thus was the room filled with emotions of love, compassion and empathy. Joan was silently receiving a message from the ETs, "Go through the Portal now!" (It was still morning, and I was wide-awake. Oh what joy!)

Next, Joan asked me if Maria could sing the note of top "A". I was able to give her an affirmative without hesitation, confident that we could go even higher than that together if necessary. So I stood up in front of the group to channel Maria's sounds. Personally, I had no idea at what point exactly we arrived at top A, having started to warm and loosen my vocal chords at a noticeably lower pitch, but Joan wrote afterwards,

"Since our DNA has ET origins, it is best activated by Sound. People are able to hear the sound of Creation within. This DNA activation is facilitated by the note of "High A" and by absorbing this frequency into the physical and subtle bodies. Our dear friend from England was here to sing us this note. Helena, a channel for famed opera soprano, Maria Callas, sang the Portal and sang our bodies. When she hit the note of "A" we all ascended into higher frequencies. Holding this vibration allowed

us to accelerate our frequencies quickly and safely. We entered the Portal of the 5th dimension and connected to the highest Beings of Light."

Following this, Joan played a CD with *Amazing Grace* on it, and Maria was happy to sing along to it with the rest of the group. She seemed to enjoy doing this, and with her ability to reach the higher notes, her voice rang out clearly. She and I were working together, so it was not perfect, but without her, I could not have sung it so freely.

When all was silent again preceding the Portal meditation led by Joan, I became very aware of another energy shift, which the singing had brought about. The sound had lifted the already present love vibration upwards. Babaji's story, followed by the music, had put us into the perfect state to enter and open further the Portal. We accessed and anchored fourth and fifth dimensional energy into the Earth. The veils between dimensions were thinner. All was more accessible. The ETs had helped greatly, and nothing on Earth would ever be quite the same for us again.

More About Babaji

The man, who never normally allowed himself to cry, was not the only person to react this way for the first time. After the seminar was complete, I heard from Celeste that she had asked someone else's group to send healing to Babaji. Many of them cried when they heard the story, including another man, who, as his heart opened, was moved to unaccustomed tears. What a service this little dog had undertaken! There was more. Celeste channelled that she felt he was losing the blood for humanity. It represented releasing the old, and making way for the new. Babaji needed his blood like the rest of us, but, it seems to me, chose to communicate a very important point to us by this means.

This is more than a theory, for during the silent meditation that morning, I felt something inside my mouth. I gently inserted a finger to find out what it was, and located a small blood blister. To my surprise, just this lightest of touches was enough to cause it to break, and for such a small blister, an amazingly large quantity of blood began to pour out into my mouth. Usually the skin over such a thing is tough and hard to break, so

248

that even with lots of pressure they do not break. I swallowed the blood from time to time until it stopped.

I was not alone. Another member of the group had had a very small injury on the underside of her foot, which bled profusely all over the bathroom floor that morning. It became clear that Babaji had really bled for all of us. Personally, in the time following this seminar, not only did I let go of some of my old behaviour patterns and opinions, in fact even the way I think; but frequently found the desire to discard material things in my house that I considered to be no longer useful to me, such as old clothes I never wear, and any other "clutter" I could find.

Celeste had two dogs. The second one, Nickea, was really upset finding himself alone, Babaji having gone to the vet. So healing was sent to him as well. Celeste told us how well he responded when we sent healing to him later in the day. He stopped fretting, as his confusion left him, and was at peace again. By now, the whole group, organised by Joan, had sent healing twice, the second time being late afternoon and including Nickea.

The big question in my mind was "What would happen to Babaji? Would he live, or was this his time to leave us?" To most of us, it appeared he would have no option but to go. The strength that he received from the healing we sent him, combined with his own will to survive was amazing. When Joan and I saw him alive and much better at Celeste's house shortly before I left the island, we could barely believe our eyes. During the healing we had pictured him whole, happy, and healthy, asking that he be assisted to stay or leave this dimension in keeping with his own wishes. His eyes were so bright, as he came to greet us at the door of Celeste's house. This was only four days after he nearly bled to death.

The vet made x-rays of him after we had sent our healing, and there was no sign of any cancer in his body anywhere. In fact nothing that could possibly have caused it showed up. So it really did appear, that just as we thought, he had bled for humanity and all that is. Whatever one chooses to believe about his bleeding, there is absolutely no doubt whatsoever, that he really had helped us on our way through that portal. So did Maria in her fashion. I cannot forget that either. Thank you Maria and Babaji.

Sperm Whales

The seminar was to last until 15th August, so we had a few days left together to assimilate and consolidate the changes, which doubtless would continue to affect and work on us for days after our departure from the Ranch if we were open to that. Personally, I feel that it changed my vibrational rate for the better, and that it prepared me for other changes that might follow in my life.

When we went out in the boats on 13th, the sperm whales helped us. Joan was so keen that this should happen, that she had even hired an aeroplane to spot them from the sky, so that the pilot could tell our boat captains in which direction to take the boats. Time passed, and none were to be found

I thought about how hard I would have taken it, were I in Joan's situation after putting so much effort into organising a wonderful experience, when it did not seem to materialise at all, but I only heard one person complain that she would have liked to have seen sperm whales. Of course, I had longed to see them, but had felt surprisingly unbothered about their failure to show up for us.

The boat captains and Joan did their best to keep us happy, and give us a lovely day, by stopping the boats, and letting us swim and play in the water with each other for hours. There were many blessings. Perhaps the biggest one I was aware of at the time was the beautiful calm ocean. We were in deep water, and knew to expect big waves out there. Yet it was so still, and where we stopped, there was a gorgeous current of warm water. Although I felt slightly seasick by the time we arrived there, this eventually went away, and then I was able to enjoy myself like everybody else. It seemed so strange that instead of returning with long faces as a truly disappointed group, because we had not seen the sperm whales, everyone appeared to be feeling bright and cheerful.

This mystery was to be solved for me later, when I spoke to Celeste. She had heard from a fisherman, that seven sperm whales had been viewed surfacing on exactly the spot where we had stopped the boats to play in the ocean shortly after we had left. Whereas I had observed nothing beyond the fact that I felt happy in that location, Celeste had felt these whales working on us, even though she could not see where they were.

250

Now we understood that they must have been resting on the ocean floor, invisible to our eyes in the very deep blue water, when we were swimming about merrily on the surface. Of course we felt happy! Who would not in the energy field of a sperm whale? As Celeste shared this story with me later in her house, talking about it gave her goose bumps all over. I knew it was true. Had they surfaced for us, and especially if they had started moving about, then most probably only a few of us would have been allowed into the water at a time for just a few minutes each. Although their energy field would have been detectable for those waiting their turn on the boats, the encounter might well have been brief. By staying still, and undetected by most of us for so long beneath us, they were able to have all of us close to them in the water for ages. This realisation explained to me why Joan and I had been so confident that they would be there.

Maria helps Douglas

It was my last full day on the island, and to my great delight, Joan and I were able to spend some time together. She arrived in her car, and drove me to the local health food store, where we enjoyed a smoothie and a chat together.

Joan had never seen Maria when she was singing, so I had brought a DVD of her, which we planned to look at up at her ranch. Eventually, we came to the conclusion that just like videos, English ones do not work in the States. As there was still plenty of time left, before I needed to return to Celeste's house, chatting together, we spoke about Maria amongst other things. Jean-Luc was there as well, for he had been helping us understand why we could not watch my DVD. In the course of this conversation, we began to wonder if Douglas would like a private session with Maria. She had already made it clear to me, that she would be interested in working with him, when she sang to the group in sections around the portal, the first time I channelled her during the seminar. Jean-Luc made the necessary telephone call, and in due course Douglas drove up Joan's driveway, delighted to make the best of this offer.

During one of my conversations with Story Teller, I had offered to channel Maria for her, but she declined to accept, because she said she did not want too many healers at once. (She was having some physical problems). I would have felt sad that she did not wish to accept the gift I was offering her in return for what she was doing for me, had she not gone on to say, "…but if you would give that to someone else for us, that would please us very much." "Us" is how she referred to the twelve beings incarnated in her body, so I understood immediately, that by "us" she meant all twelve of them. She added that someone would come to me asking for help, and that would be my opportunity to give. I had waited, and almost reached the point of thinking that no one was coming, but then on my last day, here was Douglas ready and waiting for it.

While I had been waiting for him to arrive, I had walked up the slope in the direction of the tents we had used during the seminar, and Maria had indicated exactly where she would like to be channelled, so I had placed two chairs there in readiness. Joan and Jean-Luc had both wondered if Maria would speak to him, so although I preferred to channel her sound standing, I thought that the chairs would be helpful when she spoke.

Following my inner guidance, I decided to start with sounds. I liked this idea, because I felt it would give me the chance to get myself into the right space for any spoken words that might follow.

Douglas stood up as requested in between the two well spaced out chairs, leaving plenty of room for Maria to move around him if she wished. I had difficulty getting started due to congestion in my throat. Each time I tried, I found myself standing there coughing and constantly trying to clear it. I paused to reassure Douglas that this did happen sometimes, but it often cleared, which in this case it eventually did. After the session he told me that this was a normal problem amongst singers, and I understand that it was probably nerves, as I was really anxious that this should go well for him.

The first notes that came out were really my own voice, but Maria was there guiding me to keep the pitch low until the coughing had stopped, and my vocal chords were warmed up. Then she came into me more to guide and influence the sounds. All the while, I kept the advice of Story Teller in my mind, so that this experience would be gentle for my physical body.

It seemed a curious thing to me that the sounds not only started low, but also seemed to remain low for longer than I would have expected. I wondered if perhaps men needed a lower pitch than women do, but on reflection, that was illogical, as she had sung plenty of high notes for Richard in France. I later concluded that it might have had something to do with the needs that Maria could see of my own chakras. Perhaps it was necessary that some of the sounds should loosen those up first, in order for what followed to be good, but it is also possible these low notes were needed by Douglas as well. Certainly, Maria was directing them towards his lower chakras.

When Maria felt the time was right, she took the sound upwards. I could hear it echoing back to us from the trees. The strongest echo came from the higher land uphill from where we were standing. Her sounds concluded with a remarkably deep note directed below Douglas's feet. At first I thought a sound so low could not be produced by my vocal chords, but on the second attempt, it came out well.

Following this, still on our feet facing each other, I was expecting Maria to speak through me, but that is not what happened. Instead, another voice said, "Be seated my friend!" to Douglas, where upon we both sat down. This other voice, which portrayed none of Maria's personality, said various things I had not expected to hear. There was the occasional "I" in the dialogue, but mostly it was "we", "for there are several of us", as it said. Another phrase was "Douglas, if we may call you that?" Douglas gave his consent. The messages from this voice were spiritual and simple in nature. I experienced them as being full of truth and purity, which was more or less how Douglas summed it up later.

On completion of this spoken message, my voice dropped in pitch, as Maria returned for a few words. She did not issue any additional advice for Douglas, but wanted to acknowledge those concerned for making this opening possible, and Douglas for being a willing recipient. Finally, she announced her wish to embrace him physically, while still in my body, so Douglas obliged her, and then, at her request, went on to assist her to find the chair behind her, and sit down. Almost immediately she was seated, she withdrew.

Before we left the hillside, Douglas gave me some feedback. He told me that during the sounds, he had seen pictures of pyramids, and felt something from the opera Aida coming through from Egypt. This was particularly interesting to me, as I recalled someone having told me that Maria's sounds were similar to the healing sounds used by the Egyptian healers in their temples long ago. This fitted in with the picture that Maria had given me of her mentor for this work, the one who was dressed in long white robes and the tall white headdress. (He may even have had some kind of carefully trimmed beard as well. I am not sure.) Douglas picked up a possible connection with a small tribe who lived in the Amazon. They had lived close to nature, and may have used these sounds.

The thing that had impressed him most, however, was the intent, which he said had made the whole difference to the quality and effects of that which came through. I would call it love's healing and truth. When I met Douglas again the following day, as he and Joan drove me to the airport, he told me that he could still feel the effects of the tones working in his body. It appeared to me that Maria had opened up his auric field more, as I perceived that it had expanded. There seemed to be more space within it.

Then the inevitable happened; my stay came to an end as I boarded an aeroplane to start the journey home.

Chapter 24

The Harmonic Concordance

Living in my own little world, as I do, I could so easily have had no idea that this event was going to happen until long afterwards. As it was, Norm Hacker was circulating information of all sorts around the Joan's Portal group, so I waded through pages of astrological analysis of the meaning and implications of it. I was fascinated by a picture of a crop circle, which had appeared in year 2002, predicting what would come.

There seemed to be various different ways of using this special time, but the thing that started me thinking of taking an active part was an email, about using sound to help anchor the energies available then into the Earth, sent to me by Douglas Webster. The first word to come into my head after that was "Maria!" Surely this was exactly what she was good at. I felt her presence close to me, understood why she had been trying to persuade me to start my music practices again, and wondered what I should do about it.

Should I offer to give a seminar in France that weekend? I did not want to go away so soon, but there again, if I had to…. As I pondered over this dilemma concerning how to give Maria the opening she needed to do some good, another idea sprang to mind. Why could not I organise something in my own house with just a few other people? As a complete unknown seminar leader in my own country, and with no ambitions to get advertising underway for it, I thought I stood a better chance of not being alone that night if I just asked friends, and did not demand money for it.

It was so clear to me that in this instance, the most important thing was not to be paid, but to do the work. I wanted to do that more than anything. Alone, I felt sure that I lacked the enthusiasm to take any action in this spiritual happening. I would more likely sit down and watch something on the television, if there was anything on it of interest.

So rather warily, I approached three people, and one of them, Margot, said, "Yes". When I meditated, I saw that just one other incarnate would suffice, so as long as Margot was able to come that night, and thank goodness she did, this spiritual evening I was planning could go ahead. When she accepted my invitation, Maria was clearly delighted. "Well done!" I heard her say. I was happy as well.

It seemed that the planets would be aligned in the sky to form a symmetrical six-pointed star. The astrologers were calling it the November 8th Grand Sextile Lunar eclipse (year 2003), for this configuration coincided with a full eclipse of the moon. Now I learnt from my reading that it was very unusual for these two events to happen at once. In between the years 1000 B.C. and 3000 A.D. there is no other date with this precise configuration. Maybe it has never happened before. It occurred to me that perhaps the stars and planets never repeat their patterns, but that made little difference to my resolve. If this was to be something like another portal opportunity, there was work for us to do. Some were calling the "Grand Sextile Star of David". Whereas I quickly forgot what that meant, the name had great appeal to me. I liked the sound of it.

So I began my music practices in earnest. I wanted to get my vocal chords stronger again, so that my voice would last more than five minutes, and be a suitable instrument for Maria to use, or guide. I had been suffering from quite a lot of congestion, and was finding it hard to sing. So I asked Patrick Kempe to help my throat with his healing powers, which he did, and the voice grew stronger. After breakfast was the best time. Chewing helped loosen my mouth up. As I only eat a little, I was not too full of food to sing afterwards, with the added advantage of doing it before filling my lungs with dust from the stables. Maria was present on these occasions, advising me on what and how to sing it, which I found most helpful.

I became very focused on other aspects of this. Things like cleaning the room we would use, how to make it look nice, and how to give Margot a pleasant and interesting evening.

It was just a week away, when I managed to strain something in my right hip. It did not take much working out that this meant I was not very confident about taking this next step, namely initiating an event myself, instead of waiting for someone else to ask me. Furthermore I was doubting my ability to make a success of it. Part of me was very enthusiastic, while the other part was wishing that this were not happening. In view of the physical pain I was in, it seemed unwise to allow myself even the one hike a week I had been enjoying since mid-September. I thought hiking would make things much worse, and I could not enjoy it if my hip was hurting so much.

Finally the confinement to my house became too much for me. I set off up a medium sized fairly straightforward hill one evening. I was so uncomfortable that when the shooting pains went through me, my right leg could not take my weight at all, and I would loose my balance badly, though I never actually fell. Not a person to give in easily, I continued to limp my way up the hillside. Then I noticed something interesting. The further I went, the less pain I had. By the time I returned about two hours later, I was mostly pain free and moving well.

For this reason, I gave my horse two days of rest after that, so that I could walk more to help the ligament or muscle heal. It must have stretched during an over-enthusiastic yoga session I had given myself, and the walking was helping it to return to the proper length and be comfortable. I tend to forget that my body is less elastic than it was at nineteen. An advantage I did not see in this therapy until afterwards was how it kept me away from the stable dust that irritated my throat, and made it so much harder to sing.

Saturday, 8th

As the time drew nearer, I reflected on how much energy I had already invested in my preparations, and how bitterly disappointed I would be if Margot were unable to come. Therefore I was glad when Margot telephoned at 6.30pm to confirm the time of our meeting. She arrived early. I was not quite ready for her, but her premature arrival time was a healthy reflection of her enthusiasm.

I took her into the room where our activities were destined to take place, and showed her my pack of Angel Cards. I invited her to choose one for the evening, while I finished getting myself ready. By the time I reappeared, Margot had already picked four cards. Now what really intrigued me was the discovery that the first one she had drawn was "Guardian Angel". I had found one for myself twenty-four hours in advance. My card was "Guardian Angel". This could hardly be a coincidence. It seemed to me that our angels and guides wanted us to know that we were receiving their full support with our spiritual endeavours, and it was a very good omen with which to start the evening. After we had cleaned each other's auric fields with sage smoke, I began to see and sense how many other beings were present in the room with us. Margot had brought her own lovely spiritual energies, along with her angelic guides. Mine were present also, and together they made the atmosphere feel so pure.

We started the evening with a little trance dancing, and then sang OM to continue setting the good vibrations in my little room. I was silent for a moment or two, and then commenced the toning, at first accompanied by Margot, who had already informed me that her voice was not likely to be very strong that night So I was not surprised when she stopped quite a while before I did. I knew that her presence and good intentions would suffice as well as anything, and was thankful for this.

Maria was working on the portal energies. I watched as it opened wider and wider in the centre of the room like a column of Light from higher dimensions running down into the Earth, just as I had hoped it would. The angels were still around us, and Maria's voice seemed to be strengthening and fuelling everything to happen in the right direction. She was very effective. The work was being done. I was pleased.

Towards the end of it, it occurred to me that the volume in such a small room might not be very comfortable for Margot's ears, so I stepped further away from her. When I inquired afterwards how it had been, she said, "Well it was not as bad as the sage." Not being over fond of the smell of sage myself, I was naturally sympathetic.

258

After this, Margot and I sat silently in meditation. I was still very much in an active organising mood, and found it very hard to sit still without making a sound, instead of rushing ahead with whatever I thought we should do next. Unable to relax enough to use my intuition about when to stop, I kept and eye on my watch, and forced myself to stay there for a full fifteen minutes.

Margot led a very hectic life, and I thought she would really enjoy this pause with its stillness in the evening. The time was not wasted for me. I looked at the portal, and reflected on Margot's supportive energy, and how lucky I was to have her there.

I could feel so much tension in my body that I decided to ask my guides to help me release it. Two angels moved in closer to me, and began to do some intricate work on my upper spine and shoulders. They were working with their fingers around each individual vertebra. I was fascinated! The tightness left me, and I felt much better afterwards. (The following day, it occurred to me that had I included a suggestion from Patrick concerning what we could do together, Margot and I would have taken turns to massage each other's neck and shoulders before starting, and then the angels would not have had to work so hard. I just hoped that Margot had not had the same problem.)

As instructed by the angels and Maria, I asked Margot's permission to channel the spoken word for her, as well as whether or not she was open to allowing Maria to tone her chakras. Margot said "Yes" to both. We danced a little more to another of Enya's music tracks. Then I sat down opposite Margot, and began.

I do not remember the content of the channelled messages from the discarnate beings, but one seemed to be speaking for several of them. The vibration of this communication gave me a feeling of quietness and sincerity. As my vocal chords were already partially spent, I had been sucking a throat lozenge throughout, which did not seem to get in the way of the channelling, but on finishing that, I had to crunch what was left of it quickly, because I did not think Maria and I could sing together very well if I was still sucking it and swallowing dissolved lozenge in between her notes.

In my opinion, this toning went as well as I could hope for. Margot stood still in the centre of the room while Maria and I moved around her. We both sat down at the end of it, and I was not surprised when Maria wanted to say a few words. While she was talking, I was shown Margot's auric field. Although I had not seen it at the beginning, it was clear that the combination of the portal and Maria's sounds had changed it.

Without a doubt mine had altered as well, but I could not see my own just then. I remember Maria having difficulty finding the right descriptive words, as she sat there surveying it. I knew that Margot had made a positive shift with her vibrations, and it was as if any blocks or stuck areas had been loosened. What she would do with the changes was a question of free will for her. Either way, she had chosen to come to my house and experience these things. As for me, there is probably much to say, if I knew what it was!

Knowing what kind of thing Maria often says at the end of these sessions to people, I found myself wondering if maybe I knew the drill so well, that she was not really there at all, and I was doing it for her like an act. Maria, quick to notice my doubting mind, had her own remedy for that, which was very effective.

She reached out with one of my hands for an ornamental red rose that I had laid on the nearby table top to complement the beauty of the six real roses I had bought to honour her presence, and she told Margot, (as well as I can remember it) that she wanted to give her a present. "Now I am sure Helena won't mind if I give you this, so I would like you to come over here and receive it from me." She held it in my cupped hands in front of me for Margot, who duly arrived and took it respectfully from her.

I, meanwhile, could hardly believe what was happening. Maria was calmly giving away the little red rose, made of soap with plastic petals, which I had treasured for about fourteen or fifteen years, without so much as a "by your leave"! She was, nonetheless, quite right. I did not mind, and was delighted for Margot to have it. She made the situation quite clear, as she instructed Margot that this was a present for her from Maria Callas, adding that of course, she just called herself Maria now, for although she still retained some of that identity, she had released much of it. (Some time after this, I discovered that in her lifetime, she had differentiated between "Maria", the woman and "La Callas", the artist and performer.)

Margot was then asked to lay the rose down on the table, and then come back a second time to Maria, when she received a kiss on the forehead before Maria withdrew. Margot and I decided it was time to go and sit comfortably in the other room to enjoy a cup of tea and a chat.

As we sat there, I was still close to incredulous, as I surveyed Margot lovingly cradling that rose in her hands. Had this really happened? Just giving my rose away like that, when it was not hers to give? Truly it was bound to cause me less inconvenience than if she had given away my house while I was in trance, or worse still my horse, but what a nerve this woman has! As we sat there, I passed on a little more from her to Margot. "My goodness Margot!" I exclaimed, "She really does love you!" as I had felt Maria wanting to embrace her.

So after giving Margot a hug that came jointly from Maria and I to say goodbye, I found I could still barely take it in that she was walking away with my rose in her hands! In fairness to Maria, Margot and myself, I must add that this was the most important event of the whole evening for me, even though it was anchoring the good energies into our Earth that was supposed to matter most. You see, this very clever move on Maria's part was the one thing that left me in no doubt what so ever, that Maria really had come, and I was not deluding myself when I thought I was channelling her. Therefore I thank Maria from the depths of my heart for this little piece of evidence. I certainly would never want Margot to think she had to give her present back either to me, or worse still to Maria to return to me. Seeing Margot enjoy and appreciate this little gift was more than enough reward for me.

Before I went to bed, I noticed a change in my throat. Something in it had opened up more, and I instinctively knew this was healthy. The tone of some of my lower notes was different.

Following a thoughtful night concerning how could I have done it all better, (not to mention a trip outside into my garden in the middle of the night in the hopes of seeing at least part of the lunar eclipse due at 1.20am, only to observe that there were too many clouds to see more than the occasional star,) I found myself starting to laugh out loud while finishing my breakfast. It was about Maria's behaviour with my rose. I chuckled over this little episode many times during the day, and hoped Margot had enjoyed the funny side of it as well. Maria definitely does not live by the same rules as most of the rest of us!

There was to be a more minor eclipse two weeks later, 23rd November. It was being thought of by some as a follow-up to 8th, and something to mark the completion. I did not know if that was true or not, but did not feel any urge to organise anything this time. However, that evening, I received an email from someone stating, amongst many things, that 23rd was the day of welcome and joy for the ETs. I was alone in my house, but felt moved to go and sing some kind of joyful welcoming song for them as they draw closer to our planet. I had no idea what this might consist of, but called to Maria for help.

I can't have sung for more than five minutes all together at the most, but it was powerful. The sounds were quite different from any of my previous channellings right from the beginning. The usual pronounced vibrato was almost always completely absent. Instead the notes coming through were strong, clear, pure and steady.

One top note faltered, and Maria instructed me to put some of the abundant saliva present in my mouth just then over my vocal chords. (I had just eaten a few dried cranberries). I did as instructed, and it worked like magic. This very high note came out of my throat beautifully, and was easy to sustain for as long as required.

Shortly after that, the pitch descended, as Maria connected with the energies of the earth. She raised them up from deep down below the surface, and offered them with the sound containing them and the movements of her hands to the ETs. I understood that they needed them. Whether that be for analysis, or to strengthen their connection with us, I was not told. The low sound that carried them grew softer as the earth energy was smoothly transferred to the ETs. I felt that the unusually high note had some way of making a strong connection with them, possibly as a transport vehicle to help them connect with this communication of sound coming to them from the earth. I do not know which ETS they were, but before I even opened my mouth, I had requested a connection with the "good" ones, as I called them, as well as asking the angels to be present for protection if it was needed, and to assist us.

I had an inner knowing that the work had taken place just as it was meant to. Maria said, "You were not eating cranberries just beforehand for nothing you know!" When I ate them, I did not even know I was about to sing!

The feedback for this that I was so grateful for came from Joan Ocean. I had informed her by email of these events, and she responded this way.
"I am so happy that you and Maria sent out a welcoming vibration to the ET communities. I felt their happiness in my heart to have received your tonal message of Love and Joy."

Chapter 25

Little Gems From Maria

It was mid-November 2003, and my singing was going well. I was finding Maria the most amazing character to work with. Not only was she very clever, but also both strong and persistent. Feeling somewhat insecure with this much power around me, I supposed that one day I might really have to watch that power of hers, as I felt it was very important that I remained the ruler of my life, not someone else, not even a discarnate entity. As I saw it, that was a necessary part of my agreement with her. Of course I did not know if she had read that section of our unwritten contract, and much less if she had agreed to it.

On the plus side, I could see that a less powerful soul might easily have difficulty keeping me interested, and giving me the confidence I needed to keep on working at music and singing. Then there was her know-how and invaluable guidance, although looking back, I can see how I frequently ignored her, because I thought I had heard wrong, or made the directions up with my imagination. When I was sure, I treasured every syllable.

Another advantage was that I could benefit from her tuition without even having to travel anywhere, and I could arrange the practises to suit myself. Not having to pay her any money for her help was another consideration. It occurred to me that if I was to receive tuition from an incarnated being of her calibre, the fees would be astronomical, that is if there is anyone as good as her incarnated today. Furthermore, such a tutor would be most unlikely to want to teach me, a beginner without a voice, as I saw it.

The day after thinking about these "free" lessons, just after I had written in an email to someone, "...aren't I lucky that I do not have to pay Maria for her lessons. That would be well beyond the limits of my purse strings! Oh well, I give to her in other ways." I heard her say to me, "It's all right, my dear. I do not need money now. Those days are past, and I love you anyway." Those words of hers touched me deeply. Knowing she understood how I felt was helpful as well, so I resolved to continue putting my focus into this spiritual work, and trust that the rest would follow.

One day, when I was practising singing along with a CD, trying very hard to improve my technique, Maria, whose presence I had not even been aware of, decided I needed some help. "Put your passion into it!" she said. Before I had had time to get over my surprise to discover she was with me, she jumped into my body without any further warning, and sang a couple of lines of "I know that my Redeemer liveth" for me. I felt her power surging through my veins as my body experienced a liberal covering of goosebumps, the volume and richness of the music at least doubled, and it was full of passion. I had never heard Handel's music sung like this before.

She slipped out again with the same suddenness she had entered. I was so astonished, that I could not continue to sing without talking to her first. "What was that Maria?" I exclaimed emphatically, even though I knew exactly who had done what. There was no reply from her just then. Instead she left me to practise singing with my own passion.

Then I asked her why on earth it mattered, the words and the passion, after all, our work together seemed to consist of healing sounds, not words and passion. She explained how it was important to be in touch with emotions, even for the wordless singing that we do together, because without the emotion of love, the sounds would be like an empty vehicle. My emotion free singing had sounded very dry and uninteresting by comparison. I understood how without feeling, even the potentially most beautiful music becomes meaningless.

It was the fact that she had entered without warning me that contributed to my fear of my life being taken over by her, instead of living it myself in keeping with my proper destiny. Many months were to pass before I really understood how our destinies were interwoven in the best interests of both of us. By that time, not only had my trust of her greatly increased, but also I felt secure enough in myself to lose my fear of this strong woman, and to recognise the great respect she showed me. Furthermore, because she did what she did, I have never forgotten that lesson she gave me on passion by demonstrating with my body like that.

In an email, I wrote to Patrick Kempe about how Maria alternately pushed me onwards, and touched my heart. I told him of the insights I had had after going for a walk, when my energy had all but dried up, how I had listened to her voice on a CD, singing the fast running completely free passages of Bel Canto and coloratura that go on and on, which were that there are more forms of movement to be enjoyed than just walking. If I were to work hard enough to acquire the necessary skill, I would be able to indulge myself in fast moving sound with all the beauty of a mountain stream that flows and tumbles down the mountainside to be enjoyed as well. Physical movement is just one aspect of it. The human voice can enjoy freedom and movement as well.

Another day, when I was talking to someone about my "musical guide", the lady asked me if I knew who it was. I admitted that I knew, gave the year in which Maria died, the fact that she had sung opera in her lifetime, but instead of revealing her full identity, I just said that her name was Maria. Had the questioner's interest taken her far enough to ask me directly, "Maria who?" I would have told her, but I declined volunteering the information.

Maria had something to say about this. While I was driving myself home, I heard her ask me, "What is the matter? Are you ashamed of me or something?" I took this to mean that it was time for me to become more open about her, at least in some situations. The way Maria said it made me laugh. It was as though the words had been half a joke, which helped me remember them, but more importantly, that they carried this deeper meaning about openness.

December arrived. I often start to feel a little low around Christmas time. The days are so short, and the weather does not always oblige me with suitable conditions for riding my horse, or long day-hikes in the mountains. The situation had been further exacerbated by increased difficulties finding my singing voice. I cannot say if it is caused by the winter pollution of the outside atmosphere, the food I have eaten, the central heating in my house, or breathing colder air than is good for me when I go outside. Perhaps even an increase in my caffeine intake in my efforts to keep myself warm dries out my vocal chords in spite of the fact that I restrict myself to weak teas, thus avoiding the strong Indian teas, which are loaded with tannin and caffeine. The only thing I am certain about is that it gets so hard, that some days I can barely sing a note. Nevertheless I want so much to really work at it to strengthen my vocal chords, not to mention the pure enjoyment it brings me when I can sing.

While I was going through all this, not having been able to detect Maria's presence for some time, even though she may have been there, made my spirits sink even lower. Now on the one hand, I have always tried to look at her working with me as a temporary thing in her existence and mine, but on the other hand, it was contemplating the possibility that she might have moved on to greater things, or found someone more suitable to train up instead, so that I would lose the pleasure of her company, friendship, support, and assistance altogether, which left me feeling so sad. I had not forgotten how the previous winter she had stayed with me, even when I had worse problems vocally, and had helped me find the right piano, but I was so unsure about it all. If she was gone, then I needed a replacement. I realised that I was less self-sufficient than I thought.

To help keep my spirits up, I had bought myself some pretty flowers with which to decorate my house. Those and my Christmas cards would make it a bright and cheery place to be over Christmas I felt. The flowers were also a way of loving myself, and making things as good for me as I could. Then, just as I was sitting in my favourite chair downstairs at home thinking about nothing in particular, I caught sight of Maria on the far side of the room looking at my flowers. I knew she loved flowers. "Yes, they are nice, aren't they?" I said to her telepathically. Relief filled me. My good friend was still there.

About three weeks after I had bought those flowers, Maria caught my attention again. She inquired whether or not I might care to throw them away now. I crossed the room to have a look and see if she was right. "Yes, they are rather dead, aren't they", I responded, having not noticed this before, and duly discarded them.

One day, when I was listening to a CD with Renee Fleming as the soprano, I wondered if Maria might be thinking it was like a betrayal to give so much attention to someone else's skills instead of hers. Would she be jealous? "No" was very definitely the answer. She kindly showed herself a little distance away from me displaying love and support for me. Several others stood close to her for the same reason, but she was the one closest to me. I remembered the time when she her told me that she wanted me to hear someone else's interpretation of "Casta Diva", and it was Renee Fleming who was singing it on my car radio. I could feel the benefits of listening to Renee, because she puts so much passion into her voice. That is something very close to Maria's heart, for it makes the music real. It comes alive, giving the words a meaning, not just a sound. Emotions are as important as the words and the notes.

These last two little events made me aware of something I had not realised. I had become very attached to Maria. I decided to re-evaluate the nature of this working friendship, and received some interesting insights about it. I had always known that whereas I loved her very dearly, it was not in the way one might love a man. There was the teacher pupil aspect of it, the sisterly friendship, the working partnership, and now I saw something else. She was serving me in a way my mother never had. Maria believed in me. She knew that I had something which made me worthwhile working with. Therefore she was able to enhance my self-confidence and esteem.

My mother, on the other hand, was more concerned in making sure that I never over-estimated my abilities, which, I had the impression, often seemed to be almost none-existent to her. Unwittingly, she had contributed enormously to my lack of confidence and self-belief. I remembered how when I first realised that this was what my mother had done, I had felt anger towards her. It seemed she had lied to me, even if not deliberately. Actually, she had only spoken her truth, for she was a very honest woman of great integrity. Now I could understand why she had been how she was. She thought very little of herself. How could she possibly have passed on to me qualities that did not exist in her? One cannot teach something one knows nothing about personally. Realising this, I could only feel compassion for her, not wrath.

Maria had had the opposite experience. Once her mother had realised she might become a great singer, she believed in her daughter's talents sufficiently to direct huge quantities of her energy into making it all happen. Combined with the strength of Maria herself, this produced a daughter full of determination, and before her voice left her, much more than a normal amount of confidence and courage. Therefore Maria could play a motherly role, and pass these positive qualities on to me, because she had them to give.

I found myself accepting these treasures, and taking them into my heart. I needed this support from another being, and at the moment it was coming from Maria. It was a blessing I could give thanks for.

Singing For Joan

This little "gem", I have added here like an afterthought. It is too good not to put it somewhere. So skipping on through time to 5th. October 04, here is the story.

After having resolved that I was definitely not going to sing for anyone or anything today, because I was too tired, suddenly I knew I was about to sing for Joan. I walked into the room to do it, and as I entered, I rather lost my balance, almost falling backwards. It was as though Maria, already in my body had forgotten I never wear high-heeled shoes. Therefore her balance was not adjusted for walking in just a pair of socks! Without any heels, she had toppled slightly backwards. That was how I experienced it, but actually it is most likely another clever little move of hers to convince me she was there, and about to sing. The voice was strong and rich, and when I checked the pitch of a note I could clearly remember, it turned out to be Joan's favourite top A.

Chapter 26

Maria in Hawaii, January 2004

In January 2004, I answered the call of my heart by joining another of Joan's seminars, this one entitled "*Sky Ranch with Star Beings*".

When I left home, my throat was already in a rough state, and flying through Chicago seemed to irritate it further. Therefore had Joan asked me to channel Maria, it would have been very hard, and maybe even damaging to my vocal chords.

Therefore it was not surprising that although Maria was staying very close to me, I did not even attempt to sing to myself, never mind to anyone else, before 29th, four days into the seminar. However, something interesting happened earlier in the day, when Joan led a meditation in which we were to see who our Guides were.

My Guides

I suppose that I should not have been surprised, when Maria came forward as my closest guide at that time. It seemed that she was always there, as I viewed her with a hand on my left shoulder. Her form looked denser than the other guides who followed, which indicated to me that she was the closest of them to this physical reality. I felt that this gave her certain advantages, both in communication with me, and how she could view my life and surroundings.

Next in line was the Archangel Gabriel. The name was given to me so clearly, that I could not doubt it. I felt that other angels working for "The Order of Gabriel" were probably involved as well.

Budamus came next, but I cannot be sure that I have spelt the name of this Ascended Master correctly, as Joan's postcard on which it was written had mysteriously disappeared in the course of the workshop. I recognised him instantly, as I had seen her picture of him before it went missing. I also remember that he worked with sound, and that there was a strong connection to Saint Frances of Assisi with him.

Then there was Elisabeth. I might have drawn this conclusion with my mind, as I already knew that she had helped me from time to time with my horse.

Another possibility, which may have come from my mind, was that there are others, who I would describe as specialists, because each would come forward to assist when I required their particular skill. (Elisabeth belongs to this category.) These guides would not be with me all the time, and may well offer their services to many of us. Maybe the angels call them over to whoever is in need of them most.

There were angels around me, whose function was to step in and help anytime I was in danger, or some life-threatening situation, and it was not my time to go. This was easy to accept, as I had sometimes had real evidence of this, as have many other people in their lives.

Joan instructed us to ask our guides for a message. Mine was clear, short and simple, namely "Trust and wait!"

I channelled Maria's Sounds at last!

It was another fine evening, so we were able to sit outside around the fire to make our contact with the ETs. Following the more intense part of that meditation, many of us went to bed. For once, I was not one of them. My energy levels felt good, and I was still quite wide-awake, so I decided to stay longer just in case something interesting happened with a space ship. Gradually more people got up and left for a good night's sleep.

Those remaining did not appear to be in a deep meditational state, so thinking maybe this was the right moment for it, I asked Joan and those present, if they would like me to channel Maria. Many of them had heard her before, but some had not. No one objected, and as some were clearly keen to hear her, I went ahead. It went well. Most interesting to me was the feedback that came to me from those present, especially Sandi, although she only shared a little of what she had seen and sensed there and then. Later in two emails after my return home, she gave me a lot more. So moving forward in time to life after my return from Hawaii, the following account is what I eventually managed to type into my computer.

10/2/04. Although still experiencing a large amount of jet lag, I felt inspired to write to Sandi to inquire about what she had seen, felt or heard about Maria that night in Hawaii when I had channelled her by the fire, and Sandi had not had the time to tell me the whole story. Her reply interested me greatly. She wrote:

"The violet aura, as you know, indicates the highest level of spiritual achievement in the colour spectrum, just under white. So I guess you could say that Maria has done her homework, and done it well! The feelings I got as I watched her descend into your space were those of helpfulness, joy, participation, and most of all that she felt comfortable coming into our conjoined energy fields. Her toning had a definite purpose. It energised everything. Sound is the basis of everything; it creates, expands, and heals. So I think that she helped us all by toning. I think that Maria is in the next stage of evolution, where as she turns around and helps you/us, then she gets to go to the head of her class, just as we get to the head of our class here on Earth as we do the Light work we're here to do. I don't know what specific notes she sang that night, perhaps you do, but I do know that each note corresponds to certain colour/chakra centres, and sets the vibration spin. My guess is that she upped all our spins in our chakras that night.

I had to laugh when she was singing, because it made me feel giddy, which is a very good thing. I noticed Norm laughing too. I guess you could say we were really enjoying her. Her energy signature is quite different from yours...what I mean is that to me everyone's energy field has a different feeling, a different vibration, a different hum, so as I sit here and write to you, I can feel hers...it's very loving, and high pitched.

At the time that night, I could not make out her entire facial features, only the outline of her head and body. When she pulled away after the toning, I saw her stand behind you for a minute or so, and then the colour shape evaporated. It did not go up or back or anything else, it just evaporated. I see things all the time, but some things to me are just wonderful, and that was one of them."

Sandi's curiosity had also led her to look Maria up on the web. She already knew Maria's shape, but was quite stunned to see the extent of her physical beauty. She felt she had been led to do this, by Maria, I would surmise.

After I had read Sandi's email, I was so moved by these words, that they took me to a space where I almost cried, as Maria held me lovingly in her arms. I felt bathed in Maria's love.

I wrote back to Sandi to thank her, filling her in with a few more details, although unable to tell her which notes had been sung precisely. She came back to me with more information, which was of great interest to me, and confirmed several things I had suspected, or been told about by Maria.

Sandi wrote,

"We layer upward and outward. The different octaves in each note equate to the different bodies within the chakra itself. For example: each of the twelve chakras has an etheric, emotional, mental, and astral, etheric template, celestial and ketheric body.

The base chakra resonates to the note C.
The sacral chakra resonates to the note D.
The solar plexus chakra resonates to the note E.
The heart chakra resonates to the note F.
The throat chakra resonates to the note G.
The brow or third eye chakra resonates to the note A.
The crown chakra resonates to the note B.

By the way, Maria had me spend an hour looking all this stuff up. I had to be very exact. I remember reading all this years ago, but I had to find it all again for you. I had a lot of fun doing it!

So it makes good sense that she wants you to expand your ranges; it's very healing for you and the rest of us. If a note comes out unclean, it would be my guess that there is not a clear vibration at that level of the chakra associated with the note. Getting the note clear would be getting that area of the chakra clear as well."

Maria on the Boat

The morning after channelling Maria by the fire, we went out on the boat. The ocean was quiet, and Joan decided that we should tone together during our meditation. Full of confidence, after she had been so well received the previous evening, and knowing that my throat was really healed, I had no hesitation in inviting Maria to come through. No doubt Joan had warned the captain that there was an opera singer on board!

It seemed to me that her voice was stronger, and the tone was better and smoother. The sound rang out freely. Afterwards, I asked one of the people standing next to me if her ears were still all right, or had the volume been too much for them. I was relieved to be informed that all was well. Joan, singing strongly, had been standing on my other side. It seems that when one is outside without walls to hold the sound in, there is less risk of any audience finding it too much, and yet all can benefit to the changes in vibration that it brings about in both the atmosphere and people's bodies.

Then the captain came down from the bridge, and jokingly told me that the sound had made the glasses start to shake upstairs, and I would have to pay damages if they broke. After some joyful banter between us, he finished by saying, "Just keep doing it!" He was happy, and I was delighted both with the singing, and how it had been received. I had really enjoyed myself.

Later in the week, I told Joan how bad my throat had been when I first arrived on the island. She responded that although she did not know why, intuitively she had felt she should not ask me to sing. I, for my part, had supposed that this was strictly an ET workshop, and that therefore Maria was not appropriate, so I should forget about the possibility of channelling her. However, it had been mystifying me that she was always so close to me, even though I was not singing. Discovering first that she really was one of my guides, and then feeling that the time was right to let her through that evening by the fire, helped explain my situation to me.

Maria and "Amazing Grace"

I never really wanted to sing Amazing Grace when I first heard it, but it kept on coming up at various seminars, until eventually I more or less knew the tune. By this time, I had noticed that Maria thought more of it than I did, having sung along with it once before in one of Joan's workshops. As Joan had her said afterwards how nice it was that someone could get the top notes in it, I had begun to come round to the idea.

It was the closing morning of the seminar. Maria was very close to me. I began to wonder if I dared hope that I would get a last chance to sing with her for Joan's group. After all, she was present and ready. It is not my style to ask, so I remained silent, and hoped. Then one member of the group said something about Amazing Grace, so I thought that maybe Joan would invite us all to sing along to it. She put the C.D. on with the volume fairly low just for us to listen to. It went through my mind that with the volume so very low, it would be really hard to sing along with, as even my pianissimo would be loud enough to drown it. Then I saw Lisa make a sign to Joan to increase the volume. Joan obliged. When it finished, someone asked if she would play it again, so that we could sing along to it.

Permission was granted, and as it was now loud enough, I asked Maria to help me, because I knew that when she helped, the tonal qualities of my voice, the freedom and range of notes available to me are all greatly enhanced, and therefore it would give more pleasure both to the group and myself, than if I sang it without her, which would have been very hard anyway. I explained to Maria that I did not want us to sing like the soloist, but more as part of a choir, knowing that Maria's voice can always be heard and enjoyed above everyone else's voices, even when she sings her pianissimo.

It worked beautifully. I did not concern myself with the words, but chose to focus solely on sound quality and the notes. Once or twice I heard comments from Maria, such as "Remember to take a quick breath here", and "This is really easy for us, because it fits so comfortably within our register." I felt that the practise we had had at home together had given me enormous new confidence. Thanks to Maria, I knew exactly what to do with my throat for the slightly higher notes, how to change it when the pitch dropped down again, as I enjoyed the freedom and richer rounder tonal qualities that I hear when she participates. I was so grateful. Her close presence gave me goosebumps, thus further enhancing my confidence.

Afterwards, I received lovely feedback on our performance from a thankful group.

Following that, at someone's request, we sang OM. The pitch for this was always low and grounding. Maria helped me with the sound quality, pitch, and tone of these lower notes.

When we shared in the group at the end of all this, more aware than ever of the way in which Maria helps set up opportunities for us to work together, I light-heartedly referred to "The Maria Conspiracy". It seemed to be acquiring an increasingly large number of members. There was Joan, Marguerite in France, the various members of the group who had just helped bring about the right conditions for Maria to sing Amazing Grace, and many others. So much was being done for me. Maria was able to inspire those who were receptive to her, so that these wonderful opportunities for us to sing and benefit all present would arise.

Singing Practises

After the seminar was complete, I stayed on at the ranch for another six nights to give myself a little holiday, and time for any further spiritual experiences that came my way. Sometimes I would walk up the little slope behind Joan's house, and hoping to be far enough away from everyone else to avoid causing a disturbance, I would practise singing, or channelling. The first time, on 1st February, I sang along with a few arias using my Walkman CD player.

When I returned to the house, Jean-Luc, who had heard me, thanked me for the singing. He said it was beautiful, and very good and healing for the land, which he loved so much. He felt that as Maria's voice was so strong and piercing, it was not very good for people close by, although they could be helped by it, if it were done in a big enough space. He said people were not always comfortable with it.

He then passed on something that Alexia had channelled to him. She felt that it could be used to help heal both the land, and to deal with viruses, such as mad cow disease, which she said was everywhere now. There would be many viruses coming to us, which other types of medicine would not be able to deal with. This, I consider to be a daring statement, one which only time will confirm or not. Either way, I was grateful to hear it.

The next day, I decided to tone to the land and the animals from the same spot. I did not stand close to the three donkeys in the paddock, because if they wanted to, they could come closer, and they would hear it anyway. Maria was present helping me a lot. Some very high notes came out. I cannot say how high, but certainly the highest possible for me at the time. When Maria thought we had done enough high notes for my throat, we continued using a lower register. When I wondered if we could sing some pretty little passages up and down to finish off, Maria said, "No. We cannot combine that sort of singing and this at the same time."

So I continued with the healing sounds, just as Maria wanted. She guided me with great precision, which included some animal sounds, as well as some really deep notes.

I returned down the slope, and met Jean-Luc again. He told me how, on hearing the sound, a horse on the neighbouring property had galloped up the hill to get closer to it

Meditation with Joan

It was my last day on the island. As the flight out of Kona was fairly late in the evening, there was still time to enjoy a few things as well as pack my cases before I left. Therefore I was delighted when Joan expressed the desire to make time to talk to me, and then asked me if we could meditate together in my favourite location on the slope behind her house.

As I understood it, I was asked because when the two of us get together, the energy is often much stronger than when we are alone, and Joan really needed to know a few things. Before we started, I asked her what exactly she needed answers for, and did my best to pick up any insights on it that might just help back-up or enhance the direct communication she was receiving herself.

As I was expecting the whole thing to be something to help Joan, I was really surprised when, having received as much as I could get for her, out of the blue, Maria turned up. She had a message for me. Here it is.

"I came in with fire to put people in touch with their emotions." "Now, when they know how they feel, and see more clearly, I want to focus full blast on the healing aspects. I would love to work with Joan and others to bring in ET vibrations through my sounds. Put us in nature."

You (Helena) are not doing nothing in between seminars. WE, I and others, are training you to assist with sound. This aspect will become stronger and stronger. You are not an organiser, but a very strong member of the planetary team (of Light-Workers), far stronger and more influential than you can ever realise at this moment. Do not let money bother you. It could become a restriction if you let it. Feel free to follow your heart wherever it takes you. I pledge to be with you when we can help. Our love link to each other of which you are increasingly conscious, is the quality that holds us together for our purpose, enabling us to play our part in planetary evolvement. Thank you."

During this transmission, I was picking up that Joan's energy field was such that it helped Maria to come, and I was sensing that even before this incarnation as Maria Callas, she had had strong ET connections.

Chapter 27

At Home After Hawaii

It was 9th February, the day after my return from Hawaii. I had collected two new videos of Maria from a shop in Chester, and was sitting down to watch one of them. I studied the expressions on Maria's face, along with her amazing ability to act and express emotion. One of the arias clearly expressed something more joyful than many, but as I studied the smile on her face, I felt that I could detect more than this behind the smile. "I wonder what she was really feeling?" I asked myself. "Pain and pleasure, both at once", came the reply from Maria, who I had not realised was watching it with me. On hearing these words, I realised that I was able to perceive what exactly her real emotions had been, for she was communicating with me on more than one level.

13/2/04

I was watching one of my new videos again. Part of it showed her performance of the second act of Tosca at Covent Garden on 9/2/64. I experienced this production of it as even more powerful than the previous one I had seen with Maria. I felt it was some of the best and most convincing acting I had ever known from anybody at any time in my life. I wondered what she must have been through in her personal life in order to both understand and then portray and live for others emotions of such intensity on stage. Maria, who was watching this video with me, replied, "I felt as though I was burning in my own fire. Sometimes, I just did not know how to get out of it."

I reflected on how much courage it must have taken to agree to this incarnation of hers. For she must have known beforehand how it would be. I also saw the riches it would bring to the soul living it, on account of the enormous depth of understanding of the human condition gained from it, which could later be used to empathise with others, and to help them. As I write these words, she says, "Yes. You are right. I am able to give great comfort."

After watching this just the once, I not only reflected on how draining giving such a performance must have been for her, but also how in watching it, I felt I had lived some of it with her, for I too felt very depleted, and that one viewing of something so strong was plenty for one night. When I watched it a second time, about a week later, I was less swept away by the emotions expressed, and totally entranced by the skill and focus necessary to perform it.

On another evening, when I was listening and watching her sing "Una voce poco fa", in which she flirts a little in the presence of her lover, observing the mischievous expressions on her face, I reflected on how she had not always been totally open and straight during her lifetime, if any of the accounts about her are to be believed. Therefore how could I trust her totally when she was working with me now? Maybe she still had this subtle streak in her that would make our partnership more complicated than I wanted.

She answered me. "If I had not had these traits in my character, I would not have been able to express them on stage. You have some of this as well, even though you are mostly unaware of it, because you were brought up not to live and express such things. You need to look at this, and allow the expression of it to come out. This is why I would like you to sing more of these arias. It is therapy for you, not just to train your vocal chords."

I looked at her clairvoyantly. Could I honestly say that I trusted her one hundred percent? No, maybe ninety percent, but not more than that. I told her that I would love to be able to trust her totally, hold her hand, and kiss her on the cheek, and really be there without my doubts and occasional mistrust. She seemed to accept this honest communication from me.

The next morning, she told me that her love flows much more freely than it ever did during her lifetime. She said, "I am much less selfish, which is easier now, as I am no longer focused on an earthly career of personal fame, therefore I am able to look at other possibilities, such as how best to use my talents to work with you and others for the common good. No longer "at war" with certain fractions of humanity, or myself, the door to love opens wider." I could see all this in pictures as she spoke, and her light looked expansive and beautiful.

I do not know if she sings through others, but I am aware that she inspires others to help support our work together. This is not manipulation, for all of us can resist if we choose, and the "others" receive gifts from her automatically, as a consequence of their participation.

Early March

I was busy in my kitchen preparing myself something to eat, and thinking about Maria. It still seemed so strange to me that someone who had dressed so beautifully, and was so sophisticated, should be taking an interest in me, dressed as I was, informally in "comfortable clothes", and no make-up. Maria, I understand, had usually worn lots of it. Also, as far as I knew she had never rambled all day in the mountains with her hair flying in all directions, or ridden horses, or pottered about caring for a garden, or lived a life even slightly like mine.

Maria was listening to my thoughts as usual, and regarding the sophistication issue, she said to me, "But I have not forgotten that there was a time before that." To illustrate her point, she projected an image of her former self onto my person. So I experienced her before she dieted dressed in non-descript clothes, which hung badly on her, when she was still very solid and overweight. I felt that body which she no longer has sticking out on all sides of me. I was like a slender nymph inside it! Maria says I should add the word "beautiful", so that this reads, "like a beautiful slender nymph".

A White Poodle

On March 15th, I was just about to get into my car to go and ride Starlight, when I spotted Gordon on the other side of the road with a small white poodle on the end of a lead. I had difficulty believing my eyes. Now I was so sure that Gordon did not own a dog, that I forgot to start with a polite good morning, and began with, "Is that yours?" "Yes", he replied, I have been given it."

I crossed the road and went over to find out more. While we were talking, the poodle, who had been pulling a little on its lead expressing a desire to go somewhere else, suddenly began to take an unexpected interest in me. "Now then! Behave yourself! We are talking to a lady!" Gordon informed it. By now I knew that the poodle was a "he".

Usually when dog owners considerately hold their dogs away from me, I express my gratitude, as I really dislike them being allowed to jump up all over me. For the first time in my life, I reacted differently. "Oh he is so desperate to say hello!" I exclaimed, taking a step forward towards him. I reached down to make a fuss of him, as first one, then both of two very gentle front paws were placed on my leg as he tired to get closer to me.

He was well fed, but as light as a feather. His paws were clean and dry, and the love and affection radiating out from this small creature who had never met me before had to be felt to be believed. The meeting was brief, but it affected me all day. I had never felt a warmth like that coming towards me from a dog, least of all a poodle.

As a child I had heard my mother say what awful dogs poodles were. My grandmother had quite a large black one, which she liked to bring to stay in our house. It would go wild all over my mother's precious garden. My grandmother seemed to have no control over it, as she stood helplessly in the middle of the lawn watching to see how much destruction of the garden would take place.

Naturally as soon as had I set eyes on Gordon's dog, it made me think of Maria, her love for poodles, and the fact that one of hers had been white. "Oh Maria! Where are you?" were my immediate thoughts. I had often wondered why she had been so attracted to such "awful" little dogs.

Before this encounter with Gordon's poodle, I had no idea how loving and gentle they could be, or how wrong I was in my judgement about them. Those few moments completely won me over, and my feelings about poodles have been altered ever since. No wonder Maria loved them so much. When I managed to contact Maria the following day to ask her again where she had been when this happened, she replied, "I was looking down at him through your eyes". She superimposed her image over me, so that I felt this tall person stooping over to watch what was going on in the very place where I had been standing. She showed me the spirits of three of her own poodles, two black, and one white running around us as well.

I had suspected something like that must be the truth, because the little chap being attracted to her loving vibration would totally explain this desperation Gordon's poodle showed to make contact with her through me. I had noticed how I knew exactly how to fondle this poodle in a way he would like. I felt as if I had been handling one all of my life, whereas actually, nothing could be further from the truth! Maria was showing me how. It was a gift of healing to me from her, as it totally healed my relationship with the species we call "poodle".

Five days later, as I was walking home after posting a letter, who should I meet but Gordon. He was alone, so I asked him immediately, "Have you still got the dog?" He gave me an affirmative. In the course of our conversation, I learnt that his name was Jim, and that he was a special breed of poodle, not English, but French. Gordon said he would show me a book about them sometime. I was longing to tell him why I was so interested, but every time I tried, he would start talking about something else so that I had no opportunity. I had to accept that this was an area of my life I could not share with him. I suppose he just thinks I like dogs including poodles.

When I was just a few houses away from my front door, Maria came really close to me so that I was covered in goosebumps. She showed me a picture of her with her white poodle on her lap, as the two of them interacted lovingly with each other. The emotion I could not miss was joy.

Chapter 28

The German Trip I Never Intended To Go On

On 26th December 2003, I wrote to my friend Gila Galitzine in Germany to ask if she had the postal address of an old friend of ours of long ago. Alas she did not, but this served to open some communication between us, which otherwise might never have taken place.

On January 13th, an email from Gila arrived asking me if I would like to join her in April, when she and her husband Michael would be attending an Easter Retreat. Now I read her message in too much hurry, so I understood wrongly that this was going to take place in Cologne somewhere not far from her house. I would be living with them, and we could go together each day. What a kind offer! I was not sure. I felt some attraction to the idea, but there were some things that did not appeal to me.

One of them was that she had mentioned the word "sit". As an exercise fanatic, I dreaded having to sit still all day, with perhaps only a few brief meal breaks for movement, as well as the thought that if there were any time to walk around, it would be in the town with all the traffic fumes. However, she was so enthusiastic about the "enlightened master" she had met who was leading it, that instead of saying no straight away, I wrote back asking for more information about the seminar. Then it might be easier to make my mind up.

Her reply arrived on 23rd January, just after I had left for Hawaii. Therefore I was not able to read it before February. She gave me much more information, but its content still had plusses and minuses. On the good side, there would be time to go swimming in a swimming pool, and walk around in nature, as we only had to sit for two two-hour sessions, and it was to be held in a country location near Kassel. So no surfeit of traffic fumes when out walking. However, it might all be dead flat with muddy tracks, and no trees for shelter, just endless straight lines to walk in. We would stay in the same hotel, and Gila and Michael could drive me to the seminar each day. They would also meet me at the airport in Cologne, take me to their house, and then drive me three or four hours from there to the hotel. The thought of so much driving before and after the seminar did not appeal to me at all, kind as it was of them to offer to take me.

The important thing, I understood, was to apply quickly, as it was getting booked up very fast.

I thought about it all carefully. I was mowing the lawn, and thinking it would not be so bad, if it was only two days instead of four, because I did not want to be away from home for so long for countless reasons. I felt I would not be going in order to benefit from the seminar with no whales, dolphins, or extraterrestrials, but for the pleasure of seeing Michael and Gila, who I had not seen for a number of years. If so, and if we needed a reason to meet other than just enjoying each other's company, then surely a two day seminar would be plenty of time?

This proposed seminar would take six days including the journeys, and not even help refresh or improve my German, because it was to be a silent retreat. Finally there would be nothing in it for Maria, and I wanted to stay at home to write this book about the two of us, or "her" book, as I would often refer to it when speaking amongst friends. Although there had been one positive sign I should go. This was that a training clinic I wanted to attend with my horse at home, which would have been difficult, if I went to Germany, had been postponed, so now it would be possible to fit not only that, but also the seminar in Germany as well into my schedule.

Nonetheless, on balance, I thought it a bad idea to go to Germany, and still mowing my lawn, I said definitively to myself, "I am definitely not going. I will write a nice letter to Gila explaining why not, and tell her to get in touch if ever she would like my company for a shorter event, possibly of only two day's duration." My mind was made up.

"But I would like to go", Maria said to me. I did not know she was listening to my thoughts, but it seems she had waited until she was sure I was not going to go before she intervened. If Maria wanted to go, that put a whole new light on the situation. Maybe I should reconsider. She usually knew in advance of me if something was going to be beneficial to us or not, and had successfully coaxed me into doing things before. Therefore I decided to apply for it.

So on 10th February, I applied for a place. A few days later I heard that my application had arrived too late, as it was already fully booked. I heaved a sigh of relief. I had satisfied my conscience by trying, but as I was wrestling with resentment that Maria seemed to be governing my life instead of me, it was wonderful that I no longer had to decide if I was giving her too much control or not. I thought to myself, that I must be captain of my own ship, even if I need help and guidance regarding which way to steer the ship at times when I cannot see what is best for myself. I was relaxed about life again, and content that I was apparently still in charge of it personally. This dilemma concerning whether or not I should go to Germany had been removed from me. I was so thankful.

I wrote and told Gila my application had failed. Maria stayed silent.

This was not the end of it. On 16th February another email from Gila arrived, which she had named, "Shall I try?" I had already told her that the retreat was fully booked, but I thought to myself, if Maria wants me to be there, with her energy behind it, Gila might even succeed. So I accepted the offer. By now I was less bothered about whether or not I was being controlled against my will by Maria. I found Gila's willingness to try and get me a place on this fully booked seminar a very positive sign that I should be out there. I even inquired at my usual travel agency about flights, but without actually booking anything.

Then there followed telephone calls from Gila, and to cut a long story short, with her help and Michael's, everything was arranged for me. They even lent me the money to pay for all this, as there was a problem with my credit card. Everything was so easy, and because of this, I felt that I was swimming with the current instead of against it. I let go of my resistance concerning the trip, and felt really happy and excited about it all.

When I wrote to Joan Ocean in March, I very briefly referred to my initial resistance to the plan, adding the words, "...but now I am thanking her for it." This was the moment when I recognised for the first time I actually was thankful for her guidance on the matter. Maria was watching what I wrote, and exclaimed, "Thank God for that!" Again, I had not realised she was around.

Joan's reply contained the inspired comment, "Yes. I think Maria is quite a world traveller. She will keep you moving" Joan's feeling about this German trip was clearly a very positive one.

I had not, however, completely got over this issue of not wanting Maria to control my life instead of me. It kept coming up in our interactions. One evening she was suggesting we sang together in my kitchen, where I usually practise. Feeling full of rebellion, I said "No!" After all, why should she tell me when and when not to sing? Surely that was my right, and I intended it to remain so. "I am not telling you what to do. I am offering you something." That put the matter into a whole new light, so I gratefully accepted, and the singing went well.

Another night she demonstrated her patience as she listened to me half-heartedly singing along to one of her CDs while I prepared myself some food. Then, when I decided to sit down and sing for a bit before I ate the meal, Maria asked me, "Are you ready to begin properly now?" I gave her an affirmative and my full attention, as she came closer, and the two of us worked together for a while. It was very helpful to me.

Yet another time, not realising she was around, I thought to myself something like, "Well Maria is not going to be allowed to bully me." "I am not bullying you at all, I only want to help, teach, and guide you as you wish." The next incident occurred when I was with Starlight. As far as I knew, Maria had little interest in horses, and as I was not about to sing, I was under the impression my thoughts were private. "At least I can express my own desire to control another being as appropriate when I am with Starlight, whatever I have to put up with when Maria is there." (It is necessary with an animal the size of Starlight to be the dominant half of the partnership, rather like a good caring parent bringing up a child. Otherwise he could become dangerous, especially a horse with his temperament, kind and talented as he is.) "I am not trying to control you." Maria said gently.

No escape from her, I realised. She seemed to be everywhere. (I have written so many times that I did not realise Maria was close by, or listening to my thoughts, that I would like to explain that unless she actually enters my body so that I feel her, when she is silent, and chooses not to show me herself visually, I forget about the possibility she could be present. Thus I am so frequently taken by surprise when she speaks.)

This latter incident left me thinking about it all day. Much later, sitting in my favourite chair at home, she explained to me that control was not an issue for her now. There was no dominant half to our partnership. It was about working together, and helping each other, a partnership based on our mutual free will. I wondered if I would ever really grasp that and stop fighting her. It was an important lesson for me. She had even told me not to worry about fitting in singing at the moment, because she could see that I needed the time for writing this book, something both of us consider important. She was not putting any pressure on me to work at it. The drive to get it done came from me, and she was there offering all the support that she could.

I remembered how in 2001 in France, when she had asked me to hand the reins over to Marguerite, how much I had disliked giving the control to another, even though I had reluctantly submitted. I reflected how from early childhood, I had been taught to assert my will controlling animals, namely horses. I had learnt that if I could remain in control of them, I would be safe. Accidents took place when I lost my control.

Then there were the people I had encountered throughout my life whom I had somehow failed to prevent from suppressing me in one way or another. I had fought with all the force of my will to escape from that. The very idea that Maria might be going to take my independence away from me again filled me with dread. I could not let that happen. I did not see the truth, namely that it had nothing to do with taking me over. Instead, in my freedom, I was being given a chance to work with this genius, and be guided lovingly, tenderly, wisely and with great understanding by her, a gift that many would have died for. She really is one of my guides, and stays close to me, because I am precious to her. I am truly blessed.

Chapter 29

Miracles In Germany

After an easy flight from Manchester to Cologne on the evening of 7th April 2004, I was met at the airport by Michael and Gila, and had a comfortable night in their house. The next day, Michael drove us to Gut Hubenthal near Kassel in the afternoon. We were staying in a lovely little hotel nearby. Well over a hundred people had come to this Easter silent retreat.

The programme consisted of two "satsangs" each day, and plenty of free time in the afternoons for me to go walking in the forest. A satsang is the word used for our meetings with Samarpan. They took place in a large hall where most of us sat on the floor with cushions or meditation chairs, and Samarpan had his own chair at the front with a guest chair for one of us to sit in while we spoke to him. This would be a time of the day when we had permission to speak, but only to him. There was usually a queue for the guest chair.

Samarpan had studied with Osho, from whom he had received the name Samarpan, and later with Gangaji. They are Advaita teachings. It was in 1995 during a retreat with the latter, that he became enlightened. Gradually I began to see what this curious word "enlightenment" probably meant. It seems to refer to a knowing of the truth, which was definitely high on my list of priorities as something I wanted to find out about.

The first Satsang was on the evening of our arrival. That was also when the silence started. Although I felt tired from the travelling, I thought this might be my best chance to get an audience with Samarpan, and that the queue might get very long as the days progressed, so being an opport-unist, I made my way to the guest chair.

I had a question which had arisen mostly from my resentment of Maria telling me what to do (as I saw it) and not being sure how much control to give her and when. I realised this problem occurred with relationships with other people as well, even though it was mostly her at this time. I made it a general question, as I understood from Gila that this seminar was really about earthly matters and oneself, all very important to me. Therefore, I made no mention of Maria or her whereabouts.

I explained how, as a child, I had felt very controlled by my mother, for example, how later I had rebelled, and fought really hard to prevent anyone thinking they could tell me what to do. Therefore, any attempt at controlling me by anyone seemed so threatening. I did not want to be suppressed again. I told him how this meant that when kind well-meaning advisors attempted to gently guide me in the right direction, they met with such a wall of resistance from me, that although sometimes I would eventually see that the advice was good with the passing of time, it was hard for people to help me.

Samarpan said a number of things about this issue, but there was one line in particular, which stuck in my memory. I knew this was something I had to remember. He said, "Something in you resonates with the advice which is given". I could not see quite what this meant to start with, but after I had left Samarpan, little by little, some of its meaning started to register. I perceived that the angry, sometimes fearful reaction happened because my kind guides and advisors were asking me to face, feel or do something against my wishes. Therefore my interpretation of these situations was invariably inaccurate. On some level, I already knew their advice was good, but I did not want to see it. I felt that Maria would be very glad that I was getting some help with this.

The following day, I went back to Samarpan, because I wanted to share with him the insights his words had given me and thank him.

I was so keen to have an audience with him that I made certain I arrived on the little stool where the next "guest" is asked to wait first. Having thought this was a clever move, I then changed my mind. I had the idea in my head that we were supposed to wait until the musicians, who played every day for us, had finished before making a move towards Samarpan.

So when they started up again, and seemed to be playing endlessly for ages, all through this time I felt I had conspicuously put myself in the "wrong" place.

I started my conversation with Samarpan by explaining how much I had embarrassed myself, as I had been so visible to all in the room sitting up there on the "next guest" stool at a time when I believed it was not acceptable. I told him how I had even tried shutting my eyes, as it helped a little to exclude the reality that so many people could see me sitting there in the wrong place. I had felt miserable.

Now that I had arrived in the chair just beside him, he comfortingly told me that wherever I was, it was always the right place, even if everyone else believed it was the wrong place. He said, "You never have to worry about anybody else. It does not matter what they think. It is going to be some kind of nonsense anyway." This remark lightened the atmosphere, as many of us started to laugh. "Thank you. I will stop hiding then," I replied. Feeling relaxed and comfortable at last, I went on to tell him how, before that, I had been feeling quite pleased with myself, which Samarpan seemed to find hilariously funny, as peals of laughter rang out form him. He inquired what was it I had done which was good.

"Well, I will start with the second thing. I was really enjoying the singing. What gave me such pleasure was this feeling of letting the sound come in through me, and out through the mouth. I felt there was something quite sensitive in the noise that came out. I hoped the musicians did not mind, but I sang the descant, because I enjoy it the most. So that was wonderful!"

This was as close I dared come to saying that Maria had been singing softly through me, improving the quality of the sound, making it flow, and adding the sensitive beauty to it. I still did not know Samarpan very well, so I chose to stay very quiet about the full details of this. He knew nothing about my connections with Maria at this stage, and I thought it likely I would never have the courage to tell him, in case he did not accept that sort of thing. I feel that the dread of both personal rejection, and also of something very close to my heart was a risk I was not ready or confident enough to take with him. These fears are no reflection of

Samarpan, but the result of how my life had conditioned me to think in my past.

"So what was the first thing?"

"The first thing began last night", I started, as I referred to my previous days question about things or people outside me trying to control me. I told him how my understanding of his advice had gradually expanded during the time since he had spoken to me, and how it was my unwillingness to see the truth that made me so cross, when good advice was given to me. Samarpan replied:

"You know, when we are not ready to look at something, then somebody trying to teach us is just horrible. It is disrespectful actually. When we are ready for it, then it is a gift. We are all able to see things with each other, because it is easy. But when the other person is not asking for it or not ready for it, we better keep our mouths shut."

"Then does that explain why sometimes, after a little time has passed, I can accept whatever it is very fully?"

"Yes, that is right…"

"That shines even more light on the situation. Thank you very much! This time I really believe I have (understood) it while I am still here. I don't need until tomorrow night!" (I meant I would not need more time before I could truly accept and take in what he was telling me.)

Both of us were delighted. We discussed things a little further, and then Samarpan said,

"There was one other thing I thought of when we were talking, and that is that when people say something bad about me, it does not hurt unless I agree with them."

"Oh!" I responded in tones of astonishment, for this was a new idea to me. "Well that is even more light on it! Wonderful! Thank you. I was ready for that too." More laughter from all of us filled the room.

At this point, I introduced myself to him as Helena, just in case I wanted to send emails to him in the future. We then agreed that we had both had a nice afternoon, and I went on to the third thing, which was to talk about the silent aspect of this retreat in between the satsangs, and how I enjoyed it, including the revelation that I could sit beside someone at the table, and due to the absence of speech, I could rest, even though I was so close to her physically. However, to balance things a little, I went on to say,

"Just so that I do not portray myself as a complete angel," I paused slightly, and Samarpan said,

"Now we are going to have a confession",

"Right," I continued, "I have had to talk about one or two logistical things",

"Ah… Well logistical things don't count." That comforted me greatly. Thus ended my second conversation with him. It had been lovely.

Maria Comes Through Again

The following day, I did not speak to Samarpan, but it was not uneventful. During the morning singing at the satsang, before Samarpan started to talk, I felt really uninspired. I heard Maria say to me, "Wait until the evening". I waited.

Evening came, but still I had very little voice to sing with, and I was experiencing a lot of difficulty trying to get my tongue round the strange Indian words, even though they were written up in front of us, not to mention the notes and the timing of them. The second song was no easier for me, and I resigned myself to a poor performance. My spirits were rather low. I ceased worrying and thinking about the singing. I just let the situation be as it was.

Suddenly I noticed a change. I began to sing well with amazingly clear annunciation of every word, a strong voice, and good timing. Furthermore, both the accent and the singing voice sounded very Indian. My emotional state which had been so low started to soar up to the heights! I let the obviously channelled sound come freely through me.

294

Afterwards, I asked myself, "Have I acquired an Indian musical guide as well as Maria?" I looked around with my inner eye for such a guide, but saw only Maria, who, laughing happily at my confusion, said, "I thought you would enjoy that!" She appeared delighted with the result.

For a moment or two, I queried how a voice sounding so different to that which I usually channelled could be hers. Then I remembered I had read in a book how, when she had sung opera, she had been capable of using a different voice for every part she sang, and that she was a brilliant mimic. I already knew she could act. Her channelled voice had been strong, although the volume carefully selected so as not to disturb Samarpan's satsang. On reflection, I conceded it did have her tone (one of many she can produce) and her vibration. The most interesting aspect of this was, that she had always left the words entirely up to me before when she had helped me sing. I usually had to remember and pronounce them clearly, while she looked after the quality of the sound.

Going back to the morning session, something else of interest to me was happening with Maria. She was observing the musicians. What really struck her was how much they were enjoying themselves. She had loved music, but it had often been so much hard and serious work. These musicians had fun and laughed at their mistakes. Maria found this wonderful!

I made another observation. The flautist played some very fast and difficult music with joy and playfulness. The higher it went, and the more playful it became, attracted by the music, the larger the number of fairies who entered the room.

Easter Day

I had been wondering for at least twenty-four hours if I should seek Samarpan's help over the lack of a relationship with my sister. Was it just an excuse to sit in the guest chair? Was I merely seeking attention like a needy child? Surely if I wanted to be in that chair, I did not really need a problem to get myself there? Was I just grabbing more than my share of the cake, in which case I could really deal with this problem myself, and maybe it did not really exist anyway? However, it would not go away, and was persistently bothering me, so I decided I had nothing to lose by seeking help.

Then there was my story about the fairies, and Maria's observations concerning the musicians. I was longing to share these things with others, which in the silence of the retreat, I had been unable to do. Furthermore, I felt such a need to be centre stage. How else could I share my gifts and bring laughter to others? Surely it was part of my mission to bring joy to others? I knew this ability was greatly enhanced by Maria's presence, for she was far more gifted than I. My role was just to be me.

So I gave myself the pleasure of speaking to Samarpan again, hearing and learning from his wisdom as I sat in his presence. I began like this.

"Well, although I can give myself many wise answers in my opinion, the situation between myself and my sister still bothers me."

"Sisters are hard."

"Yes" I replied emphatically. "I don't take what she does too personally, because she is the same with my brother, and neither of us have done her any harm."

"OK. So this is the rationalisation, and it does not help anything."

"That's my experience exactly", I confirmed.

"So what do you want from your sister?"

"Well, I would so love to feel it was all peace, harmony and love between us." In Samarpan's face and voice as he said "Yeah", I read something like, "This is totally unrealistic. Come down to earth", although he may have been thinking something quite different. Either way, I was immediately certain that my request was in some sense unreasonable.

"Would you walk down the street, pick any stranger at random, and demand that you feel love, peace and harmony with this person?"

"No. I'm too scared."

"Exactly! But then we have these brothers and sisters, "nest mates". They are strangers actually. I did not choose my brothers and sisters. If the truth be told, I would not choose them. I have one brother that I like. The rest of them…I would not vote for them if they ran for office. I would not choose them for friends. I have better taste than that."

"What am I to do?" I enquired in desperate tones. I am quoting Samarpan's answer in full, not only because there must be so many potential readers out there who will be comforted by this wisdom, but also so that you can understand how Maria, who had had relationship problems within her family, was able to benefit in a healing way, as she was listening to every word Samarpan uttered. He continued,

"Well, it's a hard process letting go of brothers and sisters. I know this very personally. I have one brother, who has been really difficult for me, because I wanted to be close to him, because I had some picture of him that he was something special. Somehow, I wanted him to approve of me. I wanted to be OK to him. He tells me I'm OK, but I don't believe him, because I have some idea of what it would look like if he were really OK with me. If he were really OK with me, then he would not be the way he is, at least not with me. But he is the way he is.

It was funny; I met an old friend of his. I had not known this woman before, and my brother met her while he was studying in Rome. He is a priest you know. This woman and I have developed a friendship. I have not met her in person yet. This was all by email. It was really interesting, because one time, it must have been some intuition, she invited him, "Oh why don't you come and visit?" At the time he was in America. She lives in Germany. She did not know, and I did not know that he was planning a visit to Paris, almost next door.

He wrote to me while he was in Paris, as usual, a superficial letter, you know. I was like, "He was in the neighbourhood, and he did not even let me know he was coming. I would have jumped over to Paris to see him, played a round of golf with him, but he did not want to. He is afraid to be so close to me, I guess. I mean either he is afraid, or he hates me. I don't know, one or the other. I prefer to think he's afraid.

So I had to make peace with him being the way he is. It did not happen immediately. It is a long process. So be gentle with yourself. You have to feel all the feelings."

"Um. Being cut off, and excluded and all this?"

"Exactly."

"And not to feel it is my fault, because it is nothing to do with me. Is that right?"

"Ja. This is what you have to discover in your belly. Doing it in your head does not help, and my agreeing with you does not help either."

"That is interesting, because this is where I feel it". I put my hand on my solar plexus to indicate where I meant.

"Exactly. Just give the attention there. Then the clarity happens. The peace happens. It happens by itself, and it happens in its own time. We can't hurry it up."

"Thank you so much, because I feel that you have completely understood the situation."

"Yes. We can only really understand from inside."

"And I feel that when I have had time to really absorb these few moments with you, and it goes in deeper little by little, that things will change inside me very much for the better."

"Yes, naturally."

"And for this I am very thankful, truly."

"It's my pleasure."

"And then, may I share a couple of things I have been longing to share? Quickly, because there are people behind me?" I enquired cautiously.

There was a queue of participants lined up to speak to Samarpan, who would naturally hope their turn would come to speak to him before the time ran out.

"Whenever people talk about sharing, my alarm bells go off." This I took as a caution not to waste any precious time with unnecessary chatter, but my burning desire to share a little more of myself with this newfound wonderful friend got the better of me. So I ignored that, having made a note of it, and warily continued wondering how much I dare reveal.

"Well... there are two things, and they both relate to your musicians. I would like you and everyone, and especially them to hear it, what I have to say. First of all, I am one of these strange channel people, and the lady whom I channel was with me yesterday."

"What did she have to say?"

"Well, she was watching and listening and observing the musicians, and she probably knows more about music than anyone in this room. She was delighted! She looked in amazement. It was the morning session, and she said, "But these people are having fun!"

By now Samarpan was laughing, which encouraged me to keep going with this risky story.

"And she said, "In my lifetime I loved music very dearly, but as a professional it was so hard and intense and serious!" and when she saw some of your people laughing at their mistakes, it was like a healing balm for her."

"Yes."

Next, with my courage still rising, I ventured to recount the fairy story I had witnessed on Easter Day. When I had got to the bit where I said,

"And this brought the fairies into the room", Samarpan commented in a tone that suggested this was very normal and not at all surprising,

"Yes. I saw them." Helpless laughter from all filled the room.

"Wonderful!" I exclaimed, and continued, "They were all clustered over there. I thought maybe everyone other than me knew this already, but just in case (this was not so) I thought I must make sure that everyone knows. So thank you for letting me share, and press your alarm bells. In the silence that was tricky. Thank you." More laughter. This I feel was partly due to Maria, whose presence I could feel coming through as I replaced my glasses. She had worn glasses off stage, and knew how to make a joke of it without the need for words. Finally I had finished.

You might well wonder why I was so reticent about sharing Maria and the fairies with Samarpan. It was because someone else had instructed me before I left England even, that his work was not about esoteric matters. It is not. That is true. However, I mistakenly thought that this meant I must not mention anything of this kind. I wrongly assumed that any such material would be rejected, and Maria, the fairies and I would be thrown out of the window at the same time loosely speaking.

I had managed to stay silent about these issues for several days, a great strain for me, but I felt I was hiding behind a mask almost. I was denying myself the right to be fully me. I did not want to seek advice about these treasures of my heart from Samarpan, but just to share the joy of it all, and be fully myself complete with my reality. That it, in other words, "I" would be so well received was a wonderful surprise and relief. What is it after all that separates us from these other realms but our blindness?

Maria could tell you with total honesty, that her world, the dimension where she now bides her time, is just as real as this physical one. The Earth after all, is far more than its physical tangible reality. As all other things we perceive, it is, on all of its dimensional levels, a manifestation of the Divine Source.

Meanwhile, this discussion about brothers and sisters with Samarpan was having a wonderful healing effect on me. The guilt gradually left me. It no longer felt like an area of my life which needed sorting out. There was nothing to sort out, so I let go of it.

During the evening satsang, I did not speak to Samarpan, but it was none the less eventful for me. Maria was with me encouraging me to annunciate the words clearly when I was singing, just as she had the day before. She assisted me personally to some extent, but left space for me to contribute my own effort and learn. I realised that if I made mistakes, which others could hear, it did not matter. I felt I was supporting the music, participating, and trying to feel what Samarpan's musicians were creating. I frequently looked across the room to see what they were doing. I was aware of Samarpan observing this, and maybe noticing how much I tried to tune into and work with his musicians. One of the songs had a higher bit that was pretty. I enjoyed making those sounds.

When the flautist, Nandine, played her virtuoso flute passages again, it brought the fairies back. On this occasion they brought with them some of their own instruments. They had some reddish coloured flute-like things, fairy bells and cymbals. All of their instruments were high pitched. They told me that Samarpan's musicians were providing the base for them as they provided the top notes, thus bringing earthly and fairy music together into a perfect balance. Many of them were dancing to the music, and all of them enjoyed it greatly.

In the corner of the room stood a tall, shining, silver angel holding the Light, just like a guardian for the room.

Easter Monday

This was the last day of the retreat, and we were blessed with two more satsangs from Samarpan. As usual, they were preceded by music and singing, which tended to last about half and hour. Maria was with me as usual, and chose to remind me to move my lips and face more by doing it for me for a few words, and then stepping back to see how well I could manage on my own. I did my best.

Following that, Nandine sang one of her solos, strictly in her own style, as I perceived it. Maria and I were both listening and assessing it all in our own ways. I asked Maria, "I wonder what you would do with that?" "I would bring the house down with it", she replied. I continued, "She has neither your voice, nor your technical knowledge and ability, but she is happy, isn't she? You would not want to change her, would you?"

I was recalling Samarpan telling us how happy he was having fun, when people left him alone to enjoy playing golf badly according to his own set of rules, and how it ruined this fun for him, if someone tried to tell him how to do it better. Being corrected when he did not desire it, he found so very painful, even though he had described it as an "exquisite" pain.

Maria had no doubt been listening to that story as well, and had clearly taken in his message, for she answered my question with, "No. I would not want to change anything. It is far more touching just to enjoy her as she is. This time here with Samarpan has taught me something else. That is to assess music very differently to the manner in which I was trained. It is the energy that comes with the music that counts. Without this energy, it would be like dramatic opera that held and expressed no passion, but was reduced to a mere technical exercise, an empty vehicle that was something for the mind, but nothing for the soul."

So you see, Maria and I were learning our lessons together. It was all happening just as she had wished, when she had told me long ago that she wanted us to walk into the Light together. These experiences brought us so close to one another, as she wept on my right shoulder with emotion. It was the first time she had allowed herself to be so vulnerable with me.

It was at this point that I really started to understand she had been present for each moment of every satsang, whether she had always made me aware of her or not. Furthermore, she came with an open mind, heart and soul. This made perfect sense of what Gila had told me, namely that there are certain lessons, which can only be learnt on this planet. The welcome I was giving her now made my side a comfortable place for her to be, and I for my part was receiving more from her than I had ever dreamed of. It was a truly wonderful exchange of services between us.

By the time I sat down for the music prior to the evening satsang, I thought I was completely satisfied, and that I would not need to talk to Samarpan again. Then I recalled how on impulse, just before I had entered the room, I had bought myself a copy of Samarpan's book. Now the previous day, I had watched with interest, as Samarpan had signed a book for someone else. So I left the room, and came back with my newly purchased treasure and a pen.

The musicians began to play their lovely music, and the time to sing arrived. My greatest fun was singing some harmony, which Maria was probably helping me with, as she told me to really listen. It was not so very high pitched, just a little above the melody, and probably lay somewhere around the middle of my range. Maria told me that this area of my register was lovely, and that I was gifted with it. I knew that the quality of the sound coming through from my mouth had improved in the last few days thanks to her careful tutoring.

My most interesting observation was that Maria was changing. Her need to be seen, heard, and recognised was diminishing. There was so much more humility and trust in her. The whole seminar was such an eye opener for her, not only concerning the nature of music and its energies, but also the amazing insights provided by Samarpan's truths about the human reality, and how it can be experienced.

When I felt it was the right moment, I joined the tail end of a very long queue of people waiting to have a turn with Samarpan. My mind was busy. Would time run out before I reached him? I wondered. A clairvoyant vision was instantly provided, in which I saw Samarpan very clearly signing my book. So I did my best to trust the vision, and waited my turn. My patience was rewarded, as I sat down in the chair next to him. This is how it went.

"You brought a book and a pen! Did you want me to do something with that?" At first I said "No", holding book and pen out of his reach, confident that he would not believe me. Then quickly, just in case I got taken seriously, I said, "Yes please", most emphatically. I handed him the book, and then said slowly, so that he could get it right should he have forgotten whom I was,

"I'm Helena".

"With an "a" or with…?"

"A". I then spelt the whole of it out loud for him.

"Got it", he said.

As he was still busy writing, I realised I was getting more than a signature, and sat in suspense, wondering what he would put. Much to everyone's amusement, when he handed it back, instead of asking my first question, I opened the book as fast as I could to read his words, partly because I was itching to know what he had written, and partly because if there was anything I wanted to talk to him about, I intended to find out while I was still beside him. I read the words silently.

"That is beautiful! Thank you so much!

(I did not read out loud what was written, but so as not to make a mystery of it, the words carefully printed in capitals were, "To my beloved Helena. I am so happy to know you. You fill my heart with joy and laughter", followed by his signature. Little wonder I was so moved and delighted.)

"If it were not against the etiquette here I would give you a hug."
Samarpan laughed warmly. I explained it would be a nice spiritual hug that would keep his wife happy. I looked across at her seated in the front row, and saw a lovely smile on her face. (In spite of the silence, someone had kindly pointed out to me, which lady she was.) By this time, Samarpan had blown me a little kiss, which probably only a few people could see.

With that something wonderful happened on an energetic level. A ball of pure white love came through the air, and landed itself in my heart chakra, the one in the centre of my breast below the throat chakra, but a little higher than my physical heart. It was not too much, but it was a lot, and it filled me. I went on,

"Thank you, thank you, thank you for the little kiss. OK, the next question. I write books. Please may I mention your name, and how I have experienced this satsang?"

"Oh yes please! You can mention it in the whole book. I am not shy."

He was full of humour as usual, and we were laughing. I responded,

"That is very trusting. I will not betray the trust. I will email you the relevant bits that you can read or not read according to your wishes."

"Oh. Fair enough." Then on a more serious note, he said,

"Well, I don't need to approve of anything, because it's your book, and it is your experiences of me you are talking about. I can't sensor that. They are your experiences."

"Well, you see I am not used to dealing with enlightened people. That is why I was a little apprehensive of asking. I knew it would not be a normal reaction, but thank you so much. I must tell you something else." I knew I had to talk about Maria in some way, but declined to give her name. It did not seem wise, as even if Samarpan accepted the truth of it, there were other people present as well. So with Samarpan sitting on my right, and Maria on my left, I handled the matter this way.

"There is this dear sweet lady there, my musical guide", (I pointed upwards to make it clear I was talking about someone in another dimension) "who wants me to thank you on her behalf from her heart. She has learnt so much, not just about how to enjoy music, but about life on this planet that she did not grasp during her own lifetime."

"She is so welcome."

Then out of the blue, Samarpan said, "All the angels are welcome here. They all love to come to satsang."

"Ja! That reminds me! Yesterday I saw a huge beautiful shining angel standing in the corner there where the speakers are, like a guardian for the room and the satsang. I was not going to mention that, but since you brought it up…Um. Thank you so so much!"

"You are so welcome."

"Oh well, I will now take leave of my favourite chair. All good things come to an end, don't they? Thank you."

At one point in one of my conversations with Samarpan, I have a clear memory of saying about Maria and I, "We are both so touched". I think the laughter on the tapes from something else may have drowned the sound of my words, but they were so heartfelt from both of us that I have to write them into this text.

As a footnote, when I started to type in the messages from Maria to Samarpan, I said to her, "Now help me get this right, but we have to stick to the truth, remember?" "But that's a bit of a limitation, isn't it?" she responded. This had me in helpless laughter, as I tried to carry on typing. What she says is so true, but we both know that truth is the only thing of interest to me, unless I am playing of course.

There is something else that I would like to point out. Where I have taken the liberty to describe Samarpan's reactions, or thoughts, this is my interpretation of what was going on. Samarpan might well have described the situation entirely differently, and yet both of us would be telling our truth. The conversations are mostly transcribed from tapes, as this seemed the surest way to avoid any misquotes. There is one thing I cannot transcribe, and that is the entertaining facial expressions and body language of Samarpan, which caused so much laughter; neither can I portray the humorous tones of his voice. He is a born comedian, as well as being a loving, sincere and compassionate man.

Chapter 30

The Effects of the Satsangs

As promptly as possible after the Satsangs, Gila, Michael and I left in Michael's lovely Mercedes for our return trip to Cologne. I was sitting in the back of the car from where I was able to observe Gila trying to find some nice music for us to listen to. As I had two of my own CDs beside me, I decided to pass them over to her in case one or other of them appealed to her. The choice was Verdi's Requiem with Renee Fleming and other soloists, or a double album of Maria singing a selection of arias. Gila chose one of the latter, putting on the collection of Maria's I most wanted to hear myself, although I had not told her which one that was.

I knew that Maria was with us, and I could feel how shaken she was by the experiences and revelations of truth she had submitted herself to during the Satsangs over the previous few days. She did not seem to be sure who or what she was any more. I held her in my arms for a while to comfort her. I felt I understood her emotions perfectly. After all, I had just been through a similar initiation myself, the effects of which were still active in me, and would most probably continue to be for some time. The thing I did not know was that Gila was also sensing Maria's presence in the back of the car. Gila felt her sitting beside me looking as she did in her best and most successful years at the height of her fame. She asked me if Maria had liked car rides, as she was definitely enjoying this one. "Didn't she like being driven around in fast and beautiful cars, Helena?" Well I knew she had appreciated luxury, and always went for the best in everything, but I had to get home before I could check up on this.

I found the last edition of "Paris Match" dated May 1969, which Dany had sent me, and sure enough, when she lived in Paris, she had herself driven around in a marine-blue Mercedes 600. I began to understand how enjoying an old pleasure like being driven in a beautiful fast Mercedes was the best reassurance and comfort she could have at the time for her soul and emotional welfare. It was something familiar, an environment in which she felt secure at a time when she was actually almost in a state of shock.

A huge hunk of her previous reality was no longer the only truth. It was barely her reality, and more like a distant dream, neither good nor bad. Her eyes had just been opened to an area of being strange and new to her, however beautiful it might be. It is likely that all of us needed time in which to let the changes in ourselves gently install themselves more deeply into our souls, until this new reality, this wonderful new level of truth became as familiar as the old beliefs about ourselves and our realities had been.

Speaking for myself, I definitely needed time. Meanwhile, I was riding through life on a "high". It had an almost dreamlike quality about it, slightly bewildering at times, and yet for me so welcome. I knew that an important and much needed step was just beginning. The seeds had been well sown in me by Samarpan.

It was not the drive in Michael's Mercedes that provided me with something familiar and reassuring, but Gila's kindness in allowing me to make myself some porridge exactly as I like it in her kitchen when we arrived at her house!

The following day, Michael had to go back to his job. Heaven only knows how he managed that after the strong experiences all three of us had chosen to partake in over the previous few days. Whereas Gila and I had the time for ourselves up to 4.30pm, when I would have to leave for the airport. Both of us were very tired. At one point, Gila decided to go to bed for a nap, and as I had the feeling a walk in the fresh air was what I needed most, that is what I did. Both of us benefited from our own form of tonic. In betweenwhiles, when we had the energy, we shared the processes and changes we were feeling.

When we were not discussing ourselves, the conversation was centred around Maria. Gila had made the important point the day I arrived in Cologne before the seminar, that there are some things that can only be learnt here on this planet. This was one of the reasons why Maria was with me. I had not realised this before. No wonder she had been so keen to come to Germany with me. So much of Samarpan's truth concerned life as an incarnated being. It seemed to me, that this was showing all of us how life in a body could be better than we had experienced it so far.

Samarpan emphasised many times that we had been "taught wrong" regarding the rights and wrongs of this existence. Seeing it all from an angle new to me opened countless possibilities in how I might be or become. Therefore Maria was not only seeing music from a different viewing point, but also how to live life as a human being. She understood so clearly that with her previous conceptions about who and what Maria Callas was, and how much she knew about everything were being stripped away from her. She was not Maria Callas, but a soul, something separate from the illusions of this earth. Her eyes had been opened wider than ever before. So were mine. I realised she was having difficulty finding her feet in this new situation, and I sought to comfort and support her as much as I could. Sometimes she just needed peace and rest.

When Gila and I were talking about her, Gila asked jokingly, "After all I have done for her, (helping persuade me I ought to be there etc.) do you think she would be willing to help me with my singing as well?" I was slow to grasp Maria's response to this, but saw her laughing. It was a little like a nervous laugh, perhaps because at last we were not quite so serious. "What?" she said, "How many more of you are there down there who want to learn to sing? I thought I had finished my work on the earth! Oh well, I suppose I might be able to inspire your thoughts a bit when you are singing."

She had something to say about Michael as well. "What a lovely kind and cuddly man! How did you find him? I did not know there were men about like that!" She was sizing up the relationship between Michael and Gila. She saw how good it could be. It occurred to me later, that as Michael was a tall man, and not too thin, as a tall woman, she would have felt really comfortable with him, and if she did accidentally gain a pound or two, she could still have managed to feel thin and elegant when she was with him, which she would have loved. Most of all though, it was the beauty of his soul that attracted her.

Then she added that she was so pleased to see Michael and Gila together, so there was no jealousy here, just happiness as she looked at these two lovely people sharing their lives and helping each other.

4.30 pm inevitably arrived, and soon I was wandering around the airport pondering my thoughts. I realised that although I had known for a long time that Maria was not my property, that I had at last reached a state of mind where I could let her go for another incarnation when she felt ready. There were reasons for this change in me. I no longer needed to be the woman who channels Maria Callas in order to gain acceptance, be in demand, or gain recognition from others. It was not only Maria's ideas about who she was which had changed. I was able to think about the words of Story Teller with greater perception.

She had said, "Maria is not the end, but just the beginning for you." When Maria's time to move on to new pastures arrived, my life would not be permanently empty from then on. I felt sure that sooner or later there would be other work for me to do. Who would I get next, I wondered? Would it be another celebrity, one whose past could be verified in books, or someone none of us had heard of, but was nonetheless in need? Maria had brought many gifts to me. What would I learn from the next person? I thought it was inevitable that I would grieve when and if Maria left. It would be just like losing a favourite horse. After all, the longer she stayed, the more I loved her, and she had given me so much healing. I remembered how much I really hoped this book would make people realise how much love she had and still has. Maria told me that was unimportant. Other people did not need to know how much love she had, only she.

I detected enormous changes in Maria. The biggest thing seemed to be that her arrogance, something I was barely aware of before, perhaps because I did not want to see it, had left her. The seminar had been a very humbling experience for her, but a very important part of her preparation for whatever her future held.

During my first full day at home in England, she told me that casting aside the burden of being Maria Callas was an enormous relief. Guilt was leaving her as well. Little by little she began to realise that she had lived the Maria Callas life as well as she could, and that there was no need to regret anything she had done or felt. In time, I hoped she would manage to see how actually she had served humanity wonderfully well, and given herself many jewels she could take with her, if she chose to reincarnate again.

When I thought about her enormous spiritual force, I wondered what she would do next. Having furthered her education regarding the healing possible with sound, which she had learnt in other realms since her death, and now having opened her eyes to a happier more enlightened way to be in human form, having even seen that we have some lovely men down here, what would she chose? Her potential to serve the Light was enormous. Perhaps she would be a man next time. Who knows? The whole subject was fascinating to me.

At Home in England

The first day back at home was a curious time for me. I decided it would be best to forfeit my ride on my lovely horse, as life would be much easier if I got ahead with my other tasks, before returning to my usual routine. Also, I realised that it was more valuable to give myself time away from any other projects I could avoid, just to make assimilation of my inner changes easier.

Half way through the morning, I decided to change the plan again. I felt exhausted and incapable of doing anything well. It may have been barely an hour since I finished a generous breakfast, but I thought I wanted lunch. No, I told myself, this is not hunger; it is simply a way to prevent myself from working. A much better avoidance tactic than over-eating would be to go to bed. In theory, there was no rational explanation for my being both mentally and physically exhausted. Physically I had done very little over the previous twenty-four hours, or so it seemed to me. I eventually understood, that although not jet-lagged, when the soul has so much to take in on so many different levels all at once, other activities have to stop to allow it to happen. So I lay on my bed with my eyes closed, and waited to feel ready to move.

About ninety minutes later, I arose slowly from my bed, and finished the last of the unpacking of my suitcases, before going out. I stopped in a café for a lunchtime snack, and some interesting thoughts arrived. One was that for the first time ever, when I had gone to bed in the middle of the day to rest, in spite of a long jobs list, I felt neither guilt about spending time resting instead of working, nor frustration that other things were not getting done. To me, it reflected the realisation that other people's opinions of my life, and how we should live, no longer counted. Only the truth mattered, and I had been shown another way to exist, which I preferred.

The most striking features for me of this new philosophy of being here as incarnated humans were these. There was the lack of judgement about the things we do or feel. Then there was not trying to "fix" anyone else, because it is none of our business and not actually possible, although when someone asks for help, it may be different. Also living in the present moment as totally and consciously as we could, because otherwise we miss it and have nothing. Above all acceptance of whatever we were going through at the time, no matter what it was, be it love, pain or anything else that comes our way. I could see that this opened the door to the experience of an enormous inner peace, something many of us long for. In fact, I was already feeling a great deal more of that than I was accustomed to, and it felt really good. How blessed I was.

Maria, meanwhile, had become so silent that I began to wonder if she had already left me. I tried to check in with her to see how she was. We connected. She was looking for comfort, help and reassurance, and Pixie, the little white poodle, was there, and telling her exactly what she needed to know. Even as a complete nothing and no one, she was still very, very lovable. Pixie was on her lap, licking her face as lovingly and affectionately as is possible. Fame and special skills are not necessary for a soul to be lovable. Maria was beginning to understand this.

The other poodles she had had seemed to be much more distant from her, in fact I even wondered if one or two of them had left to reincarnate. Pixie was staying really close to her. Pixie's love and obvious affection for her was so touching. Some animals seem to possess a level of spirituality that goes far beyond that which they are considered by many to be capable of. Perhaps due to being less busy with technology, complicated thoughts, and money, their access to it is easier. Who knows? I just suppose it.

As I lay in the bath that night, Maria chose to make me aware of her presence. She was showing me pictures of her in her early life when she was fat, inelegant, badly dressed quite often, and suffering with pimples on her face. I understood that she wanted me to see how she was starting to love and accept herself more and more totally, even at times when in the eyes of the world she had not been so very beautiful, or for that matter, accomplished. I felt this was a really important step in her preparation for whatever she might do next, this loving and forgiving of herself. She added, "I am letting go of my regrets about my past life, so that I can move on." She did not say to what or where. Her passionate desire was to take a huge step forward. I had this too, but I have never possessed her level of passion!

Love and Pain walk Hand in Hand

The next day found me thinking about Maria again. She told me in the morning that there were still one or two more things we had to do together. I assumed she meant before she left. I wondered if she had really said that, or was it just a wish of mine, because I was so used to having her around, and especially over those few days in Germany, when she had been so very close to me. I resolved to be extremely watchful with myself, in case I hung on to her, thus making it harder for her to leave than it should be. Doing anything to retard the progress of another soul was strictly against my principles.

So that evening, I sat in my favourite chair alone, missing her. Only now did I realise how much I really loved her, and how alone I would feel without her. I thought about how long it had been after my beloved horse Wilderness died, before I was capable of really loving another. I had had no control over the duration of my grief, so it was likely I would have a similar experience when Maria left. I decided it was better to feel my grief rather than suppress it, so I allowed my tears to run freely down my face.

I did not call Maria, but her love for me brought her. She seemed to be sitting on the arm of my chair, and gently put her arm around my shoulders. She showed me the ruby ring she liked to wear on her right hand. I knew that that stone represented love, divine love, and passion. It was a way of expressing how much she loved me. Now it was my turn to cry in her arms. She repeated that we had not finished our work together yet, and showed me a snowdrop.

I felt much better about it all thanks to her presence and her comforting love, and hoped that if the snowdrop meant she would leave me in January, although she had not explicitly said that, by then I might be in a state where I could deal with her departure better than if it happened immediately. We had shared so much together, she and I. The idea that she would eventually leave had not come from her, or from me, but from other people.

The story about what happened when the snowdrops next came out took place after the end of this book. It can be summarised in these few words. We grew closer to each other. There was no departure.

Chapter 31

Samarpan and Maria Through Emails

In keeping with my promise to send everything I wrote for the book I was writing to Samarpan, if it was about him or the Satsangs, when each bit was ready, I started to email chapters to him to read if he wished. "Chapter Thirty" was the first to go, and I sent it with this letter.

"Dear Samarpan,
It is not you who has the need to read the material I am about to paste onto the end of this email, but I who need to share it. If there is anything you want to say about it, I will read your words with great gratitude. If not, then all is well as it is.
We met for the first time in Hubenthal last week. It was a truly remarkable experience full of exciting surprises. I am deeply grateful for all that you gave us.
I have not written the chapter about my experiences during the seminar and our conversations yet, although all is recorded in my handwritten notebook. This following chapter, which I am sending to you, has gone straight into my computer. The whole thing was so powerful.
It is good to be so stretched, as through it I may learn.
Thank you!
With love,
Helena"

On 19th April, I received this reply.

"Beloved Helena,
When I read your words, "We met for the first time in Hubenthal last

week", I was somehow shocked. How is it possible that I feel you as a very old and dear friend? It was and is such a joy to meet you.
As I am reading your report about Maria tears are coming to my eyes; I am so touched.
Thank you for sharing this with me.
With all my love,
Samarpan."

It did not take me long to respond. Two days later, I wrote,

"Dear Samarpan,
I was sad to read that you were feeling shocked when you read my words. I feel so much love towards you. Had I your level of awareness and enlightenment, I would have known that you knew me.
Greatly helped by this message you have sent me, how I felt towards you all becomes so much clearer. Even the first time I made it to that chair, when I admitted with honesty that I felt nervous, looking back, I can see that those nerves were tinged with joyous excitement and anticipation of what would follow. I was not disappointed.
The last time we spoke together, I realised that in a different situation, I could have stayed on that chair, and chatted to you as to an old and trusted friend for hours in harmony and happiness. You were gentle and tender with me, each conversation gaining more of my trust.
Before I came to Germany, I had been told that this seminar would not be about other realms, but more about getting in touch with oneself, and I assumed, getting grounded. I knew intuitively that there was work to be done on myself along these lines in order to become a more suitable vessel for my work this time around.
Afterwards, I would be able to serve not only those in other dimensions, but also those incarnated on the Earth more effectively. So I came.
The most pleasant surprise of all, was your acceptance of the fairies and the angel I had seen. Then, you made my beloved friend Maria welcome. Some of my questions were actually about her, but I did not dare tell you at the time whom they concerned, or even that one of my advisors was actually discarnate.
Now your beautiful message has arrived, and I discover that you not only accepted me, but also Maria Callas, and her soul as well. This made me feel so loved and accepted by you. It meant a lot to Maria as well. In her

316

lifetime, some worshiped her, and others disliked her intensely. Even her mother had not accepted her properly until after she became famous. You were such a healing for her. She is blowing you a kiss though the atmosphere. For some reason, she is feeling a little anxious. Perhaps that is part of her personality. I do not know.

She has confirmed that she will not leave me until I am completely ready, and that it will take place at a time when there will be no pain. Someone else helped me see that. How does all this resonate with you?"

(I did not fully see that my interpretation of Maria's words about leaving me was still coloured by things other people had told me) The letter continued,

"My doubts about her staying have put me in touch with just how much I love her, and given her the chance to demonstrate her love for me, as she successfully sought to comfort me. I have never had a friendship as close as this with a discarnate soul before. I find it very wonderful, and the two of us not only serve each other, but we want to share the fruits of it with humanity to help them as well. We know we want to serve. The first thing seems to be to get this book about her written and published. Then we will see. It is like a bridge across death, from one dimension to another perhaps describes it best. I am blessed to have had such an interesting life, as I watch the story unfold. By the way, in her lifetime, Maria was capable of being a brilliant comedian, and sometimes she gives this gift to me. I do so love to hear laughter.

Have you any insights about all this, which you feel moved to share?

It should never have been necessary for you to wait to gain my trust, but it seems to me that there is this personality of mine, which gets in the way sometimes. Thank you for your part in my awakening, and your patience. I thank you for all from the depth of my heart and soul,

Love Helena

PS. When I was talking to you the last time in Hubenthal, I looked across at your wife, and on her face was one of the most beautiful smiles I have ever seen. My heart went out to her. Please tell her. Thank you.

PPS. Yes, I do believe we have known each other before somewhere, perhaps in some other reality, beloved Samarpan.

Helena."

Received 23/4/04

"*Beloved Helena,*
This was a nice shock when I read that we had only just met. We came together so beautifully and so intimately in such a short time that my poor head is still spinning. What a joyful dance this is!
Yes, I am full of joy to meet Maria through you. I have to confess that I am such an ignorant person that although I have heard the name of Maria Callas, of course, I am not intimately familiar with her work. When I told my wife that I didn't really know Maria when she was in a body, she was shocked. She said Maria Callas was really GREAT. How could this be possible that a person could go through his whole life being so ignorant? For me it is natural and easy. My hearing is not that good and my memory for names is even worse. I hear music and I don't ask the name of the performer. It is the same with films for me. Only recently have I started to notice the names of famous actors and actresses and other performers.
I am also not a fan of opera. I think that this has to do with my limited hearing. I only recognized this limitation recently. This limitation also explains why I have such a difficulty learning languages. With Nandin around I have discovered that it is possible for a human being to hear with much greater width and depth than is possible with me.
Anyway, Maria is welcomed by me as a beautiful person, not because she was famous or talented in her last lifetime. And I love Maria because you love Maria, and she loves you. It is the love that attracts me.
Yes, I see that you are blessed to have her with you. Enjoy each moment totally, because everything in this world passes and we can't hold on to anything or to anybody. Yes, I see the book as a beautiful way to celebrate your life with Maria.
Yes, laughter is a great healer. Papaji said that when one is laughing, there is no mind.
My wife, Marga, also is touched by you, and sends her love.
With all my love,
Samarpan".

Sent 27th April.

"Dear Samarpan,
Since I read this email from you a few days ago, I have been bathing in
its Light. Thank you.
Yes, I too was astonished at how quickly we came together. To think that
we only spoke briefly four times, and yet this could still happen. I never
anticipated it. IT WAS A WONDERFUL SURPRISE AND GIFT TO ME!
Thank you for being you.
The fact that you love Maria's soul, rather than the identity of Maria
Callas and her previous accomplishments is the perfect gift to her. This is
exactly the kind of love that was missing in her lifetime. On stage, she
reigned supreme, but offstage as a woman she was very unsure of herself,
thus her nervousness when she tentatively asked me to tell you she was
blowing you a kiss. When I later wrote to a friend and put, "Samarpan
loves Maria", she appeared, and heaved an enormous sigh of relief
backed up by her very expressive body language. I could equate with this
feeling so easily, that I started to laugh, and so did she. Perhaps it was
nervous relief. She often makes me laugh. It is one of her gifts. She says,
"Thank him from my heart for this soul healing I am receiving from him."
I can feel that strong passionate spiritual love of hers towards you. You
have really touched her more deeply than words can express. Maybe you
can feel it already.
By the way, I knew almost nothing about opera or Maria, beyond her
name, before the time that she walked into my life so unexpectedly in July
2001. She announced her arrival by singing through me.
Nandin must be a very interesting person. Perhaps one day I will get to
know her a little. I always loved music, but have often had no time for
enjoying it.
Did you know that there is a percussionist who is very famous alive
today, and is completely deaf? She feels the physical vibrations of the
sound in her body, and this is what enables her to play instruments as a
virtuoso. (Evelyn Glennie)
The words you wrote near the end about everything passing in this world
are so poignant for me. I have thought about those frequently in the last
few days. Thank you.
When you write things as profound as that, or other material that I feel
needs to be shared with others, is it all right to pass it on, or are emails,
unlike Satsangs, private and in confidence?

319

I am glad you wrote the line starting "My wife Marga..." because before that, I knew which person your wife was, sitting in the front row, but thought that the Marga who wrote the emails was someone else. Now I have the name and the face together.
I am thankful for her love, and send mine to both of you beloveds,
Helena"

Received, 29/4/04

"Beloved Helena,
It is wonderful that I can also be with Maria through you. I am totally touched.
Thank you for the story about the percussionist. I am very blessed to always be surrounded by excellent musicians. My relationship to music has been a funny one. In my youth, I tried to learn to play several instruments because I felt an attraction to music, I also sang in the choir for the same reason, but the best way I "make music" is through others.
You are welcome to share my words with others. You are correct that letters are personal in that they are like arrows aimed at a particular target, but often these arrows will find their way to the hearts of others as well. My fondest wish is to touch as many souls as possible before this body disappears from the earth.
With all my love,
Samarpan"

Sent 29/4/04.

"Dear Samarpan,
Thank you for this reply. I am quick to answer this time, because Maria wants me to share something with you.
First, some other things.
Before life became too full, I studied violin and piano, and even sang in one or two choirs, in spite of a certain lack of expertise. I only realised how little I knew about singing since Maria came into my life to give me some "proper" education! I gave up all this wonderful classical music in my life in my early twenties, believing I would never really be any good at it. Now in 2004, I see that it does not matter if I am good at things or not. I only need to be me, who I already am, and that is enough for me,

320

even though that does seem to include getting better at things, which bring pleasure. I find having something to work for can be nourishing and uplifting. I just have to love the original material I am as well. Have I got to the truth here? What do you think? (I was born 10th July 1946, so twenties are not very recent!)

Thank you for the permission to share the words you write. I thought you would say yes, because of the good it will do, but wanted to be 100% certain before I did.

Now for Maria's bit.

I was just about to go outside and work in my garden, when I heard the beginning of a poem being given to me by Maria. I knew I would never remember it accurately if I did not write it down straight away, so I grabbed a piece of scrap paper, and scribbled this down before I went out.

"A Poem of Love"
How sweet the sound of sacred kisses,
It's music to my ears.
I hear the sound of human voices,
But now allay my fears
That perhaps the love I craved in lifetime
Never to me nears,
For I have heard those sacred kisses
The ones that touch my soul and heart,
The type of love, which never misses
That my heart gladly doth impart."

Then she added,
"Send my love to Samarpan again will you, along with this little poem. My heart heals, and not only mine, but yours too, Helena, I see".
With that she appeared radiant, full of joy, and handed me a red rose. So now you have heard from both of us,
With love and laughter and thanks,
Helena"

"Beloved Helena,
Beloved Maria,
Yes, it is true that it doesn't matter how good we are in our music making. Yesterday, my wife and I were walking through the village and passed a local celebration. A man was singing a lovely happy song that inspired everyone to dance. I too could not resist moving my body to the music. The energy of this simple native music was so full of joy.
Yes, we only can be who and how we are. This is the true joy. The "better" happens just naturally by itself and needs no "will" on our part to make it happen. As soon as I "try" to do it better, I feel tense and burdened but when I am simply enjoying the moment to its fullest I notice how effortlessly this instrument develops by itself.
Thank you, Maria, for the poem and sweet words of greeting. Yes, Love and Truth heal all wounds.
I am so happy to be with you both.
With all my love,
Samarpan"

I had just sent the Chapter, "Miracles in Germany" to him, and this was his response on June 27th 2004.

"Beloved Helena,
Beloved Maria,
          I am totally touched by what you wrote. Your faithfulness to what actually happened and to the accuracy of the words spoken by both (all three) of us is remarkable.
My heart is singing. I am so blessed to have met you both.
With all my love,
Samarpan"

I responded,
"Dear Samarpan,
Your feedback is touching. We are both delighted about the harmony between the three of us.
Yesterday, I woke up with the awareness there was something else I wanted to tell you. You already know how healing your acceptance of both of us is, bringing increased levels of peace, joy and love. There is more.

Your work has strengthened the mutual trust, as well as these other qualities just mentioned in my deepening friendship, and working "help-each-other" partnership with Maria. This is mostly because of the help you gave me with the control issue, which was the first question I ever asked you. All that stuff about resenting advice from other souls that came with it has largely dissipated. It is as though you helped me sweep away the debris that kept Maria and me apart, the bit that stopped us working together, apart from spasmodically, in the love, joy and harmony that now can flourish. It was always meant to be, but had to wait until I was ready to take this step.

(Maria) "For me it is the same. I too have mellowed greatly since I met Helena, and you Samarpan have done me a great service. Although she has some reticence concerning channelling good things about herself, I wish to tell you that I have never met anyone like her before. So many times I have asked myself how a soul so tender can live on the earth, and give thanks for her presence and the privilege of working with her. As was predicted, she has softened my character, and gives me an opening through which I can express my great love on earth, but in a purer form than it had when I lived as "La Callas". I give thanks to both of you. Let me add I can still be playful, but that heals, for it is fun. I respect your knowledge and wisdom Samarpan, Maria."

I plan to include a chapter about this friendship, which has developed between the three of us, but not yet. When that is done in the distant future, I will share it with you.

I have signed up for Christmas and New Year retreats at Oberlethe in north Germany. My feelings about Christmas need healing, and that will bring it to them, assisted by you I hope.

I feel you are well and happy. Is it true? It is really good to be connecting with you again. I am going away for three weeks in July to connect with ETs, dolphins, and whales in the Azores. The seminars are run by one of my favourite friends, and there will be others there whom I know. By the way, we connect with the spiritually advanced loving caring extraterrestrials, which I add, because some of them get a bad press. I will take care to keep my feet on the ground! I did not get brave enough to mention ETs to you before, so I suppose my trust level has risen. They do love us, you know.

As you are already aware, we both love you very much,
Maria and Helena"

Samarpan replied,

"Beloved Helena,
Beloved Maria,
It totally touches me to hear that I have made your relationship to each other softer and more productive. I agree with you, Maria, that Helena is a rare jewel. It is an honour and privilege to be with both of you.
I am delighted that we will meet again at Christmas time. I look forward to this.
Yes, I am well and happy. My life is so full of everything, and my body is also becoming fitter. Perhaps it will remain on this earth for some more years. I am certainly willing.
I am happy that you are in contact with ETs. Yes, of course the ones who are loving would naturally be attracted to you.
With all my love,
Samarpan".

Chapter 32

Maria After The Easter Retreat, 2004

It is so very evident after reading the previous chapter that I was going through a tough time emotionally. I had thought that I was good at letting people and animals move away from me. Having Maria depart just now seemed like losing a horse in its prime years. When they reach old age, and seem to be suffering, to allow or assist them to move on to other realms can be seen as a final act of love and compassion both to the animal and to oneself, as hanging on to them for too long is not doing oneself a kindness any more than it helps the animal.

Maria's love and reassurance as she showed me the snowdrop the previous day had definitely given me great comfort, but she seemed to think I needed more, so she made herself visible again. She gave me a picture of the two of us sitting on a rock high up in the Welsh mountains.

"I want to enjoy the mountains with you," she told me. "Perhaps I should come back as a hermit next time, and live high up in the mountains".

"No, I do not think so, Maria. There must be something much more important than that for you to do with your gifts."

"Now who is telling whom what to do!" she said in good humour, as she kissed me on the forehead, so that I could be sure she was not really annoyed, but just teasing me.

"Besides, I am not ready to go just yet".

I understood that she actually needed to stay with me longer for her own benefit, and it was really important for me to know this, so that I could stop worrying about whether or not wanting her was holding her back. This was a great relief to me. No one likes to lose a good friend.

Progress in the Kitchen

It was May already, and I was walking home after doing my shopping in Chester. As my thoughts strayed randomly from one thing to another, the words "I would like a blender" entered my head. Now this was very odd because there was nothing I wanted to blend, and my mind was not occupied with food issues when the thought arrived. Also, I have emphasised for many years that I cannot cook, as well as feeling confident I did not want to learn how. There had been times when I started to learn a few culinary skills, but particularly the last time was not a happy period of my life, so I preferred to forget all about it, and live very simply where food was concerned. I knew no one else would like my food, but as nobody was being asked to share it with me, this did not matter.

I could not be sure if this desire for a blender came from Maria or me. The fact that it came in the first person, "I", made me think at first that it might be me, whereas later Maria came higher and higher on the suspect list! She may have managed to convince me it would be a good idea when we chatted and discussed things while I was sleeping: thus this surprising change of attitude of mine.

It took at least two weeks before I got round to actually buying a blender, but after I had, I wasted no time in getting to work learning how to use it. Soups were the biggest success, as I became intrigued by the different foods I could combine to make it. The texture provided by blended potatoes was particularly satisfactory. Even more important to me was the fact that I could make myself tasty soups inside half an hour. Previously, I seldom had potatoes in the house, but my next-door neighbour gave me a large bag of them just before she went on holiday, as she did not think they would keep until she returned. What on earth could I do with that many potatoes? I asked myself. Soup? I tried it, adding other things for flavour.

326

My friend Dany sent me yet another Paris Match with pictures and writing about Maria in it. There was to be a grand dinner for four hundred people with Maria as the guest of honour. Maria was to be asked for advice about the menu, because she was quite skilled in cordon bleu herself. When I put this information together with the fact that much of my life was being influenced by a creative genius, it seemed that it was even more highly probable that this was Maria's influence.

Besides, I was beginning to see cooking with rather different eyes. It was yet another outlet for my own creativity. I felt that the ideas concerning how to make soups came from incarnate friends, and some from myself. I even enjoyed decorating my soup by sprinkling marigold petals from the garden on the surface of the finished dish. By now, I felt so confident that Maria was behind it all, or at the very least supporting this strange new development in my skills, that I felt I had to put this story into her book.

The climax came when I decided to try and make rather more soup than I needed, so that I could take a cup of it round to my next door neighbour's house to show her what I had learnt thanks to her gift of a bag of potatoes. She was very quick to notice that I do not use salt in my kitchen, (it makes me swell up slightly if I eat too much salt) but after adding some, she liked it enough to ask me to tell her how to make it, becoming especially interested when I told her how little time and work it took. She does not like to spend all day in the kitchen either! I wrote it all down for her, and passed the information on. This was really a triumph. I was thrilled.

Maria's Poodles Again

It was 21st June, and I was busy preparing my breakfast and thinking about Maria's poodles. Dany and I between us had counted five now. There was Tea, Toy, Toby, Djedda and Pixie the white one. We thought Toby might have been black. Maria was listening to my thoughts as usual, and as I pondered this little matter of her poodles, she said, "Amusement for the children!" She obviously found it very funny. Dany and I were the children! This had me in helpless laughter for at least a whole minute, so that I felt I must share this little comment with Dany.

Dany's research resulted in this little extract from her email,
"*Ari* (Onassis) *gave her both poodles, Pixie, white, and Djedda, brown. Maria named the latter after "the Saudi Arabian town where Ari was doing business at the time." Am I not a good Sherlock Holmes?*"

I should add here that when I see things clairvoyantly, although a lot of it is amazingly accurate, I cannot always distinguish between dark brown and black, even though it all comes to me in full colour.

During this time at home, I saw an hour-long documentary about Maria on British television, in which statements such as Maria's "great love", and the fact that she could do it on stage, and "to have so much power!" were mentioned. It was wondering about how she had come to be so strong and have all that power that really set me thinking one day towards the end of June, when I was out hiking in the mountains of Snowdonia.

I thought about my life and Maria, but more particularly about her and this power that she had and still has. With it, she had succeeded in changing opera for all time. One can see in modern productions how the singers really act now, something seldom seen before Maria demonstrated this to the world. At least, that is what I believe to be true. To have such an impact, just one person in one lifetime, how did she get all this power, determination and drive?

As I continued wondering about these things, the insight came to me that perhaps the soul of Maria Callas was not just one simple soul, but a conglomeration of several souls. Her work was so important that she is still around with her spirit influencing those who need her, whether they know it or not. It seems to me that when there is something really important to be accomplished on Earth, a number of souls come together, each bringing something needed for the task in hand, and form a really powerful person who can complete the mission required.

No sooner had I thought these thoughts, in fact before I had really had time to consider their implications, I became covered in goose bumps all over, and knew that I had come upon a great truth. This explained not only how she came to have such love and inner strength, but also why one of those interviewed in the documentary said that he often felt that she was still present amongst us.

In early July, an email came from Marguerite Vidal saying that I could come to France in October to give a seminar and a conference etc. She wanted to know what I would plan to do so that she could start organising the publicity for it. I was very busy, but managed to write back explaining that I could not say at this point what would happen in the seminars, because I did not know if Maria would be with me or not. Maria promptly asked me to tell Marguerite that of course she was coming. Then she said to me as well as I can remember it,

"You and I are married to each other". Maria spoke of a spiritual marriage, and reached out with her left hand to show me that she was wearing a golden ring with a ruby in it on the wedding ring finger. Then clairvoyantly, I noticed I was wearing a plain shining gold ring on the same finger of my left hand. I understood that she spoke of a spiritual marriage, not the earthly kind. I have noticed that when she really wants me to understand something, she sends both words and pictures to me, so that I am less likely to dismiss her communication as part of my imagination.

Meanwhile, I was enjoying my soups, which Dany told me were good for my throat. Also my trip to the Azores for Joan's seminars was coming up, and I felt gently encouraged to start a little singing again, something I had not done since Easter. Maria let me know as I sang that she was with me.

Chapter 33

Maria During Joan's Azores Seminars, 2004

On 8th July, I left home for the Azores. There were new adventures to look forward to, but most of all, I wondered what would happen with Maria. I was full of hope and expectations.

I had left a little early, as I wanted to have some time on the island of Sao Miguel, before flying on to Pico where I would join Joan. So after an interesting day, mostly spent hiking in the mountains there, I flew on the following morning to Pico Island. Joan was leading two weeklong seminars, the second one following on after the first with barely a pause, but just enough time to rest and so on as I wished. The first week was based in the town of Madalena, and the second one near Lajes in hotel Aldeia da Fonte, where we had stayed last year. Both weeks were to include swimming with dolphins and watching the whales.

Changes in Me

I experienced quite strongly how my willingness to welcome more of Maria, or to give up my physical body entirely to another walk-in, if that would be for the best, brought about changes. It was like a form of surrender.

I was willing to express myself more as a woman. I found myself asking for a bikini wax, and when the lady asked me if I wanted my underarms waxing next, (normally I just shave them) I went for that as well. Next came the desire for red fingernails. Maria had had them, and now I fancied some, even though I usually kept my nails very short. So having not had time to do anything about them before I left home, I bought nail varnish in Lisbon airport, and in no time at all, my nails had turned red. (In various degrees of unevenness with some of the varnish all over my fingers as well. After all, I had had no practise at applying it since my twenties!) Soon after noticing Joan's pretty varnished toenails, I painted mine red to match my fingernails, and was delighted with the result. This desire to express myself more as a woman had seriously affected my packing. Shorts for daytime and boats, but not a single pair of trousers, only skirts! Astonishing! At least I had skirts to take, even if they normally never left my cupboards.

The desire to sing came more strongly than ever, as I managed to make time nearly everyday to train my voice again following a long silence. Tutored by Maria, I started about eight days before I left home, and managed to continue with private practises during my time away. (I should add, that in spite of Maria's guidance, I do not train, as she must have done with many vocal exercises, as though I were heading for the opera house.) My voice was gradually growing stronger again. I sang arias with the help of a CD Walkman.

Although there was at least one person in the group who loved Maria Callas, there was no outlet to channel her or the ETs in the seminar. So by the end of the week, I had to admit that my heart was bleeding. I must emphasise here that there was no agreement with Joan that any of the participants in either of her groups were to channel anything. It is just that I look for openings sometimes, and when they are not there, well, my heart bleeds.

However, as it happened, in spite of my efforts to restrict the sound of my singing practises to my room by closing all the windows first, the sound was getting out, and several people told me how much they had enjoyed hearing the music. "You were singing my favourite aria, O Mio Babbino Caro!" someone told me. Because of this, I asked Maria to help me sing it extra well on one of the following nights, in the hopes that this man would have the pleasure of overhearing it again. She did help, and unusual as it is when I am alone, she reinforced my voice with her own for the whole of the aria. Actually, the man was too far away at the time to enjoy it, but this experience left me thinking.

I asked myself what the point was for all this effort on my part, if it was only for me? Shouldn't others be benefiting from the fruits of it all? Of course, my efforts to sing were very unpolished due to lack of serious consistent long-term study, and no doubt countless other reasons, but they seemed to be affecting other people in a positive way. The seminar I was to lead in Alsace was not until October, so it seemed a bit early to be doing it all just for that.

So I finished the first week having enjoyed the dolphins and seeing whales, but thinking that however much of a holiday it may have been, "What on earth was I here for?" I found no real purpose for it. As you will see, I had to wait another week to get the answer to my question.

The Second Week

The second week at Aldeia da Fonte had a completely different group apart from me, as nobody else was staying for both weeks. During the sharing of the first group meeting, I spoke openly about Maria and myself. This created a lot of interest, so I found myself answering many questions about it over dinner that night.

The following morning, Joan had some important logistics to tell us about the afternoon boat trip, but as two of our group were very late arriving, the perfect opportunity to channel Maria was created for me. I gave no explanation concerning what it was all about, apart from asking the group to tone with me while my vocal chords were warming up. They did, but they stopped quite quickly, I assume because Maria had so obviously taken charge, and we were away without the need for their vocal support any more. Joan told me afterwards that Maria had sung some whale sounds. I had not noticed this. The timing of the completion of Maria's performance was perfect. Seconds after she had finished, a waitress entered the room with water for someone, closely followed by the two latecomers, and Joan was then able to get started on the logistics.

Feedback from the morning came from various sources. Toet said she could see how Maria's sounds came from deep inside me, (not the throat) and then rose up through my body to be expressed through me. (Not her words exactly). She said that from the body language, it was really clear that this was something sacred. During my conversation with her, she commented how much I had changed since the previous year when we were also together in the Azores. I was more grounded, and much more interested in people. She felt I was stronger, and that instead of always talking about myself, I listened to people now. The word stronger interested me, just in case it had some relevance to my prayers for more power to be used for good.

Jim, a hands-on healer, told me that when Maria was singing for the group, he had observed how the sound was helping to shift a lot of "stuff". I understood him to mean bits of negativity, or emotional debris in the auric fields of some of them, and he had seen several people in tears, something I had been unable to observe myself with my eyes tightly closed, and being rather distanced from my body to give Maria space.

She, on the other hand, most probably saw all these things, thus enabling her to match the sounds to the needs of the group. Jim and one or two others told me about how they had heard my private practises, and enjoyed or been touched by them, to which Jim added that anyone who was meant to hear them had, and been helped in some way by it. He encouraged me to keep on practising at home, and not to worry about who could hear me, as they would benefit from it.

Then there was Sarah with whom I was sharing a room. To my relief she had a high tolerance of the singing, or so I thought, until I realised that it was more than that. At one point in the week, when she had told me she was going through some kind of spiritual transformation, and needed to rest a lot, I had sung with her consent. Admittedly it was behind a closed door with the window shut, but Maria must have known that she could still hear it very well, and adapted the quality of my voice according to Sarah's needs.

She told me a few days later that she had been feeling very low just then, and the sound had really lifted her up, so please would I thank Maria. On hearing this, Maria chose to come through me with her spoken words to say how she considered it a privilege to work with Sarah, and then kissed her on three of her chakra points, third eye, throat, and heart.

Other Notes

I kept a diary during this trip in which I wrote down everything I thought should be remembered, or would be part of Maria's book.

For example, at dinner on 19th July, the words definitely came out of Joan's mouth, "You are Maria Callas". I did not analyse what this might mean, but just made a note of it. Another time, she said, "You and Maria are perfect together! When do you suppose this agreement to be together was made?" "Since before the beginning of time", were the words that came out of my mouth, before I had even had time to consider her question properly. It felt as though this reply from me was half channelled.

Someone else had called me Maria instead of Helena at the beginning of the week when she was still trying to learn my name. Another time, when trying to get my attention at the dinner table, the same lady had called out Helena twice without my hearing it, so she resorted to "Maria", and immediately got my full attention.

Then there was the time when I was walking to and from the kitchenette area of our apartment to the sitting area. I knew there was a step somewhere, but where? I must learn its exact whereabouts and memorise it, so that I would not fall or trip over it, almost thinking I had to count the number of steps to reach it. Then it dawned on me that this must have been exactly how Maria had to think on stage. She performed without her glasses, and was so short-sighted, much more so than I am, that she had had to learn her way around the stage almost like a blind person, or so others had said.

At another point during the second week, when just as I often do, I was questioning whether or not she was still with me, Maria showed me that not only was I wearing the gold ring on my left hand which I had seen before, but also a ring on the middle finger of my right with a large diamond in the middle of it. "A diamond is forever", I thought to myself.

This closeness with Maria made me wonder so much about what was actually happening with me. I kept on wanting to be able to analyse it all and have some mental clarity on the matter. So at Joan's group meeting on the evening of 21st, I decided to try and get Joan's opinion. Joan made several suggestions. Maria and I must be very compatible, more so than with Helena number one before I walked in. This statement made sense of Maria's message to me a year previously, which was that she preferred to work with a walk in, because it was easier, and that she had known this would happen before she painstakingly prepared the way for me with the previous Helena.

Joan's second point was that the changing vibrations on the earth were making the veil thinner, so that communication with other realms was getting easier now.

Joan's ET Night

Even before we got as far as "ET Night", I had experienced a brief contact with one of them. It happened one afternoon during a group meeting when Joan was talking to us about the low frequency sound that the military put into the ocean. An ET slipped into my body, not to speak, but just to look around at the group using my physical eyes for a moment or two.

I was able to perceive his appearance. He was a greenish hue with a large head consisting of a much larger brain than humans have. The shape was different as well. The left and right brain lobes were clearly defined with an obvious cleft (or dent) down the centre between them. The eyes were visible, but I did not see much nose, and the mouth area was small, as though little used. When I shared this description with Joan, she told me that it was similar to a drawing of one of the Arcturians in Elaine Thompson's book, including the colour.

This was an exciting revelation for me, because up until now, I had had no means of knowing with which ETs exactly I was communicating. To some extent it had not mattered as long as I enjoyed their vibes, but in a world where so much use is made of words, it was lovely to have found one to go with my pictures and feelings! It occurred to me that this would only work if they continued to come in the same form, for I know that many ETs can change form at will.

It was the evening of 20th that Joan decided to hold an ET contact night outside after dark under the stars in the exact location where I had channelled Maria for her group in 2003. It seemed the perfect site for it. Dinner was always a leisurely affair, because the restaurant was invariably busy, so more time was passed in conversation while waiting for the food than actually eating it. Therefore one had to count on the whole thing taking roughly two hours. It was a very good way of unwinding if one needed to. After dinner I usually had a bath and went to bed, so back in my room preparing to go to ET Night, I commented to Sarah, "It's bedtime already, and we have not even started!" "Well you know you don't have to go, don't you?" "Yes," I replied, "But I would not feel right in myself if I missed this out." My intuition was telling me that it was important for me to attend, no matter how much I fancied bed. I made the right decision. This is what happened.

I was aware of an ET presence. Several of the Arcturians were standing around me with their ship hovering close by. I felt strangely connected to that ship. Once I started communicating with them, all the protocol that Joan had mentioned beforehand went right out of my head. So I plunged straight into a discourse with them about what I wanted from them. I listed a whole string of requests, mostly about my physical needs. Could they fix the lump on my right foot please? Could they help my throat, so that I could sing better? Would they mind making my energies and vibrations more compatible with Maria's, so that I could channel her better?

It was only when I paused to wonder if there was anything else I wanted, that it finally dawned on me that I was only concerned with my own needs, and it was time to open my ears, and ask what they wanted to tell me, or what they wanted from me.

They informed me that I was one of them, and I had recently chosen to take on human form on Planet Earth. "Why?" I asked. It was to help anchor the Light on this planet. Just being here was what was required. I perceived my own ET self superimposed over my physical body as confirmation of what they were telling me. Whereas I had felt that it did not really matter from which constellation I had most recently come, there was nonetheless a growing curiosity in me to know a little more. I also felt that Maria's soul was connected to them at some point in its history, and time being an illusion, her links to them would still be powerful. So no wonder Maria had chosen to work with a walk-in, and no wonder she accepted so happily the presence of any ETs who might visit me.

It was at this point that I decided to take another look at my watch, and saw that it was now very late, taking into account that we were going to get up early the following morning for another boat trip with the dolphins. So I said to the Arcturians, "It is definitely bedtime for me now, so if there is more communication necessary, please can you follow me to my room, and continue there while I am sleeping if you wish to." I am not aware that any further discourse did take place just then. I had received enough information for the time being already it seems. It is worth adding that as I typed this into my computer a week after my return home, the Arcturians told me that they came here to Earth now through a window. I saw that they came from a place of great Light, and that an opening, which they were calling a window, took them through both time and space to reach our reality and communicate with us to serve both us and the Light from whence they came.

During the last evening group meeting with Joan at the end of the week, as Joan was speaking to me, I learnt more about the Arcturian way of being directly from them, or even from myself, as I am an ET. The Arcturians do a lot through their eyes, which includes communication, and scanning what is before them to give them a sense of what things are, rather like a dolphin with its sonar.

I saw lines of Light coming out through my ET eyes to make sense of the reality about me. It reminded me of the way in which Joan had looked at me earlier in the week after I had shared that my heart was bleeding. No doubt she was wondering what was going on, and trying to see.

Regarding Maria's connections to these things, I recalled how a day or two previously, I had seen Maria dancing around chanting joyfully, "I'm a dolphin too!" repeatedly. Although I did not get any real answers, I wondered how many close times together in dolphin or Arcturian realities Maria and I might previously have had together. Maybe time would tell if I needed to know.

Now I had seen that there was little I could do to further my skills with Maria during Joan's groups, but the answer to my question concerning "What on earth was I there for, in the Azores with my good friend Joan?" was apparently this; I needed to be there in order to allow Joan's presence to assist me in realising and furthering my ET connections. This side of my life needed to be nurtured as well.

Chapter 34

Licinia's Jungles and Maria

It was already 23rd July, the day after Joan's seminar finished. Highest on my list of things I wanted to do, in the few remaining days before I left the island, was to climb up Pico Mountain. I had looked longingly at it so many times. Nonetheless, this did not seem a good day to do it. I felt very tired following two seminars in a row, and secondly the clouds were low, and I so much wanted to go up there on a day when I would be able to enjoy the views. So I settled for a much less ambitious hike at a lower altitude.

I had not realised quite how much damage a bruise close to my right hip joint had made. It happened when the waves banged me against a rather hard bit of the boat just as I was getting back on board after swimming with the dolphins during the first week on the island. I had suspected (rightly as it turned out after someone diagnosed it properly when I was back in England again) that my pelvis had been knocked out of alignment by the blow, and walking with a twisted un-level pelvis, even just for my "easier" hike, made it extremely painful the following day to climb even gentle slopes.

I sadly realised that even though I had arrived on the island very fit, Pico Mountain was out of the question for this trip. If I did climb it, the best advice I could give myself was to postpone it for another year. I thought boat trips were best avoided for the time being, in case I aggravated my body even more, much as I would have enjoyed the dolphins or some scuba diving.

Reluctantly I resigned myself to a quieter less active lifestyle, and took pleasure in singing more often with Maria at my side, as well as catching up with my notes for this book. Desperate for at least some form of exercise, I walked down to the beach, and swam off shore. I was thrilled. Swimming did not hurt at all! The moment I immersed myself in the water all pain ceased! Wonderful! I could practise my free diving, and enjoy the refreshing ocean, as I snorkelled about enjoying the view of the fishes and underwater terrain. Also, there was no schedule, so I could do it exactly when I felt like it. So this was my exercise for the remaining days of my holiday.

Walking back up the short slope to the hotel still hurt very much. The pain recommenced the moment I surfaced into the fresh air. So I decided that as I had time on my hands, I would organise a massage for myself the following day. I felt that my body was not happy, so I turned my attention more towards looking after it with tender loving care than wondering what else it could be used for.

Licinia arrived on time with her massage table at the door of my hotel room. To my delight, I found that she spoke good English. Although she had been born on Pico Island, she had lived much of her life in the States, where English had been a necessity for her.

Surveying her, bright eyed, and very ready to get straight on with her work massaging me, I realised quickly that I did not have to apologise when I took my clothes off for not having any underwear underneath them. (I might have felt obliged to mention that at home.) I always prefer to be massaged completely naked on the grounds the even brief knickers get in the way, and fresh out of the ocean, I had not seen any point in putting any on. A pair of shorts and a top was ample clothing for a warm sunny afternoon. Her attitude to this, which we never needed to discuss or even mention, was very refreshing. I think it often comes with people who are really in touch with nature, no matter what cultural conditioning has also been inflicted on them.

Licinia asked no questions concerning why I wanted a massage, so I decided to tell her about my hip. She agreed to pay special attention to this, and telling her definitely did help. It also led to various interesting spiritual conversations about the healing power of thought, and other even deeper truths.

Finally, Licinia asked me if I would like to visit one of her two houses, the one where she had what she called her "jungles". Once I had understood it was wild and remote, little could have kept me away from it. I could see that there would be plenty of time after leaving the hotel before going to the airport to visit it. Licinia was completing a massage for someone else about the same time as I would be checking out, so she offered to let me follow her car to her house so that I could find it.

Rather typically, I regret to say, I was a few minutes late for her, and as I apologised for this, she instructed me not to hurry, as that would bring me out of my peace. "We are supposed to be in peace, and we have plenty of time, don't we?" This was not the reaction I expected, but whereas I do not condone keeping people waiting and being late, I felt there was a lot to learn from her attitude. Looking into her eyes, I had no difficulty believing that she was really sincere, not just pretending she did not mind when she did, as some might have done. This was a really unusual person. I found it very interesting.

This was the second time that I had been invited to visit someone's private domain on Pico. Last time it had been Sonia's fairy-filled garden, and I had been able to channel Maria for her and all that was there. Would I receive the same privilege with Licinia? Only time would tell. I did so hope I could.

My longing to do more with Maria was very strong, but I knew it had to be at the right time, and where this gift would be welcomed. It seemed to me that my spiritual gifts were really underused. Surely they had been given to me to be shared more for the benefit of others.

Aside from that, I had been struck by how giving and generous Licinia was, and so longed to give her something, not my remaining scanty supply of Euros which I would need to travel with, but a part of myself, if only this would be acceptable to her. As far as I was concerned, it was my love and my spiritual gifts I wanted to offer if it felt right. Either way, I sensed this visit as a gift from the universe, for which reason I was accepting it. It felt as though it belonged to my spiritual pathway.

In her car, Licinia lead me slowly along a lovely scenic route over the mountains, and down narrow winding roads on the other side of the island, until eventually we reached her front drive. Her steady pace had given me a wonderful opportunity to admire the beauty of the route, and drive the car safely at the same time.

From the road, the entrance to her property looked like a gate to nowhere, I observed, as Licinia opened it to let us in. House and garden were hidden from public gaze by countless trees and vegetation on the steep hillside. The driveway was steep and quite short, but on arrival at the top of it, a small and ancient building came into view, which was her house. Unconnected to mains electricity or running water, the simplicity of her life style, when she was there, was obviously a source of pleasure.

Some of her previous work had been building houses, which stood her in good stead for doing any repairs or improvements with her own hands. Clearly, this was a very capable woman who was strong both physically and spiritually. Bountiful rainfall kept her water tank full, dead wood collected locally provided fuel to heat water and cook with, there was a generator to provide electric light for parties, whereas when alone, she was happy with candles. Chickens and ducks gave her eggs to eat, and the fruit trees in her garden supplied her with fruit.

Her "bathroom" outside the house in a separate little building had a bucket of water there for flushing the lavatory, or pouring into the washbasin to wash one's hands. It was clean and nice. Hanging from a tree was the shower. It was a special bucket, just like the showers we had used so gratefully after a hot dusty day on Safari in Africa. The only difference I could see was that this one had no curtain or tiny tent around it, as there was nobody around to see her when she used it. I could easily have believed that it was a million miles from the nearest house or person, if I had not known otherwise.

After a tour of the house, I was taken slowly round the bit I most wanted to see, her garden, or her "jungles" as she called it. There was a brief moment when both of us managed to stop talking at the same time, as we sat side by side on a seat under an archway looking out towards the sea, and it was then that I felt the peace in that place. The birdsong was beautiful, and had there not been more to see and do together, I felt I could have stayed there silently for hours just taking it all in and enjoying it. I already knew that happiness did not come from money, affluence, recognition, crowded cities, and mod cons. Licinia knew that as well, and mentioned it.

The garden was situated on a steep gradient, but luckily, as we wandered up and down her many pathways through it, my hip was already healed enough not to spoil the visit, and we were only going slowly, so there was no strain involved. It was full of nature spirits. This was just the kind of setting they seem to love. Flowers were abundant. Many of them I knew, because although the climate supports plants that can only be grown as houseplants in colder climates, it also had many I knew or grew in my own garden. There were trees as well as flowers, which I always feel improves a garden. They seem to provide balance, as well as giving shade.

I was thoroughly enjoying being in the company of a fellow gardener, as she shared with me her ideas, enthusiasm, and joy concerning each time she discovered yet another ancient walkway through it lying hidden beneath the vegetation. The property had been let go, and run down before her arrival there three years ago, and little by little, mostly with her own hands, she was making it beautiful again. It had magnificent views of the ocean, and one could see about three of the other islands across the water on a clear day. She told me everything about everything, or at least as much as possible in the time.

As my tour of the property was nearing completion, I began to feel that this might be the right moment to offer her the gift of my channelling. I hesitated, having had the impression so far, that just like me, she preferred to be the one who was talking and sharing, rather the silent one who listens, even though I knew she had listened when I told her about my hip problem the previous day. Perhaps it was being a little alone spiritually, and her delight in showing me her creations that kept her talking so much.

I remembered being exactly the same when I showed other people round my garden, to the point where one friend had actually asked if she could just go round it on her own. I suppose this was the only way she thought she could get enough quiet to tune into the fairies and the peace that is there!

Anyway, I was in for a surprise. As soon as I told Licinia that there was something I wished to offer her, if she would like it, the talking stopped. She stood there motionless and silent, waiting for me to reveal what this gift might be. I offered to channel Maria Callas for the benefit of the nature spirits, the plants, all of the life within earshot, and not least her dog and her. Without hesitation she accepted.

"Wait!" she said, "I will go and get something for us while you fetch the songs, and then I will show you the right place to do it."

"I don't need to fetch anything, because I am not going to use any words. It is more like toning, with healing sounds for the benefit of all that is. I never know how it will be beforehand, because it is different every time. I do not control it, because it is channelled, and not I who sings".

I cannot remember if those were my exact words, but it went something like that. I wondered what Licinia would return with for us, and waited full of curiosity. It was a white cape for each of us to place around our shoulders, as she felt it might be cool under the trees, and could even turn to rain. I wore it rather like a stole, just as Maria had often worn one on stage. I adjusted it from time to time as I sang. Licinia was obviously expecting me to sit on a little bench beside her, but I chose to sing standing up.

As I started the sound while waiting for Maria to take over, the first notes did not sound promising to me at all. My throat was not very clear, and I wondered if the top notes would be completely absent. Yet I did so want to do this. Luckily it was not long before I was convinced that the sound was flowing through me, and I had nothing to do with the choice of the notes any more.

Then I was able to relax, because I felt relieved to know that the responsibility for the sound was no longer mine. I just let it happen, and observed a little of it from somewhere slightly outside my body. It seemed to go on for quite a while. I had noticed the chickens being quite noisy at the beginning, but apart from that I knew nothing of what was going on around me in the third dimension.

Towards the end, I began to wonder if Licinia was still beside me, or was I now standing alone on the hillside? I continued to listen to the sounds. There was hardly any vibrato, which was unusual. There was an amazing moment when the sound went up far above my personal vocal range, and a prolonged high note was sung softly with amazing ease. I felt Maria, or something, use muscles in my throat I am not capable of controlling myself to produce the right shape for passing air to create this high pitch, which reminded me how the pipes on an organ for the top notes are smaller and narrower than those for the lower ones.

Before she had finished, I asked if Maria could manage to sound a bit more like herself, for I wondered how on earth Licinia would know I had been telling her the truth if only sound so unlike opera came through. I too needed a little reassurance. I had no doubt it was somebody, but was it really Maria? She responded to my request by coming even closer, so that I could really feel her vibrations clearly. Well, of one thing I could be certain, it was not I who sang! It finished with the blessing of the earth.

Knowing it to be complete, I opened my eyes to see if I still had an audience. Actually, it had doubled in size. Not only was Licinia still there, but also she had been joined by Lucy, her dog. One of the things that had worried me beforehand was whether or not any of Licinia's animals would be upset by the noise. Lucy was being restrained so that she could not touch me, but was wagging her tail joyfully, obviously wanting to make contact. The fact that she was there, happy, and had not even barked delighted me.

"As soon as you started making a noise, she came racing up the hill, and wanted to lick your feet, but I would not let her in case it disturbed you."
Now Lucy had been left in the car with the window open, and firmly instructed to stay there, so that she would leave us alone. Normally she always obeyed this request, and Licinia was very surprised she had chosen to jump out, and I was surprised she had not made a sound! That is what astonished me the most. Had she gone anywhere, I would have

expected her to run as fast and far away as possible, especially when the high notes came out, or the volume was loud. Now Licinia did use sound to call her, (I was given a demonstration. She had cupped her hands around her mouth, and let out a loud long sound) but Lucy would have known immediately that my sounds were different, for they carried a different vibration, most probably a mix of Maria's and mine, and therefore could not be mistaken by a sensitive dog for Licinia's. Lucy was racing around excitedly, which was commented on several times, so I supposed this was not her normal behaviour, but her reaction to Maria coming through me and the sounds.

I asked Licinia about her ears, just in case the noise had had too many decibels. No problem. "I went right into a meditational state as soon as you started. I enjoyed all of it. I was right in there." I could see by her face the experience had moved her in some way. As far as I remember, Licinia said that it seemed to her that I was communicating with nature with the medium of sound. She felt that in another life I had belonged to a tribe of people who did that. Certainly, I had asked for nature to benefit, so what she said fitted in neatly with my intentions.

We spoke briefly about what I had been doing, and then Licinia decided to try. One thing was very clear to me. This was not a timid lady. She seemed to have no fear of being heard, quite unlike me when I first started! Her performance did not last long, but certain aspects of it were very striking. I decided to go into a meditational state while she sang, in the hopes of picking up some information for her.

As she began, it sounded like a release of any residues she had of personal pain. What interested me most was the fact that she did not sound like a beginner. She must have done it before I felt, as pictures of her with dark skin during a past life in Africa began to emerge in my consciousness. There was also a gorilla, and other African animals, which helped me to draw my conclusions. This use of sound was surely an ancient art, one that most of us are no longer in contact with. When she had finished, she told me that it made her feel good. Looking at her, this was easy to see.

"You looked pretty good before you started, but now you look even better!" I confirmed.

My next privilege was a demonstration of the music she played on a little mouth organ produced from her pocket. It was tuneful, and I felt I could have danced to it given the space. She had had no musical training, but just played whatever seemed to come through her. "But where does it come from?" she kept asking me. I was not sure enough to tell her, but I felt it was probably channelled through her, and I realised afterwards that I had been sensing the presence of a man who had been involved with that type of music during his lifetime.

Her vocal toning could of course, have come from a part of her own soul, which is what I felt about the first part of it, although what followed may or may not have been channelled. There was, however, one point I was certain about. It was wonderful and beneficial that she did these things.

We walked back down to the house, where we munched happily on apples she provided as we continued talking. She repeated that our meeting, and all that had happened between us had made an impression on her. She intended to continue with the vocal sounds. Unlike me, she had the perfect place to practise without reservations, as there were no neighbours to consider. She remarked that it was so rare that one could be with someone, and let all of it out. This appeared to have touched her in some way.

She offered to help me find the airport by following her car again, but I rightly felt that I could manage that alone, and I did.

The fact that I did not manage to write all of this down during my flights home, partly because I felt so very tired by then, turned out to be an advantage, for it kept me thinking about the time spent with her, and what it had brought me. I could see how the hip problem had led me to our meeting, as I thought I needed the massage to help it heal. Had I stayed well, I would doubtless have climbed Pico Mountain instead, not had time to be massaged, and therefore never met her. It was so clear now that the longed-for hike was not important, whereas my meeting with Licinia was.

It was the effect that Maria and I had had on her, and her personal performance that made me think. If she could be so helped, then how about other people? I had been wondering what to do when I led my two-day long seminar in Alsace in October that would make it different from the last one, and now I felt inspired. Maria had said to me during the last one, "You must let the people sing, or they won't develop." Licinia had opened my mind to ways of doing this.

At home again, as I pondered over these things in my kitchen, I thought about Maria, and wondered how this visit and tour of "The Jungles" had affected her. "I found it very interesting. It put me in touch with my distant past," she told me. Yes, surely Maria and I were walking together towards the Light, for the time being anyway.

To complete this chapter, there is a truth I have instinctively known for a long time, but have never found the words to express it in full. Licinia said it so well during our conversation when we were eating the apples. She commented, "We never win wars fought with violence. The only things we can ever win are people's hearts".

Chapter 35

Another Trip To France Looms Up and Begins

Plans and arrangements had been made for a third trip to France. There were various things to do out there, but what concerned me most was the two-day seminar I had agreed to run. It was not that I did not want to lead one, but simply how was I to cope if Maria did not want to attend? I had persuaded Marguerite not to include her name in the publicity, as I was not sure it was right to tie Maria down to an earthly commitment like that. Furthermore, she is always free to leave me for good at any time she wishes.

I remembered having read how severely she was criticised during her lifetime for not keeping commitments, even at times when she could not help it, and thought of the pain this lack of understanding must have caused her. For her to be put through that again after her physical death was not something I intended to inflict upon her.

So supposing she was not with me in France? Should those attending be given their money back and sent home? There did not seem to be much that I could do without her. As it was advertised as a seminar about the use of vocal sound for spiritual purposes, and I did not know if I could sing at all in her absence, I asked if I could have a sign that she was still with me. Also I decided to start singing again to get my vocal chords strong enough for over me to be able to sing for much longer periods of time than an unprepared voice could ever hope to manage, and wondered what would happen.

The first sign I had did not specifically promise me Maria's presence, but it served to give me the confidence I needed. I had gone for a few hours walking in the hills, and not expecting to stay out long, I had only limited provisions in my backpack. The weather turned warm and humid. The cooling breeze dropped, and all this was noticeably depleting my energy. I wanted so much to make my walk longer, to add another loop to it, but it seemed to require so much effort. I struggled wearily up the next small summit, thinking I might perhaps pause for a drink of my water, and perhaps even eat some of my emergency dried food rations, which I always take with me, when I made a remarkable discovery.

My hungry, rather dehydrated, self saw what to me was manner from Heaven. Another hiker, who could not have known I would need it, had considerately left me a lovely ripe juicy pear! Now it was getting late, and I felt I was the only one left in these hills. Meanwhile this treasure, I noticed, as I picked it up to examine it, was slightly squashed at one end, probably from being in someone's backpack. By the morning, I reasoned, it would either have been eaten by an animal or pecked at by a bird.

Its previous owner obviously would not be returning so late to collect it, and I guessed it had been abandoned deliberately, because of the slight damage near the stalk, and clearly someone felt he or she neither wanted nor needed it any more. Instead of hurling it into the middle of the heather where I was unlikely to have found it, this kind person had laid it down where I could not avoid seeing it. "This is a gift to me from the Universe!" I exclaimed delighted. "What a wonderful Universe we live in!" I marvelled.

I walked a few steps away from the summit to seat myself on a welcoming rock, where I could comfortably enjoy this newfound treasure. It was delicious, and far better suited to my needs than anything I had brought with me. The juice re-hydrated me, and the natural fruit sugars put the spring back into my step. Happy and joyful, I continued my walk, able to go as far as I wanted.

With a quiet mind, I was easily able to contemplate the meaning of all this. It was a powerful sign for me that my needs would be met in a similar way in France. Therefore I became aware that if Maria were absent, then another would come in her place to inspire and assist me with the toning and my group. Peace of mind was mine again.

There followed little signs from Maria. She was quick to observe that showing me pictures of herself did not serve to convince me she was really present with me, because I frequently told myself that it might be just my imagination and wishful thinking. So twice, when I was wondering which note to start an aria on, or how low was the lowest note in something, she gave me perfect pitch, which I could then check on the piano or a CD. This is not one of my gifts, so I really dared to start hoping she might still be with me.

One day, for a very brief moment, I felt her vibes clearly in my body. I knew that this was not imagination either. I was still ready to go to France without her if she did not want to come, but I realised I loved her, and that whatever wonderful being might take her place in my life, it was her I had become so comfortable working with.

So it was still in this trusting state that I arrived in France. When I heard, however, that I had fewer bookings than my last visit, I began to doubt a little, or at least to question the purpose of my being there. "Why on earth am I here?" I wanted to know. Only time would tell.

As it turned out, everyday had a purpose. It seemed to me that no time was wasted. During the week, I sometimes practised singing the arias I was growing so fond of in my room with a CD Walkman to sing along to, but there were also many opportunities to work with toning as well.

The very first evening, Richard, Marguerite and I met to send healing to Marguerite's daughter, Emilie. Each of us worked in our own way, and in my case that meant channelling healing by singing tones. On that occasion, it was not the highest notes in my repertoire, because I was guided otherwise.

The next morning, inspired by a conversation with Marguerite, in which she had expressed her thought that it could be useful if I worked with toning more often, and not just the arias, I sang alone in my bedroom for Starlight. I had by this time received the insight that it was not just fear of frightening the animals and upsetting the neighbours that had been causing me to hold back, but also the fear of enlisting the wrath and disapproval of the owners of pets who might become upset should that happen. I felt safe singing in Marguerite's house, especially upstairs alone in the bedroom.

That evening, the three of us met again to send out healing. I channelled sounds for Emilie, Richard, and Marguerite. We all noticed how the sounds for each person were different. In Richard's case, much of it was to open his throat chakra more. Little did I realise at the time that Maria was already starting to prepare him for the seminar at the end of the week.

Before going to bed I had a question for Richard, which I asked just after he had given me some soothing healing. Did he think the sounds I had made were channelled? Yes, I was guided, he told me. Then still wondering if Maria was really still around me or not, I went to Marguerite, and asked if she thought it was still Maria who was helping me. "Helena! How can you still doubt that after all this time? What is the matter with your head?" Her absolute conviction reassured me enormously, and opened the door for me to pass on a few words to both of them from Maria, who, it seemed, had followed us into the kitchen.

I informed them that she was presenting them each with a posy of wild flowers as a token of her appreciation for having given me the answers to my questions about her. I was so happy and relieved to find myself totally accepting the reality of her presence again. She had never left me. It was just that I had ceased daring to really believe she was with me. I fell asleep very content that night.

Wednesday morning arrived, and I began my day with another aria practise. I decided to follow this with toning for my house, but stopped when I noticed that my voice really needed a break. What moved me to sing for my house was a conversation with Marguerite the previous day, in which I told her how much easier it was for me to sing in her house than mine. She made the point that many healings had been carried out in her house, and this provided very good energy for doing this kind of work in it. I wrongly understood that she had meant for her house. Therefore I was hoping healing sound would help my house.

Although I had stopped almost immediately because of the fatigue in my voice, accompanied with the feeling it would be more effective for three of us to send it healing at once, I had managed to observe how cramped the space felt at home. Its auric field needed to expand so that it slightly overflowed the physical boundaries of the property, and gave me the feeling of comfort and space in which I could freely sing.

A friend of Marguerite's called Noëlle came to join us for lunch, as she had booked a private session with me in the afternoon. During this session, I felt Maria's presence the moment Noëlle entered the room. I felt it in my body language, which became overshadowed by Maria's. She looked Noëlle up and down as she assessed her.

I tuned into Noëlle's vibrations a bit, and then asked her what she wanted. "Something useful for me" was the only guidance I got from her. So I began by using my clairvoyance to see what information was forthcoming. Then, as I surveyed her, helped by Maria, I was strongly inspired to tone her chakras and auric field. I understood that what would follow would be more effective, if these were worked on first. Maria and I sang together, and much to my surprise, she included a few lines of the aria, "Un bel di vedremo", but without the words, in the middle of it.

Later, Noëlle told me she had recognised that aria, adding that the very last note of the toning had been beautiful! The singing complete, she was given a short time to reflect on what she had just experienced. Then, to help her access information for herself, I asked her to close her eyes, and as inspired, I toned very softly some notes to assist her.

Afterwards, I invited her to share the experience with me. Unable to answer all of her questions adequately with my own knowledge, I closed my eyes, and channelled the angels, which took us exactly to the end of the session.

Over some tea with Marguerite, Noëlle told us how for the first time she had been able to see her own auric field. It happened during the meditation with Maria inspired toning towards the end of the session. She said she had never seen anything before. This was very encouraging for me, and just what I needed to hear.

That evening, the three of us held another meditation after dinner. When it was my turn to lead something, I chose clearing, cleaning and expanding the auric field of number 49, my house. This was to include the ground beneath it and the garden around it. I asked that each of us set about this independently in our own style. In my case, it was sound again.

The pitch of the toning was really deep at the beginning, which felt to me like a cleansing of the earth and foundations of the buildings (house and garage). This was providing a good firm platform, which could support the space above ground. Little by little the pitch rose.

Then came a moment when I felt strongly guided to stop, and say to the others, "Don't forget the fairies!" When I started toning again, the sounds were different. I had the feeling that I was deeply in touch with their moods, and how they felt, and that the sounds coming through me were part of their own fairy language.

Following that, the pitch rose up again, and I felt a connection to the birds and all of nature around my house. Marguerite said afterwards, that she had recognised many animal calls as well in Maria's sounds. Close to the finish, I felt Maria about to slip into another aria, so that I could easily accept it was she behind all this. It was an answer to my unspoken question, "Are you here tonight Maria?" The instant I accepted her presence, the necessity of singing me an aria was no longer purposeful, so it never happened. Instead, the sounds came to a natural peaceful close.

The following healing was proposed by Marguerite. This time it was to be distant healing for a sick child who the doctors thought would definitely never get better. We decided to include the parents, not just the child. The father did not accept the spiritual side of life, but only science and allopathic medicine. The mother was deeply distressed both by the doctor's prognoses, and the attitude of her husband towards spiritual healing. For my part, I was using channelled sound again. All of us noticed how each person to receive was sent different types of sound according to their needs.

It was the father who needed the most help with the toning, and healing energies from Marguerite and Richard. I sensed him as though he were walking through life in a straight jacket, refusing to look left or right for other possibilities or ways of being. When I sang for the mother, I felt great tenderness and pain in her, because of the situation with her daughter and the closed state of mind of her husband. So the sounds were to help heal her tattered emotions.

I had the impression that the needs of both parents were greater than those of this 18-month-old infant, who appeared to me like a shining soul with an energy field brighter and cleaner than either his father, or his mother. This child was still relatively untainted by earthly life, and this was reflected in the purity of the sounds. So I was easily able to accept Marguerite's inspiration that this child was here with this illness to help the father learn to accept the reality of other dimensions, spiritual healing and all that goes with it. In short, it was to help him evolve.

Chapter 36

Marguerite's Sixth Interview With Maria

During this third stay in Elsenheim, Marguerite was to ask me three times if I was willing to let her have an interview with Maria. This chapter includes the first of these. Confident that she was following her intuition accurately, I willingly presented myself as channel for these on each occasion. I never asked for this myself, as I did not know if that was still a useful part of my existence on this planet or not. The first of these took place on Thursday 21st, and we recorded it. In my own words, this is how it went as I wrote it down in my little notebook soon afterwards.

Shortly after 10 a.m., we sat down facing each other, and Maria slipped smoothly into my body, announcing her arrival verbally. As she continued speaking, she exhibited a certain restlessness, stood up almost immediately, and proceeded to move around the chair she had been sitting on, using it like a prop on stage to orientate herself in the room. She spoke slowly and clearly, and like any good public speaker, seemed well acquainted with the art and value of using a silent pause, when she felt she had said something important, which she wanted her audience to have time to take in. I could feel her physical mannerisms. She was making it quite clear to both of us that it was really she, but I was the one who needed that reassurance the most.

It was only when Marguerite asked her for some personal advice, that she stopped acting her former self, sat down quietly to reply thoughtfully to the best of her ability, and changed her tone to one of greater intimacy.

The conversation finally returned to herself again, and the subject of Onassis came up. Before expressing my reactions and feelings about that, it is helpful to read the transcription from the tape of this interview. M.V. = Marguerite, and M. = Maria.

M. *I am here.*

M.V. Hello. You are welcome in this house and in this world.

M. *Thank you. Have you any questions?*

M.V. I have no questions. I just wanted to invite you to talk and express things clearly for Helena, and maybe for other people and for me, but you can express yourself.

M. *That is very kind to invite me. It has been a while since I have spoken this way.*

M.V. Does it help you if I ask questions?

M. *Yes.*

M.V. What sort of advice could you give to Helena for her daily life related to sounds?

M. *The most important thing is that she stays open to other possibilities, open to changes in her life however small. It is possible to help her. I enjoy working with her very much, even when she doubts my presence. She does not think she works alone, but because she loves me very much, she likes to know if I am there or not. I understand this, and it is touching. It would be true to say that we touch each other's hearts. Time with her is a pleasure. I love to show her the things she does not know. I enjoy giving her little surprises, suddenly helping her with something, pointing something out, showing her her progress; these things. These things are special to me.*

You are right, Marguerite, when you say that sometimes I inspire other people, but it is working with sound in this special way that attracts me the most. I enjoy still the arias. I see the healing, which they can have when Helena sings them. I see the pleasure it gives her to sing. Each tiny little piece of progress with the art of singing opera is a pleasure for her. I wish to give her this. It is like presenting her with a beautiful bunch of roses. I do that so gladly. I love to see the smile on her face. It is something special for me, and I am really touched by it.

(She is) someone who has never had the time, never had the opportunity to study opera as I did. She is right in thinking it would not have been the best career for her. As a soul, she was not ready to take that on, but this is a dream (of hers). I can fulfil it for her quietly at home. It is not necessary for her to undergo the stresses and the pressures that I underwent. For Helena it can be a pleasure. It can be something of beauty. All the time as the technique develops, her throat becomes more flexible, and then when it is time to make the special sounds as we did together last night, she is much more open to allowing me to change the shape of things in her vocal chords, to change the shape of things in the whole of her structure to produce the fairy sounds, the birds, the animal sounds, the most useful way in which to produce sound.

Sometimes it is very close to opera, and she has learnt that one cannot hold the throat and the vocal chords in the same position for every note and every sound. She has learnt that this must change from one thing to another, from one sound to another. She has learnt that if it is necessary to do it in a special way, which seems peculiar to her, that is not wrong, it is good. She can allow herself to do that. It is not less than singing opera. Oh no! It is something, (slight pause here) one could almost say it is more.

Last night I was pleased. She understood and permitted this. She needs to learn to trust, to trust and not to judge (and ask), "Is this correct?" when the sound comes. For her this (sound) is much easier than the spoken word. There is no script, written in advance. No one can say, "Ah! She missed one out!" Therefore the fear of judgement is so much less. This is why this special soul we call Helena is so well adapted to this type of work.

Then, just as I have, there is a deep love and appreciation of music. She enjoys the adventure. She enjoys feeling the sound. She enjoys feeling the vibration. With her spiritual gifts, she is able to sense and see the ripples of sound as they move out. She is beginning to see more and more the effects of the sounds. She is beginning to understand how they can help, how they can clear and cleanse energy fields, how they can create space! This is a revelation for her, and it is a joy for me.

I do not know everything. It is no trouble for me to admit that, and I am learning many things through working with her. I am learning through being with her. It is so interesting to see this world, this planet, through the eyes of another being, in this case, Helena. Her perception of what it is or how it is, is so different from mine. It is as though I see everything from a completely different way, a new viewpoint. This is my adventure with her. This is what she gives to me, and her study of spirituality, the time we spent together in Germany over Easter; it helped my soul so much! She thinks she knows that, but she does not realise how much it helped.

She has written already how I was greatly helped by it, and that I was changed, and deeply touched by it. Ah...but now it is more than that. This is why I wish so much the privilege to hold her hand, to help her walk through life, to give her my gifts. It is a fair and balanced exchange. It is a partnership. It is, as I have told her before, a spiritual marriage.

Someone said to her, "Ah! But Maria will leave. Maria will leave you!" No, I will not leave her. Even should a time arrive where there is no longer work for us to do together, or there is no longer the chance for us to play together, even if that happens, the contact between us will always be there. These times, (as) I have been told so many times in the spirit world, these times are for the in-breath of God. They are for the unification of the Divine Essence, not separation. That is something of the past. Yes, it still exists in our little heads, but life is not about that now.

The Divine plan is about the Divine essence knowing itself, knowing that we are all one. The pleasure of the dance of life is that each one of us is different as we dance together. That is why it is so interesting to look around at the different kingdoms, and at the people too, and see how everyone else is doing, to lend a helping hand to one, to accept a helping hand from another.

All of us can advance, and forget not (how) those whom one may perceive as evil are not so. Their behaviour on this planet also serves a purpose. It wakes the rest of us up. We look, we see. They express our shadow side. We all have this. It can have a useful function for each one of us, if we learn to channel the so-called darker energies in a useful way. We all know how sometimes when anger burns inside us, if we look at what it is that makes us angry, makes us react in this way, we can then see how this very thing moves us to action. It takes us away from apathy, where no progress can be made.

I do not suggest we go out and treat others unkindly. Far from it, but we need, as Helena knows in her heart, to accept our failings, and see how they can be tools in our personal spiritual development. It is that. Every so-called flaw in the character of anyone of us is not only a little aid, (but) something we can learn to understand, and accept. Then it goes away.

Because we see we have these things if we are honest, it gives us the ability to empathise with other beings around us, to understand why they are how they are, to let go of judgement. One no longer looks at one's neighbour, and says, "Oh, so-and-so is awful!" One looks and sees, "Ah! That is the reality of that person. That is where they are now." One might even see if there is a possibility of help, or whether one needs to leave them until they are ready to be helped. That is something for our Divine guidance, never forgetting that offering help to someone who chooses to resist it is not helpful. If they choose resistance they have a Divine right to choose that. It is not for us to intervene, and say, "But what you should be doing..." No. Now this is something.

There are those who begin to understand that, but then when somebody comes and says, "I have really reached an impasse in my life. I know not what to do", and holds out a hand for help. That person is worth all the time one can give. I saw Helena hold her hand out. Her life pattern seemed to repeat itself. Nothing much happened. "Where am I going?"

she asked. "What do I do? Am I really on the pathway? Am I really on the pathway? Should I really be living differently as my mother thought?" all these things.

I felt, I Maria, I felt that a guiding soul behind her, beside her, someone still close to the earth, someone still in touch with what it is to be a human, what it is to feel passion, all the passions, all the emotions, the dark and the light and the in between, she needs that, and I saw the extreme difference in her manner of being on this planet when compared with how mine was, and I could see that if we came together, I had something to give her. One could say, the gifts from my past, my incarnation. And to find a soul so tender, and yet shutting out the world, well, it melted my heart. Of course, this coming together with her was prearranged. She knows that, and so do I. But somehow it was so perfectly right.

Do you have another question?

M.V. Do you have a piece of advice for me regarding Lyme's Disease? (This is when Maria changed her tone to one of greater intimacy, and decided to sit down again.)

M. *It was without doubt a great gift for you. It has changed your life. You have seen that.*

M.V. I have seen things, but maybe I did not see everything. If I may share with you, it allowed me to stop doing too many things. It allowed me to rest, because I did not allow myself to rest before, and my body invites me to rest more. By rest, I mean not doing nothing, but doing nothing physically. In another way, I am open to other things such as thinking, and allowing what has to come, come, for writing, insights, and so on. Then it also allowed me to feel love for these very small animals who gave me that disease, and that surprised me as well. I could feel love for them.

M. *You have many insights, and they are good. Lyme's Disease is a gift for you. It will stay with you for as long as you need it. When you pass through the lessons it brings, there will no longer be a need for it, and it can leave you, or remain so dormant that you do not know you have it. It is certainly something for you to make friends with. Not just to love the tick who brought it to you, but friends with the disease itself. Everything has a purpose as you know. I am saying, if the time comes when you no longer need it, it will leave. If it does not leave, accept it and live with it in a loving way. Know that you will always be perfect. Be at peace with it. I do not mean cease to do things to help you overcome it, but to have complete peace in your soul concerning its presence. Let us suppose that it was far worse than it is, and that you passed into another dimension, that you died,*

M.V. Yes I know…

M. *It is not serious. It is just a change of dimension. That is all.*

M.V. Last year I was so bad when it broke out, that I was ready to die, and I thought, "If it is the right moment, I will not fight". I was really ready, and I understand it was a spiritual death, or a human death, but in another sense. Thank you.

M. *That is the most important advice you can be given, to be at peace with it. What ever your situation is, do not judge it as good or bad, just be at peace with it. Acceptance is the key. That does not promise you losing the Lyme's Disease, but it does promise you inner peace, and that is a far greater gift than even physical health, far greater, and others will learn greatly from you. I must say that to give this advice just now, I, Maria, was aided by the angelic realms, the healing realms, those with more insight than I have.*

But I would tell you, Marguerite, that in my incarnated life, I often had illnesses. My health was not good. You know already that I died relatively young. I certainly lost the will to live, because there was nothing here for me. There seemed to be nothing left. I had done all I could. My voice had gone; my lover had died. What could I do? I thank the good Lord I had my poodles, and I thank the good Lord I was supported by those who served me in my house in Paris. They knew my wishes.

Then there were the friends who tried to help, but could not. They felt, and I felt I was really beyond help. It was a very sad time for me, and I wish very much that in respect of these illnesses, I had had the spiritual maturity that you have shown Marguerite. I did not have it. However, in spite of the enormous sadness and pain that I felt during that time, it is so clear to me, the lessons of compassion for others I learnt from it.

Because I underwent that, and I speak now for my own benefit mostly, because I underwent that, it is possible for me to see others in similar situations, to totally love them, to totally understand how they feel, to totally understand the depression, the need to try and hang on to something. One does not know what to grasp for. If everything one takes hold of crumbles in the hand, there is nothing there. It is like a vast, vast emptiness, which nobody other than oneself can understand. This empty hell, this emptiness is the worst. How can one run from it? One cannot run. One can try to mask it with strong medicine. I did.

One can try to pretend that all is well for short periods, but the truth always catches up. Somehow in one's more aware moments, it shows its ugly head, when one has to look and see that no, life is not how I wanted it. It is not how I think I want it. That is what I felt, I myself. I emphasise Marguerite, I am not giving advise to you or Helena now. I am not advising you, either of you. I am expressing myself. I am expressing how I felt, how helpless I felt, how I grasped for things, how when the time when it seemed my only hope was death, and yet, I could not deliberately kill myself.

I knew I could welcome death. When it came, it was a release. I saw the people on the earth, and wondered to myself, why on earth do they love me so much more now than they did when I was there, and I was longing to be loved? There were those who loved me. I know this. That is the enigma of incarnation. Little by little, I moved into greater peace.

I began to understand, at least to some extent, that it is not the love of others that makes a person content. It is love for oneself, recognition of oneself for being the beautiful a soul one is, recognising myself for being so perfect in the eyes of the Source. Seeing that I am beautiful, just as I am, and seeing that if the rest of creation thinks I am hideous, that changes nothing. I am still beautiful. I am very beautiful, and I do not speak about physique. I describe my own soul. I saw this. I see it still. I am exceptionally strong and powerful.

Yes, there are others equally powerful. I do not deny that. There are others more powerful. I do not deny that, but that still leaves me strong with much power for my use, for good. Then I think, what can I do? And I begin to see how I can help those left behind on the earth. I begin to see how I can work positively to help creation. It is the same for many of us in this dimension. We know that our happiness is not complete, when we are aware of suffering, of spiritual blindness amongst those and that which is of, and exists in the earth, and in other universes also.

There is much to be learnt in other universes. There is much to be learnt in this universe, more than the finite mind could ever hope to comprehend. The more I travel a bit, here and there. (She meant she was learning during her travels around universes, etc.) I have my extraterrestrial contacts who bring me great joy. I see the ET in Helena. I see the ET in me. I see that that strengthens our connection even more, although of course it is not essential that we have that, but we have.

But for now I smile on Helena. I give her my blessing. I give her my kisses. I have no desire to leave her now. I love her for her willingness to release me if and when I need to go. I love her understanding that I do not belong to her. That of course is not entirely true. We belong to each other. I love her willingness not to do anything that could hold me up on my spiritual pathway, which of course continues in the dimension in which I live, and through my contact with earthly beings. I love her for all that, but I see also that this partnership I have with her can be of great mutual benefit to us both.

I see also how during the last few years the trust builds up, the ability to work together builds up, and this at the moment is more useful for her than if I were to leave and she were to start again with another. At the same time, it is good that she welcomes other entities also, but I would have her know that I am the one who chooses to stay. It is my wish to be with her just as much as it is her wish that I am with her. I cannot say often enough, how much I appreciate her willingness to finish the partnership at any time I might choose to terminate it. That is really unconditional love, but I do not choose that now. As I stand firmly on the earth (in Helena's body,) I am there, it is my pleasure to be there. I will support her in her comings and goings. We will help each other, and I will guide her in the writing of books, and her spiritual work.

Now I have something very important to say for you to hear Marguerite, and that is my deepest felt appreciation of the support you and Richard have given to Helena. My deepest appreciation of the welcome my presence receives here, my deepest appreciation of the openings you make for this special work with sound to come. You give me my heaven on earth. For this I thank you.

M.V. Thank you.

M. *Other questions?*

M.V. For you Maria, is it time for you to express something else that you felt when you were living on earth that you never expressed?

M. *There was the extreme anger I felt towards Onassis. It was so great, I could not safely express it. I would have been dangerous, which, as others know is why the role of Tosca was so powerful for me. She, an innocent young woman, killed Scarpia. I understood how someone intrinsically good could reach a point where there is a readiness to kill, even though, as another said, I never killed my Scarpia in life.*

There was always this desire with Onassis that I wanted him, and I wanted him, and I wanted him, and I needed him so that the world could see that I really was a desirable woman. There was that, and " Ah Maria, well, she's not so nice. That's why she's alone." So I wanted to be seen with someone who really loved me. Of course we did enjoy the sex, but at the same time, this man was so dangerous. It was like a dance with danger. At the end I felt I lost, I somehow lost in this dance.

When I look at him, and what his soul was doing, I can see that he was in a position where he felt more than one woman, changing women, using other people, all this to him was common sense, the intelligent way to go

365

through life. I could not accept that. It was too hard for me. It broke my heart. It really broke my heart, and yet I could never let go of the hope that perhaps, perhaps he might come back to me, but then he died, and then it was hopeless. I knew he could never come back. Even if I loved and hated him both at once, there was no one else at that time, and as I have said, my voice had gone. So I could not throw myself into opera again. My voice was unreliable.

Helena understands that. So many times her voice won't sing. I do have the power to help that enormously, and I do. It warms my heart to see her pleasure when I help. There is something that I ask of you and Richard. Help Helena to move to a point where hers and mine (energies) are more vibrationly compatible. She does not really mind which of the two of us makes the changes. She wishes to maintain all that she has that is good, but (at the same time) to become so compatible with me that my energies are not too strong for her, and that we can work as one being in her body, without any risk of damaging either her physical form, or her etheric structure, or astral body, or any of those things.

Her own fears were not originally those. Her own fears were those of being controlled by a being far stronger than herself; me. She feels her strength is not compatible with mine. Little by little this is changing, and she does ask in her soul that her energies become more refined, making her an even easier and more suitable vessel for me to come through. What she does not see is that there have already been changes, big changes. She does not see that it is already better. She does not see that she carries more light, but...while she is here, she needs to see more of the truth of that. I will explain it to her more directly when she is alone. Should you feel moved intuitively by your higher self, confirm the things unspoken, which I will convey to her directly, and this would be useful.

Going back to Onassis, your question, the difficulty I had with the anger I felt was that I was so much in my emotions, which were an enormous source of pain, much (of which was) expressed, but much more unexpressed. I already expressed more than many people around me, and yet somehow with that it seemed so hopeless. I felt I lost hope. I hung onto hope for as long as I could, and then somehow, around when he died, how could I hope any more? I lost hope with (his) death. That was too much pain; the hate and the love together.

366

But because I was so much in my emotions, I could not see it from the outside, as they say. I could not see that here were two people, Onassis and Maria with completely different personalities, different needs, different beliefs about how to be, and well, different ideas about what was intelligent and right, and what was not intelligent. I was so much more deeply in my emotions than he was. I could not see that this was not so (much) because I was a woman, as I thought, and he thought. I could not see that it was because the two of us were different.

Sometimes opposites come together, and it is truly beneficial like the partnership between Helena and I, but it (ours) is based around love. I had love for Onassis, I had great love for Onassis, but I was very needy. It was not unconditional. There was so much I wanted from him, and he had his own ideas. From that experience, I have learnt a great lesson. It has given me huge understanding of other incarnated beings in similar situations. As I have looked around, I have seen their grief. I have seen other people's disability to understand each other. Oh yes, I can say the mission of Onassis for me was to assist me in this learning, this very important learning. He achieved this with great thoroughness.

I do not say that with bitterness, for I speak the truth. It was a very hard lesson, very, very hard, but as with many hard lessons, the gifts I have received through it are great. It is only with this new understanding which I did not have before my death, that I am able to say, "Well, thank you for that. It was a gift", although I must admit, even with this understanding, the pain of that has not completely left me, but it does help to speak. I would like, with your permission, to make sounds for myself through Helena, because I feel I could release some of this through her.

M.V. You are reading my mind, and you can of course release whatever is ready now to be released.

Maria, who was sitting down again by this time, got to her feet, pushed the chair back a little to give herself space, and standing beside it, started to tone her pain and suffering in sound with my voice. This lasted about six minutes, before she was composed enough to say to Marguerite in correct French, "I will come back this evening". Marguerite, however, was expecting English, so she did not understand. Eventually, after some faltering incorrect French, because I, wanting to help, became too present for a moment or two, Maria spoke these words in English, and was easily understood.

M.C. I want to come again this evening, because the release I have made needs time, and a big opening. I need to go to the angels, to be in the heavenly space to assimilate the changes in myself. In time, I will stay close to Helena today. I wish to be with her, to comfort her, to thank her for all that she has done for me, but especially for this morning. I am very touched by both of you for providing this space. I thank you.

M. *I thank you too for having accepted the invitation, and be at peace.*

M.C. It is finished.

Marguerite had emitted a soft humming sound at the end while Maria was still gasping for breath in my body having finished her toning. The sweetness of this sound was unbelievably comforting for her. It was not wasted on me either. From somewhere close to my body, I sighed a sigh of relief. At the time, I had marvelled at the way I was not feeling any of this pain transmitted by sound. All of it was audible to me, but I remained untouched by it.

When I returned to my body, I could feel no traces of it left behind. Energetically, I felt clean. As Marguerite said, "She did not want to give it to you, just to release it into the physical dimension." I asked if we should now do something to transmute the vibrations released, or send them into the Light, but Marguerite said she had already done that as the sound came out.

I cannot finish this chapter without first writing more about the experience of listening to it as the emotions Maria released were expressed by these vocal sounds. I could barely believe what I heard. She let out her feelings of suffering and despair. There was a whole series of truly terrible sounds, including moaning and groaning, such as one could easily imagine coming from the fires of Hell. It was utter despair and the agony of the soul, truly unbearable pain. Intermittently I heard shrieks of frustration coming out with the complete hopelessness of it all.

Quite near the beginning, Maria had placed her (my) hands over her eyes, so that the little bit of me still present in my body could experience the utter darkness that had seemed to fill her life at the end, for as no daylight could now pass through my eyelids, it was as though the light had been turned out, and only this pain-filled dark vacuum remained. Thus was I becoming aware of the misery she experienced towards the end of her life. It seemed to me, through the body language, that she wept, even though no actual tears were shed.

I felt it all coming to a conclusion at the point when she seated herself down on the chair again, and took so much comfort from the gentle humming of Marguerite. The fact that none of this pain stuck to me had happened automatically, and was nothing to do with the energetic cleansing of the negative energies by Marguerite as they came out.

Afterwards, I pondered over how amazing it was that a healing such as Maria had received could be achieved in this way. Even more remarkable was the fact that it could happen through me! It did not seem so many years behind me that it was pointed out to me in somebody's workshop that I was a very reserved, and a severely suppressed straight faced "nice" English woman, who was anything but authentic. Yet here was a woman with Maria's level of passion able to express it all through me. I had not become like her, but the changes in myself must have been greater than I had thought. Life is truly amazing!

Over three weeks later, I was ready to transcribe the text from this tape, and rather reluctantly put myself through the ordeal of listening to Maria's pain coming out again. I knew I was afraid to hear it, because I remembered it as sounding so terrible. It was no less terrible. In fact, fully present in my body, I experienced it even more keenly than when I was in France.

To think that Marguerite had been capable of listening to all this as it happened! It takes great courage and compassion to be with someone in that much misery. I turned that volume down, for fear that the neighbours might hear, and think either I was in serious distress, or else that I was torturing some helpless small animal.

I do not really believe I am thought to be capable of that, but even so, it was not in me to inflict that kind of worry about me on anyone else. I wondered how it was that Maria thought I would allow her to do express all that through me. Not having had time to think about it first was a big help. That way, I could not get frightened. She told me later that she had trusted me, and knew that this experience would be helpful to me, and not just to her. It was the revelation it could happen like this that helped, and the fact that my beloved Maria would be happier and feeling more comfortable with herself afterwards, combined with the satisfaction of having actually found something I could do for her, not forgetting Marguerite's part in all this of course. It seemed to me that it brought more balance into our friendship.

As a footnote, I would like to add that Maria is pleased that these personal things are included in her book. "It must go out fully", she told me when I came to write it all out at home later.

Chapter 37

The Seventh Interview

As it turned out, Marguerite and Richard were both out on Thursday evening, so it was Friday afternoon before Maria could be interviewed again.

M. *We can begin.*

M.V. I welcome you Maria, and I hope you can tell us how you are feeling today.

M. *Much better, lighter, less worried, more peaceful. It was not just Helena who needed a rest after yesterday,* (but) *I also to assimilate the changes. Yesterday you had questions. Have you more?*

M.V. Yes, if you are ready.

M. Yes.

M.V. I would like to know, when we meet somebody in despair, as you were, without any hope, what can we say, or what can we do to help him, or to assist him? What would you have needed at the time, for example?

M. *I would have needed someone I trusted to explain to me that all was well, and all was perfect, as it was. I would have asked, but what can I do with this pain I feel, the emotional pain? The answer from a good angel would have been, "Just accept it. There will come a time when it will pass. Just accept it." Every adversity has its gift. This is something the human race still experiences much difficulty with. I mean many of them.*

Things should always be perfect according to their own ideas. They cannot see that we are here on the earth, when we are incarnated, to experience everything, not everything in one life time, but as much as is appropriate for each soul. I could not see for example, the real love and compassion that my pain would attract to me. I was not at peace with my life. It is a very common thing in the human condition, which those incarnate endure to have a lack of self worth, something they are longing to disbelieve.

Part of them would prefer to believe they are wonderful, but when that becomes too difficult, they look for the outside worshipers, those around them to say, "You are wonderful! You are beautiful! You are loved!" When it comes from others, it is like nectar, but the comfort does not last. The next day the emptiness returns. They need more. They always need more, more love from those around them. The moment it is not there, or they are alone with themselves, the despair is still there. It does not go. One can distract oneself in this life. One can distract oneself from that by performing marvels.

One can distract oneself from that by achieving the things that the human race consider beautiful, wonderful, marvellous, to draw in the admiration of others, but it changes nothing inside. For those without hope, one could ask, "Now tell me my dear, what is your greatest fear?" If they say illness, one can say, "But that is normal for the human condition. It is painful, yes on one level, but it will not harm your soul. Always remember that. Always remember it will pass.

Do not forget that inside of every person, and every thing lies the Divine spark, something equally beautiful, and equally radiant in all of us. If our soul has chosen to experience suffering, you can be sure there is a reason for it. Welcome the suffering. Welcome the hopelessness. Embrace it. You will learn. Much is said among those who would progress about the Light side of each of us, and our shadow side. It does not work only to accept the Light side. One must accept the shadow side as well. One must love that too. It has a purpose. Things only go awry, when the shadow side is given total power, and is not guided by the Divine spark. That is what causes the cruelty in this world. It is that. It is ignorance. It is spiritual blindness.

For every so-called character weakness, or bad things we do not like to look at, there is a useful purpose. It is like a pair of scissors. If you wish to make a dress, a pair of scissors to cut the cloth can be essential, but if you go out with the scissors in your hand, and you use them to stab your friends in the heart, and kill them so, that is the wrong use of the scissors. The scissors are neither black nor white. They are a tool, as is our so-called shadow side.

All the experiences we have in this life have a purpose. They are all part of the Divine plan. When a soul has really experienced enough of that thing, of one particular thing, that soul can be ready for another experience. It might be joy. It might be anger. It might be frivolity, playfulness. Who knows? It might be sadness. It could be deprivation of something that this person thinks they would like to have, but whatever it is, it is a gift. It might be love. It could be hate.

How can we really understand the human condition, if we deny ourselves the opportunity to feel all of these things. When I look at what I went through, I see now how much, how deep it was. My experiences were very intense. I was known for that. It was as though each lesson had to be very thorough, intense despair, great anger, and also great love, great love. Great love for many, many things. I did learn compassion. That was one of the gifts of that life as Maria.

Why was it all so intense for me? Well, it is perhaps not a truth that everyone wants to hear, but sometimes when there is something very important to achieve on this earth, the energy of several souls blends together to form one who is exceptionally strong. There have been many people throughout history, who have been exactly that. That is what I was , and what I am, and what I continue to be.

Power goes two ways. Power is very capable of many things. The question is, "Does one use this for the Light, or just to serve some kind of ego, in which case it can be painfully destructive and damaging to the soul energy?" Now that is a lesson that some have to learn, which can only be learnt through experience. That is why not all (of) powerful people are so very good.

But now, I speak for myself, I am very consciously walking towards the Light. It is not that I wish to take Helena there, or that she wishes to take me there, but I do know that when we all walk together, thus I have inspired others also, it is more powerful, just as I am powerful, because I am more than one soul.

So I would say to those who are in despair, and depressed, "It passes, and when a soul has chosen to undergo this at a sacrifice of personal happiness done in service of the Light, if a soul is in deep despair, and not consciously looking for Light, this condition, this despair, this suffering, can cause them to turn around and look towards the Light." Whether that happens before or after death is another thing. It is not so important whether that happens before death or after death, so-called death. It will happen at the right time for that soul.

So I would say, Marguerite, that if you wish to comfort such a person, and you feel it is appropriate, you may be able to call on whichever of the words and thoughts I have just given you on the matter. Use them for these people. Some are not ready to hear that. Others are. Those who are not ready to hear it, the fact that you are somebody who cares, and that you come with love, is the most that you can hope to do, and it is not a little. It is a great thing.

You can only move... you actually cannot move those there (other people). You can guide. You can give them rays of hope, but it is for these people themselves to decide when and if they are ready to accept that. We all decide on a soul level. That is not the responsibility of another. One can only give help where it is desired, and where the recipient is ready to receive it.

M.V. If you don't have anything to add to this, I have another question.

M. *Yes.*

M.V. It is a question about you. Did you meet the soul of Onassis after you left the earth, or your physical body?

M. *I did ask about that after I arrived here. I saw that his needs on this plane were very different to mine, and that it was not appropriate at the moment to spend time with him. I did pass quite close to him, just once or twice, because in some senses I found him very alone. I...with my love I did not wish that he should feel totally abandoned. I wanted him to know there were those who cared. It was very painful to go near him, and I wept many tears. There are others with him. I wished him well, and whilst making the sign of the cross, I turned away, and asked that he receive the help he needed. He had served me in many ways. I knew that in spite of my pain. It is still painful to think of him somehow, and yet I do feel love.*

There have been other things for me to do, things for me to learn here, other people to help, more service to give, but it is not unbalanced. I receive greatly. And because I have followed Helena in her spiritual studies, I am much better able to answer your questions than I would be otherwise. You see, not all of the answers come from the angels. Some do...but there are certain things that need to be learnt about the earth on the earth, and this is why for many a disincarnate person, it is so helpful to return without incarnating just to see what is happening down there? What are they doing over here? What is that about? and if one is very close to somebody vibrationally, as I am to Helena, it is possible to tune into the environment, to hear all that is said around, and to learn, to watch, to observe.

Observations are very important. I am seeing many things through Helena's eyes. In this way she and I have learnt together. She is still learning. There is a great deal she does not know. I am learning also. If I play with other people, it is the same thing, learning, seeing what happens. It is also very interesting.

M.V. I have a question if I may? For a wounded soul, how is it possible to heal a soul as you see it?

M. *We all know that love is the greatest healer. It is always good to remember though, the things I have already said. We cannot heal a soul, even a wounded soul, who does not feel ready to be healed. They may come and ask for help, but that comes from the mind sometimes. If that soul is ready to be healed, the best healing you can give that person is* with love, love and empathy, and lending your ear, those things. You don't have to tell them what to do. That is their own business. If they ask for advice, you can give your opinion, but to anybody wanting to help, I would say, do not go to another and a say, you should do this. You should do that. That is not helpful. Try and find out what they want to do.

M.V. It was not the sense of my question. Maybe I expressed myself in the wrong way. Well practically, talking of you, or about you, last time I saw how you got your self-healing, and I just wanted to know how are you going to, if you know that, how are you going to achieve the healing, as you said you felt still a little pain?

M. *How am I going to achieve healing?*

M.V. Do you know? Yes.

M. *Your question still is not clear.*

M.V. Your soul, your soul self, well the part of you we name soul. Yesterday, you did a great healing, and it is not finished. Do you know how you are going to complete this?

M. *I could express more with sound. The possibility to speak openly, and not be judged, the wish that if I speak of something in me which might not be admired, you will not stop loving me. That is healing. The feeling I do not have to get everything right for you, the knowing that when I answer your questions, if I cannot answer them as well as you had hoped, that you will not regard me as useless, because you will know that I have done the best I can, and that surely is all that any of us can do.*

So, one could say, just by being you, you are able to help me. Knowing I am being supported in my spiritual work. The acceptance of this is good, but I also have to learn, that when I do things just to please myself, even though they perhaps go unrecognised, that is sufficient. I would like to be totally free of the need for any outside recognition.

However, I would say here that I do understand that to serve Helena anonymously is not right for her at the moment. Somehow, she receives great comfort from my presence. It is as though the child in her still needs a mother to hold her hand. I am willing to do this for her with both of my hands. I know she hopes that one day she will have more strength, but remember, in my lifetime, I wanted children. There was the one who died very young, the one the world did not hear about for many years, but I never had children to nurture. The mother in me was unsatisfied, and although that is only one aspect of my spiritual marriage with Helena, and by the way, there are no rules.

One can have a spiritual marriage with more than one person at a time without being unfaithful, but I certainly have that with Helena. That is just one of the things that nurtures me, being able to do that, and then at the same time, there can be a sort of sisterly relationship with her, and from her the sharing, just like being a good friend, those things. Have you a question? I think your question is what can you personally do to help me now. Am I right?

M.V. At the moment, no.

M. *What is your question?*

M.V. You have answered. It is what can you do for yourself.

M. *Ah, ah!*

M.V. What can you do for yourself?

M. *Loving Helena is definitely part of it. Needing someone to love who does not run away, and yet at the same time, to give her her freedom, or rather, to recognise that she has freedom, for I cannot give her what she has not got in that respect. She has it. Recognising that, just as she recognises my Divine right to leave her at any time, even though she would rather I did not. Are there other questions?*

M.V. Yes, another one, the last one I think. It is about Richard. I feel he is blocked in his throat, and he never sings, and when I invite him to sing with me, and even when it is only sounds, not just when singing other things, but sounds, he is blocked, and nothing comes out, only very rarely, and well, we never worked on this matter, and I am wondering how it will be for him this next weekend. Is there a way to support him, or to give him confidence?

M. *Yes, this beautiful man! He does not feel comfortable in that area. Deep down inside he is afraid of it. He knows it is not good to be blocked, but at the same time, there is a deep subconscious fear of moving the blockage. But, being in a group, where he can let things go a tiny bit without really being noticed, and we do not know yet how many times that will take, that is a way he could open this. But do not be concerned about it.*

When the time is right, all will happen. It is not for us to say when the time is right. One longs to help, one longs to aid. With his mind he wishes to be unblocked, but remember, the mind is only part of the human condition. Deep down inside the question is what does his soul want? What does his soul need? What is he ready for? These are not questions for me to answer. All we can do is make sure that, if he wishes it, he can be put in situations where something could begin, just like making a tiny weenie little crack in a solid wall. And then, little by little, it can happen for him that that begins to open up.

M.V. Well I just had to insist a little for him, because he did not even want to come to the workshop, but I told him it was to support Helena.

M. *Very diplomatic. Very good. His energy will support (her) in any case. So what you said was not completely untrue. It will help him if he sees both the successes and difficulties that others have, because in some ways, that man feels alone. Of course all of us have problems of our own, which are special to us. No one else has it quite the same, but there are always many people with things that are a little the same. It is just the balance, the intensity (that is different), the slight variation. That is all.*

Who thinks Helena had an open throat chakra? Even now it is often closed. That is one reason why she cannot always sing. That is one reason why she is very dependent on me to be there. Otherwise it does not work for her, and she is depressed. But that is normal, because she would like so much to do it.

378

Yes, the human condition is a difficult journey to make alone. We can only be there to support each other in so far as we are capable. That is the best we can do with our love, and yes, you have done much for him, which is very wonderful, and not only for him, but for many.

M.V. Thank you. I have no more questions, but now you are free to stay, and do what you feel you have to do, or sing or express.

M. *I would like to make sound for the benefit of all who will be present at this workshop, you and I, Helena, Richard, and others who come.*

M.V. Noëlle, Geneviève and Georgia.

Maria stood up, and toned for five minutes. Then, sitting down again, she continued speaking.

M. *That is enough.*

M.V. Thank you. Thank you very much.

M. *I bless you Marguerite.*

M.V. I bless you as well, and be at peace.

M. *Thank you.*

M.V. You are welcome.

M. *It was my pleasure.*

Chapter 38

The Two Day Workshop

I seriously wondered how I would cope with this, as it followed a very late night giving a conference which had lasted two hours in Montbéliard, which I had finally managed to bring to a close with some difficulty, as the enthusiastic audience had more questions than there was time to reply to. I had spoken about the spiritual aspects of animals, and their purpose and place on the planet, just as I had experienced this personally. I had illustrated it with as many stories as I could manage in the time, and finally climbed into bed back in Elsenheim at about ten to one in the morning, following a lovely hot bath.

In view of this, it was hardly surprising that I suffered greatly from acute abdominal pain for the first two thirds of the first day of the seminar. The interesting aspect of that was, that when I slipped into a sufficiently trance-like state to channel Maria's voice for the group, in spite of the severity of the spasms in my abdomen, I became unaware of them, just until I stopped channelling. I later heard someone used to performing in public in England say that when one is performing, very often one does not feel the pain.

We called this seminar,"*Healing and Communication with Vocal Sounds.*" The group was very slow to assemble in the group room, so I decided to begin the morning with trance dancing to music, so that the less late members were occupied while waiting for the even later ones. We were only five this time, but as I could not help noticing, I had exactly the "right" people present, those being the ones who needed or were ready for the experiences to follow. The small number made the whole thing very intimate and personal, so that each participant had plenty of attention from Maria and me. Although the exact order of events had already escaped from my memory by the time I made my notes on it, I could remember the different things we had done.

The morning included "Body Flow" as I had learnt it in the workshops of Rhea Powers and Michael Barnett years earlier, introductions, toning low sounds together to warm the voice and activate the chakras, some higher sounds, chanting a second time as a group, and some more dancing while the music "Bones" was being played. Then there were Maria's individual toning sessions, and a number of pauses between events for each person to share their experiences and feelings.

Lunch was served for all by Marguerite, and before we had finished the meal, Georgia arrived to join the group, so now we totalled six. I spoke to her to find out a little about her, and gave her a résumé of the events of the morning. Before we left for the forest, we reassembled in the group room, so that, supported by the group, Maria could give her a personal toning. As inspired by Maria, I told Georgia when to join in with her own voice. The harmonies and the complete sound made by all six of us were wonderful! For feed-back, Georgia said, "It was like being bathed in sound."

In the Forest

I directed the group to go in silence and alone to find a tree that he or she felt attracted to, ask for its permission and support to sing there, and then to sing sounds without words to express any suppressed or buried emotions to release them, asking that the negative aspects be transformed in Light.

I spite of a short healing session from Richard during a morning tea break, which had given me some temporary relief, I was still enduring sharp pain in my abdomen, which felt very hard, stretched and strained, it seemed to protrude much more than usual, and there was no way I could hold myself properly with that level of pain, and the muscles in tight spasm. I had eaten lightly at lunchtime, because I felt my system was not coping with food, and gave thanks that my legs were still working. Thus, I proceeded slowly and alone through the trees. Being by myself, I was at last able to relax in other ways, and to my huge relief the worst of the pain began to abate. I ate lightly again in the evening, and although still sore inside the next day, I knew that I was on the mend, and could enjoy myself at last. I sang a little in the Forest, but not much, as my voice was weak just then, and it did not seem so important for me. What I needed was exactly what I gave myself, the time to relax and be alone doing very little.

The group was slow to return to the cars, which pleased me greatly, as I took it as a sign that they were enjoying themselves either singing, or just being out there with nature all around them. While waiting, I noticed some lovely flowers growing wild beside the car park, and took great pleasure in gathering some to take back and place on the dining table.

Back in Elsenheim, we gathered in the group room for the final sharing of the day. I was pleased. The first day had reached a satisfactory conclusion, and without the pain in my intestines, I could start to really enjoy myself.

Maria had felt so present all day, doing her special work aiding, balancing and harmonising the sounds we made. As I heard expressed by one of the group whilst they were talking amongst themselves, "La Callas était là". (Callas was there). Hearing this was music to my ears. The results coming from the group during the day had touched and impressed me greatly. There was always a lot of power in the room, which helped everyone. It seems to me that when the auric field is really open, the power and Light belonging to all of us that is the Source becomes available, and can be used for the good of all creation, which of course includes both ourselves, and all of the other kingdoms everywhere.

Sunday

A new day dawned, and there was a happy me to go with it. Full of enthusiasm to see what wonderful things would happen during our second day together, I took myself punctually down to the group room. I found myself alone down there for ages. Although apparently content with the seminar and what it was bring them, the group showed a strong preference for a late start. I went upstairs, and found them barely halfway through their breakfast. Strangely, this did not bother me at all. I just said, "Come to the group room when you are ready".

382

Returning downstairs, I decided to enjoy this unexpected free time by listening to Maria on a CD singing "*Ombra Leggiera*" in Italian. (It is known in English as the shadow song). It is one of my favourites, and I was loving every syllable of it. One of the group was later to tell me that when she had heard it from upstairs, she thought it was me singing. Naturally, I took this as an enormous compliment. Who would not? My original plan had been to start with dancing, so that the late-comers would not have missed anything too important, but in view of the fact that some were almost still chewing the last mouthful of breakfast, I decided it would be better for them to begin by listening to this beautiful recording of Maria that I had just been playing to myself. There were sighs of relief all round! Several of them were moved to tears by the beauty of it. When, at Marguerite's suggestion, I invited them all to share whatever they wanted about that, I drew attention to the words in this aria meaning "Sing with me", as I felt they contained a message from Maria for all of us.

"Bones" had been a hit on Saturday, so I decided to use more of this music for some of the dancing. I noticed I could not dance too well to this myself, so as inspired, Maria and I started walking around helping each person in turn with silent energy work, to further open the chakras, and especially in most cases the throat chakra to aid the freedom and quality of the voice. Those not being worked on were still trance dancing to it. I marvelled as each person, none of whom had had any prior warning that this was going to happen, understood without a syllable being uttered, that it would be best to stay still until we moved on to the next person. There were one or two more cases of tears, some I think, because people were moved by the beauty of the experience, and maybe for others, they were private pain being released.

During the sharing which followed, it became evident that one of the group needed some extra help, so as guided by Maria, I instructed her to stand in the centre, while the rest of us chanted for her sending her all the love we were capable of. When all was quiet again, before allowing her to sit down, Maria inspired me to ask her to go round each one of us, and ask he or she to give her a hug. She was about to sit down at the end of this, but as directed by Maria, I forbade this. "You still have not received enough love", I told her, "so you must go round a second time asking each of us for a second hug." I knew full well that this was quite an ordeal for her, because, as Marguerite pointed out to me afterwards, she lives her life helping others, but although she wants love, she does not ask for it. The interesting thing was, that the second time, the hugs seemed to be even more meaningful on all sides, and never just a mechanical exercise to appease me. I was pleased.

Then the group sang together for Nature, and this was followed by something I would never have thought of myself. Maria suggested that each person who was willing, stood up and chanted a wordless duet with her. They were given the freedom to select a subject themselves, so that we were singing with a purpose. It could be anything. I thought the task of singing a duet in front of everyone with such a famous opera singer would be so daunting, that it was possible that no one would have the courage to come forward.

I was only left in this painful suspense for an instant, as the one who had just been put through the hugging exercise, bravely stepped forward, and asked if it could be for herself. The rest of the group remained silent in keeping with Maria's wishes. Everyone did this! I was amazed! What a brave group! I could not have felt more support both for Maria and myself.

The subjects chosen included things like Creation, and expanding its awareness, and also the dolphins. I could hear the difference in the moods and tones used for each one. In the dolphin music, for example, whale song was included by Maria, and Georgia, who sang with her, commented afterwards that Maria's voice had given her the feeling she was in water, even though she was not familiar with whale song herself. She had recognised the dolphins' voices.

For me, partially present, it was like working with a horse. It was always a partnership, never just Maria or I trying to impress, but a real team effort. I was thrilled, and found this new experience fascinating.

Afterwards, we took it in turns to share how it was, and then danced or moved peacefully to "*My Lapis Heart*", which I played twice, because it was so obviously being well enjoyed by all.

Lunch time again, and I was sighing with a relaxed contentment inside me. Marguerite wanted to know what we were going to do in the afternoon in the forest, but I had not yet received the inspiration myself, so she had to wait. By the time we left, I was able to tell her what type of environment we needed. We wanted trees to sing amongst near a car park away from the road and the public, so that when we sang, we would both be undisturbed, and disturbing no one. I promised further instructions on arrival. I was still waiting for mine.

The perfect spot was selected by Marguerite and Richard. When we arrived, I only knew about the first thing we had to do. So I led the group just a few steps into the forest undergrowth, where we could form a circle around a very small and rather dead looking tree. We all sang together for Nature.

On completion, inspired by Maria I am sure, but also in keeping with my own wishes, I told them that I, Helena, would like them to sing again, but this time for Maria, who would remain silent. I wanted them to give her their love and appreciation for all that she had done in this way. This would be the first time the group had sung together without the support and assistance of Maria's voice. I understood from Maria that it was important they had the chance to discover that they could sing without her before the group split up, and they were on they own. I also understood the emotional need for them to express their thanks to her in some way, and sound was a gift she could receive and accept, even in her own dimension. It was an opportunity for both of us to listen to the fruits of the last two days, without having to take part.

I stepped outside the circle with the intention of keeping myself completely out of the way until if was finished. Maria could go wherever she liked. Someone sang the first note, and the others joined in without hesitation.

Meanwhile, contrary to my expectations, Maria slipped into my body again, and we walked into the centre of the circle. This was definitely the best place to be. She and I could listen to the toning together. We could hear and feel the wonderful gentle loving sounds and vibrations wafting into the centre of the circle where Maria had based herself. These people were not fully-fledged opera singers, or even professional singers. Some may have tried before with limited success, one of them with two years of classical training, which had not been fruitful. They were amateurs!

Yet they were showing themselves capable of putting the love and feeling into their music, which is the very essence of healing, and sending it out for whatever purpose they chose. Maria was receiving all of it. I remembered the words one of my spiritual guides had given me in the early 1980s, "All we really need to know is how to love". Once, someone had the need to let out a scream in the middle of these loving sounds, which Maria totally understood, and chose to support energetically during her own silence.

Meanwhile, Maria was bathed in sound. With my physical eyes half open, she surveyed the singing group. She was sensing our dimension. For her, as she looked out through my eyes, it was as though she saw it all through a thin mist. This dimension is of course denser than hers, so maybe it was still having a foot in her own reality, that made ours appear so misty, and yet she could see it almost as though she were incarnated. All the time, she placed a hand on the little tree in the centre of the circle, thus using this to orientate herself in the same way she had used the chair when she walked around or stood beside it when being interviewed by Marguerite.

I felt her feelings, most of which were expressed to the group when she chose to speak to them after the singing ceased. She was very touched in her heart by this "present" they had given her. (Later I was to read in a book that presents of any kind had always been very special to her during her incarnation). She said she enjoyed being there with her feet in my hiking boots, and feeling the earth beneath them. She had looked up at the sky, observed the group and the trees, in fact really been able to experience a moment in our earthly reality. She noticed how beautiful it can be here when one is encircled by love. Each person in the circle was acknowledged by her in turn, and given his or her own little message. She was delighted with all of them.

During their singing, she had carefully noted the fruits of this little seminar we had given, observing with pleasure the results. Later, she showed me pictures of her in the group room, and how she had spent time going round each person busily supporting them, and aiding them by organising the energies in their auras to help with the singing. It was clear to me that she had put her whole self into the process of seeing what could be achieved. For her it had been extremely rewarding, and totally absorbing.

She knew that the group did not want to lose her, so she told them that there was no separation, and that she was not going anywhere. She would always be with them. She deliberately declined to finish her speech for that very reason, and therefore did not say good-bye. She just stopped talking, and stepped out of my body. There was time left for all of us to take a short silent walk alone to absorb the events of the weekend, and especially the afternoon. Again, some were late returning to the car, and we joyfully sang encouragement to the last latecomer who arrived running! How much they all enjoyed those trees on that lovely sunny afternoon.

Back in Elsenheim, we had a last group sharing, after listening to part of the CD of whale song, which I had given Marguerite on a previous visit. After some tea, three of them left to go home, and just Richard, Marguerite and I remained for the evening.

Before dinner, I went for a lovely walk in the forest and fields, the second half of which was in the moonlight. I did not use a torch, for the moon was bright. I saw three deer, who had warily come out of the trees into the fields, thinking no doubt, that the humans would have gone indoors by now. The first two were in a field together, and later, when I saw the third, it was in a field a little distance apart from the first two. I shared this with Marguerite, and she commented that for her, it symbolised two other people in my life. I was the one a little apart, and the other two represented Richard and her. I experienced a lot of peace during that walk. The workshop and other engagements behind me, it seemed there was nothing left to do that evening apart from enjoy myself.

After dinner, Richard channelled that it was time for me to release any baggage I no longer needed to carry, and also that I was perfect for what I was doing now. The first comment was helpful, and the second reassuring, and very good to hear.

Chapter 39

The Eighth Interview, Special Sounds and My Departure

The morning after the seminar, I rose early. More sleep might have been welcome, but I had many notes to write about Maria, and wanted to finish them before leaving France while all was still fresh in my mind.

I mused over the manner in which the group had thanked Maria with their singing in the forest, and thought she most probably she had never been thanked quite like that before. I wondered what she had thought of it. Maria, reading my thoughts as usual, commented, "Well, it was certainly better than being mobbed by the crowds on my way out of the theatre!" I put my pen down immediately, as I laughed out loud at her humour, something that had been absent during the last two days. Having shared this comment of hers with Marguerite and Richard, I returned to my notebook, and finished the notes.

Just as I was wondering what to do next, I met Marguerite in the kitchen, and she asked me if I would like to let her have another interview with Maria. I gave her an affirmative without hesitation, having taken it for granted that following the two busy days of seminar she would have too many other things to do for anything with Maria to be possible. I also thought that if such a thing was meant to be, Marguerite would suggest it, and she had.

By the time we were ready to start, I was very conscious that my energy felt extremely low, and had few expectations for a good result. However, this was the last chance for heaven only knows how long, so it was not to be missed. It would be the eighth time Marguerite had interviewed Maria. This is how it went.

I knew that Maria wanted to start with sounds. She and I were both aware that I needed something to still my very busy mind, although as it turned out, there was more to it than that. This lasted for six minutes. Maria brought her energy, which filled my body, and made what followed much more powerful than I had thought it would be.

M.V. I welcome you.

M. Thank you. I wish you a good morning.

M.V. Thank you. Now may we know what the purpose or subject of your sounds is?

M. *Yes. First of all, it was a connection with the stars. There are special beings up there with whom I am connected, and it was my desire that they should be present in this room for this interview, bringing the special vibrations that they have. They understand the language of sound, which is why it is possible for me to reach them in this way. Of course there are other ways, but if I were not in Helena's body, I would have used sounds similar to those you have just heard, but in my own dimension. Everything has sound. Thought has sound.*

So if you think, maybe some people would have called them with telepathy, but then you remember that everything has sound, you will see that telepathy and sound can be the same. The sounds I have made were visible. The higher notes were lines of light connecting us to the stars, connecting us to the star people, connecting us to the extraterrestrial peoples, the spiritually advanced races. With those notes, one does not reach the less spiritual realms, because they operate on a different vibration. So you can say it is like a telephone line, and when one knows which number to dial, then the destination is assured.

So, I made the connection with the stars and the star people, and also the angels, the special angels who dwell in those realms, that they come here also. We know that there are already angels present in this house, but those I called are guests you have not had before, and we ask that you welcome them also.

M.V. I have already been aware of the presence of two beings, who were not angels in our bedroom one morning when I woke up, and I was very surprised, because our presence in the bed did not disturb them at all, and I did not feel disturbed either. I realised that there were at least two houses here, the physical house, and, in another dimension, a house of light with these people. Then I walked around my house with more respect, but I did not have any more conscious contact with them.

M. Yes. There are several different realities existing in the same space like parallel universes.

M.V. Yes, I saw that. I understood that they are not elsewhere, but here as well.

M. Yes. This is so, and as the veils between the different dimensions become finer, more and more often, you will be aware of these other realities. It is just, as is well known, in some parts, there can be elves and other beings whose homes are in the rocks, so it would seem. They are also part of another reality. They are not visible to those without extrasensory perception, but they are nonetheless there.

The other purpose of the sounds, the lower sounds, was the preparation of Helena's body for the channelling. The whole exercise was beneficial for her, because as she knew, something was necessary for her to move out of her mind. The sounds also served the purpose of clearing her energies, expanding her auric field, and allowing the energy that she has to flow, thus making this transmission much easier for both of us. There was that also. And one or two of the notes, at Helena's request, were especially for you.

M.V. Thank you.

M. It is desired, Marguerite, that you have more and more opportunities to experience different energies. And quite apart from quickening the vibrations by the presence of the star beings, which surround us now, quite apart from that, their presence in the room is part of giving you such an opportunity, so that your spiritual horizons continue to expand.

It is very good that you are already connected as much as you are to the fairy kingdom, and the flowers, the daffodils are something special for you also. Have you considered planting a yellow rose in your garden?

M.V. Many years ago, yes, but I never did that. We suggest that you look for one beautifully fragrant, and full of health, (for) many strains of rose now have much better resistance to disease than the older roses; and that you choose this rose for yourself, and plant it with blessings in the garden. I feel the colour yellow is needed more in your garden, yellow daffodils, and a yellow rose, but remember the fragrance, for what is a rose without a sweet perfume? Remember also, that just before the petals fall, (you can) gather them for making rose water, or decorating your cuisine. You can eat them.

Choose your rose carefully, using intuition. Ask for spiritual guidance. That way, the petals will taste sweet, and not bitter as if you do (choose without intuition). It does not have to be a big rose, just large enough to please your personal preference, and able to share its beauty with you in the sunshine.

The fairies will come. "What is this she has planted? What is this? Ah! Oh yes! We would like to work with this. Oh yes, and how pretty the leaves are with the dewdrops on them! Those little bits of water capable of reflecting all the colours of the rainbow. Oh yes!" say the fairies, "We would like this! It does not matter that it has thorns. That is not a problem for us," say the fairies. We ask that you take care of your pretty hands, because of the thorns. We would not like you damaged, but we would love it if you could enjoy this plant. Just one would be enough.

Yes, it is the fairy voices speaking. The friend of roses, Maria, she is also here, and it is she who speaks now," for, as you know Marguerite, all is one, so I Maria can tell you that to speak the voice of the fairies one minute, and to be myself the next is perfectly natural. I do not have to leave. I step back very slightly, I tune in to the fairy kingdom. It is almost as though, but not quite, that I Maria, am channelling the fairies using the body of Helena. Not how's that? What do you think?

M.V. Yes, that is natural.

M. *The fairies, (are) very happy.*

M.V. It does not seem strange to me.

M. *The fairies, (she claps her hands) they are clapping their hands with joy.*

M.V. Yesterday night, I could not sleep, and I was inspired with ideas of writing a story, and now that you speak about star people, I wonder if they were inspiring me, because it was an insight, which did not come from earth. It was as though I saw people on earth from very far away, and as if I made a report on what was going on, on the earth, from another point of view?

M. *Yes. It was exactly that. Just, in a way, as I see life on Earth from another point of view, when I look through the eyes of Helena. When I look from the perspective of her life, and it is just as it was for her yesterday, when the group was singing for me. Then (as) I was speaking to the group through Helena, she was able to see how this dimension appeared through my eyes, and how I experienced it all in her body, and how it was different and beautiful from what I had...from what I would have expected before. It is like that. Marguerite, your perception is very good.*

M.V. It will be a new adventure.

M. *Yes. If you would like to trust it, trust it. You have the capacity to receive ideas from other dimensions, which no one on Earth has given to you first. And just as you have accepted this one, the communication with the star people, the star people, the angels, all...*(Here the tape was turned over, so we lost a few words, but she may have said, "all according to your wish".)

M.V. Thank you for the confirmation.

M. *The star beings are asking me to ask you, "Is there anything more you would like to know about us?"*

M.V. Yes.

M. *For example?*

M.V. Well, I don't know. I don't know. What do they think I should know about them that I don't know? If I don't know, I can't ask.

M. *Yes, yes.*

M.V. Tell me something that I need to hear now.

M. *They have understood the question very well. They thank you very much for asking, because for them that shows an openness to hearing. They are impressing upon me the importance of writing down everything that happens with them. Little by little, these experiences with star beings, and/or other realities will start to form a picture. You will find, when you look back, that you have a clearer larger picture of the whole, of all that is, or perhaps more precisely, of more than "of all that is", for there are lots of everything, although not just yet, than you had before. This will greatly enrich your spiritual life. This will enable you to explore new pathways, without even leaving your house. This actually is one of the treasures that is coming to you, for which you can thank your disease. Had you continued the way you were going...*

M.V. Of course not.

M. *Exactly. It would have been far harder for you to get these precious treasures that are coming to you now. They say again, these star beings, "Tell her to keep on and on writing, (including) the tiny little details. They suggest just put the date, then write what comes into your head about what you are experiencing with them, or concerning any other new adventure in these realms. They want you to know that there is a reason for this. It is for this connection that is starting with you with them.*

It is not really something to satisfy your curiosity. It is something that will not only help your own spiritual pathway, but it is a very important part of the coming together, the unification of all consciousness. They are part of that, just as you are, regardless of whether you perceive them to be something present here in this room now, or something a million years and a million galaxies away, bearing in mind time and space are both illusions.

It is just becoming aware, and being able to exchange gifts with them. Little can be more beautiful than that. And then, as you receive these golden treasures full of sparkling jewels, if you look around, you can see whose eyes are open, and whose are shut, and who is merely slightly curious around you, and to those who you feel would like to see, would like to hear, you can say, "Look! This is what the star beings gave me", and, "Have you seen this? They have this there. They have this there; they have music.

They have a wonderful, wonderful music, different to yours, but their perception of the sound language is very sharp, very keen, very good." Music is a language of all the universes. It does not just belong here. It is true, Earth has had music for quite a while, speaking in earthly terms. As earth evolves, the ability to use sound, or you can say music, either, combined with this very special emotion called love, will evolve and increase.

And this work with sound and Light, for sound and Light are connected, as are colours; this work will help to build what we can call, "the light net". The Light net is the fabric made of Light like etheric threads that crisscross, crossing like a net, the substance that holds the whole of creation together. Any work strengthening this net can lead to greater awareness of all of creation on all levels everywhere.

It is this that not only brings heaven to heaven, but ultimately can bring heaven to earth. This experiment, for lack of a better word, one could choose many words, which the Source makes, and remember, we are all the Source, is simply a means of experiencing itself.

Forgive us if we repeat what you already know, but our words do serve the purpose of further clarification. I say "our" and "we", because, as I explained with the fairies, I, Maria, though I am not really Maria, but then you understand that, (As I Helena understand it, she means that Maria was the identity used during her previous incarnation, although she is no more Maria, than I am Helena.) am serving as a channel for the other realities, just as Helena is serving as a channel for me. So you see how the connection descends from them, (and they get (receive) more from even higher realms) through me, through Helena, and then they (messages, information etcetera) come out in the spoken word, and also, as you may have perceived, with energy in the Earthly dimension.

For if you look, you can see that this energy, which comes through with this vibration is full of very many colours. Everything shines and sparkles. It is more than the colours of the rainbow, but one cannot fully or adequately describe it with words, but for those who can perceive it, it is beautiful. For those without the ability to see it, it is tangible like any atmosphere in a place. So that if there were someone with no clairvoyant vision, no clairaudience, etc, that person, just by being quiet enough, would feel these energies that we are bringing through, as I explained this morning.

And we ask permission to let some of these energies, these beautiful fine spiritual energies, these structures of Light, to allow them to penetrate this area you call yours, and descend though here, to anchor themselves in the centre of the Earth.

M.V. Of course you can.

M. *We thank you greatly. We would have you know that as these energies descend, not only does it further strengthen the Light net to which I have already referred, but it will aid all the beings who dwell in the Earth, who I believe you call in French, the "intraterrestres". They will be grateful. Right now it is not always so easy for them, because although they do a lot of work themselves to bring the Light into the Earth, many of them, there are so often these blocks on the Earth's surface, these areas of relative darkness, where the vibrations are very dense, fixed. They need not be.*

395

There are other places; here (Marguerite's house) is a good example, where because of the spiritual work, and healing that has already taken place here, the vibrations have become less dense. And this is one reason why the star beings are choosing this place to anchor Light into the Earth. They surveyed from afar, they looked down to this planet, aided by beings who were naturally closer to it, to find places where with reasonable ease, the Light could penetrate to reach the very centre, the core of the Earth.

We would remind you, that some of these "intraterrestres" who live in the centre of the Earth, are not living in a fiery furnace, as many are led to believe, but in the hollow space around the central sun you do not see from here. That is where they dwell. They have been successful in purifying their own vibrations. They are spiritually advanced, and they live in a beautiful place. They have found ways of exiting the Earth, and returning at the poles, where the energies are not blocked. They have often asked, "Could something be done about the humanity living on the surface?" It is all so close to them. It need not be as difficult as it is. This is really a time for change.

When I saw that after my death, the physical death, it took a while, it did take a while, when I was ready to be less absorbed in myself, and to look around a bit, I saw that there was a great deal of work to be done on Earth. It was explained to me that however painful my previous incarnation may have been at times, it was nonetheless a perfect preparation, when combined with the studies I have made since my death, to come back and aid and assist.

I really did not want other people to suffer as I suffered. Even in my successful times there was suffering. I may have kept myself so occupied, I could barely feel it as success reigned, but had I stopped. Oh my! The emptiness I sometimes had inside, I would not say I was always unhappy. There were times of great joy, when I felt things were going as I wanted them to. The emptiness inside me, this was my downfall. When the things I relied on for my happiness were lost, it was as though the lights went out, and I felt abandoned, alone in total darkness.

There were those wishing to offer friendship, but I felt that no one could reach me, and I was so thankful for my little poodles. In their simplicity, with their unconditional love, I sometimes felt they were the only beings on the Earth who really understood me. I repeat, others tried so hard to help, but really I moved beyond help, such as humanity could offer. And I certainly did have a wish to die, because nothing was left to live for. Who would want an eternity of tears, I ask you?

M.V. No one.

M. *Yes, and how could it pass this situation, if I stayed alive? My voice had gone, Onassis gone, I did not dare try to perform on stage. I knew I had not got it any more. My confidence, gone, the things that had kept me alive were all gone. So, whereas I did not kill myself, when death came, it was sweet and welcome, very welcome. I died in a state of great peace thinking, "At last! At last! It is finished! What a relief!" At last I was able to experience peace. Yes.*

Why or how could I help other people to not have to go through what I went through in the last years of my life? Well, thanks to the lessons I have learnt since, especially through my communication with Helena, and my view of her life as we have learnt together from others, I have began to see that had my spiritual values, and I did have some, had they been in better balance, had my spiritual awareness been greater, no matter what would have happened, I would have been too enlightened to be anything other than at peace throughout my life.

The need to prove myself to the world as someone wonderful, a wonderful opera singer, and then a truly feminine woman, those things would not have been there. The need to feel I was physically beautiful, that would not have been necessary. However, I also see that my ignorance has served both me, and the world very well. For I am able to accept that I did change opera for all time, as men say, and that through my music, when I was alive, I touched many people.

I awakened their hearts, I stirred their emotions, just as you saw people weep yesterday morning in the group room, when Helena played a CD with my voice on it. That happened so many times when I performed.

Each time somebody was in some sense a little bit healed by it. I did not fully recognise that always, but I do now. I can see that being in touch with one's personal passion, all of it, not just the love, deny nothing, accept everything you feel without judgement.

I can see that that is the first step that humanity needed to take to move further towards enlightenment. You see, as Samarpan could tell us, the mind is a very useful little tool for an incarnation. It tells us how to find our way around the metro. It helps us learn a language. It helps us know what to do in the kitchen with the food, but, humanity as a whole has identified itself with the mind. One is not one's mind. It is a false identity. One is something far more beautiful than that. This is why it is of no importance, in one sense, if one has intellect or not.

And as you have noticed, Marguerite, sometimes someone with less intellect finds it easier not to be stuck in the mind, than those who have more. But having more can also be a gift, providing the mind is kept in its proper place, providing one does not identify with this mind, but uses it as a God-given gift when it is required, and that the higher self it is who rules, not the mind. Yes, and getting in touch with the emotions is the first step for getting out of the mind.

Music and sound can help greatly with that, as well as with many other areas, as you know. I would like to clarify with you that we are aware that we often say things to you, which you already know, as you have observed, and that we have recognised that you are, at least in one sense, not a beginner; and that this is because we still have the wish to give you confirmation.

M.V. Thank you.

M. *Have you any other questions? Is there anything else that I, Maria, can do for you before I leave? I have time if you wish.*

M.V. Your presence is a gift. Your vibrations are a gift, and I have no question, I am just receiving, and my mind is resting.

M. *This is very beautiful and perfect. Very beautiful! For we have offered you a glass of spiritual wine, the very best, and we see that you are drinking all of it, just as we hoped you would. We are so happy, and I speak for myself. I could speak for Helena if she was here. I speak for the star beings. We are so delighted that our messages be so well received. And the fairies also, they want to know, do you think you might buy them a yellow rose?*

M.V. Of course I will!

M. *They are laughing. They are laughing, because they say, "We knew it, but we had to ask. We had to ask, because we know, we...(laughing slightly) we know that when Marguerite makes a promise, she always tries to keep it!"* (Maria was struggling to keep her laughter at bay, so that these last words could be spoken.)

M.V. Yes, even if it is not right now.

M. *"Yes! Oh that is all right. We can wait", they say, "We can wait!"* (*Then, still trying to keep her own laughter under control, Maria continued with their words.*) *"But please, please bring us a yellow rose"*

M.V. Okay.

M. *They thank you very much. They have a very light, lovely sort of energy. They want to communicate.*

At this point, my body felt fairy light, as I jumped to my feet filled with their energy. I feel Maria had stepped out slightly to give the stage to them. Without hesitation, they made sounds through me. These lasted less then a minute, were very quick, and seemed to dance freely up and down in what I assume was some kind of tonal language of their own. None of us knew what they had said, but it was very uplifting to hear them.

M.V. Very nice and joyful!

(A warm deep laugh came out of Maria, who was back in my body the instant following the cessation of the fairy sounds.)

M. *I am Maria, and I have noticed they have a lot of energy.* (Maria laughing again)

M.V. Yes.

M. *I have enjoyed this "interview", if I may call it that, very much, very much.*

M.V. So did I.

M. *I am very thankful, and very grateful. And, I would...even though I am to some extent disconnected from this human way of being, I would still like to have the pleasure of holding you in my arms.*

M.V. It would be a pleasure for me as well.

They embraced each other.

M. *Until next time, Marguerite* (said in French)

M.V. Thank you.

Helped by Marguerite, Maria sat down again. I have noticed how much she enjoys little bits of help like that, even if she might have been able to manage on her own. As soon as she was safely seated, she left, and I was back. Having observed how she moved in those last few moments, I exclaimed, "My goodness! Isn't she graceful!" after which we stopped recording.

As there was still a little time before lunch and my departure, Richard was able to join us for some toning. I had requested that Starlight be helped, so we started singing together for him. To my great delight, there was enough space left on my tape to record both this, and the following toning that we did for me. Starlight's sounds lasted five minutes, and mine for about four minutes. I join in with my own sounds as well as

Starlight's, because it occurred to me that Maria was doing it, and she would know, as usual, exactly what I needed.

After that, I rushed upstairs to do more packing, then we had lunch together, and shortly after that and a breath of fresh air, the three of us piled into the car and left for the airport.

On arrival there, with my head so full of all that had happened, I felt noticeably spaced out, and was finding it hard to adjust from having someone to guide me everywhere, and having to try and focus and think for myself again. Marguerite kindly directed me to the right escalator, and as I waved good bye, and ascended without her, I prayed to the angels to help me get myself onto the flight to Manchester. I knew I needed more help than usual. I prayed again, when I noticed that holding my focus well enough to drive my car safely from the airport to my house was equally hard. All was well, and as I thankfully entered my own front door intact, I knew that all I needed was quiet time alone, and little by little, I would automatically return to a normal state of consciousness, which is exactly what happened.

In the February 1st email from 2005, Marguerite wrote,

"As far as your third stay here is concerned, it began very differently, as YOU emitted the idea of coming. What a change! (I think Marguerite had forgotten that I had said I would let her know when I felt ready or had time for another visit before I left the country after the previous one. At least, that is what I had intended to convey to her. So having waited for over a year, I thought maybe it was time to start planning something, in which case I must let her know I was willing, and when I would be free. Helena) As usual the workshop took place at the end of your stay, so we had time for other things before. We had a sort of warm-up with meditations. We sent our vibrations with those of Maria and our guides to several persons during the meditations. Then I waited for you to express something regarding Maria, your collaboration with her, to ask if we could look for more information... I waited and waited. No question, no request came from you. Were you shy? (A little bit perhaps, but I was both totally unaware that Marguerite and Maria wanted to talk to each other, and full of trust that Marguerite would suggest anything that "ought" to

be done. Helena) Eventually, four days after your arrival, as you didn't express any wish concerning some support I could give you and Maria, I asked you if you were ready to let Maria express herself. You said something like "You mean an interview?" and as I nodded, you agreed immediately.

All interviews were of highest interest to me as they gave me light and comprehension on many subjects. A healing liberation for Maria took place that I longed for her since the first time we met. This was a lesson of patience as well as a demonstration of "things come when they have to, not when we decide they should come".

I realize that right from the beginning, I had the idea of helping Maria Callas to heal her life wounds. Everyone coming to us looks for help and it was quite natural that I tried to do the same for her as well. In our lives as human beings, the wounds seem to remain as long as the emotion is imprisoned in the cells, which store a great amount of information. I saw, in these encounters with Maria Callas through you, Helena, the opportunity for her to release her sufferings, as if she would let them drop like a burden at the side of the road, she would then be able to walk her path with a renewed energy.

As it didn't work as I thought during your first stay here, I was aware that I wanted to do something but, as usual, I was not leading the dance! I was just following the rhythm of the Great Composer...

During this third stay in France with us, Maria could express her despair so openly and so noisily that I had some seconds of surprise at the beginning. I didn't expect anything and there it was! She was now ready and could release what she had hidden for such a long time. I was so grateful to her for allowing herself to do so, and to Helena for letting this avalanche come through in spite of the "noise". I also realized how deep and how powerful these unexpressed feelings of great pain and despair in one's life and after life can be. How courageous for Maria to go inside and express them into words first, and then let them burst into sounds, just like an animal would do when he suffers. Every feeling can be expressed with sounds, but since ages mankind has been taught it was not fair to show feelings, that it was a sign of weakness etc.

After a short while, when Maria began to express her sounds of despair, the room was full of these vibrations. The invisible beings present and I, with the vibrations of love flowing out of us, supported and enveloped the whole. Some of the particles streaming out melted, some went in the earth or upwards for transmutation. My intuition or my inner knowledge led me to sing gently as a mother would do with her suffering child, to calm and bring peace. And it was effective! I didn't decide with my brain to do it, but I just had to do it, as well as I let my hands move the way they went, without trying to decide what to do and why. I was just present and part of the whole movement; it all occurred in a very natural way.

As I said before, I was not alone with you and Maria there. Both worlds, the visible and invisible or whatever you may like call them, are simultaneous and at the same place. For me it was a confirmation, something that I had been already aware of at some moments in my life. While writing this I am in the same room we were in, and there are two "empty" chairs in front of me. I know I am not alone right now, and a peculiar warmth fills the room and me. It's a perceptible sign of presences and I am so grateful for them to be here each and every moment, even when I'm busy with material things, when my human mind is focused on other thoughts or actions.

For the third workshop, it was clearly announced that it would have something to do with sounds, even though nothing about Maria was mentioned on the leaflet. I had verbally told the participants about your channelling so that they could be prepared. No one had an idea of what was going to happen, but I must say that it was beyond what one could imagine, even if I didn't imagine anything. I was present and very attentive to what was coming. When Maria began to lead the workshop, I thought, "Now Maria and Helena are in their path. That's it." The maturing time was permitting a marvellous opening of sounds here on earth...

The duets with Maria and each one of us in turn were amazing! Everyone felt the humility to accept her invitation, and it was very moving for me to hear the others. Each person had to find a subject for healing and I wondered what I would choose. I looked for one with my intellect, but none satisfied me. So I abandoned the idea, and waited for something to come up in my mind. When the third person was singing with Maria I saw two spirals descending from the sky to the Earth, which were connected to both. Then the idea came: to bring healing for the humans, to help them recover the memory of who they really are, to have a larger inner sight of themselves.

What struck me during these duets is how synchronised they were. It was as if the soul knew the score, the intuition knew perfectly what to sing, but the intellectual part of the brain didn't know what note was coming next. It just came naturally. The harmony between each participant, albeit no one was a singer, and Maria was impressive. Tears were to flow quite a lot for some of us during this workshop, but it was not sad at all! Love was flowing continuously from everyone, and we gave each other healings. Sounds express what words will never be able to, and they have a real power.

Something important occurred when Richard and I came back from the airport after taking you there for your return home. As we had some free hours, I suddenly felt like going to the cinema, without knowing what films were on. On our arrival at the cinema, we saw a list of about 8 films. I was attracted by one whose title was "*L'histoire du chameau qui pleure*" (The story of the crying camel) even though I didn't know what it was about. We saw it. What a sign after the workshop! You won't believe it: it was about sounds! How sounds (or singing) were or are used in Mongolia by the farmer families living in yurts: to pray, to thank the universe, to calm, to bring balance, to heal... What a confirmation! It reinforced me in my power and desire to use my voice in any situation. (Just before I received this email, I had watched a documentary on television about nomadic Mongolians living in yurts. I heard them sing, and when asked what it was that made them so happy, one of them said, "It is the work that I do, and the peace in my heart" Helena.)

To summarise the film, it is the story of a female camel that suffers so much when giving birth to her baby and then sees he has a different colour (he is white) that she rejects him, and doesn't want to nurture him, in spite of all the efforts and love of the owners to bring them together. Eventually a local musician with a violin plays music to the camel, in full harmony with the voice of the young mother of the family, in a beautiful duet, sometimes together, sometimes separate, until a tear appears in the camel's eye and only then can she let the baby camel come under her and suckle. I was so moved that a flow of tears was pouring on my cheeks!

Anyway, seeing this film was no coincidence at all... Life is simply a marvel...

We continued to develop sound meditations after your departure (we could also say singing sessions) and it always brings us in a higher state of spirit, of well-being. What I like in it, is that it helps me to put aside my intellect. It cannot judge, or evaluate etc. It can only hear the sounds... That's fantastic!

These life experiences during your three stays here have brought me further on my path of understanding people, on what is going on after the body's death, and much more. I learnt a lot and experienced many openings on many levels, which has brought so much into my life. I am so grateful to... whom? To you, Helena, and Maria of course, to so many others, and to me for welcoming all this, but who is behind all that? Life? The Universe? God? No matter what we may call it, the most important thing for me is the love I feel, which is both filling me and radiating out of me, and at the same time entering into me. Where am I... in all?"

Chapter 40

Starlight's Sounds and Tigger's Turn

Starlight's Sounds

After my return from France, I was curious to see how I could progress from here, and how I could make some of the new possibilities, which I had become open to work for me at home. I took the recordings we had made, and found that it was not Maria's spoken words I wanted to hear the most, but the tonal language of the fairies as they had come through in the last interview between Marguerite and Maria. Hearing them again was wonderful!

Next, it occurred to me I wanted to play the sounds made by all three of us together to help Starlight evolve. Whilst doing this, I asked that he receive yet another dose of them telepathically. My next inspiration was to play them again, and this time I asked Maria to add a fourth voice using my vocal chords "live". That was fun! It also occurred to me to play back the toning we did especially for my own evolvement, and then to add a fourth voice to that one as well. So far so good.

Why not take my cassette recorder to the stables, and play Starlight his very own music? It seemed a good idea. So I went shopping for the necessary batteries, and the next day I took it with me.

"Great!" I thought to myself as I looked around the yard, "Nobody here except me. So I can make as much noise as I like."

I rode Starlight first, and to my dismay, on my return I found two people, both friends of mine, with the horse two boxes away from Starlight's. It was unusual that either of them should be there at this time of the day, but one of them was holding the horse, while the other one gave him a massage. Tigger is his name. By this time I was looking forward so much to playing Starlight his music, that I was not going to be put off easily, so I told them what I was about to do, and asked them to tell me if it was a problem. None of us thought it would be.

I started the music, and Starlight stood as close to my cassette recorder as I allowed him to. After a minute or two, my friend Wendy put her head over the door, and said something like, "Please could you turn the volume down, because Tigger is wild with fright, and it has become very difficult for Katerina to massage him?" I was very surprised, but turned it down as requested. Wendy, Tigger's owner, had hardly been able to believe her eyes when she observed Starlight's reaction to it just before she left, "But he loves it! He really loves it!" she exclaimed. Shortly after that she had to return and ask me to stop it altogether, as Tigger was still afraid.

As I had played so little of it, I felt deeply disappointed. I had another idea. I took Starlight and his music away to a spot in the middle of the fields far from Tigger's earshot, I hoped. I let him hear the rest of it, and then I played it a second time, adding a fourth voice. Blissfully content, he grazed the grass around my feet until I had finished, when I put him into his own field for more grass and a frolic.

On returning to the yard, I discovered that Tigger, with his sharp ears, had still been able to hear the distant music, and had remained too tense to enjoy his massage properly. In fact he still looked as though something was bothering him. I was so sorry and full of apologies. The two ladies were both very kind to me, and we agreed we could not be certain that the horse was not aware of something else we did not know about, which might be the cause of his tense state, and not the music.

My original plan was only to bring the music once to the stables, but I was so intrigued by Starlight's enthusiasm for it, that I decided two days later to play it to him again. I chose a moment when all the other horses who live there were out in the fields, and would not be disturbed by it. Tigger lived in a very distant field.

This time, I decided to trust Starlight not to destroy the cassette recorder with his teeth, and if he wanted he could come closer to it. As soon as I entered his stable, he came over to inspect this little black thing I held in my hands. I thought he might jump when I pressed the play button, and suddenly it omitted sound, so I turned down the volume switch slightly first. The end of his nose was only half an inch away by this time, but he never flinched. I turned the volume up, and asked for Maria's help in adding a fourth vocal line to it especially for him. She obliged.

At the same time, I was able to remain aware of what Starlight was doing. He spent a lot of time with his muzzle actually touching the cassette recorder. I supposed it was the vibrations that fascinated him. Then, as Maria led my voice up higher, and I wondered if the sound might be too shrill for him, he moved his nose slightly, so that he could place his left ear as close to my mouth as possible. I wondered about the welfare of his eardrums, but he was clearly enjoying it, actually even more so than the first time without the possibility of grass beneath his feet to eat! I was delighted.

Bearing in mind that his sound therapy had been started while I was still in France, it is interesting to note that I found his temperament changed for the better on my return. He was more mature, mostly more relaxed mentally, and therefore coping with tricky situations more confidently. In fairness, two other points need to be taken into account. The first is that Patrick Kempe was still helping him with distant healing, and the second that his holiday might have helped him mentally as well. He had had time to digest and think about the events of the previous summer. I feel, however, that the change was bigger than that, and therefore believe that the sounds had made a real difference.

Meanwhile, Wendy, who understood that Starlight's sounds were made especially for him, was curious to know how Tigger would react to channelled sounds sung to suit his needs. So was I. Therefore, finding her so open to trying something, we made a date for it there and then.

Tigger's Turn

So on Monday 15th November, I came early to the stables to ride Starlight first, and then after a drink, I went to see Tigger.

I had already tried to contact him the previous evening by telepathy from my home to tell him I was coming with something good for him. What really surprised me, because he is such an introvert that I doubted my message would reach him, was that he had replied without any hesitation, "Yes. I know". I wondered who had told him? Did he get that from Wendy? I had not said anything. I promised him I would bring him something nice to eat, as I debated between the possibilities of carrots, polo mints, or an apple.

Well I had run out of apples, so it had to be one of the other two. I asked Wendy if he liked carrots, having carefully prepared some for him, and made a point of giving some to Starlight as well. I had enlisted Starlight's help with this, asking him to send telepathic messages to Tigger that sound was all right, and in no way dangerous. I feel Starlight did help. The food for Tigger was partly to gain his trust, and partly because if a horse is chewing something, it helps he or she to stay relaxed. Alarmed by Tigger's apparent unease and fear level when I had sung for Starlight, I was doing all I could to help him overcome it.

"I thought I should introduce myself to him as a friend", I said to Wendy, presenting him with the first piece of carrot, which he accepted eagerly. With the bag of carrot pieces in my pocket I entered Tigger's stable. The organically grown carrot was a real "hit" with him, so no matter where I went to try and get far enough away from him to be able to sing without frightening him, I was hotly pursued by a delighted carrot-loving horse! "Perhaps the carrots weren't such a good idea", I said to Wendy, asking her to keep him further away from me. "Oh no, this is good. It is good that he wants to follow you", she replied. I could see her point. Singing for a horse in flight would have been much harder.

Then with Tigger restrained by Wendy at one side of his box, and me as far away from him as I could get on the other side of it, I gave Wendy her instructions. I requested she asked the angels and Maria to come and give us lots of guidance to help make this session as good as was possible for

Tigger. Then I asked her to hum gently to him, so that the first sounds would come from someone he knew and trusted. Then I told her that when I felt it was the right moment, and I had observed he was accepting this, I would in join in, most probably on a different note, and it would be fine for her to stop as soon as she thought Tigger was settled. Wendy obliged, and Maria began very soon afterwards.

Although in semi-trance state, I managed to remain more aware than usual of what was going on with my subject. There were various sounds distracting him from time to time, but these were things going on in the yard outside. I was finding it difficult not to worry about whether or not he was accepting his treatment without getting stressed, because of his restlessness, but Maria told me I was doing fine, and explained he needed time to get used to it. That was all.

I trusted her, stopped concerning myself with whether or not he was moving about, just hoping that we were not having to compromise the notes too much just to keep him quiet. Maria's understanding of Tigger's mentality was brilliant. She started off at a sort of medium fast tempo. Quite lively, but using notes from the middle of my range mostly, and almost establishing a sort of little theme tune which she could come back to in order to reassure him after each new bit, so that he would recognise it, and remember that that part was not painful last time, and relax because of the familiarity of it. I felt that he found this an interesting experience, and that somehow it was making him feel more alive. Remembering what Maria had taught me about passion, I added my own thought, "We love you", to the sound. I did not see how he could continue to feel fear of sound carrying that vibration.

Then there was a marked change in tempo to something much slower. This gave the music a relaxing quality, and I was inspired to use my body language as though I was almost going to sleep leaning against the wall in the corner of his box with my eyes shut, so that he would know that at least I was not afraid, so maybe there was nothing for him to fear either.

Just occasionally I was inspired to open an eye to see what he was up to, and sometimes I went over to him still singing, and just as one of the more shrill, to him possibly threatening sounds was coming out of my mouth, he received a carrot. The message was, "Loud relatively high sounds bring nice carrots." That was a bit more of Maria's clever psychology.

With my knowledge of equine body language, I was able to perceive more and more signs from him that he was starting to trust and relax. This helped and encouraged me enormously. I would hear little things like him chewing and licking his lips, even when his mouth was empty. Had he been afraid, his jaw would have been too tight and tense for that. By now Wendy had intelligently prevented him from looking out over the door into the yard, so that his attention would go more specifically towards Maria's toning.

Then, as Maria and I sang some much lower sounds, Wendy allowed him to come closer to me, and as I momentarily opened my eyes, I observed him looking at me with wide, open eyes full of interest. He was showing no fear, and he wanted to be with me. These low notes were not only needed by him, but he was very comfortable with them, so just like his theme tune, they were something which could be returned to from time to time to reassure him in between higher or faster bits.

Then there was a moment when he placed his tail close to me. I knew somehow, that this was exactly right, and that he needed that end of his auric field to receive help. He was standing more and more with his head lower, (a sign of relaxation) and although the volume had to be kept down for him, Maria and I were able to get more and more adventurous. We had won his trust, so now we could really work on him.

It was at this stage that I started to see clairvoyantly where the sound was going, the colours of it, and the shape and size of each note along with the energy density that each one carried. The higher notes, although smaller, consisted of much more compact particles of energy. The lower ones may have held at least as much, but the components of it were more spaced out. There was a whole line of sound starting just between his ears, and travelling at a steadily descending pitch to the top of his tail, where after a quick breath, it was continued in a swoop just clear of his physical body behind his tail, and down into the ground. I realised that we were working more on his auric field than his physical body at that point, and this line of sound was helping to make a continuity of connections throughout the whole of his being, as did many of Maria's sliding sounds at other times.

One of the notes, amber in colour, was directed to his loins. This note was quite big, and of a wonderful smooth texture, as though it was healing and smoothing something out. Wendy told me afterwards, that he had a problem I had not known about in his spine just there. The higher notes used were more light-coloured, varying from slightly golden light towards a whiter one.

There was also an extensive wide-open green note, of more diffuse nature, which was directed towards his intestines. I felt the urge to sing more directly into the different areas and chakras, but wondered if too much close physical contact with his physical form would destroy the carefully built up trust we had achieved. I did, however, find myself guided to move further forward, as a wave of sound went in a gentle ark from his ears over the front of his face. He was looking very much more relaxed, and little by little I moved in closer, watching his reactions, and feeling my way.

Next, no doubt strongly moved to do so by Maria. I sang quite a high note straight into his right ear. He accepted it very well. Maybe he was enjoying the vibrations he could feel in his body. Maria guided me to squat down just in front of him. This was a very clever move on her part. Tigger could perceive me as something totally none-threatening and smaller than him on the ground, and to get closer to the source of the noise, namely my mouth, he had to lower his head still further.

I felt his treatment coming to a close, as Maria sang a gentle low note straight into his nostrils. When horses make friends with each other, the introductions often begin by breathing into each other's nostrils, so this would have seemed to him like part of his own language.

Opening my eyes fully, I turned to Wendy to see how she was feeling. Happiness reigned on her face. Her comments were something like, "That was wonderful! It was really beautiful!" She pointed out to me how his nostrils were still quivering gently, which is something Tigger likes to do after a healing therapy he has enjoyed. "You are a good boy, Tigger", I said, handing him a carrot, and now fully myself again.

I discovered that Wendy had not only been open enough to allow this to happen, even though popular opinion had been that he might be upset by it, but she was deep enough into her spirituality for me to be able to share with her all that had happened with the colours, and so on, and how it had been for me. The whole thing had taken the best part of an hour, and I had thoroughly enjoyed it.

"I have never sung so quietly!" was my immediate reaction. "Even when I sang for a cat, it was not as quiet as that, but I realised about three-quarters of the way through it that Tigger did not need volume, and that it would be just as effective for him sung softly." Wendy told me that Tigger had often been afraid of therapies of other types when first introduced to them, and learnt to enjoy them later. It may have been partly this that gave her the confidence to follow her intuition and ask me to sing for him.

In spite of all the wonderful things that had occurred in France, this was another step, something else new for me. The reason was that as Tigger was not in a position to speak out loud if he did not like it, I had to be present enough in my body, and in contact with the physical dimension almost throughout, so that I could observe everything that was happening with him, read his body language, and not disappear so totally in a trance-like state that I had no idea of what was going on around me at the same time. In short, I had to be much more multidimensional. Yet Maria was there, singing, inspiring and helping just as much as before. This was fascinating!

Then, having left Tigger, I chatted to Wendy in the tack room about it, sharing how I had contacted him the night before telepathically to warn him I was coming. Wendy said, "Yes, he was expecting for you. Normally, when he comes in from the field, he goes straight to his hay net (to eat), but this morning he stood with his head out over the door waiting for you." This was very interesting, but it still did not explain how he knew before I told him, that I was coming. It was about the following day at home, when Maria confessed it was she! She had been to see him, and help prepare him mentally for what was to follow. Later, when I mused over the fact that Starlight had maybe done his supportive role for Tigger as well, Maria said, "Yes, he did help a little, but not half as much as I did!"

Wendy was able to report that Tigger seemed very relaxed and happy afterwards. I was delighted; as I had been worrying a lot about the rumours going round that Helena's sounds for Starlight had upset Tigger. My confidence to come out openly with what I was doing had felt noticeably undermined, but now it had recovered, and left me open to whatever other adventures might follow at the right time. Helping Tigger had healed and helped me.

It is worth mentioning how very different these two horses are in personality. Starlight is, and always has been very vocally expressive. He has no inhibitions about neighing across the yard when he has something to say or ask for. Tigger, on the other hand, is a much quieter more reserved animal, and I could not help wondering if loud vocal sounds, in his distant past before he met Wendy, were associated in his mind with angry or violent humans shouting aggressively at him.

Chapter 41

Christmas and New Year in Germany

Nobody had to persuade me to attend the two weeklong seminars that Samarpan was going to give over Christmas and New Year in Germany. I knew I wanted to go this time. I assumed that Maria would benefit as well, and she did. In fact, as the time for my departure grew nearer, she expressed her joy and excitement about the adventure we were about to embark on wholeheartedly. My enthusiasm was greater as well.

When the first of the two flights from Manchester airport was delayed due to technical problems concerning the baggage, I started to feel some concern about whether or not mine would be successfully transferred to the second flight, or would I arrive somewhere yet again without my suitcase? As it was, I had to run as fast as I could from one terminal to another to catch the flight after the flight I should have been on. If I had to be so quick, then what chance was there of my case keeping up with me? My good friend Maria tried her best to comfort me, by showing me a picture of herself following closely behind me and my luggage. I wanted to believe her, but it was almost impossible for me to avoid thinking that this was part of my imagination, and merely what I would like to happen, not what was going to happen. When the case arrived at the proper time on the conveyer belt in Bremen, I was not only thankful to have it, but thankful to Maria, who I felt had put some of her energy behind it to ensure its arrival.

Hello to Samarpan

I spent the night at a comfortable small hotel called Wardenburghof, for which I was very thankful. The next day I left earlier than necessary by taxi to make my way to the seminar house at Oberlethe. Out of character as it may be for me to go anywhere early, it felt so right that I had to do it.

After I had settled myself in, I made my way to the tea-making facilities. It was while I was thoroughly enjoying myself totally engrossed in trying out as many different drinks as possible that were there for us, that I heard a voice behind me. "Helena!" I turned round, and there was Samarpan. He was greeting one or two of us with a hug, (hardly anyone was there because it was so early). This encounter was completely unexpected by me.

We exchanged a few words, as I reminded him that it was Maria who had brought me to him the previous Easter, and as we spoke about her a little, he mentioned how much she touched him. The truth and sincerity of his words shone out of his eyes, and I was touched to see this love for my friend. Just after he left, I recalled having had a vision earlier in the day, when I had seen myself greeted by Samarpan with an embrace. I did not believe it was foresight at the time, because as far as I knew, he always kept himself out of range of "the masses", when not giving Satsangs. Therefore I had both dismissed it and forgotten about it completely. When it happened, it felt so good to be received as a friend, and to speak about Maria to him. Maria and I were both loved and accepted.

Samarpan's Clarity

The next happening, where Maria was involved, took place on Wednesday 22nd December during the evening satsang. I was talking to Samarpan, and started to share an experience, which had taken place the previous day when discussing something with him in another satsang. I explained how during our conversation, I had been shown a vision of his clarity like a large area of his auric field around him, "...and", I continued, "It was as though in that moment, I was reaching out to something I have, but which I am not enough in touch with yet. I thought that it was a bit like one candle lighting another, and if I spend enough time in this chair, (next to him) I might become less unenlightened!"

416

"It is a very good description that you are making. It is really like that. It is as though you are borrowing my clarity, you are borrowing my ability to see from the truth, and little by little, it just becomes your own, where it lights up your own. Then it just grows, and it is natural. It works like this."

"I felt that I did not take anything away from it, but simply that it, well… helped to ignite my potential clarity."

"Your potential becomes awakened. So it is there, it has always been there. It gets activated."

"That is what I felt, but I wanted you to confirm it".

"I am happy to confirm it."

Now temporarily, I was happy to take the credit for this analogy of one candle lighting another that Samarpan liked so much, but the following evening, I wanted to tell him where that had come from, and explained how Maria had prompted me to use this. (Just as when I was in France the previous October sharing her work with those around us, she had shown me as a large yellow candle burning brightly, which could light all the other candles around me who would then grow, and pass on the Light, and what they had learnt from Maria and me to others who could pass it on further. I did not give Samarpan the full story, but just enough to put the credit where it was due.)

My Christmas Day Massage

One of my biggest reasons for joining Samarpan over Christmas and New Year, was that I wanted to heal my Christmas. Although I knew that many people had to pass the holiday season alone, it always made me sad. Other days of the year I was happy to be alone. I like my own company. At Christmas, I did not want to impose myself on someone else's family life, or be invited by someone to lunch, because they felt sorry for me. In short, I did not know how to avoid feeling increasingly miserable alone on 25th December every time it happened, which was always since my mother died in June 1994. I had not enjoyed Christmas very much even before that, in spite of my mother doing her best, but now it was worse.

Samarpan helped me understand how this idea that Christmas was a social time for those who "got it right", is merely part of our conditioning. Actually, it is the same as any other day. The truth is that we do not have to be happy if it is not convenient! (I have put this into my own words, not those of Samarpan.) I could see that buying into the concept that Christmas Day should happen just how we have been taught it should be, maintained that belief, and all the pain that goes with it if we fail to make it like that. I was determined, however, that at least this time, I was choosing happiness, someone to talk to, and giving myself all that I could.

So when I discovered someone who was willing to give me a massage on Christmas Day, I was delighted! I had not expected anyone to agree to work at such a time. After all, we are taught that it should be a holiday, are we not? Meanwhile Samarpan was helping us accept it like any other day by banning Christmas decorations in the dining room, and sparing us from being force-fed on Christmas carols. I found that unbelievably refreshing!

So at 11.00 I met Ujjavel, who took me to the room where he gives massage. I clearly remembered that on the notice I had seen about it, one could choose to have a Hawaiian massage using lots of hot oil. It seems very odd in retrospect that I had failed to take in the bit about it being a massage with toning! I had experienced a Hawaiian massage before, but never one where sound was a part of it.

The first part was done in relative silence, but just before the toning started, I saw Maria arrive. She was powdering her nose, and putting lipstick on for this man. She liked him! Throughout the toning, she stayed very close, almost leaning over the massage table to get the best view possible of what was going on. For me it was really great to be on the receiving end of sound.

Ujjavel toned with a rich deep resonant voice with varying pitch and vowel sounds. I noticed how each variation affected me differently. He

418

worked on my chakras moving up and down my body, and I noticed with interest how the pitch was higher for the upper chakras than the lower ones, just as it usually is when Maria works this way. I was so impressed that I gave myself the pleasure of a second massage with him the following week.

Meanwhile, on Christmas Day, I felt I had to break the silence to tell him what Maria had shown me concerning how much she liked him. She was asking me to, and I observed afterwards, how it helped fulfil my need to talk on Christmas Day, the thing I had felt so deprived of other Christmases. (Not an easy thing to arrange during a silent retreat). Ujjavel looked very happy about this, and asked what she thought of his singing. I was able to pass on a good report, as he used his throat, lungs, and vocal chords very well. Maria was keen to encourage him with this wonderful work he had started. He explained that about ten years ago he had started to play with his voice. No one had given him lessons, and he had just let it evolve naturally. I was delighted with it all.

Anger and Power; Maria and Smoking

Having not reached the stage where I had really integrated the concept that Christmas Day was the same as any other day, I was determined to enhance it with another talk to Samarpan. My first attempt after lunch failed, but had its gifts, for while I was endlessly waiting just in case I could reach his guest chair, various insights took place.

Someone else had discussed her power and the issue of anger. She was afraid of both of these, and had seen herself with a sword, which she did not trust herself to use wisely. Spontaneously, I noticed that I carried a sword, not a long one, but a sharp tool with which I felt perfectly comfortable. Unlike the other lady, I was happy to carry and own mine. (It is very likely that at one time I would not have been.) I could see how anger could move me to action, to using my power to make things good or better. It does not have to be destructive in a negative way. It can shake me out of complacency. I saw how I could use this sword to cut myself free if tethered or stuck anywhere, to hack my way through the jungle, clearing a path for myself to walk along to reach my goal or destination. Anger can act like a motivator for me, when I am otherwise left in a passive powerless state. It can bring me to use my power in a positive way.

The long wait in the queue to reach Samarpan seemed endless. I was physically uncomfortable, cramped into small spaces sitting on the floor, and my body was complaining about it. Maria, close by and observing everything carefully, decided that this was the time to talk to me about smoking, a habit I had difficulty understanding in others. First of all she showed me a cigar, and then a cigarette. Sitting there full of frustration at this drawn out unsuccessful wait, she explained to me how people smoke to relax themselves thus bringing relief from exactly the sort of state I was in.

This made it easy to see why those who give up the habit often go through a period of feeling very irritated without the nicotine until body and soul adjust. For the first time in my life, I felt some kind of empathy towards smokers, although I continued to think it was not a good idea, and had no desire to start myself, no matter how I felt.

That evening, I joined Samarpan's queue even earlier, and was rewarded with reaching that chair! At last I had my Christmas Day talk with Samarpan!

The next day 26th December, while listening to Samarpan talking to someone else, he spoke about God coming fully into these bodies, the final descent of God. So it is not about leaving to join God, but bringing the Light into this three dimensional reality. (I have expressed this in my own words) When Maria heard this, along with my thought that I was bringing more of my soul and spirit here into my physical body, she commented, "So am I, but respectfully", She reminded me that I had agreed we could blend in this body of mine, which I felt so happy to share with her, and that we can move into the Light together, which it seems is the same thing as bringing more Light into this dimension here on Planet Earth. Also, together we have more power to use for good, and put in the service of the Light, and therefore ourselves.

Meanwhile, Samarpan's comment that "Life is more fun and more interesting if I don't take it too seriously", is well worth remembering and mentioning, even if I do so out of context like this!

That evening I discovered that even though I am happy to carry a sword, or a dagger, I had not yet owned all of my power. I suppose there is always further to go.

On 27th, I went out for a walk in the morning, just as I always did during these two weeks, and I received some insights, the most noteworthy of which was, "When judgement goes, love flows." Another was, "Where love flows, energy goes", but the more important of the two for me was the first one. I felt that this letting go of judgement was the key to loving all sentient beings, and all that is , no matter how things appeared to be. This would be very important for any future work I might get involved in with people. Since then, I have seen how important it is to remember this when considering Maria. It brings us closer together, and increases the mutual trust, when there is no judgement, but only love abounding.

Maria's Questions

The evening satsang on 30th was the most potent regarding Maria, and how much Samarpan helps her. Starting the previous day, and feeling rather as though I were her secretary, I had begun to list her questions, and had a total of three in my notebook to ask Samarpan on her behalf. I had to sit in the queue for a long time to reach the interview chair, and began to wonder if I would ever get there before time ran out, and Samarpan had to stop.

While I was waiting, I was shown a comforting vision. I was sitting underneath a Christmas tree, and presents from it were raining down all around me. When I decided I dare not really believe this positive sign I would actually reach Samarpan that night, I was shown another picture. It was of him handing me an extra big present, beautifully wrapped in Christmas paper. This is how the part of my interview went, which concerns Maria. Having discussed something else with him in response to his questions, I continued,

"...and the other thing was, I thought if I ever get to that chair tonight, and I have," (unsure how Samarpan would receive this request, I hesitated awkwardly, but recovering my voice quickly, I went on) "I promised my friend Maria, that...she asked me if I would ask you something, and I would like to know too. She got interested when you were talking to someone else yesterday, who said how she felt her dead mother came, and first of all, when Maria heard you acknowledge that you accepted that the various dead people the other lady spoke about were here, that again touched Maria, and she wanted me tell you that although she had not got them physically of course, she was giving you a bunch of red roses."

"Um, yes." Samarpan sounded pleased.

"And today in the Satsang at two o'clock, you said something else. Unfortunately I have forgotten what it was, but that touched her as well, so she added some white lilies to the roses, and asked me to give you those as well."

"Lovely!"

"This is what she would like to know please. You told the other lady that if she healed her life, it would heal the lives of her ancestors, like her mother. Now Maria had a very difficult time with her mother, and she did try in her lifetime to heal the situation, but it did not work. It got worse. So this for her was like a dream opportunity come true, and she would like it confirmed that if she really heals her life through attending your satsangs, and the other things she is doing, will this heal her mother?"

"Absolutely! When Maria feels her feelings, and makes peace with her life, then this peace just spreads, like throwing a pebble in a lake. This peace just spreads in every direction."

"She thanks you very deeply from her heart for that. She would also like to know, and I am interested as well, does this work with siblings as well?"

"Oh yes, but it works in its own way, and in its own time. So we have to be infinitely patient, especially with our siblings and our parents. You know we tend to get impatient, we want to push them; we want to get confirmation from them. It does not work this way. The way it works is that we make peace with ourselves first. We make peace with our feelings, with our feelings of not getting what we wanted from our parents or our siblings. Then out of this peace, and out of this deep, deep patience, slowly, slowly it works. It is working with my siblings. I have friends who are saying that they are experiencing the same thing, but it is so slow! We have to be really, really, really, really, really, really patient. We can't imagine how long it takes. So we have to just stay in peace. This is the magic, to stay in peace, we keep coming back to peace. We know that we don't need anything from anybody. When I don't need anything from anybody, then the love is unconditional."

"That is the key, isn't it?"

"Yes, that is the key. That's right. That is the power."

"Now I think that answer would apply the same to her third question. She wanted to know, does this extend to Onassis? Onassis is the lover she wanted to marry, but he would not marry her, and he's dead too. He went off and married somebody else, which nearly broke her heart."

"Well, you see the (her) love was not touched by his decision to marry another woman. Love is still alive. So nothing was taken away from her. That is the secret."

"Oh, she had not realised that!" (Maria was communicating her responses to Samarpan's answer for me to pass on as the conversation went along.)

"I know. That is what we miss. We always think that when our lover goes off with somebody else that our love gets lost, but it's not true."

"Well, I can see her now with tears of joy at hearing that, and she sort of says, "Tell him I just want to fling my arms around him and love him!""

"Um, yes!"

"I think she wants to give you a kiss just here on the forehead." I pointed to my own forehead to show him.

Samarpan responded by sending her a kiss, directed into the air in front of him.

"She got it!" I exclaimed, delighted with the outcome of this discourse between Samarpan and Maria, "Well thank you for helping my other "other half", the bedroom "other half", and this "other half". (Maria)" (Laughter from the audience). I was referring to the lady who was sharing the bedroom with me for the week. Both of us had aired our sharing difficulties with Samarpan, and both of us had been helped. So temporarily I had two "other halves", this lady, and Maria.

"My own question, I think it is an interesting one, and we could..."

"I don't know if Anchie is going to let you continue. I think she is going to fight you."

"Who is Anchie?"

"The lady sitting next to you."

"Oh, well I'll gobble it out very quickly. I have only got one question. Our dark sides; I know one has to own one's dark side. I have got that far, but then there is... I mean if one is going to own it, is it a case of learning to use it in a positive way, or does one just own it, and remember not to use it?"

"What's dark? Isn't dark just a judgement or something?"

"Ah ha."

"Without judgement, it's not dark is it?"

"Um, well I suppose it isn't" Obvious surprise was expressed in my voice as I said that. It was a completely new way of looking at it for me.

"That's your homework."

"Thank you Samarpan very much, and especially for helping my friend. Thank you, for helping Maria."

I bowed to Samarpan several times. It was as though words alone were totally inadequate to express my gratitude. There was obvious affection in my voice as I spoke Maria's name, and also my satisfaction at having received so much help on so many issues for both of us in one session was very evident. Finally, I gave up my place to Anchie, who had kindly restrained herself from fighting me!

At the end of these two weeks, I went home, where I was unbelievably tired. I could not be sure what the main reason for this was, but certainly I had brought many spiritual treasures home with me, and I needed time to absorb them fully. Maria's benefit was equally great, and because of it all, she and I drew even closer to one another. Letting go of more of my judgements, thus allowing love to flow was perhaps the valuable treasure of all. I had many interviews with Samarpan during that time, each one bringing Maria and I something special, but where the questions were solely mine, I have mostly not included them, because these along with the learning we had from everyone else's queries and experiences as well would fill another book! Eventually, I recovered my energy, as little by little more of this trip was taken in, and able to be put to good use.
Maria and I were so thankful!

Now there was something that Samarpan had said about angels needing to come to Satsang, which I could not get out of my mind. So on 19th February, I wrote this email to him.

"Dear Beloved Samarpan,
By the evening of the last day of the Sylvester Seminar, I already had another question for you, but you had gone home, and I was about to! I intended to ask you as soon as I reached my computer, but then realised there were some other things I had to see to first. This question continued to haunt me in my quieter moments on a regular basis, and now I know it is time to find out why you said,
"The angels need to come to satsang."
How come? I have a few ideas about it, but that is not the same as knowing. So please will you tell me why that is?

I understand why Maria benefits so much when we are with you, and the angels, like her, are not incarnated at present. As I understand things through direct communication with the angelic realms, one or two of them have incarnated at some time. It affects the appearance of the auric field they have now. It takes on a white misty look, whereas the others have auras of a completely clear transparent nature.

This may seem like a question for the mind's entertainment, but I am looking for the truth. It is high time my eyes were open to that. Please help.

Meanwhile, thank you so much for all that both of us received from you at Oberlethe. It was a wonderful trip. We learnt so much, and love each other more because of it. What a gift!

Both of us love you greatly,
Helena and Maria."

His reply arrived on 25th February 2005.

"Beloved Helena and Maria,
What a lovely question you sent to me!
In all of the realms, dimensions, and forms that are possible, there is only one "reality". It has been said that our planet is the only one where people have a sincere desire to awaken from the dream. In all of the other places, there is no desire to know the Truth.

The story was told that Papaji was walking in the Himalayas (on a road that was said to lead to heaven) and he met two gods. The gods bowed down to him and touched his feet.

Yes, the gods and the angels come to Satsang because they too wish to be free. If there is any idea of being somebody who is separate from God, (from the Source) there is still something missing, no matter how lovely his or her existence may be. If I think I am one of God's angels, then there is a separation between God and me, and this is simply not the Truth. God is all that is and there isn't anything or anybody separate from THIS.

I embrace you both.
With all my love,
Samarpan"

426

Epílogue

This story of the journey of two souls is unending. Maria and I are still together, still interacting and helping each other, and I know there is more for us to do and experience on our pathway. Waiting for the end of an unending story would deprive the world of the opportunity to share in all the wonderful things which have already happened, and are carefully described in this book. Therefore I am finishing here, and feel strongly that those who read this far with open minds will be the richer for it. It is my pleasure to share all this. I do it for Maria as well. How could I ever have dreamed that I would come to love her so much? It is what she wanted, and it is the golden gift and greatest treasure of my lifetime so far.

When in the final stages of putting this book together, I was communicating with Sarah Diane Pomerleau about leading a possible seminar she had suggested. I had sent her various chapters, and feeling rather pleased about the amount I had achieved, I wrote playfully,

"I am a good girl, aren't I?

I've done lots of work in spite of my lazy nature. Maria says I should not have written that, because I am not lazy. I knew something was not right as soon as I had written it! She goes on (to me) "and you said that I should stick to the truth!" "Sorry Maria, I did not realise it wasn't the truth until you pointed it out!"

Isn't it lucky I have a helper to keep me on the straight and narrow? Perhaps if I said I was a slow worker it would be nearer the mark. Maria seems much happier with that way of putting it."

Sarah replied,

"She is a kind of guardian angel... except she has been incarnated...."

Many have supported us on our journey, but perhaps no one as much as Marguerite Vidal, so it seems appropriate to include a few more of her words that came to me by email here. Sarah Diane Pomerleau had written to ask me if I would be willing to lead a seminar in the United Kingdom for a group of her pupils. She knew almost nothing of how my life was going at the time, and there was no mention of Maria on this invitation. Worried that perhaps Maria and her music would not be welcomed, and unwilling to go anywhere without her, (far too painful, and not true to myself either) I wrote to Sarah to find out if Maria was welcome. I told Marguerite what was going on, and in her reply were these words:

"As for what is coming with Sarah or whatever you will do in your life, please, PLEASE look at this thing you wrote, "...ask if Maria is invited to this party", and remember she is always with you. When somebody invites you, or when you go to Samarpan or to Joan Ocean or anyone, Maria is with you. You are living a duet with her, and for us, for Joan also I suppose, and for all others who can accept this idea that you are living this experience, it is no doubt that you are here together. Of course, strangers don't know. But now, any group you will take part to or lead will know. It is something natural and if this proposal of Sarah comes to a physical reality, sure that Maria and you will lead the journey. You know that! You are the one who is permitting all this with Maria. Thanks to both of you!
Be inspired, as you always are.
Love,
Marguerite"

Other books by Helena Hawley:

The Other Kingdoms Speak - What the Animals, Plants, Crystals, Extraterrestrials, Angels, Mermaids & Fairies Have to Say
Helena Hawley

"Inspirational...a joy of a book." Susan M. Phillips   *"...an unusual and marvellous woman.... in Hawley's view, almost everything carries an underlying hint of cosmic truth and, quite often, humour....refreshingly original."* Alaskan Wellness   *"Helena's efforts inspire and uplift us in every chapter...leaves the reader feeling lighter and brighter as a spiritual quality shines out from the pages....I am sure many readers will find something of value in these books"* Jeannie H. Judd.

This is a book of communications from the spiritual dimensions. The diversity of themes covered includes the "Council of Animals", dolphins, whales, tree consciousness, mermaids, fairies, angels and interaction with extraterrestrials with wisdom and learning from past lives. The need to recreate the balance of the planet is explained, but more than this, our true place in the scheme of things, part of the whole, no longer needing to be apart from it. The other species on many levels of existence all offer us their loving help and energy in making a great leap forward in human development. The energies of wisdom and love are extended to the reader through the medium of both words and inspired artwork, including full colour plates. ISBN 1 898307 062X
£10.95

My Inner Life, the Animals and the Angels   Helena Hawley

Helena opens a magical door into the animal kingdom in the spirit world, taking us on a fascinating journey into the secret realms of dolphins, mermaids, fairies and angels. As you share her experiences, they will give you a heightened awareness and clarity, enriching your life with new appreciation and understanding. Her gift to them is sharing these experiences with the world. Describes touching encounters with The Council of Animals, also contains communications with the Sun and Earth and Ascended Masters. Full colour pictures. Helena's inspired watercolours bring the energies of the animals directly to the reader.   ISBN 186163 121 9   £10.95

My Spiritual Journal - Book Three in The Other Kingdoms Speak series
Helena Hawley

"This is a truly uplifting read..... If you are ready to receive such information, and need hope, this book will give it to you" Psychic Voice

In this, her third book, Helena shares more of the messages and channellings from the other kingdoms, taking things further as the teachings evolve. Communications with fairies, including a description of life as one, encounters with mermaids, a giant, the spirits of animals such as dogs and horses, trees and ETs are all simply described. Also spiritual communication with wild dolphins and whales which Helena swims with, linking her amazing spiritual revelations with physical experiences in the ocean. Helena has had immense support from leading workers in this field such as Joan Ocean, and readers of her books throughout the world. The simple, but meaningful messages are highlighted by Helena's inspired colour paintings and photographs. Full colour pictures. ISBN 186163 1901   £13.95

FREE DETAILED CATALOGUE

Capall Bann is owned and run by people actively involved in many of the areas in which we publish. A detailed illustrated catalogue is available on request, SAE or International Postal Coupon appreciated. **Titles can be ordered direct from Capall Bann, post free in the UK** or from good bookshops and specialist outlets.

A Breath Behind Time, Terri Hector
Angels and Goddesses - Celtic Christianity & Paganism, M. Howard
Arthur - The Legend Unveiled, C Johnson & E Lung
Auguries and Omens - The Magical Lore of Birds, Yvonne Aburrow
Asyniur - Womens Mysteries in the Northern Tradition, S McGrath
Beginnings - Geomancy, Builder's Rites in the European Tradition, Nigel Pennick
Between Earth and Sky, Julia Day
Caer Sidhe - Celtic Astrology and Astronomy, Michael Bayley
Call of the Horned Piper, Nigel Jackson
Can't Sleep, Won't Sleep, Linga Louisa Dell
Carnival of the Animals, Gregor Lamb
Cat's Company, Ann Walker
Celtic Faery Shamanism, Catrin James
Celtic Lore & Druidic Ritual, Rhiannon Ryall
Celtic Saints and the Glastonbury Zodiac, Mary Caine
Circle and the Square, Jack Gale
Come Back To Life, Jenny Smedley
Compleat Vampyre - The Vampyre Shaman, Nigel Jackson
Creating Form From the Mist - Wisdom of Women in Celtic Myth, L. Sinclair-Wood
Crystal Clear - A Guide to Quartz Crystal, Jennifer Dent
Crystal Doorways, Simon & Sue Lilly
Crossing the Borderlines - Guising, Masking & Animal Disguise, Nigel Pennick
Dragons of the West, Nigel Pennick
Earth Harmony - Places of Power, Holiness & Healing, Nigel Pennick
Earth Magic, Margaret McArthur
Egyptian Animals - Guardians & Gateways of the Gods, Akkadia Ford
Eildon Tree (The) Romany Language & Lore, Michael Hoadley
Enchanted Forest - The Magical Lore of Trees, Yvonne Aburrow
Eternally Yours Faithfully, Roy Radford & Evelyn Gregory
Everything You Always Wanted To Know About Your Body, But So Far
    Nobody's Been Able To Tell You, Chris Thomas & D Baker
Fairies and Nature Spirits, Teresa Moorey
Fairies in the Irish Tradition, Molly Gowen

Familiars - Animal Powers of Britain, Anna Franklin
Flower Wisdom, Katherine Kear
Fool's First Steps, (The) Chris Thomas
Forest Paths - Tree Divination, Brian Harrison, Ill. S. Rouse
Gardening For Wildlife Ron Wilson
God Year, The, Nigel Pennick & Helen Field
Goddess on the Cross, Dr George Young
Goddess Year, The, Nigel Pennick & Helen Field
Goddesses, Guardians & Groves, Jack Gale
Handbook For Pagan Healers, Liz Joan
Handbook of Fairies, Ronan Coghlan
Healing Book, The, Chris Thomas and Diane Baker
Healing Homes, Jennifer Dent
Healing Journeys, Paul Williamson
Healing Stones, Sue Philips
Herb Craft - Shamanic & Ritual Use of Herbs, Lavender & Franklin
In Search of Herne the Hunter, Eric Fitch
Intuitive Journey, Ann Walker Isis - African Queen, Akkadia Ford
Journey Home, The, Chris Thomas
Legend of Robin Hood, The, Richard Rutherford-Moore
Lid Off the Cauldron, Patricia Crowther
Lost Lands & Sunken Cities (2nd ed.), Nigel Pennick
Magic of Herbs - A Complete Home Herbal, Rhiannon Ryall
Magical Guardians - Exploring the Spirit and Nature of Trees, Philip Heselton
Magical History of the Horse, Janet Farrar & Virginia Russell
Magical Lore of Animals, Yvonne Aburrow
Magical Lore of Cats, Marion Davies
Magical Lore of Herbs, Marion Davies
Magick Without Peers, Ariadne Rainbird & David Rankine
Masks of Misrule - Horned God & His Cult in Europe, Nigel Jackson
Mind Massage - 60 Creative Visualisations, Marlene Maundrill
Mirrors of Magic - Evoking the Spirit of the Dewponds, P Heselton
Moon Mysteries, Jan Brodie
Mysteries of the Runes, Michael Howard
Mystic Life of Animals, Ann Walker
New Celtic Oracle The, Nigel Pennick & Nigel Jackson
Pagan Feasts - Seasonal Food for the 8 Festivals, Franklin & Phillips
Patchwork of Magic - Living in a Pagan World, Julia Day
Pathworking - A Practical Book of Guided Meditations, Pete Jennings
Personal Power, Anna Franklin
Places of Pilgrimage and Healing, Adrian Cooper
Planet Earth - The Universe's Experiment, Chris Thomas
Practical Divining, Richard Foord
Practical Meditation, Steve Hounsome
Practical Spirituality, Steve Hounsome
Psychic Self Defence - Real Solutions, Jan Brodie

Real Fairies, David Tame
Romany Tapestry, Michael Houghton
Runic Astrology, Nigel Pennick
Sacred Animals, Gordon MacLellan
Sacred Celtic Animals, Marion Davies, Ill. Simon Rouse
Sacred Dorset - On the Path of the Dragon, Peter Knight
Sacred Grove - The Mysteries of the Forest, Yvonne Aburrow
Sacred Geometry, Nigel Pennick
Sacred Nature, Ancient Wisdom & Modern Meanings, A Cooper
Sacred Ring - Pagan Origins of British Folk Festivals, M. Howard
Seasonal Magic - Diary of a Village Witch, Paddy Slade
Secret Places of the Goddess, Philip Heselton
Secret Signs & Sigils, Nigel Pennick
A Seeker's Guide To Past Lives, Paul Williamson
Seeking Pagan Gods, Teresa Moorey
Spirits of the Earth series, Jaq D Hawkins
Stony Gaze, Investigating Celtic Heads John Billingsley
Subterranean Kingdom, The, revised 2nd ed, Nigel Pennick
Talking to the Earth, Gordon MacLellan
Talking With Nature, Julie Hood
Taming the Wolf - Full Moon Meditations, Steve Hounsome
Teachings of the Wisewomen, Rhiannon Ryall
Tree: Essence of Healing, Simon & Sue Lilly
Tree: Essence, Spirit & Teacher, Simon & Sue Lilly
Understanding Chaos Magic, Jaq D Hawkins
Water Witches, Tony Steele
Weaving a Web of Magic, Rhiannon Ryall
Wheel of the Year, Teresa Moorey & Jane Brideson
Wildwitch - The Craft of the Natural Psychic, Poppy Palin
Wondrous Land - The Faery Faith of Ireland by Dr Kay Mullin
Working With the Merlin, Geoff Hughes
Understanding Past Lives, Dilys Gater
Understanding Second Sight, Dilys Gater
Understanding Spirit Guides, Dilys Gater
Understanding Star Children, Dilys Gater
The Urban Shaman, Dilys Gater
Your Talking Pet, Ann Walker

FREE detailed catalogue and FREE 'Inspiration' magazine

Contact: Capall Bann Publishing, Auton Farm, Milverton, Somerset, TA4 1NE